World Communication:
Threat or Promise?

World Communication: Threat or Promise?

A Socio-technical Approach

COLIN CHERRY
Henry Mark Pease Professor of Telecommunication,
Imperial College, University of London

WILEY–INTERSCIENCE
a division of John Wiley & Sons Ltd
London · New York · Sydney · Toronto

Library of Congress Catalog Card No. 79–147195

ISBN 0 471 15343 5

Made in Great Britain at the Pitman Press, Bath

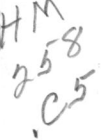

Apology and Acknowledgement

No technical knowledge is required for reading this book, beyond ability to interpret a simple graph.

Our subject is World Communication, a socio-technical subject which arouses a great deal of interest nowadays, even concern, and sometimes anxiety, for in certain ways it is a highly emotional subject. It cannot fail to be so; much of the technology of communication is firmly related to war, whilst all of its values are, in some way or other, human values which affect us as individual people, personally, and collectively as nations. Passions have been aroused over television, strong feelings over telephones and newspapers, and mixed emotions over tourism. Words like 'propaganda', 'mass-communication', 'the Press', seem easily to trigger-off people's most unreasoned opinions. It is a subject having a whole popular mythology of its own.

It was then with full knowledge of the dangers into which I was moving that I set out to write this book. It has been based upon my last 20 years of travelling in many countries, on visits to various Communication Authorities and on lecture tours, among linguists, sociologists and technologists. I am heavily indebted to so many people and so many Institutions, that I cannot list them all here. Instead, I have referred to them in the text and Bibliography and would like now to offer them all my grateful thanks for many discussions, for giving me facts and data, and for permissions to quote from their work.

Most books about Communication have been written either by engineers and scientists, as technical experts, or by sociologists, philosophers, linguists and other humanists. This book makes a modest attempt to throw a bridge across the chasm and to guide the layman back and forth. I hope that it doesn't collapse under his feet.

'Tillingbrook'
Rectory Lane,
Shere, Surrey,
England.

COLIN CHERRY
The Salisbury Hotel
Nairobi,
Kenya,
E. Africa.

Contents

Introduction ix

1 ON THE NATURE OF HUMAN COMMUNICATION

1. Society regarded as 'People in Communication' . . . 1
2. Persons and personifications 8
3. Communication as an act of courage 11
4. 'World languages'—Linguae francae 12
5. Clichés and slogans 17
6. The significance of literacy: the sense of 'historic time' . . 20

2 ON COMMUNICATION, ANCIENT AND MODERN

1. Our changing view of the world 26
2. Our present day obsession with the clock and the news . . 27
3. Notes upon communication in antiquity 29
4. The coming of mass-communication 33
5. The Press and advertising 36
6. Mass-communication media. A new medium does not replace
   an older, but only some of its functions 42
7. Speed of communication and social stability 53

3 THE COMMUNICATION EXPLOSION

1. Post-War expansion of world communication 57
2. World news. The spread of News Agencies 60
3. 'Inland' (or national) communication. Comparision of countries 69
4. International, intercontinental and overseas communication . 80
5. Airways traffic, air mail and tourism—post-War phenomena . 94
6. Technology both satisfies and creates demand. . . . 96
7. The logic of growth: the expanding rich–poor gap . . . 98

4 COMMUNICATION, POLITICS AND PLEASURE

1. A vision of world communication in the year 1866 . . . 103
2. Modern communication media and our personal attitudes . 104
3. Overseas and international broadcasting 108
4. On propaganda 113
5. The growth of International Organizations 121
6. The planning of world communication 126
7. Worldwide telecommunication. The Rome Plan and the Mexico
   City Plan 132

5   COMMUNICATION AND WEALTH

    1. Communication and wealth: the advanced countries   .   . 137
    2. Communication and wealth: the developing countries   .   . 145
    3. The falling costs of communication   156
    4. 'Trunking' of communication traffic offers advantage to the
       richer countries 160
    5. Satellites and the poorer countries   163

6   SOME SOCIAL ASPECTS OF WORLD
    COMMUNICATION

    1. Communication, nationalism and internationalism .   .   . 166
    2. On tourism as a mode of communication   .   .   . 170
    3. International relations are institutional, not personal   .   . 173
    4. International communication is both slender and institutional . 175
    5. Will world broadcasting lead to extinction of minority languages? 179
    6. On books in the 'Age of Television'   185
    7. Democracy and the mass media   194
    8. Thoughts on the future of world communication: a summary . 201

BIBLIOGRAPHY   207

INDEX 221

Introduction*

In the year 1271 A.D. the young boy Marco Polo, together with his father and uncle, set out from his native Venice to carry the Christian message into Asia.[204] From Acre they crossed Persia, Afghanistan, Turkistan and then in thirty days they passed over the Gobi Desert to reach the Great Wall of China. Entering through, they finally reached the city of Shang-tu, near Pekin, after four years travel across the longitude of Asia. There they came face to face with the Lord of Lords, Kublai Khan, whose grandfather, the terrible Genghiz Khan, had swarmed his armies over the whole face of Asia, from the China Sea to the Baltic, right up to the boundaries of Europe. What fate could these brave Venetians, highly cultured and civilized men, reasonably expect from the hands of this heathen Tartar? Strangulation, maybe? Or 'to be shaken between two carpets until their spirits left their bodies'?

As we all know it was quite otherwise. The three travellers were treated most honourably and kindly, the boy becoming a great favourite. But why? Mainly because Kublai's grandfather Genghiz, by bringing his hordes to the edge of Europe long before had thereby exposed them to influences of the Christian culture. A few travelling friars and others too later passed into AsiaK ublai Khan wished to learn more, for he saw in Christianity a possible means for civilizing his people. The Polos were expected and were welcome.† [78,204]

Let me now cap this story of successful communication with another, of less success, but equally relevant to the theme of this book.

Some seven hundred years later, I myself was travelling in the U.S.S.R., in far greater comfort than did Marco Polo, for I had all the aids of modern transport and communication to ensure that I did—aeroplanes, telephones, telegraphs and other things, all far better than horses, camels and elephants; besides these, but hidden from my sight, were navigation aids, radio, computers, even closed circuit television, a vast complex of electronic technology to ensure my safe passage.

One fine afternoon found me sitting in a bus, sight-seeing in Moscow. We had a most courteous Russian lady guide who told us in faultless English of the various sights as we passed. Coming to a certain church she gave a thumbnail history as we passed and then, solmenly and without apparent malice said: 'I don't quite understand it, but I believe that this Church was named after an unmarried woman who became pregnant in rather unusual circumstances'.

The whole bus load of us sat aghast, shocked into silence for the moment, both Christian and pagan alike; then a few giggled from embarrassment. It was the sort of silly, literal, word-by-word interpretation of a translating machine. Gone was all the mystery, the symbolism, the allegory and all

---

* Some paragraphs in this Introduction and in Chapter 1 have been taken from the author's two (unpublished) B.B.C. 3rd Programme talks, entitled *Living with Telecommunication*, produced by Mr. Laurie John, broadcast on 10th and 11th July, 1969.

† The two elder men had made the journey before, a few years earlier. At the start of the second journey, the boy Marco was only 17 years old.

aspects of the specific culture out of which the story of the Virgin birth had sprung. The ground had been suddenly cut from under our feet; we were in two worlds at once.

It was only a matter of *words*, of course. Oh, yes, the interpreter had learned the syntax and the vocabulary of English, and spoke fluently. But a language is far more than a dictionary and grammar book; however skilfully we may learn a foreign language we cannot *be* a member of its society. I was reminded then of Benedetto Croce's remark *traduttare tradittore*: 'translation is betrayal'. So, once again, with the aid of aeroplanes, navigation aids, radar, computers, telephones and all the rest I got me back to Britain, where things are said and done as Nature intended.

With all these 700 years of history, from Marco's day to mine, with all our technical progress in means of communication (most of it made during the last 15 or 20 years only), Asia and Europe, with its Western historical derivatives, are farther apart than ever. They have never been closer together, in their *wish* to understand, than in the late 13th century. Is this technology's fault? Of course not. However, to ask whether our modern means of communication aggravate or alleviate the position is to open a whole field of discourse, filled with opinions, half-truths, and a great lack of evidence.

Of all the revolutionary changes which have come upon us since the Second World War, few are likely to be of greater long-term significance to the world than those deriving from our vastly increased power for communicating. This is a sweeping statement, but it is said here not with specific gadgets in mind, like telephones, aircraft, television, computers, satellites and . . . whatever next? nor from conjecture about what each is likely to do to us. It is said rather from consideration of the nature of human communication itself, the basis of social existence and awareness, and of the real nature of technology. In Chapter 1, Section 1 'society' will be regarded as 'people in communication', the means of communication which are possessed being a major determinant of the forms of the various social institutions in any society, whether they be within a peasant society, a nomadic society, or one which we pride ourselves in calling an 'advanced society'.

To take an example, money is a technical means of communication, the invention of which permitted totally new forms of social organization. Its coins, notes and bills are tokens of exchange, readily convertible to numbers or words on paper accounts. Money, like other media of communication, telephones, telegraphs, computers, data links, offers 'power to organize' various forms of social institution. All the media of communication which are today pouring from the cornucopia of modern technology offer power to relate one set of human activities, at one place, to other sets of activities, at other places: i.e. to *organize*. Looked at this way, they may be regarded as the most recent and important extensions of the values of the division of labour principle: over whole countries and, increasingly, internationally. Printing is another obvious example, whose social consequences need hardly be mentioned. Both are ancient technologies yet, far from becoming outmoded, both are coming into increasing and widespread use, nationally and internationally. The coming of the telephone in the last century was equally revolutionary, not just because it raised the speed of communication, in one step, from that of the horse to that of electricity, but because it enabled people to move about with greater security—it added as much to personal mobility, as did the wheel, inasmuch as it made *conceivable* the movement of people's bodies whilst they remained, in mind, at home. Again, the primary importance of the invention of radio, at the turn of the century, was that it immediately changed the future of naval warfare—because ships could disperse out of sight of one another.

These two examples, the early telephone and radio, may illustrate one of the most important aspects of technology, often overlooked by the general public. It is that the original purposes and values of a new technique, which may so greatly excite the people of the day, soon become overtaken by totally new, hitherto unconceived, values and purposes. The new techniques permit new modes of action and totally new forms of social institution come to be created, having new purposes and values.

This very week (July, 1969) three American astronauts have journeyed to the Moon and two of them have landed on her. T.V. programmes have kept us informed of every step of that voyage and of more technical details than most of us can comprehend. At the same time there has been a flood of speculation, often in high-flown language suited to the excitement of the moment, of what this 'means for Mankind, etc.' The truth is that no-one knows what the longer-term values to society will be, what new forms of organization will be created, or how we shall come to change our ways as a consequence of this epic voyage.

Technology is not comprehensible in isolation, but only within a social, political, environment. It is a major determinant of our environment today and its success or failure cannot be judged by technical or even by economic criteria alone. People and institutions are always involved in these judgements; their happiness, their security, their beliefs and social attitudes. It is always a social affair.

It is by taking such a viewpoint that this book may be said to differ in approach most markedly from the writings of Marshall McLuhan. Whereas that writer seems to be dealing, using great imagination, primarily with the psychological, internal, subjective results of a person's involvement in the communication process (both person-to-person and person-to-medium), my own book aims to examine the global, social, aspects. Perhaps it is complementary to McLuhan's approach, but it gives us a certain advantage in that evidence and data are fairly easy to come by, for Government Yearbooks and International Organizations publish facts and figures in immense quantities. We shall here be always mindful of individuals, but also of their creation by their society and its institutions, as Emile Durkheim first urged us to do.*

'Communication' has become a subject of great popular interest today, and often of concern, for very good reasons. The various new media, as they appear, offer a certain feeling of *threat*, because they all imply a possible disturbance of the familiar social order, a change of social relations and hence a threat to one's own feelings of self. Many questions are raised: will world communication help unite or divide us? Do radio, T.V. and the Press control us or not? Is T.V. really increasing juvenile delinquency? There is now a whole mythology of so-called 'mass-communication'. What is modern communication doing to us and what new media are around the corner, yet to come? Will increasing national and global communication services inevitably lead to greater centralization of power and so to loss of the individual? If this is feared by some, then why should centralized 'world government' seem to many to be a desirable aim? Is there not some contradiction here? In recent years, millions of transistor sets have poured into

* For those who may not know of the work of this pioneer sociologist, the book: *Emile Durkheim* by Robert Bierstedt, Weidenfeld and Nicolson, London, 1966 is recommended.

countries of Africa and the Middle East; what effects will they have upon these traditional societies, for better or worse? As another example: radio may be used for what is often called 'propaganda', on one hand, whilst the 'hot line' (see p. 54) to the Kremlin may possibly help to counter its results. The word propaganda is flung around today too readily, without close examination of what it really means. How will our future world-coverage satellites change this propaganda—for better or worse? If the so-called 'advanced' countries own the bulk of our intercontinental systems of communication how will the poorer countries fare? Will these systems be lifelines of assistance or vehicles of propaganda?

The great enemy to rational discussion of such socio–technical questions is generalization. It is as useless to generalize about the values of, say, television or radio as it is to generalize about those of books. The values of all media are as varied as the winds and depend upon people, purposes and circumstances. Words like 'mass-communication' and 'propaganda' are words that we shall need to examine carefully (see pages 33–113), for they are themselves generalizations and, as such, can create these feelings of threat. They are blanket-words, very useful to people who argue in vague, general terms, more often than not in a derogatory sense. The *blessings* of mass-communication are rarely mentioned, only the curses. Another source of confusion can be failure to distinguish between the uses of communication media in (a) the *economic*, or public, sphere (e.g. by industry, business, government, airways . . .) and in (b) the *domestic* sphere (as in the home).

Chapter 1 is particularly concerned with the question: what is communication? It is argued there that 'communication' does not mean simply 'sending messages' nor 'bringing people together'. Human communication may sometimes bring us together in agreement, but it can equally well keep us apart; you may breathe words of love into a telephone or you may shout abuse. When communicating you can agree or disagree, assent or dispute; you may fraternize or you may quarrel.

What is this 'communication explosion' we hear about so much? It stems from the sudden flowering of our technical means of communication which has come about mainly during the last ten to twenty years—a very, very short time, before which the ways of communication for most of the world's people had changed little for thousands of years. It will be examined in some detail in Chapter 3. It is an explosion which has hit us in one generation, and is still continuing. We are living in the middle of this revolution and so we are in no position to be confident of the social outcomes. As our means of communication have improved and spread round the world so, in many but fortunately not in all ways, we have become increasing strangers. Our expanding world communication systems have brought nations which are not truly contemporaries into increasing contact, and we see each other over great historical gaps.

It is upon our very varied world, with its immense variety of languages, and of physical, social and political conditions which have evolved and changed over the centuries, that technological inventions have sprung. Inventions happen suddenly, often the creation of single individuals, and they usually come in advance of recognized social needs and readiness. The two worlds, the human and the technological, are different in their natures in this way: man is evolutionary; technology is revolutionary. All modern 'technological societies' must therefore develop under constant shock and strain, at least until we have learned to develop institutions of government, education, law, business . . . of family, and all other life, which will have vastly greater abilities to adapt than those we have inherited today.

The expression: 'this shrinking world' is a commonplace today but it is another deceptive one. The world is shrinking only in the sense that travel is much faster or that events in, say, Vietnam, are reported in cities all over the world or seen on T.V. News Bulletins within the hour. That is, the world has shrunk as a result of faster communication, but only in *time scale*. On the contrary, in the sense of personal existence and experience, the world has vastly expanded: at least it has done so in the minds of those people who have access to books, newspapers, radio or television or who are able to travel more or fly overseas. To such people, in their increasingly greater numbers and with their rising educational standards the world has not shrunk, but vastly expanded. There is far more to read about or to see. They are increasingly called upon to make more and more critical assessments, to take more and more personal views upon more and more issues, to try to understand the doings and affairs of more and more peoples in ever-more regions of the earth. The world increasingly expands and faces us with more dilemmas, whilst our emotional capacities do not. We may read the news about millions of people, or see their faces on the T.V. screen: but we do not always feel *personal* relation with those images. We can put the paper down, or turn to the crossword puzzle, just as we can switch off the T.V. set and blot out the news.

How many friends can a man have, in the sense of real personal involvement and with compassion? A dozen? A hundred, maybe? Something on a village scale of size. On no account can he have a million or a thousand million friends, known as persons, by name, with their *individual* hopes and tragedies. The world can never be my village. It is true that, on very special occasions, some special person is brought to the attention of millions simultaneously by, say, television, as by the assassination of a President or the flight of an astronaut. But these events are rare, and these people are special: public figures. World communication offers no possibility of bringing together millions of people into a sense of *personal* involvement with one another.

This may at first seem to be a depressing thought, but the viewpoints taken in this book aim to show that it need not be. It will be argued that pre-occupation with the many emotional values of national and global communication systems can divert our attention from the real, concrete values which our media offer for *organizing* new forms of social institution. It is their enormous powers for organizing, that are of primary value and importance. They offer us the means, for the first time, of forming and operating many new institutions, especially on a global scale; institutions which deal with the practical constraints of life, of international trade, finance, health, law and many others, and the removal of practical frustrations upon both national and international developments.

In summary, it is the purpose of this book to make some examination of the nature of human communication itself, if only to get away from the naive idea that it consists of people sending messages to one another, and then to look at various aspects of today's so-called communication explosion and its implications for the future. In particular, the different values to countries of different socio-economic conditions are distinguished in Chapter 5 (values to the rich countries, who create and own the bulk of the technology, and to the 'developing countries' who, in certain respects, will increasingly depend upon it). The broad, general conclusions are that our fast-expanding global systems of communication offer, as their main values, great organizing powers with which new and practical institutions can be operated, for development of trade, exchange and international law.

A brief history of the International Organizations, and of their phenomenal growth since the close of the Second World War, is given in Chapter 4. They are referred to again in Chapter 6, where opinions are offered concerning the future of world order; an idea sharply distinguished from that of centralized world government.

1

On the Nature of Human Communication

'Man is the only animal that laughs and cries and knows why'
Morris West,
'Life,' March 19th, 1965.

This opening Chapter makes some examination of the very broad question: 'What is human communication?' It cannot be deep, but aims only to highlight a number of important aspects of this difficult question and, at least, to get away from the technical idea that communication is explicable as the process of 'sending messages'. These various aspects of human communication are relevant to subsequent Chapters in which some trends and values of today's 'communication explosion' will be assessed, both nationally and globally.

1. Society regarded as 'People in Communication'

We all know the fascination of turning over a stone lying on the grass with the toe of our shoe and suddenly revealing a remarkable sight—myriads of little black ants, vibrating about over the patch of bare brown earth. After a moment's watching the movement is seen to possess structure; the whole thing seems to have purpose.

If we were unkind enough to cut open the ground we should see the object of this purpose: the complex of tunnels forming the nest, the system of self-preservation of the colony. But we should not credit any single one of these ants itself with organizing this great labour force, nor with planning the nest nor, above all, with having any knowledge of what it is doing. It has no choices, no conscious decisions to make, not even any concept of its actions.

It is we who have interpreted the whole business as constructive, planned, orderly, purposeful, not the ants.

Enough of ants. Let us now put on our wings like angels and fly up to Heaven, to gaze down upon the human race. Millions and millions of people scurrying about in all directions, very busily doing millions of different things; we shall have to watch them for a very long time before we can see any overall pattern in all this business. In fact we shall find endless different patterns, but out of all this movement no one single united purpose will show itself. Furthermore, we may notice something radically different from the ant society. The various patterns of relationships we may see, from family to continental scale, do not stay the same for long at a time, but are in a continual state of change, though the extent of these changes varies very much among them. What is more, many of these men and women seem to belong to one group at one moment, then this group dissolves and they reappear grouped in another way. Over large areas of the world, if not everywhere, any one of these people seems to be adopting a number of different *rôles*. Each seems to have very many different purposes, whilst new purposes, groupings and rôles are continually being created.

This great variety of rôles which humans are able to adopt seems to be mediated by their phenomenal powers of sign-usage, above all by those of language. It is their powers of language which set them apart from the creatures by a gulf, a gulf which Susanne Langer has seen as 'one whole day of Creation'—a whole chapter of evolution.[175] All races of man, all nations, all tribes everywhere have language. Some live amongst all the complexities of an industrial city, some live 'next to Nature'. All have language, and there is no reason to believe that the 'simple' people have 'simple' or 'primitive' languages. There are just no general relationships. Apart from their distinction of language, humans share with the creatures a host of other signs: many simple reflexes, some forms of ritual and some complex artefacts or 'inventions'. For example, our striking clocks, closely analogous as indicator signs to the sign systems used by bees, are referred to later in this Chapter. A woman can blush and she can adopt the dress fashions of the day, but animals and birds too display patches of colour. A boy can yell or point, just as a creature can indicate alarm. With such non-linguistic signs, humans can *indicate* states or *inform* or *threaten*, just as can the creatures. But with language they can further *explain* themselves, or *justify*, *argue*, and otherwise *express* themselves.*

What, then, is 'human communication? Strictly, the word communication comes from the Latin *communico*—meaning *share*. *Share*, notice, not 'I send messages'. Communication is essentially a social process. Sharing does not mean simply passing something, some sign, from one person to another, it implies also that this sign is mutually accepted, recognized and held in common ownership or use by each person. Communication always has this dual nature; it is part of each person's own mental make-up, the signs constricting his own thoughts, and equally it is those persons' union, a union mediated by those signs. Language symbols and all signs are then not only the means whereby one person gets in touch with another; they are the essential qualities of each of these persons. 'A man's essential life is made up of his communings,' was Charles Peirce's expression.†[97] What is 'me' is all my private internal musings and talking-with-myself, such as goes on in my head all through my waking hours—all personal *awareness*.[255]

To be an individual, a person, a 'self', one must be a social creature as well, a member of society and of various sub-groups, playing various rôles, adopting different loyalties and, in a self-deceptive way, seeing oneself as different on these different occasions. 'Self' and 'society' are the two inseparable sides of the coin.

When a child is born it is part of its own mother who, by verbal and other play, begins to teach the child awareness of its own separate existence and identity. Unlike any of the animals, even the apes, babies show great propensity to babble[175] and within a few months each one is babbling mainly in the phonetics of its own mother. It has by then already started off along mental railway lines which will carry it further, separating it for life from those of other languages, countries and cultures.

A child is then taught, first by its mother, by members of the family, and later by teachers and other elders, through the language, symbols and signs

* The writer has argued elsewhere[102] that a motorist is deprived of expressive outlet through language, in relation to the world outside his car, and is constrained wholly to communication by indicator signs (e.g. as by law in Code Book) and aggression signs (hooting etc.).

† The American philosopher, creator of Pragmatism as a method, and one-time teacher of William James.[97] A remarkable and eccentric character who will be referred to later on page 21.

of their culture and their specific groups. Necessarily this teaching represents a continuity from the past, with an inherent content of past and outmoded attitudes and ideas. These vehicles of language, symbols and signs inevitably ensure an adherence to his own kind, his early group loyalties, his basic beliefs and his feelings, and so ensure, in turn, his segregation from other groups, to greater or lesser degree. To exist, with a personal awareness and image of this existence, a man must also *belong*, largely as he has been taught to belong when young, to various groups—to a country, a social class, a family, a religion, a tribe, a language group and others . . . within which he plays his various rôles, thereby seeing other people as being, somehow, different.

As a child learns to talk with his mother, in early months and years, so he also learns to talk with himself. As Charles Peirce[97,252] pointed out, talking with oneself is also a social process, a form of conversation. Thinking, that is to say, is also a social activity, whilst one's knowledge of oneself is fundamentally no different from one's knowledge of other people. 'I', 'me' and 'myself' are all the creations of society.

It was the great sociologist Emile Durkheim, who first argued clearly that an individual and his society are inseparable;*[293] that he cannot have any concepts of his own separate existence, identity and nature other than those expressible within the language, symbols and signs taught him by his society. Both his awareness of himself and of other people is created, not by his direct observations, but by the sharing of a common language, cultural symbols, social habits, rituals, tokens and many forms of sign.

Similar views have been expressed too within the physical sciences. Thus the great physicist, Erwin Schrödinger,[268] has pointed out that any person's private image of the world is not mainly the consequence of his own personal observations. What he sees and notices, or does not, what is important and what is unimportant to him, his relations to other people, to the animals, the trees, the sun, moon and stars are rather the result of his teaching and upbringing. They are socially derived, through language, symbols and signs, first from his mother teaching him to speak, with legends and fairy stories and all the traditional forms of his culture. He is *taught* to see and understand the world, and to create his own peculiar images, through his own social encounters.

If that person lives in a literate community he may partly build his image of the world through books and printed records, giving some possibility of comparison (in so far as anyone can have real historical comprehension), a sense of social change perhaps, of the 'historic arrow' of time, and even of 'progress'. (Discussed further in Chapter 6, Section 8.) But in acquiring his knowledge and feelings about other countries and peoples, through literature, he cannot fail at the same time to acquire outmoded views of them; for it is a sad fact that our knowledge and images of foreign peoples must always be to some extent, great or little, old-fashioned. It is sad too to think that tourism may do little to update our views of other countries and of their institutions, for we are likely to visit them not to be *retaught* by them, but merely to 'see for ourselves' what we have already been taught to look for, and so to confirm our antique beliefs.†

---

* E.g. see Bierstedt, R., *Emile Durkheim*, Weidenfeld and Nicolson; London, 1966, for an excellent bibliography and account of this pioneer's work.

† Tourism is considered further, as a mode of global communication, in Chapter 6, Section 2.

It can scarcely be repeated too often that language is socially derived, by exchanges between people, in endless daily encounters, and with it categorizations, ideas, viewpoints, knowledge; we are each taught to think and feel as members of our particular groups, not only about the world and other people, but about ourselves too: who we are and what we are like.

Even within our own countries or language groups, as we change our social rôles during the day or over the seasons, we may change our ways of speaking and writing. You do not usually speak to your wife and children as you would write a business letter; the language of the Club is not that of the lecture room or the Church, though all may be classified as 'English' or 'Spanish' or 'Russian', etc.

If you watch, unobserved, two people holding a conversation it may suggest that they are engaged in some form of encounter, or game, each trying to influence the other in some way. Sometimes that conversation leads to some mutual course of action as a consequence—they 'agree'—but sometimes not. On another occasion, it seems that they may not *want* to agree; one speaker may be struggling to understand the other, who may refuse to let him and struggle equally to conceal himself. It is a great mistake to regard human communication as necessarily being a process of 'sending messages', or 'passing information'. Nor is conversation necessarily a 'goal-seeking' process, not only because the two conversants may have quite different objectives in mind, but often they may have none in mind at all. The two speakers may be sharing a common language but they may not be sharing a common purpose. There can even be occasions when their conversation seems to be wholly a matter of self-expression, each talking about his own feelings and beliefs, but with no attempt to understand the other; the mere presence of the other seems then to be the real need.

Language can sometimes bring people together: but equally well it can keep them apart. With language you may *enquire, inform, dispute, negotiate, agree, assent, dissent, quarrel, commune, insult, admire, ritualize* in endless ways, and . . . how many other categories of social relationship may be created?

It is this vast range of categories that, in principle, today's 'communication explosion' is spreading over the globe, such as will be described in later Chapters. What will be the consequences of this technological revolution? Even to discuss these likely consequences rationally, the dual nature of human language must always be borne in mind; as expressed in earlier paragraphs, it is both *social* and *personal*, being acquired through one's society and also being used to create one's own thoughts and self-images.

The extension of language and other signs by technical means of communication therefore has also a two-sided result, both social and personal. Where the means exist, not only can you telephone friends and colleagues or get help by sending telegrams, etc. *but you assume that you are able to.* You have learnt to speak of 'telephones' (for example) and to take for granted a host of liberties that they offer you. They have become part of your mental make-up, of the familiar world. So too with all the technological devices upon which people in the industrial countries utterly depend. These things are built into their thinking, into their feelings of security and of what they are free to do, and into their language. The way they regard themselves, their security, their status, their freedoms of action and their relations with other people are determined to a major extent by these facts. It only requires a failure of a telephone line, or of the newspaper delivery or, for that matter, a rail strike to remind us sharply how we take for granted many facilities, as if they were part of Nature; that is, in the industrial countries.

The full effects of some newly introduced mtehod of communication thus cannot be predicted solely in terms of its likely contribution to people's social contacts, to message traffic *per se*, unless at the same time its likely effects upon people's individual private worlds are also considered; and it is the latter which may often be so significant, yet more difficult to assess. One interesting illustration of the truth of this appeared when the idea was first suggested of introducing television into the British House of Commons. When Mr. Crossman (then Minister of Housing and Local Government) introduced the proposal to make a closed-circuit T.V. experiment in Parliament, as a preliminary trial before broadcasting to the public, there was uproarious debate among the Members concerning the effect that it might have upon *themselves*: 'That well known T.V. personality Mr. Quintin Hogg was among the many who felt that the cameras would change the nature of the place. . . .' 'Good for their egos too?' asked Mr. Pannell; 'Parliament', he argued '. . . is not for performers.'*†

However, in certain two-person situations which are highly ritualized where the persons are playing specific rôles (e.g. doctor and patient), the arrival of a third person may have minimal effect upon their relationship (e.g. when a nurse enters).

Let us return to the question posed at the beginning of this Section: What is human communication? It is for the various reasons which have been outlined here that the writer prefers not to answer the question in this form, but rather to turn it round and to define *society* as *people in communication*. The various types of society, sub-society and groups depend upon the modes of communication they possess: upon rituals, upon signs of personal relationships, or of vocation or function, codes of behaviour and symbols, upon extent of literacy and numeracy and, most relevant here, upon their possession of various technical media of communication—newspapers, radio, telegraphs, telephones, cinema, television, etc.—and, especially, upon the extent to which they can create their own media-usages, write their own books, make their own films, produce their own programmes.

In the sense that the term social 'groups' is taken here, endless examples could be cited. Within industrial countries we might think of a Trade Union, or a religious sect, or the local home-town, or a language-group, or a family, or a trade, or a social class, or an 'income bracket', . . . or a country . . . or motorists and pedestrians . . . endless groups. But these groups are not groups of different people; they are different sets of rôles. The people change, but the groups remain. We are all, as individual persons, involved in many such groups at different times, playing different rôles. Each rôle requires different habits of us, different loyalties, different styles of language maybe, and the adoption of various signs of identification, including ritual signs.

It is precisely for this reason, the extent to which he is aware of being able to *choose* to change his rôle, that a person can feel himself to be an independent being, but it is a freedom always restricted by constraints, seen or unseen, of taboo, economics, ignorance, fear or mere lack of motive. But the duality is always there, the apparent contradiction—to be an individual, a man must belong; it is his awareness of the constraints upon his choices

---

* *Guardian*, November 25th, 1966.
† Ref. Goffman. E. *The Presentation of Self in Everyday Life*, Doubleday Anchor Books, New York, 1959.

of rôle, or belongings, that is the source of his feelings of freedom or of frustration.

The word *ritual* has been mentioned. Today this word is often used in a narrow sense, to mean ceremonial or other formal behaviour, particularly related to religious practices. This is unfortunate, for such restricted usage may create misunderstanding, or even antagonism. In its broad sense the word ritual can be used to mean all forms of sign-usage indicating memberships of social groups (both animal[107, 117, 167, 194, 290, 292, 348,] and human), temporary or long lasting, symbols of our various belongings. Few people who would cast out ritual (in its ceremonial sense) would at the same time deny the values of such unconscious signs as handshakes, spoken courtesies and other social customs, or of some professional jargon, or of the traditional rules of conducting a lecture or of eating a meal. There may of course be good and bad* rituals, or outmoded forms whose significance becomes lost as traditions fade or change in changing industrial societies. But rôle identification requires an element of ritual of some kind or other, significant of the nature of the assumed situation in which the rôles are being played.

Human language itself has, among its many values, a ritualistic function, though unfortunately it is not species-wide, but confined to specific groups: classes, sections, nations and other groups. It is perhaps most consciously noticed in specialized jargons, such as those of the law, of medicine, of the Church, or of science. In common words, if you know the rules of talking within a group you know 'where you stand', you are accepted, listened to, liberated to speak your mind within that group. You are 'one of us'. Inasmuch as a form of language has universal significance within a group, whether this be a profession, a social class, a district, a family, an institution, or a nation, it is a force for integration, a force which may be regarded as ritualistic. The rules are obeyed, conformed to, and embarrassment fades, so that from that firm ground of social confidence, you may then personally argue, even disagree, and so employ all the personally distinguishing uses of language. You can 'beg to differ', or to 'give an opinion' without being cast out. Language is then, socially, both integrating and distinguishing. You may conform generally, but disagree personally. The dualism is always there; by virtue of being a member you are the more free to be an individual.†

The importance of the ritualistic function of language, as determining social identity and loyalties, is never more clearly demonstrated than by the passionate adherence of minority language groups to their threatened languages. Battles have been fought over languages. Riots have occurred in Belgium, with fighting between the Walloons and the Flemish. The Welsh have battled with the British authorities to ensure that the application form for a Driving Licence is printed in Welsh as well as in English. History shows endless examples. And no-one living within the security of a dominant language group should raise an eyebrow in astonishment or moral rectitude.

Unfortunately, this very belonging to groups inevitably divides a member from all the other groups, however little. If he feels loyalties *towards* a group he must be to some extent antagonistic towards other groups, or, at the very least, distinguished from them in some way or other, greater or less.

A man of liberal mind may deny this; he may say and feel that he is *tolerant* of other groups, and not opposed (for example, an educated white

* E.g. some clichés and slogans, a point to be discussed in Chapter 1, Section 6.
† E.g. see discussion of the changed meaning of the word *individual*, in Chapter 6, Section 8 (page 204).

person, speaking of the coloured races). If so, he has shared with them certain signs of relatedness but, in so doing, he has automatically divided himself off from those other white people who are not tolerant in like way. Groups, to be groups, must be distinguished. Loyalties to one imply loyalties *against* others, however little.

There is a common cliché: 'man is an aggressive animal', which is frequently offered as an explanation of fratricide and violence; but it is really no explanation at all. Strictly speaking, people are not particularly aggressive as individual *persons*. Certainly, one cannot deny that there are murderers, thugs, bullies, burglars, robbers and rapists, but their numbers are very few of the many millions of us who are, on the whole, peaceful, law-abiding people. Most of us, as individual *persons*, are not murderers, thugs, bullies, burglars, robbers and rapists. Men are not, as the cliché so often tells us, 'aggressive animals', their major aggressions are *group* aggressions. The aggressions which cause the majority of us such concern are committed by groups, by armies, by mobs, by gangs; an individual person, when involved in such groups, seems readily to become transformed into something else— something whose behaviour is certainly not typical of the behaviour of the vast bulk of human beings. If we seek the sources of human aggression then, we should seek them not in individual human nature, but in the structure of such groups, in the signs and rules which characterize these groups. In other words, in their specific forms of communication.[209]

A human being cannot fail to be a member of various groups, whether he is consciously aware of them or not. He then knows 'himself', what is expected of him and his relations to others. Call it what you will—nationalism, culture, class-loyalty, professionalism, race-consciousness, gang-membership, and many other group-attitudes—he will seek to close the ranks in defence of his own identity. He may see those of other groups as in some ways strangers, whom he cannot readily understand. Furthermore, he may not want to, nor try to. He can be *proud* of not understanding other peoples, with their curious ways, customs, sayings and other signs of their distinction. He builds emotional walls around himself, not so much to keep the others out as to contain himself, his kind, and his identity. Man is inevitably segregated into groups; his loyalty towards any one logically implies that the group must be distinct, separate, sometimes opposed to others in certain ways; *opposed*, that is, in the literal sense of 'counter-distinct', in some way or other, and not necessarily with active hostility or aggressiveness. Furthermore, it so often seems that he can adjust himself to those of other groups only in ways which his own language, signs and symbols allow, ways which have so often led to violent aggression, conflict and destruction. On the whole, although the higher mammals are sometimes aggressive towards their own kind, they have avoided mass fratricide; their signs and rituals play no small part in this. Unfortunately for the human race it has little or no common ritual, significant of its unity as a species, but it has very many different rituals, significant of its fragmentation and helping to maintain it. It would be a rash assumption that even smiles, frowns, tears and other facial gestures are interpreted *everywhere* the same.

Man has endless uses of language, signs and ritual, significant of the fact that he is a member of a nation, or a class, or a tribe, or a race, of this or that group; but he has no common language, few signs, and virtually no universal ritual significant of the fact that he is a member of the human race.

2. Persons and personifications

The global spread of communication media such as News Agencies, overseas broadcasting, films, television programmes and other services available to the public has come about with great speed, in most cases since the end of the Second World War*. One obvious consequence of this is sometimes referred to as 'the overpressure of news'. However, not only are we expected in countries of high literacy to read and understand an overwhelming torrent of news items, from all corners of the earth towards which national interest of the moment turns, but this news is mostly about distant persons whom we have not met personally and never shall. Whereas in tribal society, or in Western village communities we 'know' our fellows, with their various doings, their hopes and failings, by personal encounter, we can only 'know' the multitude of people abroad indirectly through reportings in newspapers or visual reportings on the screen—necessarily fleeting glimpses. That is to say, we may know our own kind by direct encounter and the shared experience of living with them, but we can 'know' other people only by their *descriptions*, as interpreted and reported by word or by picture. Yet this is what we are increasingly called upon to do, as global communication fast expands: to adjust to unknown people through 'knowledge-by-reporting'.

In the writer's opinion, one of the greatest dangers into which these post-War developments of world communication can lead us is the delusion that, as the global network expands, so the walls of our mental villages are being pushed back: the delusion that increased powers of communication will bring us all closer together into better understanding and a sense of human compassion. There is no foundation whatsoever for such an emotional belief. For though this fast-expanding network increases our 'knowledge-by-reporting' it adds little or nothing to our 'knowledge-by-encounter'.† And there are worlds of difference between sharing experiences with others, of joy or suffering, and reading about them in the newspapers; between starving to death and seeing pictures of it on the T.V. screen; between being under bombardment and watching a News Bulletin. One can put down the newspaper, or turn over the page, or one can switch off the T.V. set and blot out the news, and the blame is not to be laid upon 'human callousness'. It is inherent in modern long-distance and large-scale world communication media.

'An earthquake produces what the law promises, but does not in practice achieve . . . the equality of all men'. So said Ignazius Silone. Nothing integrates us like disaster. But the news which forms such a major part of the background against which Western society lives is to a great extent news of other people's disasters, in which we who are reading these reportings are not directly involved in any immediate and personal way.‡ The ever-mounting volume of news that presses upon us requires us at least to adopt some personal attitudes towards millions of different people. We cannot know them individually as persons, but read about them only as names and activities. We can see them only as classes and types, as institutions, as abstracts, and speak of *the* Biafrans, *the* Chinese, *the* Arabs, as though such populations varied little among themselves, as persons! We sometimes need to speak of

---

* Some facts and figures are presented in later Chapters, particularly in Chapter 3.

† If the words 'global communication network' be taken to include transport (e.g. aircraft), then true personal and lengthy encounter may be assisted for certain privileged persons, such as diplomats, travelling scholars, members of International Organizations, people of multiple domicile, etc. In Chapter 6, Section 2, the case against *tourism* as a successful mode of 'knowledge-by-encounter' will be presented.

‡ For discussion of newspapers, their history, News Agencies, etc., see Chapter 2, Sections 2 and 5 and Chapter 3, Section 2, in particular.

the Americans, as though every one were alike, or, worse, of *teenagers*, the *black races, students* . . . a host of gross generalizations in increasing numbers, as world affairs come to interest and concern more people. So long as these are recognized as generalizations, classes or abstracts, false arguments may be avoided. But there is growing danger that they can be discussed as though they were persons, rather than personifications (as they really are) and the sins of one member, or small section, of any such group can become read as being the sins of the whole group. The sight of a single foreign face on the T.V. screen or a single ugly incident in a vast crowd, picked out by the newsthirsty cameraman, may create symbols falsely representing something 'typical' of whole populations or crowds.

Such dangers of regarding pictures, or news items and other reportings, as symbols and not as pieces of reality are not the creation of our modern mass-communication media. They are nothing new, to be laid at the door of television, newspapers, or the cinema. For precisely the same thing could be said about literature and history books. We may read about major events of the 14th Century, or of Islam or Imperial Rome, or of social conditions in the Industrial Revolution and, from these few reportings, inevitably few, we may receive the impression that we know what it was like to have lived then, as a particular person. Our modern communication media present us with ikon symbols in increasing numbers, coming from wide areas of the world (and, nowadays, from outside it) in a way closely analogous to the way in which our old, familiar history books and classical novels presented us with symbols gathered over wide centuries of time. They merely extend this old process. In all such 'one-way' media of communication, ancient or modern, from books to television, specific events or persons have to be selected as being particularly significant and presented to the reader or viewer as symbols. Nothing else is possible in any form of 'one-way', non-conversive, communication-by-reportings. The person reading or viewing is not involved in the events symbolized, whereas in true conversive, 'two-way' communication he is, whether this be face-to-face conversation, telephone conversation or correspondence.

It was Jean-Paul Sartre*[293] who distinguished these two classes of communication, in terms of the ideas of 'watching' and 'being watched'. Thus, when you are in conversation with somebody you are fully aware that he or she is of the same nature as yourself, i.e. human. This recognition instils into you certain attitudes and feelings, which do not exist when you are quite alone, with only tables, chairs and other objects for company. You and your partner are *watching* each other and are aware too of being watched. You are mutually involved. Tables and chairs do not watch you. This may have been quite different in the days of pantheism, or even where it exists in the world today. Whether non-animal nature *watches* you depends only upon your belief. To non-pantheists it does not. Your relations to a real person are then quite distinct from your relations to objects. This distinction made by Sartre can be seen in terms of our *embarrassment* or *self-consciousness* when confronted by others. We feel that way when we are 'objects of scrutiny'. We cannot be embarrassed when alone, in privacy, though we may feel shame.[196] Briefly, we communicate with persons but merely observe objects.

When watching people on, say, a television news bulletin reported by a

* See his *Being and Nothingness*, New York, Philosophical Library, 1956.

roving camera, you are not watched by *them*; you are not mutually involved. You can then so readily watch them as symbols, as ikons, as *things*. You can watch scenes of battery and butchery, without feeling to be part of the immediate situation, *as though* those people were things. It takes a conscious, deliberate intellectual act to respond to them as persons.

Sitting in front of a T.V. set, watching these fleeting images, you are neither alone nor in company, but in a highly artificial situation. This artificiality is a characteristic of all 'one-way' communication media, to varied extents to all media which are loosely termed the 'mass-media', and it is partly responsible for the strong emotional attitudes so often aroused towards these media. In particular, newspapers, advertisements, radio, television, and all other one-way communication-by-reporting media often arouse, in the minds of those at the receiving end, fears which are expressed in words such as 'being manipulated': a fear akin to that of being under the eye of officialdom, bureaucrats, over-remote directors and other faceless bosses.

Such apparent manipulation is, however, not exercised by the performers themselves whom we are watching on the screen nor by the persons we are reading about in the newspapers. It is rather the authorities behind them who appear to have this power to manipulate us: the broadcasting authorities, the newspaper editor, the publisher, and all other one-way media comptrollers. They all, without exception, necessarily require some form of organizing authority.

One direct consequence of this fact, that all one-way media (including books and plays) require organizing authorities of some nature or other, is that the people at the receiving end are involved in dual relationships—relationships with those persons and events being reported upon and with those who do the reporting—and it is this which creates the artificiality which can lead to feelings of manipulation.

The charge is often made against domestic television that it keeps people riveted to their seats with their eyes glued on the screen for hours on end, watching with fascination whatever images appear. There may be little truth in this popular view, though it raises some interesting points. The question is, when watching a face on television, who is watching who? The viewers in the sitting room may feel that it is they who are 'being watched', not only by the face on the screen but also by the authority behind, unseen. It is the authority who is the great manipulator. They themselves are certainly viewing but they are not 'watching' in the existential sense for they cannot reply, answer back, challenge; all their gestures made seem to be totally ignored by the face on the screen. Therefore, these viewers may feel sometimes that they are being treated as inanimate objects rather than persons. It is they who are being watched by the face on the screen, in their own minds. All such 'one-way' media may therefore become imbued with a characteristic of authoritarianism. All one-way media come from them to us and we cannot answer back, but are frustrated, however little. There is no discourse or conversation, no true communication in the sense of human interaction.

It will be argued later that the conditions of the Western industrial countries, at least during the post-War years of the communication explosion, have both favoured and needed the development of such one-way, centralized media, whilst areas of economic and political affiliations have expanded. It will also be argued that these centralizations and expansions are not the inevitable and sole consequences of modern communication technology; rather, communication technology, in its various forms, can equally well assist processes of decentralization. It depends upon the particular medium and upon its usage. Centralization has come first, but democracy requires also decentralization. The two processes are not incompatible and there are today many signs of decentralization (local, regional) being both demanded and supplied, now that they can at last be *afforded*. In the poorer countries, the needs for better communication may be otherwise. See especially, Chapter 6, Section 7.

3. Communication as an act of courage

Conversation, or even casual remarks, all have purpose; they seek to greet, persuade, correct, ask, explain . . . , though the speaker may not always know his purpose. In many different ways one person seeks to change his relation with the other and, through him, to change himself. Conversations are not just signals passing back and forth between people: they are, to some degree or other, matters of personal involvement.

Conversation with another person is an act of acceptance and of committal. Before you speak to a person a decision has to be made by one of you to choose the other to talk to, whilst he has to accept. You face and see one another and recognize instantly that the relationship between you is now a special one because of this selection, a very special one indeed, perhaps recognized by a sign such as a smile. You are, to some degree, *committed*. You have to go on with it. He has your attention and anything you say or do will leave an impression upon him, perhaps permanently. You know too that he will be speaking to other people later. So what you are going to say to him commits you, however little. What you will say, you cannot unsay; you may of course withdraw the remark, or apologize, or correct yourself, or bite your tongue, or wish to sink through the floor. But nevertheless it has been said and thus your relationship will to some extent, however minor, be changed for better or worse. Furthermore, so will his own relationship with the rest of society be changed; he may 'speak about you' to others in some new way. Through him, therefore, so will your own relations with society be changed. What's said cannot be unsaid; *human communication is irreversible*.

Imagine yourself walking along the street, looking for something in particular, say a certain shop. You decide to ask somebody. Walking around you on the pavement are dozens of other people, strangers, wholly indifferent to your existence. You have now to make some conscious choice and select one person who looks agreeable to you in various ways. Some appear to be in too much of a hurry, some look like foreigners, some look the kind of person that you judge to be aggressive or stupid, or simply the kind of person you don't get on with. Your gaze hops from one face to another and your steps falter; eventually you do catch the eye of one of them—and ask. This selection of another person, however trivial the occasion, is an act of *courage*, however little. For you are deciding to become involved with that selected person, hitherto a distant stranger.

Naturally, he may dismiss you with a quick answer and say: 'Round the next corner', but sometimes you get involved in a minor conversation; if so, then breaking off the conversation requires another decision too. Indeed, many people find considerable difficulty in saying goodbye. Both starting and stopping conversations are acts of courage—however minor.

This embarrassment at approaching another person or parting from him is essential to the nature of human communication. These are conscious *decisions*, which are known to be irreversible; they are decisions to expose one's private self to another in various ways. Having decided and acted you cannot *undecide*. Social bonds of language are thus not casually or lightly made; they most often require some courage, however little, both to make and to break. This can be brought home to you very clearly when misdialling a telephone number and finding yourself encountering a total stranger. Such victims often sound most offended too, as though you had misdialled them purposely!

In Sartre's terms, this fear of approaching another person arises from exposure of ourselves to him as an *object*; we become objects of scrutiny; when alone, we appear to ourselves as persons.[293]

Can we ever feel this transformation more readily than when making a speech, giving a lecture, standing on a stage: pinned there, committed, exposed and unable to retreat or escape? Speaking for myself, I feel naked when sitting before a T.V. camera, its staring lens scrutinizing me like the one great eye of the collective audience of viewers.

4. 'World languages'— Linguae francae

Conversation, the two-person interaction, is the fundamental unit of human communication. Speech is something which is spoken *between* persons, rather than *by* persons. Even in soliloquy, or thinking, you, talking to yourself, are engaged in a social activity. (This point is taken up in Section 5.) First comes the mother/baby relationship, teaching the child its first steps towards language and, with it, knowledge of its own existence as a separate being, with a name. Then through all the child's relationships with others and, in youth and adulthood, meeting with many more people: arguing, discussing, persuading, demanding, pleading, it so *develops* its language, forming its own image of the world and of itself.

This possibility of development of human language reveals its great distinction from animal sign-systems. Human language has an apparently unlimited possibility of development.[97] Whatever you say, I can always choose to say something different. We can always add to our language, constantly bring in new ideas; language and thought go together and these are learnt socially, by exchange one with another. There seems to be no limit to the degree of modification and extension of languages and thoughts. Whereas the signs used by animals, birds and insects always seem to have the same referents, the sounds of human speech, spoken words, can have an unlimited number of different referents, or the same referent but in an unlimited variety of contexts. Not only can a man shout 'Help!' one moment, but he could on another occasion use the same word and say 'Please, can you help me?' or again he might quote: 'Help yourself, and Heaven will help you'. True language requires more than the instinctive or learned signs of animals; it requires that the sounds be used symbolically: i.e. that they can be uttered in different situations yet consistently interpreted.

Bees have fascinated people by their methods of communication, possibly more than any other creature.[93,191,192,272] Watch a flight swarming; they seem to be totally involved, in some one single purpose. Well known is their 'dancing',* on the vertical comb in the dark, signifying the direction and distance to nectar and pollen (incidentally, this is very similar to our use of striking clocks for telling the time).[93,52] It should not be forgotten that bees

---

* Aristotle commented on the 'wagging' dance of bees. (Ref. 78.)

do have various other purposes, each calling for communication. Thus they must 'decide' to swarm at some time. More interesting, at that time 'scouts' are sent out who return with information about alternative possible sites for swarming and their merits (e.g. dampness). A hive 'decision' is made, rather like voting, and a site selected. We are here near to language, but very far removed from *developable* language in the human sense.

So with all creatures. If you say 'boo' to a goose, that bird is most likely to hiss at you with outstretched neck. But if you are to walk up to *me* and say 'boo', we shall get involved in a conversation lasting until bedtime.

In great distinction from any animal species, Man has evolved thousands of different languages, dialects, symbols and sign-systems. One species we are, yet so utterly varied in this way.* Other creatures have a common 'language' throughout their species, although 'dialects' exist.[272, 290] But Man has so many, very different, ones. Kenneth Oakley distinguishes Man as being able both to make and use tools.[224, 225] In this sense, Man's signs and language are tools; he can both make them and use them.

The sounds of speech, words, phrases, exclamations and other utterances are examples of *signs*, a name indicating that they are *significant*, not only in semantic content, but significant of the speaker's mood, for example, or of his social class, or his attitudes, or fatigue and other things. It is not only what is said that matters, but where and when it is said, and to whom. The power of language does not spring entirely from its formal semantic content: if it did, then United Nations Assembly debates might proceed more smoothly. It has ritualistic power, aggressive power, publicity and many other symbolic values. It has powers for nationalism too; however, though spoken language is essential to the feelings of nationality and of nationalism, it is not their sole basis, for one language may be native to several countries (e.g. as are English, Spanish and Arabic. See Ref. 69).

The bulk of our own waking thoughts are in our language, rambling partially-connected phrases, every moment of the day. Truly, we can 'visualize' and thereby think in pictures or patterns,[99, 100, 101] but we certainly don't think in pictures for much of the day; we most likely will when day-dreaming, or when sitting alone meditating, or contemplating, or for delib-erate reasoning. The mental formation of any visual image will, if really vivid, inhibit one's awareness of the surroundings. You can test the truth of this by trying now to recall and visualize a friend's face. (Don't do this while crossing the road.)

Language is used not according to any imposed or rigid rules or laws but according to social habits; 'Custom and custom alone' as Hume said. We *conform* to habits of using these, to various ways socially and historically decided. Many studies of language statistics have been made which illustrate our verbal habits (e.g. of word frequencies and orderings, etc.). These are mostly based on written language. A few references are given here: 158, 207, 246, 274, 298, 348, 353, 354, 363.

The creation of symbols and language signifies Man's essential powers of forming concepts. Conceptualizing is the basis of human communication; Man has seemingly unlimited power for making concepts. When a new idea comes to mind, its very newness means that it is distinguishable from the

* It is impossible to give full references to the subject. A selection are numbered: 17, 18, 19, 115, 157, 258, 348–350. For those non-specialist readers who may wish to study vocal production and the physical sounds of speech there is no better starting point than Paget's classic book *Human Speech*, recently reissued.[235]

others and thereby it is already identified or categorized; i.e. signified or symbolized and so is *expressible*. The private and the public natures of language and symbols cannot be separated, for one implies the other. Concepts are created and symbolized within us in thought as the result of intercourse with other people, and, in turn, these symbols are used for communicating with others and so having effect upon them and upon their own symbolized private concepts.

Man often refers to himself as 'the rational animal', and so he is for part of the time: a very small part. The rest of his day is spent on actions innumerable, trivial remarks, greetings, daydreaming, chattering: having little to do with rationality. He can sometimes be rational but he can also be artistically creative, imaginative, speculative, inquisitive, self-assertive, sensitive, meditative, restive, hopeful . . . all these and more. No, it is not rationality or intelligence that marks Man from the animals, but something much deeper, underlying all these qualities. It is his supreme power of forming symbolized concepts and of relating them in ordered, customary ways of usage upon which rests not only his rationality but all his other consciousness and awareness of the world as he sees it.

Deliberate, reasoned argument is not easy. For the bulk of human beings conversation has little to do with reason and logic, in any formal sense; a *yes* can be turned into *no* or a *maybe* by a smile or by one person's intimate knowledge of the other. Very few people are trained in reasoning and even those who are can become most unreasonable in their daily chatter, if they are emotionally involved at all deeply.

Apart from our natural language, however, we humans use many invented systems of signs for communicating, which are imposed upon us by law, or by formal rules laid down.[216, 217] Many of these *sign-systems* and *language systems* are cross-cultural, international, and do not raise difficulties of interpretation, for their usages are restricted and formally defined. It is characteristic of formal sign-systems that breaking any of the rules usually involves the user in some kind of direct penalty.

One example is mathematics. Strictly speaking, mathematics is not a language, but rather a *language-system*.[50] A language-system[216] uses formulated signs and known rules which must be *obeyed*, within some closed, restricted class of people or culture, whereas a human language (English, French, Arabic . . .) is open, its rules of syntax may be extensively broken, not obeyed but rather conformed to only generally or on an average. But if, for instance, you say $2 \times 2 = 5$, you have broken a certain rule *laid down* in books of arithmetic. If you persist in saying $2 \times 2 = 5$ certain penalties would fall upon you, such as paying 50 new pence for 2 tickets worth 20 pence each, thereby losing 10 new pence. Rules of the road are another example; if you drive past a red light, or on the wrong side of the road, you could be fined (or killed). Clocks too; if you read your clock and mistake the long hand for the short, you might miss your lunch. Or telephone dialling; if you dial wrongly, you will get the wrong person. All such formulated sign-systems work with definite, prescribed *rules of obedience*, the breaking of any of which lay the user open to direct penalties of some kind. Most such language-systems have some definite and restricted purpose or 'universe of discourse'. Their rules of operation are, in principle, known to their users; say the rules of arithmetic, or of established mathematics, or of the road, or of reading the time, or dialling telephones . . . many such systems. On the other hand few people could *state* the syntactical rules of their own language;

they don't need to be able to. Strictly speaking there is no absolute, sharp division between languages and language-systems. But the gulf is very wide. Incidentally the so-called 'computer-languages' like Fortran or Algol, are not languages at all. They are *codes*. They convert one type of sign (e.g. those of mathematics) into others suitable for operating the computer.

Many language-systems are cross-cultural, e.g. clocks, arithmetic, international road-signs, and are used internationally over wide areas. The use of sign-systems is one form of international communication which does not raise the difficulties of national attitudes, history, emotion and all the important overtones of ordinary languages. Certain forms of ceremonial provide another example of widely-used international sign-systems, although the *significances* of these may vary among the nations. Guards of honour, inspection of troops, bands, banquets and other formal rituals fall to the lot of all diplomats and visiting dignatories; many, if not most, of such international ceremonials derive from our most common internationally shared experience: the experience of war.

All formal sign-systems seem to offer possibilities for overcoming the difficulties of language differences. They are, to a major extent, cross-cultural, for the simple reason that they are *defined*. But their fields of relevance are also highly restricted; with mathematics people can discuss mathematical affairs; with the language of science, only quantitative scientific affairs; ceremonial recognizes the existence of diplomatic relations, but does not solve the problems of international tensions. They are all restricted to their fields of discourse and cannot be used for expressive discussion.

Then what about an international language, a *lingua franca*? This is a question so often raised in this context, for it seems to many people today to offer possibility for international understanding. However, in the writer's view, this hope seems to be based upon a misconception of the nature of language, a misconception arising from confusing *expression* with *understanding*.

Several *linguae francae* or artificial languages have been designed and are well known, having the aim of providing easier paths for international and cross-cultural conversation (e.g. Esperanto). But there is no universal, worldwide *culture* whose changes and development might sustain such languages and continually modify and adapt them consistently everywhere. A universal artificial language may have undoubted value for specific and limited purposes, but the difficulty is that people of different cultures live in very different circumstances and don't always want to talk about the same things! The true values of any artificial language are like those of the 'translating machine'; they are values for *practical* purposes of many kinds. Nevertheless, such practical purposes are not to be scorned. On the contrary, as will be argued later in this book, our global communication media have very limited values for improving international relations if used solely for trying to convert each other to our own various beliefs, principles and attitudes (i.e. propaganda); their real and positive values lie rather in their contribution to practical matters (i.e. organizational powers). See Chapter 4, Sections 4 and 5 in particular.

Where such practical affairs of international organization are at present proceeding (affairs of trade, diplomacy, law . . .) it appears that the international languages being used are not invented, artificial, *linguae francae*, but are usually one of the natural, real languages, English in particular. But it would be quite false to conclude from this fact that 'everybody in this world will soon be speaking English'! On the contrary, only a small minority will have the need to, and even they who live outside the English-speaking countries will be bilingual or even polylingual. Evidence will be presented later in this book that even the global spread of broadcasting, which affects millions of people, as yet shows no threat of destroying 'minority languages'. (See Chapter 6, Section 5.)

Difficulties of mutual understanding arise also in the field of translation. Strictly speaking, translation is, at best, a compromise and the fact that it can so often be done so well is another reflexion upon the practical, rather than the emotional, values of language in conduct of our daily affairs. Travellers can get about and satisfy most of their needs, with perhaps only a poor grasp of foreign languages. It is of course in political and cultural relations between countries that all the difficulties of translation appear. The difficulties can lie not so much in the formal word and syntax transcriptions themselves, but in all the implied connotations of the words used, stemming from the different histories, surroundings, literature, legends and political faiths; all aspects of their specific conditions and cultures which give people their emotional attitudes and their feelings of relatedness, of loyalty, of kinship and unique identity. A person's language forms a major part of his own identity, of how he sees himself in relation to his friends, colleagues, fellow-countrymen and foreigners. It is one source of his pride and self-respect.

Even though seemingly exact dictionary translations of the names of simple common objects may be found, these words do not necessarily indicate the true *significance* of those objects to other peoples (e.g. water, a loin cloth, a black face, a bowl of rice). Again, within a country's own borders: it is only recently, after 45 years of broadcasting, that the importance of word choice is really becoming appreciated. Broadcasting for the first time enabled the talk of one man to be heard by thousands of listeners, whose education and background were unknown to him. It is now being realized that many words commonly used by broadcasters to people of their own countries are unknown in meaning to many listeners. Because of limited word understanding, lack of comprehension on the part of listeners to broadcast talks and news bulletins has been going on for years.* If this is so with internal, national broadcasting, what about overseas broadcasts in foreign languages? What misunderstandings have been innocently created?

There may be no better example to illustrate cultural mistranslation than the word *Red*. To Westerners 'the Reds' conjures up images of blood, fire, fierceness, e.g., *red with anger*, *red in tooth and claw*, *seeing red*, but the Russian translation *krasniy* has a very different aura. For example, to a Russian:

krasniy	= beautiful†
pryekrasniy	= exquisite
krasnaya ryiba	= fine fish (e.g. salmon)
krasnoye zoloto	= pure gold ('red' gold)
krasota	= beauty

Until recently, I had imagined that Moscow's Red Square had got its name from the blood shed by Peter the Great in 1698, when he slaughtered the entire Streltzy Regiment there, which had revolted against him![78]

* See also Ref. 193, in relation to the Press. This information is kindly supplied by the External Department of the British Broadcasting Corporation. Their studies have also included reports from the broadcasting authorities of other European countries.

† I am indebted to Mr. D. Rutenberg for these examples.

Rather than *Red*, a far, far better symbolic translation of this word into English is *Golden*, as in *a Golden opportunity, Silence is Golden, a golden-haired little child, The Golden Age*, etc. No doubt a Russian might translate this word back again into Russian to mean 'the colour of money'! And so we go on. I once received a card from a Russian friend, printed with a *blue* Father Christmas. It is *ours* which are red! Again, I was once highly embarrassed when using our common term *Red Indian* (American Indian, in British usage) to an American audience, some of whom took it to refer to an Indian Communist. Colours are no more translatable than words.

5. Clichés and slogans   Much of the ritualistic function of language is constructive and not just a waste of time. 'Hello' on the telephone indicates that you are there, though invisible. Greetings are important, as are many gestures and facial expressions; so are courtesies and other nonsemantic words and phrases, because they can identify you as a member of a particular group or groups, or they disclose something of your present mood and your attitudes to the others, or for many other reasons. Many such expressions are no more than conventional phrases, enabling people to know 'how they stand', to reduce embarrassment, to comfort and to put labels on specific situations. Other conventional phrases, although ritualistic, have aggressive values: e.g. swearing.

Perhaps the most dangerous forms of ritual-phrases today, or potentially dangerous, are those called clichés[240] and slogans, especially those of international significance. They can serve as excuses for not thinking or, more dangerously, as a means of *self*-deception: the utterance seems to relieve the speaker of further responsibility, like an insincere prayer wiping away sin. At worse, clichés and slogans may not be recognized as such; they are little more than linguistic reflexes. Incidentally the word *slogan* is from the Gaelic, meaning 'war-cry'!

A cliché or a slogan can be used, knowingly or self-persuasively, to conclude a discussion, to avoid self-exposure or to conceal ignorance. There would be little danger if they were used only as dismissals, but so often, especially in the political field today, they become acts of moral evasion, or plain lies. The consequence of this is that one's attitudes and outlook can become hardened and closed, leaving us less amenable to influence from any subsequent arguments. Clichés are *refusals* to think or to listen. 'The Chinese are inscrutable', somebody says; 'That's about right', says the other, and the matter is closed. But what they really mean is more likely to be: 'I don't know how to scrutinize the Chinese, because my school taught me nothing of Asiatic history, neither did yours. We're both ignorant. So let us agree to halt this embarrassing and futile discussion.'

We are all ignorant today in many aspects of world affairs; how can we expect to have real understanding in any depth of the flood of news which pours upon us daily from all corners of the earth? The cliché: 'this shrinking world' is valid if it refers to the increased *speeds* of travel and of news, but it can also deceive us into believing that we have a smaller world to understand, so that we may feel we can grasp it better and have a greater sense of personal involvement with all its other people. We are obliged today to read newspapers, or to watch news bulletins, and to speak of the affairs of people whom we have never met and shall never know as *persons*. We must increasingly generalize and speak of them as abstractions: as nations, classes, groups, types, and clichés are the natural language of such discussion. The impersonality of news today arises not from any greater callousness on our part, but from the sheer volume of news. We may increasingly wish tragic situations to become resolved, and our desires can obscure reason, for few of us have either the ability or the knowledge to do anything to help.

Politics is often said to be the art of dealing with insoluble issues. Statesmen may adapt to working under such conditions, but most of us are not such people; for most of us politics and world affairs are not our main job, but merely the background against which we live and work. We may have passionate desires that this or that situation should be tackled and resolved and we may democratically express our opinions upon how it could be done. And here the cliché and the slogan provide the amateur statesman (and many politicians too) with escape routes, by providing ritualistic, socially accepted phrases with which he can align himself with groups and thus share his over-loaded conscience and feelings and conceal himself. And he may not always know that he is doing it.

Clichés and slogans therefore provide us with socially accepted formulae which appear to justify our beliefs and actions, or to solve unresolvable problems, or to attain our ideals in our imaginations. These formulae can delude us into believing that we have attained the ends which we may truly wish. We leap to those ends over the unknown grounds of ignorance and frustration, muttering or shouting the phrases. 'The War to end war!' we once said, and believed it; we talk today of 'the Welfare State' and thereby comfort ourselves that no-one is left out.

As if the human race did not already have enough languages to divide it, highly educated people are continually inventing *jargons*; to those of the Sciences, Services and the medical profession there are increasingly offered those of the Law, of computer users, of journalists, of sports and endless other closed groups. With these jargons as badges, the members close their ranks in self-defence and to the exclusion of others. Jargons identify them and help preserve their privilege. One cannot *blame* them for this, any more than one can blame a national minority group for hanging on to its language when threatened with extinction. One can only blame jargon-users when they refuse to attempt translation into English (German, Russian . . .) when necessary. They might at least take the trouble to be bilingual. But no: jargons are seized as badges of clan loyalty and treasured with pride.

Clichés, slogans and jargon are examples of what has been called *impoverished language*, not so much meaning that the phrases are 'poor stuff' but rather that the same phrases are used unselectively by everybody within a particular group. There is no personal variance in them, no personal opinion is being expressed. They are simply commonly accepted phrases used symbolically, containing nothing peculiar to the person uttering them; they are as ritualistic as badges or flags, being used in specific situations where a person wants to identify with some group and express his membership of that group without any personal commitment.* Political slogans do not commit a person to a specific set of beliefs, nor do badges, any more than going to Church necessarily commits one to Christian beliefs. Such acts merely identify the person and are acts of submission to the others of the group: to the group *personified*. The personified group then appears to be the other 'person' to whom the speaker has submitted and may become a terrible tyrant. Heidegger calls this personification 'the One', who can censure or

* Business English, for example.[104] 'With reference to yours of the 15th inst.' etc., and much professional jargon.

dominate an individual.[293] The tyrant shows itself as 'the One', in such phrases as: 'One doesn't expect such behaviour nowadays!' or, in the plural, as 'They': as in 'They say that Danish bacon is best' (i.e. if you buy any other you and your bacon must be inferior). The One or They are not persons of high authority, but abstracts which can dominate us.

Clichés, slogans and jargon are the language of people who cannot, or dare not, commit themselves as individuals. It is his language and the way in which he commits himself to definite beliefs and novel policies and actions which mark off the statesman from the politicians. All human progress is made by acts of *daring*, moral and intellectual, as well as physical, by courage to go against the tide of popular wisdom and beliefs, by defiance, by contradiction and disobedience, by those who can say: 'No!' or 'You're wrong', or 'I don't quite agree', or who in some way dissent, or disagree, to a greater or lesser degree.

Certainly, agreement has value, but to keep on saying 'Yes', 'I agree', 'You're absolutely right' is only to concur with a suggestion which has been made by some other person. It does not require us to say anything more. But disagreement, argument, dispute, are vitally important because to say 'You're wrong' or 'I don't agree with what you say', opens you to challenge to be specific and to say *why*, or *how* or in what way precisely, or to contribute some new proposal or a modification. There are thus far more ways of disagreeing than of agreeing, more ways of dissenting than of assenting, and a statement of reason, a responsibility, can then be demanded.

It is in this sense that disagreement, however minor, can be constructive; a *creative* suggestion requires that one does not wholly concur with current opinion. 'All great truths begin as heresy' was Samuel Johnson's way of putting it. Human communication does not always mean 'getting together' and coming to agreement; argument, ditpute, disagreement are essential forms of communication also, and ones that lead to new ideas. This may sound an aggressive opinion, but it is not so if we distinguish verbal from physical attack; war is not the extension of dispute, but a refusal to dispute.

The statesman may himself *create* new sayings in just this way, which get taken up by the people as slogans afterwards and then the slogans may serve them as badges of membership or loyalty. Slogans, although they do not commit individuals to personal beliefs, can sometimes have at least that value. There can be certain circumstances where such ritualistic function is of great help, as providing symbols of unity, for example in war (both for civilian morale, and as Army slang is used). Often the phrases themselves may be nothing more than passwords; it is not their semantics but their mere utterance which is significant.

The so-called mass-communication* media, radio and printing above all, have of course done more than anything else to make us widely aware of other people's slogans, and they also spread slogans and clichés within our own countries and smaller social groups. Although we ourselves may each be far less aware of our own usage of slogans and clichés, as part of our daily surroundings, we can be only too acutely aware of those used by people in other groups or countries. The reason is not that they are bigger nonsense, but that the sayings of other groups can strike us as totally irrelevant to our own situations. Their strangeness and incongruity may strike us and force

---

* The terms mass-communication and the masses are discussed later in Chapter 2, Section 6 and Chapter 6, Section 7.

our attention more upon their literal semantic interpretations than upon their ritual usage as *slogans*.

To give two familiar examples: the Thoughts of Chairman Mao*[202] may read to Westerners as very simple sayings and slogans which, so we are told, are chanted in unison by the Chinese at every work-break, or shouted from loudspeakers at every street corner: the most massive mass-circulation in history, among 800 million people. The biggest circulation of newspapers and advertisements in the West looks very small in comparison! What does any one of these people really feel and think as he chants such things as: 'All reactionaries are paper tigers!' together with his comrades? How much is semantic and how much is ritual? How many of those who wave the little Red Book are illiterate, so must learn it by heart and chant it because they cannot read it?† I must confess that I have no idea, but neither do I know what the liturgy, chanted in Latin, meant to a peasant of, say, the 14th century.[2]

To turn the tables on ourselves, perhaps we might also wonder what a Chinese diplomat or visitor makes of our British commercial-culture when he sees plastered on wallboards all over our cities such strange heroics as these, all taken from well-known advertisements:

'Put a Tiger in your Tank'
'Go to Work on an Egg'
'Drinka Pinta Milka Day'

('Inscrutable people, the British—do they really believe this propaganda?')

6. The significance of literacy: the sense of 'historic time'

It is a mistaken view to distinguish speech and writing merely by classing the first as an aural medium and the second as a visual medium. Admittedly, speech 'goes in' at the ears, and our telephones and loudspeakers stimulate our hearing, whereas writing 'goes in' at the eyes, through books, newspapers and letters giving visual stimulus. But this distinction is trivial compared to the importance of the mental imagery which is formed. Speech does not produce only sound images, nor reading only visual images. There can be as much sound imagery conjured up by writing as there can be visual imagery in speech, depending upon your thinking and imagination. Likewise, the popular terms: 'the visual media', 'the sound media', the 'written media' can be deceptive overgeneralizations.

Speech is an inherent part of human nature; it may of course be consciously developed, vocabularies can be extended and finer distinctions of phrasing acquired. On the other hand, writing is an artefact, an invention, possessed to varying degrees by nearly half the human race.[33, 319, 322] Speech is not 'spoken writing'; there are many distinctions to be drawn between the two. The question of confidence placed upon news, for example, can depend upon whether it was read or learned by word-of-mouth, a confidence which varies much between people and circumstances. Rumours, too:[4] we usually speak of hearing a rumour, not of reading it. Rumours are passed by word-of-mouth.

It is true to say that we know far, far, more about the earliest scribings and the beginning of writing than we know about the origins of speech, for the obvious reason that one makes a record, and may be seen and referred to, whilst the other has wholly vanished into thin air. This is the basic value of

---

* See article by F. T. C. Yu: *Communication and Politics in Communist China*, appearing in Ref: 248.
† Merrill quotes the number as 300 million in 1959.[211]

writing, scribing and making pictures, that with such records events of the past and the present can be brought into relation and *comparisons* made, of various kinds. This is true not only for the distant past, but also for the immediate past (e.g. in mathematics, when at some point reference is made to a preceding equation). It is the *recording* of knowledge that has led to the present day scientific, industrial world. Leonardo was so successful, compared to others of his day, because he carefully recorded his thoughts and findings. When and where Man has evolved scribing and writing he has deepened his concept of 'historic time',[174] not just the past and the present, but their relationship, the past *compared* with the present. When we look at the magnificent ancient cave drawings of the Dordogne, in France, or others in Europe, or those of Tanzania or Central Africa and India[103, 171, 305, 352] we may feel these artists to be a long, long, way away from us. But it should be remembered that they may have looked equally far away to the people who first rediscovered them, who themselves seem ancient to us. And so it will be to our distant descendants when they come to examine the libraries and archives, microfilms and punched card records which we are storing up in our own generation. These records which we are making now are *intended* to communicate with the future, and are written in a form we hope they will understand, and so, by writing and other recording, past, present and future can be brought together into a single moment of thought. Animals and fish too can make records, by leaving scents at one place which may either serve the purpose of attracting or repelling others or to enable them to return to the same place later. For example, deer or salmon. They are recording for the future. (The Pragmatic philosopher G. H. Mead deals with the past and the future as being in the present moment. E.g. See his: *Mind, Self and Society*, Univ. Chicago Press, Chicago and London, 1934.)

Whose moment? Yours and mine: the 'present moment'. But it is only in terms of our ideas of today that we can interpret past records and predict the significance of today's records to future generations. On no account can we feel and think as an ancient when we read their writings. When you read Herodotus you don't really know what life was like in Western Asia in the 5th century B.C. For one thing you probably read him in English. Furthermore, Herodotus describes only those things and affairs which *he* thought significant in the course of his travels. You and I, today, would probably notice others; we shall never know. So too with the future. We may read science fiction, predicting the world in the year A.D. 5000, but writers can invent that world only in terms of the concepts that we can form with the language and symbols of today. Great imagination may have been used by the writers when creating these fantasies but, nevertheless, the people of A.D. 5000 will have thoughts which would be just as unthinkable to us today as many of our thoughts would have been to Neanderthal Man.

The moment therefore is ours, the present moment, when we read a text and create in our minds images of times past or of times yet to come.

The picture which you or I have of the world, here, today, of what is significant, how we relate to others and to ourselves and to all the elements of Nature, what are life and death, what is funny and what is tragic . . . this mental picture we have created is very different from that, say, of an ancient Egyptian. The great physicist Schrödinger has put his finger on this point.[268] Like others before him have done, including Peirce,[97, 241] and Benjamin Lee Whorf,[350] he has emphasized that only a small fragment of your picture of the world, which you share with friends and others of your culture, comes from your own sensory experience. The majority of it has been passed on to you by others, in language. That is to say, what you see and notice is what you have been taught to see and notice, by your mother and those around you; another part is passed to you by literature; that is, if you are able to read, for we should remember that about 40 per cent of the people of this world, over 14 years of age, are illiterate*,[33,319,322] although the number is reducing. (See also p. 106.)

These two methods of acquisition are fundamentally distinct. The literate person learns from his parents and friends together with books and newspapers. The illiterate person, living in an illiterate society, only has the former, and so comes to see the world solely through the eyes of his mother, father, friends and other illiterates. The man who can read really well has access to unlimited sources of outside knowledge. However, not only does the illiterate man, living in a 'traditional society' see the world much as his parents and grandparents and others before them, but he sees himself too in a similar way,[187] as an element in the life of his society. Literacy and industry may have vastly raised our wealth, but they have increased our loneliness too.

The literate, educated man sees himself as different from others in many ways; he feels different from his parents, and sees them as differing from his grandparents. He has an awareness of social change, of a sense of history, of life, time and being as 'dynamic', giving him the expectation and desire for further change. He *hopes* that 'things will be better for his children', that 'they will have a better chance in life than he did'.

These hopes and expectations are not without their price. A rapidly changing society, progressive or not, lives under a continual demand for personal readjustment. There must always be some sections of the population, great or small, who feel and express a sense of outrage, being always under challenge. A highly literate, changing society must always be dissatisfied, to some extent or other. Heaven lies in front of it, but is never reached; things ought to get better or, if they do not, people get angry.

Who knows, television may be returning us to some of the blessings of the verbal tradition? It is not only making people more visually conscious, but more aurally conscious too. We sit around the set as illiterate natives sit around the feet of the travelling storyteller. Television may increasingly help to preserve present day events as fables and legends of the future, giving a sense of ancestral continuation which the torrent of print has so largely helped to destroy. Reading books is a private, withdrawn, intellectual occupation: watching pictures is more a social, exposed, emotional experience. It is far too early yet to say; television has as yet produced very few really new art forms, but still relies very heavily upon the traditions of the earlier media such as films, newspapers, books, advertising and the theatre.

To the man living in a traditional, illiterate society, the world seems different. The concept of 'progress' or of 'historic change' may itself be absent.† He sees his world as interpreted through legends and tales told as though the events they relate had occurred that very morning. He sees himself as part of that everlasting, continuing, unchanging process. He is not a vulgar or stupid person. He sees the seasons come and go; he sees the moon wax and wane; significant personal or family events, births and deaths, mournings and festivals may give him the sense of individual life. But he lives in a social context having no *expectation* of change.[187]

* The term illiterate may mean several things.[33] See p. 198.
† See notes on the word 'progress' on page 204.

By contrast, we who can read may compare the literature of different ages, we may read our newspapers daily and, in consequence, sense the changing nature of the world we live in. Life, history, time, are all dynamic, an everflowing stream. We live by the clock. Time is a concept deeply set in our minds. We are timetabled, from birth to death.

One of my students, a native of Kenya, once told me that, at home in his village, if the bus came to collect people it would wait until they all arrived. On no account would it drive off on time and leave any passengers stranded. Then he said to me: 'You don't use your buses and trains in London as transport really, you seem to use them as *clocks*!'

This great consciousness of time in our Western minds stresses our separation and individuality. We each regard our life as 'a slice cut out of time', with no deep sense of integration with our ancestors, nor responsibilities for our descendants. Our attitude, as we look at antiquities, ancient monuments and things of the past is little more than curiosity. We are born, we live, and we die. This sense of finiteness, of a slice cut out of time, seems to be the inevitable consequence of our literacy, giving us the ability to compare and so develop the sense of change; time then becomes a clear reality.

Since the end of World War II great changes have come about in, for example, the Middle East, especially among illiterate populations in their attitudes and ideas about 'foreigners'. Professor Daniel Lerner[187] presents an account of such changes in traditional societies, of Egypt, Iran, Jordan, Lebanon, Syria and Turkey, due not only to the spread of literacy, but to the newer techniques of film and radio. These techniques however are producing a new phenomenon, being that of the *overstepping* of literacy, that is, direct visual and spoken presentation to preliterate communities of things and affairs previously inconceivable, without the prior necessity of their learning to read. In the Arab countries, for example, radio is racing the newspaper. Daniel Lerner[187] has quoted President Nasser as saying that 'literacy counts far less, politically, than it did 20 years ago. Radio has changed everything.' Again, the anthropologist Doob[71] has written that it was the 'pressure of communications (which) has brought about the downfall of traditional societies'. In modern China too, the loudspeakers blare out from every street corner, all the time, giving political slogans and general education from which there is no escape; the communication media are used as *forces* for change.[248]

The *Arabian Nights Entertainments* (*the Thousand and One Nights*, 'translations from the Indian through the Persian, made as early as the 9th century'[78]) were stories created by the most versatile and vivid imaginations of people living in the verbal tradition, who had for centuries been accustomed to word-of-mouth tales and legends, songs and recitations, for their expression of 'reality'. The impact of modern techniques, radio and film, may prove to have an effect upon the Middle East quite unimaginable to the Westerners who are so addicted to writing and print. Legends, stories, narrative verse and other verbal modes have been the methods of crossing boundaries, over whole continental areas, for long centuries past. Radio comes along today in the wake of all this. The effect upon traditional societies may be to introduce them to the outside, foreign world, or to change their imaginings of it, in ways not yet predicted, and sometimes not to mutual benefit, as well as to change their views of themselves: their self-awareness and political consciousness (see Chapter 6, Section 7).

Within industrial countries the situation of small groups of illiterate people may be quite different. If they have traditional bonds linking them into close and clannish groups, as gypsies have for example, they may be proud and self-respecting communities with their own codes and symbols of identity (which might include illiteracy itself). The forces of compulsory State education may nowadays be changing the situation, but previously illiteracy could become a source of defiant pride. However, the attitudes of isolated individual illiterates towards themselves can be very different. Such people, unable to read or write and having no social support or group identity, living within an educated community, can feel a sense of shame. It has been reported by those responsible for teaching them, that they come to look upon their deficiency as a disease; they fear that their children will be ashamed of them and they feel juvenile through constantly having to ask other people to read for them labels in shops and destination signs on buses.*

If it be accepted that the coming of literacy, radio and films changes the people of traditional societies so as to see the world and their relationship to it in a radically new way, we may next ask: what will be the effects of television? For television is beginning to penetrate into some of these communities.[320]

What specific qualities has television got, that films do not have, to distinguish it? There are two obvious factors. First, there is its immediacy in time, for television can show events whilst they are actually occurring and, second, television can show these immediate events to whole populations simultaneously. In contrast, films and books can deal with affairs only when they are over, perhaps long over.

It is commonly argued that in the more politically mature countries television has little effect upon politics. This may well be true, for such countries have long political traditions and many established institutions; furthermore the people are exposed to many different sources other than television, such as newspapers, placards, demonstrations, magazines, books, trade union meetings, education and constant reminders of past conditions and political events. At the present time, television is primarily regarded in the home as a mode of entertainment. In the emerging countries, however, the effects of television could possibly be different. In so far as people can be made consciously aware that things on the screen are actually happening *now*, the effects of this immediacy could be stronger: 'the leader is with us, *now*'. Perhaps we should not overestimate the importance of this point, because it is not easy to feel and accept emotionally that events being watched on a T.V. screen are actually happening to real people (see Section 2, p. 8); it is only too easy to watch a T.V. news bulletin as though it were a film or play or story and to become emotionally involved only in a closely similar way. As regards the second point, that T.V. is seen by whole populations simultaneously, this fact is not obvious to people viewing in individual private homes; a Western viewer is not particularly conscious of all the unseen thousands of others, of being one of the crowd, or of the masses. By contrast, where television is used at all in emerging countries and seen by native populations it is likely to be viewed by collective audiences of a few hundred people in a village hall which probably also serves as a schoolroom and as an occasional cinema. (See Refs. [320, 314] and other Unesco Reports concerning values of T.V. for emerging countries.) Each viewer is then surrounded by members of that village audience of personal acquaintances

* *The Guardian*, November 21st, 1966.

closely aware of one another, a collective audience engaged in social experience.

Although literacy may not be essential to the early stages of political development it is essential to industrialization. It is certainly true that intelligent illiterates can be trained as motor or radio mechanics, etc., this was a factor of considerable importance to Armies and Air Forces during the 1939–45 War, in many remote theatres, but the running and development of industries require far more than intelligence and skills. The ability to read books, manuals of instruction and technical journals and to be able to write instructions, to keep records and accounts, to make plans and records, is an essential prerequisite for that section of the people who assume the leadership of industries, of technical development and other institutions. Politics have proceeded without literacy for centuries; but literacy is an essential prerequisite for its responsible progress towards mature, 'democratic' forms.[33] (See Chapter 6, Section 7.)

Perhaps we in the English-speaking world do not always appreciate how fortunate it has been for us that, when William Caxton set up his printing press, in 1476, in the shade of Westminster Abbey, he immediately started the tradition of printing *lay* books, rather than religious works as elsewhere in Europe. These were sold in large numbers, though a major fraction of the people were illiterate. Merchant middle classes evolved and the literary tradition flowered early in England as nowhere else. By mid-eighteenth century, when the Industrial Revolution was beginning, England was the most literate country in Europe and its publishing trade was the most prosperous.[2,155,295,346]

There is considerable evidence to suggest that by the 16th century already something like 30% of the people of England could read to some extent and that reading of Wyclif's Bible and the Church *Primers* (liturgical texts), was possible for many poor, humble people, who could not read Latin, for both were printed in the English vernacular (only those people who reached the Grammar Schools were taught in Latin).

2

On Communication, Ancient and Modern

'Television? The word is half Latin and half Greek. No good can come of it.'

Attributed to C. P. Scott
of The Manchester Guardian.

1. Our changing view of the world

In Chapter 1 we have examined, to some extent, the nature of human language and of its significance to individuals and to society, in an attempt to destroy the over-simple idea that communication consists only of our sending messages one to another, and to replace it by the concept of human *involvements* of many kinds. Our present day systems of communication, such as radio, films, television, newspapers and others, have introduced the possibility of extending human relationships, and involvements, over larger areas of the globe, thereby giving rise to many completely new social questions. I have said 'possibility', for how we adapt to and use these systems now and in the future are totally different matters. In order to discuss such questions rationally and to avoid only too common emotional judgements heard about 'mass-communication', it is well to consider not only the way in which our modern communication systems spread their tentacles over the globe, but also how this has come about; that is, something of the dynamics, the history, of the change. So many of the questions raised today, concerning mass-communication, are meaningful only on a comparative basis; judgements are better made, not so much as to whether today's mass-communication systems are good or bad, but rather whether they are better or worse, and how our personal and national relationships have been changed by them and changed so rapidly within one generation. In this Chapter, therefore, I shall present some part of the history of communication technology.

So accustomed are we, in the advanced industrial countries, to accepting our riches and annual growth rates that we may easily forget that we have not always been in that happy state: at least, most of us haven't. Historically speaking, the economic gulf between today's rich and poor countries is fairly recent, say a few centuries. During this period of economic climb we, as countries, have become increasingly involved with the others, yet as individual persons we have had very little contact, or real knowledge, at all. At the height of the British Empire, only a minute fraction of our population had visited the countries coloured red on the Map; the bulk of people had neither been there nor seen any of the natives; they were known only as stories in books, as maps, as places where cocoa and tea came from, as abstracts. Our politicians and statesmen have spoken of their world responsibilities, but most of our citizens have been concerned with local and domestic affairs, with the struggle of living.

For endless centuries the mass of people have lived, mentally, in small communities; in farms, villages or towns. There have of course been a few large cities in antiquity; Rome, for example, had about a million citizens at its height. But the majority of people have lived in small circles of kinship, friendship, work and interest, all their relationships within comparatively closed and small communities. Wars, invasions, occupations, migrations have brought strangers into contact but, at any one time, it is true to say that a man's personal circle was small. Now, within a single generation, this state of affairs has been utterly changed, through two particular causes. First, the Second World War which enforced global movements of masses of troops and second, the rapid spread of radio and television, together with that of news agencies, all over the world. The change has been fast. Our newspapers today are filled daily with the affairs of many nations; we see the faces of people of all colours and creeds on our T.V. screens. We are flooded with news, and confused by its sheer variety; we struggle to make sense of it. However, although we may become increasingly aware of world affairs, in all their complexity, I personally doubt whether radio, T.V. and newspapers have greatly increased our sense of *personal* involvement. It is still easy to switch off the T.V. and blot out the image, or to turn our newspapers over and do the crossword puzzle, and 'sleep o'nights.' Our sense of involvement may have become greatly extended, but I question whether it has been deepened in proportion. Not only have we in the advanced countries been suddenly called upon to take a non-imperial world-view of affairs, and to establish quite new relationships, but to do so whilst so many of those in the poorer developing countries are coming to learn a great deal more *about us*, and through exactly the same means: about our affluence, our values, our attitudes. It is one of the great tragedies of today that the majority of these people have acquired this knowledge, at the point of their release from colonialism, by war (when great troop movements took place over the continents) or, if literate, by reading *our* newspapers.

Since our knowledge of ourselves, our own 'self-images', must stem from our knowledge of other people, it is not surprising that our recent and sudden awareness of so many other people of this world and their conditions has led us to change our image of ourselves. The last few years have been marked by a great self-questioning and heartsearching of a kind rare before the Second World War.* Industrial Man in the mid-20th century is like a person taking a thorough look at himself again after a long time, and he doesn't particularly like all that he sees.

2. Our present day obsession with the clock and the news

In an earlier century people within those countries we now consider advanced and industrialized saw far more clearly their relationships to each other, both in family, work and social class. They knew where they stood, their appointed positions in life, man for man.† But now, after two World Wars our relationships are in a state of continual shift and change; changes within families by virtue of the rapid rise of educational standards, sometimes opening up a gap of strangeness between parents and children; changes by virtue of increased occupational opportunity and class mobility; and changes internationally, for we are all far more aware of each other. But our knowledge of other peoples is always partial knowledge. The more I know about other peoples of this world, the more I cannot help but wish to know more about them. Our demand for news increases and our demands

---

* But less commitment and action. For example, our financial aid to the developing countries has been *reduced* during the last few years, in proportion to our rising wealth. (See U.N. Document E/4438, *The External Financing of Economic Development, International Flow of Long Term Capital and Official Donations* 1962–66.)

† This is not to say they necessarily felt more *secure*, of course.

are increasingly satisfied. We are all obsessed by the news today, living in a state of continual expectancy, buying newspapers, listening to radio bulletins, trying to make sense of a world in this state of everlasting change. Where do I stand today? What should I do? Where are my loyalties now? To Britain (a national group)? To Europe (an historical group)? To the Western Alliance (a political group)? To Mankind? To the Cosmos? My grandmother felt she knew clearly, I don't.

These two obsessions of the industrial countries which I have mentioned, with *time* and with *news*, are of course closely related. Time exists only when there are passing events to mark it out, even though they be only the ticks of a clock. But with our eyes regularly on the T.V. screen, or on our newspapers, we live today in a world of continuous change, from event to event, from news of crisis to news of crisis; we live day by day, happy only when we *can* get the news every morning and evening. If our daily newspaper fails to be delivered, or we miss our T.V. news bulletins, we can be ashamed if our ignorance of some event of that day is exposed by others. If we 'don't know the latest news' we feel inferior. So our lives are ticked away.

This is not to wish for return to my grandmother's day, to be untroubled by this weight of world news upon me today; far, far from it. It is very important indeed that I should have this wider view of the world and know so much more about other peoples. I am commenting only on the fact that we have allowed these better opportunities we have today for learning more about other peoples to lapse into an obsession, to develop into something we call 'the news', a kind of daily ritual with the regularity of mealtimes.

How has this lapse, if that be the right word, come about? A conventional reply would be that it is the result of mass-communication. However, it is difficult to see how it could be otherwise; if we truly desire a better and more peaceful world it is ignorance of one another that must be fought. Can we then genuinely learn so much more about each other without reading and listening to so much more news?

I can only offer my opinions, which are these: first, that our present day far-flung world communication networks (radio, telephone and telegraph) gather far more news daily, from all corners of the earth, than any human being could possibly read and understand, even if it could all be printed. It falls upon news editors, therefore, to select the items to be published. All news that we read or hear *must* be selected news, it cannot be otherwise today. There is a second unavoidable consequence of this however; it is that the newspapers may appear to seize upon some tragedy on one day, say an earthquake in Turkey, and concentrate on this, reporting in great detail, with pictures and advertisements for a Relief Fund, etc.—only to drop the subject altogether after a few days, and to take up another, say a coalmine disaster in Wales. This apparently flighty hopping from one tragedy to another, accompanied by the daily strip cartoons, fashion reports and crossword puzzles, can call upon the heads of newspapers the charge of insincerity and shallowness. But this too seems unavoidable; if a newspaper did not drop one subject before picking up another, it would get thicker and thicker each day.

But one aspect of news reporting which seems to me to be more insidious is the absolute *regularity* with which newspapers are published; morning after morning, evening after evening, we expect them, regular as clockwork. This implies in us an *expectancy* of there being tragedies, disasters and major events enough each day to fill the papers: ('I wonder what's happened *today*?')

I fully admit that I have no idea whatsoever as to how the situation may be changed. I wish only to emphasize the significance of this *regularity* of newspapers, a regularity shared with all other aspects of our modern industrial life, and to suggest that, subconsciously, our expectancy of getting our morning or evening paper may have become more important than the news which it contains. Perhaps we feel it to be more important to *have* a newspaper than it is to *read* it; and, again, more a duty to read it than to understand it; yet, again, far more possible to understand the facts we read than to feel any real, deep sympathy and compassion for those whose tragedies and disasters are reported. However, this is not to say that 'the media' have become 'the message'. They have merely become habits of *duty*.

If there be the slightest shred of truth in this, then we should expect newspapers to serve other purposes which depend upon their regularity, rather than news reporting. Indeed they do: strip cartoons urge us to open our papers and see the next instalment of pictures, crossword puzzles become an obsessive habit and, with this regularity established and habits set, newspapers provide the most happy ground for the sport of *advertising*. (See Chapter 2, Section 5.)

In our pre-industrial society, it was largely the agricultural calendar which marked out time; this was, together with events such as religious festival days, a man's 'clock', a clock made somewhat irregular by the vagaries of the weather. With the coming of 'collective' factories (with moving shafts and belts, requiring many workers to be at one place at the same time) it was the boss's hooter* that regulated a man's life, not annually but daily and accurately to the minute. This sense of *regularity* has become increasingly enhanced by very many different customs in modern life: meal-times, children's school hours, shop hours and other compelling appointments, all deriving from the necessity for regular work hours and collectivization. Television and radio have merely continued the process, with their regular programmes at specified times of day on specified days of the week. To see our favourite programme we must keep our eyes on the clock.

Until recently, in our B.B.C. evening T.V. news programmes, for example, the face of a clock was shown as introduction, with a third hand ticking off *seconds*. As 8.50 p.m. approached, a spoken announcement was heard, after which the announcer's face suddenly appeared on the screen at 8.50 p.m. *exactly to the second*.† *Punctuality* has come to be regarded in industrial countries as a principal virtue and merit today (and lack of it is one of the customs of some Eastern countries which a traveller soon notices).

3. Notes upon communication in antiquity‡

When modern mass-communication systems and their influence upon us are discussed, it is most usual that their speed is mentioned, together with such things as 'the stress of modern life' (whatever that ridiculous phrase may mean§). Speed certainly is very important indeed, but *not* only because

---

* Perhaps *siren* is the modern word.

† This point is raised again with reference to lonely people.

‡ This Section and the next draw upon material from an article by the author, published in the *Proc. I.R.E. Fiftieth Anniversary Issue*, Vol. **50**, No. 5, May 1963, p. 1143. (Ref. 49) with kind permission.

§ It has been stated on reliable authority that the 'proportion of persons suffering from definable mental disorders and psychological abnormalities' is little related to culture, or to 'time, place and community structure'. A moment's thought tells me that if, by magic, I was suddenly reincarnated to be one of many millions in, say, parts of Africa or S.E. Asia, I should be neurotic before very long. See Arentden, K., 'Industry and the Mentally Ill', *Progress*, **50**, 1964, p. 169.

it enables affairs to proceed faster (see Section 7). Two other important social aspects of modern communications derive first from their great reliability and second, from their universal availability: meaning that their use is no longer confined to authorities.

Table 1. List of Main applications of radio

1. Land based	(a) *Public services*	Inland microwave telephone links
		Sound broadcasting
		Television broadcasting
		Overseas radio-telephone
		(Mobile) radio-telephone
		(Mobile) radio-telegraphs
	(b) *Government, Industrial*	Aeronautical, fixed services (navigation, safety)
		Radio telemetering
		Police radio
		Radio and telephone-line data transmission
		Military, Naval, Air Force communication
		Closed circuit television
	(c) *Private*	Amateur radio stations
		Amateur services (training)
2. Maritime		(Mobile) ship stations (ship/ship/air; ship/shore)
		Port operations service
		Coast stations
		Ship emergency transmissions
		Survival craft (e.g. lifeboat) stations
		Distress calling systems
		Radio navigation (land and mobile)
		Radar
		Radio-telephones and telegraphs
3. Air		Aircraft stations (air/air; air/ground)
		Blind landing systems
		Radio altimeters
		Radio direction finders
		Radio beacon
		Radar
		Radio navigation
		Defence early warning
		Air traffic control
4. General		Radio astronomy
		Meteorological aids
		Radiosonde
		Standard frequency transmissions
		Time Signal Service
		Medical (diathermy, etc.)
		Industrial processings
		Experimental (research) work

In earlier historic times long-distance communication certainly existed,[221] linking whole empires, but its use was confined to military, diplomatic and governmental purposes, by generals, governors, emperors and other privileged élite: those in control. This has been true from the days of the Persian Empire to the coming of the railways and it is only comparatively recently that common man has had personal access to long-distance communication aids.[49] But the structures of our advanced societies today (our institutions and how we regard our relationships with one another) are very much determined by our personal use of such things as telephones, telegraphs, data links and the postal service, T.V., together with 'official usage' of these and other facilities on our behalf for such things as aircraft navigation, weather bulletins, by the police, fire brigades, industry, government and many other institutions. (Table 1 lists a number of uses of radio alone.) And it is their *reliability* and *universal access* to 'the common people' or their agents which makes our modern industrial society possible.

The widespread use of radio, telegraphs, T.V., data links etc., is at present largely concentrated in areas of the world having high literacy rates (although radio is fast spreading elsewhere). Literacy is an essential prerequisite for the *active* adoption of technology on any scale not only because of the need to read technical instructions but because of mental attitudes.*[261,262,266] I say 'active' meaning technology in the sense of productive industries: the mere *possession* of transistor sets is another matter. We should perhaps remind ourselves that today some 40 per cent of the world's adults are illiterate.*[33,319,322,329]

Indeed I would go so far as to say that *societies can develop and advance only as far and fast as they can acquire, use and maintain systems of communication: systems of acquiring, recording, assimilating and disseminating information.*

'Recording' is particularly important, whether this be on parchment, on paper, or in the magnetic store of a modern computer.

Man's progress from the earliest communities of the East and Middle East, through the great empires of antiquity, up to the highly complex industrial societies of today has been one long story of extended and improved means of communication.[146,221]† As these have developed so have people's effective interrelations, i.e. their organizations, bringing all the advantages of the division of labour and production of wealth, of broadened cultural horizons, of law and order, and especially the possibility of increased personal *trust* and *security* over far wider circles than a family or a village.‡ I stress the word *possibility* here. At the same time, military development also has come from the same sources of improved communication. As communication within a country improves, social advancement is made theoretically more possible, because institutions may be organized more flexibly, though there is no reason to assume that it is certain to happen. (To take a modern example, it may be argued that crime can be reduced if the police are provided with more and better means of communication; this is true, but this will not attack the primary *sources* of crime increase.)

The importance of *recording* has been emphasized, as the first artefact or technology of communication. The earliest Mediterranean scripts were in pictograph, ideographs and hieroglyphic, giving direct picture-representation of objects and, by associations, of names, actions and ideas of all sorts. But it was the evolution of phonetic writing, during the Coptic Period, which was the great step; speech and writing became closely linked. The civilizations which did not adopt this technique (e.g. China) have been handicapped in certain ways throughout their history.

This simplification of script did not stop there, however. For example, ancient Hebrew was written without vowels. Deliberate condensation is not

---

* See 1966 edition of Ref. 312.

† For a short, interesting, factual history of all forms of communication, from prehistory to satellites, Ref. 221 is recommended.

‡ This may seem a surprising statement to some readers, and it will be discussed further, on page 201.

confined to present day newspaper advertisements (Dsrbl fhd rsdnc; all mod con; gs, elec . . .)* but was tried in numerous ancient writings: Church Slavonic abbreviated common words in much the same way. Shorthand too is not modern, but is said to have been used by the Greek slave Tyro for recording the lengthy speeches of Cicero. This looks not unlike modern shorthand, but was based on spelling; it continued to be used in Europe until the Middle Ages.[49, 50, 78]

Together with other invented systems of recording messages, other remarkably early methods were found for transmitting them. Polybius, for example, is well known for his description of telecommunication using torches and other visual means, as well as for his coding of the alphabet. The classical historians Herodotus,†[119] Xenophon and Polybius each stress the need for communication services for the control of scattered empires and for waging wars.

How were the great empires of antiquity, such as that of Rome, held together? How did Caesar know what his generals were doing, when they were spread over half of Europe, from the North African coast to the borders of Scotland? It was done by a postal service, the forerunner of our modern services.

The postal service of the Romans was preceded by that of the Persians, by which official letters were carried on horseback in relays between established postal stations, a system which was later introduced into Imperial Rome by Augustus. The Roman Empire was 'held together' by an elaborate network of couriers, on horseback or in carriages (similar in form to the old Romany gypsy caravans) with relay posting stations at regular intervals along all main roads. Each posting station kept 40 horses and grooms[243] and the speed would have been about 50 miles per day,[249] with accurate fixed times for collection and delivery. A similar system was used by the Great Khan Kublai, as described by Marco Polo.‡ (The earliest known postal service was probably that of semitic Babylonia, about 3800 B.C.[78])

I have referred to the Roman Empire as being 'held together'. Considering the great continental scale of that Empire and the extent of its activity in warfare, roadbuilding and governing, the bonds must have been very loose indeed, by our present day standards of national and civic integration, first because of the limited number of messages that could be sent per day and second, because of the great *time delay* between sending and receiving them. Time delay is very important. It means that in any day's interval between sending some order and its receipt, events may have taken place which rendered that order useless, or wrong, or even dangerous. Similarly with the time delay between sending a return message to headquarters, asking for instructions. This situation, with long time delays between the two ends, is well known to control engineers today as being a situation which can become 'unstable', that is to say, out of hand.§ It can only be concluded that the Roman Empire consisted of many strong *local* governments, dealing with all day-to-day affairs, and associated with Rome only for matters of general policy and important decisions. One of the characteristics of today's industrial societies is the high *speed* of connexion between Authorities and the Public, for governmental and social purposes of all kinds; when we use the

---

* In full: Desirable freehold residence; all modern conveniences; gas, electricity.
† 5th century B.C.
‡ See his *Travels*, J. M. Dent, Everyman's Library No. 306, p. 207 *et seq.*
§ The socially stabilizing values of fast communication are discussed in Section 7.

phrase 'by return of post' we literally mean the next day, or day after, whilst the telephone is virtually instantaneous.

4. The coming of mass-communication

The great importance of *reliability* of communication has already been stressed. Various accounts of the ancient postal services all emphasize these points: precision of timing and certainty of delivery. Caesar, no less than any present day authority, had to know that messages were received and when he could expect a reply. Truly, the speed of communication has been increased many-fold in modern times, to be virtually instantaneous, but of first importance is the fact that we have also increased its reliability. People may now travel about with a greater sense of security, *knowing* that they will be able to telephone or telegraph home if necessary. In fact, if someone does find difficulty in getting swift contact on the telephone with the right person, he may get righteously angry about it. It has become an assumed right, taken for granted, as much a part of Nature as the air he breathes.

The Roman postal service was carried into Europe by the Roman occupation forces, and stayed there in various centres long after their withdrawal, at the collapse of their Empire.[243, 249] Indeed the system remained substantially unchanged until the late Medieval period. At that time several postal establishments in various States of Europe were run by the Universities! The University of Paris, for instance, ran a postal service from the early 13th century until the 18th.[243]

From the earliest days, postal services seem to have been organized under government control and used for carrying the King's messages. Even today, in Britain, we speak of 'Her Majesty's Mail'* and all our stamps must bear an effigy of the monarch's head, symbolic of the security or protection offered.

It was not until the 17th century that the full *social* needs were recognized, for the postal service to be used by government officials, merchants, all but 'the common people'. In 1633 a regular weekly mail was set up between London, Antwerp and Brussels which took four to five days. By the time of Oliver Cromwell (1599–1658) regular services were running on all main roads of England, under licence from that remarkable new Institution, the English Parliament. It was during the same century that the Press developed, the original purpose being for *advertising*, which then was not distinguished from news. We shall look at its history in Section 5.

Surprisingly, for those times, several attempts were made by private persons to set up postal services. John Hill, for example, organized a 'penny post' throughout England, but it was regularly attacked by Cromwell's soldiers. As early as 1680 a private London and suburban postal service was established (by William Dockwra), with hourly collections, sorting offices and postboxes, which was later incorporated into the state system. Similar developments took place in America, at much the same date.

We may read of constant efforts being made, throughout this early history of postal communication, to improve the reliability of the mails, and of growing public confidence. By the time of Queen Anne (1665–1714) regular mails were reaching England's scattered colonies and security was, officially, ensured. Whereas under Cromwell's regime, foreign mails were read by a Board of Examiners, now only Secretaries of State had authority to do this!

---

* The word *mail* comes from Old French *male*, meaning a bag for travellers.

Attack and robbery on the highways were steadily defeated, by higher speeds of travel and by arming the coach guards, so that public confidence further increased. But it was the coming of the railways which finally established the postal service as part of the life of every man, woman and child, as something utterly reliable and always available: that which we today accept as our due.

To quote my own country, Britain, by the time of Sir Rowland Hill's Post Office Reform Bill (1837), letters in the mails totalled 88 million per annum (whilst today there are over 11,000 million packages of all kinds per annum).[123] The *postage stamp* was invented in Britain, in acknowledgment of which it is the only country in the world whose stamps do not bear the name of the country (although the Monarch's head must always appear). Britain is also the main printer of stamps for the world, for no less than 125 foreign countries. (e.g. see *Guardian* for 29th November 1966).

The railways* were dominant, not only in the development of the mails, but also in the early history of telegraphy. It was the railways which were first to adopt the new electric 'telegraph', as an alternative to the post: the first invented 'electronic' system of communication. Although the suggestion that messages might be sent over a wire (by discharging a Leyden jar) was made† as early as 1753, the first really practical trials were made by the railway companies (starting in 1837) and for a long time telegraphs were used only by the railways.[146] Even today we still have the familiar sight of telegraph poles and wires through our railway carriage windows.

Soon companies were formed. In 1851, the year of the Great Exhibition, the Stock Exchanges of London and Paris were connected by telegraph so that prices could be rapidly compared for the first time. The Atlantic was crossed by telegraph successfully in 1866 whilst by 1871 there was a connexion to India. Public confidence grew further and people were prepared to pay high prices for telegrams but for some period during the middle of last century the service was still confined to those towns and cities which were connected by the railways.

Of the story of the coming of the telephone little will be told here, for it is widely documented and it brings us into relatively modern times anyway.‡ It is worth remembering that there are people alive today who can recall living in a world without the telephone; also it may be worth observing here that the telephone came into truly widespread use only after the Second World War. (See Figure 3.9.)

Technically speaking, the telephone is an extension of the telegraph. Indeed, the first microphone made, by the German Philip Reis§ in 1861, operated rather in the manner of a very high-speed telegraph, the soundwaves of the voice 'making' and 'breaking' an electric current (popularly called today the bang–bang principle).[114, 221] Credit is usually given to Graham Bell[13] for the first practical telephone, though others were working upon the same idea independently, including Elisha Gray and the lesser known Daniel Drawbaugh.[114, 146] Early experiments upon electric voice transmission had already been carried out by Page in Massachusetts (in 1837) and by Bourseul

---

* The world's first railway (George Stephenson) was opened on 27th September 1825 between Stockton and Darlington. The famous 'Rocket' followed 5 years later.

† By an anonymous writer to the *Scots Magazine*, Vol. **15**, 1753, p. 73. See Ref. 78 under Telegraph.

‡ Robert Hooke constructed a mechanical 'telephone', using a stretched wire in 1664.

§ Who devised the word 'telephone'.

in Paris (in 1854).[78] Thus the telephone was conceived very shortly after the telegraph, and that had developed alongside the railways.

It is these three modes of communication (rail, telegraph, telephone) introduced within such a short period of time, that ensured the coming of the kind of industrial world which we know today, with its huge and complex industrial organizations.

Something quite new in the history of communication was called for when telephones came into use, that is, some kind of *subscriber organization*. Every telephone in a country cannot be connected to every other telephone, so a *telephone exchange* is required. Telephone books, and a regular system of central accounting, etc., are needed. The first patent for a 'central station' to which houses could be connected had already been taken out in 1851.

The coming of radio at the turn of the century introduced something new again: simultaneous communication between some *central* (broadcasting) Authority and a large number of receivers. Other users of radio today, (e.g. naval, military, police, etc.) operate similarly, see Table 1: that is, *broadcast*. Radio is somewhat analogous to the Press as a medium of communication, if only in this respect. It is to be expected that radio, and T.V. later, have come to serve some of the functions of the Press: entertainment, news and advertising, though in essentially different ways. The various natures and functions of the different modes of communication will be examined in Section 6.

It was the coming of broadcasting,[24] as a supplement to an already established Press, into our society, by then highly literate, though of widely varied standards of education, that has created in many people's minds the symbol of *mass-communication*, which is certainly one of the most important characteristics of our advanced societies today. It is a phenomenon, no less. But the name mass-communication is a very misleading one, and it will be discussed later in Section 6.

The coming of electrical communication, starting with the telegraph, enforced two great breaks from the traditional modes, such as horse and railway. The first was due to the immense increase in speed with which messages could be sent; in one step, *the speed was increased some* 10 *million times*, so that virtually no time delay occurred. The second was due to their availability for use by the common man.

'Use by the common man' is a phrase which may be taken too literally. Certainly the older modes, the post and the *inland* telephone, are widely used today, but the intercontinental routes (e.g. the transatlantic telephone to the U.S.A.) are mainly used by authorities, for very few people out of our population have as yet any reason to make private intercontinental calls. The 'common man' does not much *use* these world-systems, any more than he would have used the *cursus publicus* in Roman times, though the systems are now *available* to him, not withheld. The difference between *use* and *availability for use* may seem a quibble, but in my opinion it is not, a point which will be elaborated later, in Chapter 3, Section 7.

In all industrial countries the use of telephones, telegraphs and radio increased steadily, but slowly, until the Second World War; then afterwards, starting in the late 1940s, their usage within all advanced countries increased suddenly, in a way which can only be described as 'explosive'. This 'explosion' will be examined in the next Chapter in more detail, for some of its aspects are surprising.

Radio and television are now used by people of all classes in the advanced countries. The voice and vision of Authority in many different forms now appears in nearly every home, to entertain, provide news, education or propaganda, to inform or to deceive, to inflame or to hypnotize, to initiate clichés and slang, to model our heroes or set our norms . . . in fact to do all those things that books, magazines and newspapers can do, and much more besides, but in totally new ways.

Mass-communication has many wild things said about it, both in popular conversation and in a good many official statements. It is often deplored as being the producer of 'mass tastes' and even as the source of 'increasing juvenile delinquency', etc., etc. Sometimes it is praised as being the most powerful means yet found for education, or as being the only hope for 'mass-education' of all kinds in the developing countries.

What then is the nature of the beast? As usual, when such conflicting opinions are expressed, often with strong feeling, the beast has many natures. Mass-communication is not one thing, but many, all distinct in their natures. It may be useful to examine something of their distinctions, but, before doing this, we should perhaps glance at the history of our oldest form of mass-communication, one to which we have so far given little attention: namely, the Press, with which is essentially involved another form, advertising.

5. The Press and advertising

When considering so-called 'mass-communication' it would be quite wrong to restrict it to electronic means, the radio, T.V., etc., and not to refer to the history of newspapers and journals—the Press.[118, 247]

The Press is inseparably mixed with another social institution of great importance, advertising. If present day newspapers were not so heavily financed by advertising, your daily paper would cost you many more times its present price. Not only this, but you would be deprived of many sources of information of great value.

The word advertising conjures up in many people's minds a rather unpleasant image, an image of present day commercialism, pressure to consume, etc., as something to be deplored, as one of the bad aspects of industrialization. It has become a somewhat emotional term. Unfortunately, this one word 'advertisement' is used to mean several quite different things; it is ambiguous. Thus the word advertisement may refer to a Situations Vacant entry, or to a forthcoming Concert, or again to a House for Sale, or to a village Fête or to a new detergent which does nothing more than all the other detergents, endless quite distinct functions. It is its application to the high-pressure selling of consumer goods that causes some people concern, especially to the suspected forced selling of totally unnecessary junk to a helpless 'consumer society.'

Another concern arises by virtue of the false images created by some advertisements today (e.g. for cars, or women's clothes), images of an elegance or snobbery or luxury which give a very wrong view of what life is really like: an invented dream world. It may then be worthwhile to glance briefly at the origins and history of newspapers and advertisements.

The need for some way of bringing people's attention to various sources of goods for sale and services, in order to effect a better distribution was recognized by the great French essayist Montaigne in an essay published in the year 1594, *Of a Defect in our Policies*, which stimulated the setting up of a bureau and publication of a Journal later, in Paris, in 1612, comprising a list of buyer's wants, together with public and legal notices. In 1611 a *Publique Register* was set up in England, though it did not last for long. It was not until the middle of the 17th century that it was finally established, and then it was supported by what we would nowadays call advertisements.[247]

It was towards the middle years of the 17th century that the 'news sheets or 'weekly news letters (or pamphlets)' became firmly associated with advertisements; in England, it was in the year 1625 that the first publication at all resembling a modern newspaper in idea was started and issued weekly, the *Mercurius Britanicus*.* But not until mid-century did advertising and news become closely linked, when Henry Walker set up an 'Office of Entries' (a public Register intended to bring sellers and buyers together). Very soon the benefits of advertising became clear; the earliest notices being for books and patent medicines,†[247] followed shortly by that newly introduced commodity, tea.

It is worth calling attention to these origins of our newspapers and advertisements if only to observe that these early publications existed both to serve the purpose of advising potential buyers where they might obtain the goods, or the services, which they needed and to report major happenings. They were for *advising* and they were, in fact, called *Advices*. (It was not until 1655 that the word *advertisement* first appeared.) In other words these original publications of the 17th century *regarded the desire of someone to buy or sell something as news just as much as the other events of the week, even the reporting of a battle*. The public needed Advices to inform them in many different ways; all were, in different senses, *news*.

Thus it was at about the time of the Civil War (1642–1646) in England that the 'newspaper' emerged, with news reporting and advertising linked together, as they are today, though printed then in a far *less* distinguishable way, with uniform print and, of course, without pictures. The fact that Mr. Smith of Cheapside had a crate of tea for sale was news just as the burning down of his house would be news.

Such early stages of journalism and advertising served the public valuably, encouraging commerce and material progress, with no sense whatever of the artificial pressure feeding which some people feel exists in modern newspapers: pressure *both* for news consumption and goods consumption. It may be asked: when did any sense of alarm arise concerning the possible growing power of the Press—political and commercial power? The earliest signs of serious alarm were shown by none other than Dr. Samuel Johnson, a little more than a century later.‡ Dr. Johnson realized that, unless other legal and social forces came to bear upon it, advertising could be used antisocially. 'Promise', he wrote, 'large promise, is the soul of an advertisement'.§ He even spoke of other aspects of the Press which are so often heard today: horror, violence and sex! But his criticisms had little effect upon standards which became, if anything, worse.

Already, by Cromwell's time, in the 1640s and 50s the political values of advertising were recognized and concern about *monopoly* led to the setting up of a Surveyor of the Press in 1663 who could issue licences giving permission to publish.

Thus some of the concerns we hear expressed today about such things as advertising (in papers or on T.V.), commercialism, political control, forced selling and others are far from modern. There is another concern of importance,

---

* As a 20 page book, with pages about the size of those of this book.
† See Ref. 78 under Advertisement.
‡ Addison too.
§ See *Oxford Dictionary* quotation, entry 277–35.

implied by the term mass-communication. This is frequently used today in a derogatory sense, implying that people's thoughts and tastes are forced upon them by the commercial giants of the Press and T.V., and suggesting that independent thought and action are getting less and less possible. 'It's all this mass-communication today which causes our children's delinquency and violence, etc., etc.' is so often heard. Whether or not this is true can be discovered only by careful study and research, not by emotional judgement.[121, 267, 303, 306]

When we discuss questions of so-called mass-communication today we should essentially bear in mind the comparative sizes of populations, and comparative literacy, between these earlier centuries and now. In the mid-17th century the population of England and Wales was about $5\frac{1}{2}$ million[295] and literacy was then confined to a fraction of these (see p. 25). Furthermore, even amongst these people the amount of buying and selling of goods or services was proportionally very small. The Advices which were published then can scarcely be called mass-communication. In simple fact, the masses of people then were very poor and many were illiterate. I, for one, have no wish to have been born in the 17th century; and half the world's population today is in a far worse state than that.

Today, the value to the poor countries of the so-called mass-media, (that is the Press, films, books, radio and others) is immense, as Unesco documents,[300, 301, 302, 307, 308, 310, 320] and reports of sociologists acting in this field will testify.[248, 262, 266] There can be little doubt that the mass-media techniques are essential for helping the peoples of the developing countries to pull themselves into the 20th century, for several reasons. I say the *techniques*, used in the various ways each country may need, the techniques only; the *contents* of these media should not necessarily copy ours. On the contrary, the introduction of Western films and newspapers can be, and often has been, disastrous, though it need not be.[248] Wilbur Schramm[262, 266] has emphasized that the various developing countries differ much from one another and need to use mass-media in different ways; there are no universal rules. We ourselves in, say, the industrial European countries and America have also been developing countries in our own different ways not so very long ago (and in certain respects we still are). The same argument has been seen to apply; it was first the introduction of printing in the 15th century, especially its use for lay books,* and then the early realization of its values for effecting exchanges of all kinds, commerce and news, the Advices which I have described, the precursors of today's newspapers and journals, which have made possible our highly literate industrial societies.

Mass-media make 'progress' possible, but they themselves do not create progress, as Wilbur Schramm emphasizes. Our advanced industrial countries have each had very varied political histories, and each has developed a Press during the last few hundred years to assist their varied forms of advance, political, industrial and educational. The social values of the Press have continually changed, from their original use as Advices to the complex tabloids and journals of today, as we approach a point of comparative material saturation: what Professor Galbraith calls the Affluent Society.[96] The trend of the changing Press, as popular education and wealth have spread through the advanced countries, may be towards serving an increasingly *political* function.

* When printing was introduced into Britain, by Caxton, it was applied immediately to *lay* books. (See Chapter 1, p. 25.)

This is not to say that the political function of the Press is at all recent, for in the 17th century the values of the old Advices for politics were soon recognized. In England this was largely owing to the Roundhead/Cavalier Civil War, 1642–1646, and the political troubles preceding this.[247, 295] Rather it is that this political function of the Press has grown to be so significant today, whilst it tries to serve its various earlier functions at the same time, i.e. advertising, of many different kinds. The Press nowadays tries to serve a very wide range of distinct functions, of very different natures. Sheer entertainment is one, crossword puzzles, reports of funny events, strip cartoons, etc., although, to be fair, such lighthearted items occupy only a small space in most Western newspapers. Analysis of newspaper content made in 1949, revealed that straight news occupied between 75–98 per cent of space in all London Dailies; in the picture papers and tabloids it could fall to 60 per cent.[125] However, most of the remaining space, other than for advertising, was taken up by pictures.[126] (Further analysis of newspaper contents has been published by the *Economist Intelligence Unit*.[77])

In today's industrial world, we have had to adapt to the habit of reading newspapers at *convenient times*, mostly very short, whenever they happen to occur: in the commuter's train, during lunch breaks, in the evening, waiting in queues, etc. Unlike those educated people of the 17th century, who could expect an Advice to appear once a week, containing its list of local affairs, and who might perhaps choose their time to sit in the coffee-houses to read them, the modern man is expected to understand both local and world news, every day, gathered in brief snatches.[193] Small wonder that it has become an obsession!

Rather than the daily newspapers, it is perhaps the weekly or monthly serious Journals that best serve this political function today; they are read by the more educated section of the people, who have a week or month in which to read them. The journalists who write the various types of article often become well known to their regular readers, and their particular political bias also becomes known. Again, many of our Journals are written in a spirit of criticism or commentary rather than for selected fact reporting, made for quick reading.[193] I would predict that as T.V. takes over more factual daily news reporting, newspapers will become increasingly devoted to criticism, commentary, explanation—i.e. a mediating function.

The steady and continued industrialization of a country such as Britain, from the mid-18th to the 20th century is mirrored in the changing forms and appearances of its newspapers.

This change of appearance, from the old Advices to today's garish tabloids has not come suddenly; it does not just represent 'the vulgarity of modern times'. The first addition to the sober regularity of print in the Advices was probably made by John Houghton, a Fellow of the Royal Society, who introduced the pointing finger ☞ and later, shortly after the year 1692, *Italian* script. During the next century, new forms of layout were tried and various other eyecatching tricks,* though pictures did not appear until well into the 19th century, including strip cartoons or comics.[294]

The history of printed pictures for advertisements is interesting. Some of the earliest to be printed in England were drawn by great artists, including Hogarth, in the early 18th century, some said to have been 'of exquisite

---

* In *The Tatler*, September 14th, 1710, Addison comments 'The great Art in writing Advertisements, is the finding out a Proper Method to catch the Reader's Eye . . .'

beauty'.[247] These, however, were not printed in the Advices, but on nothing more than tradesmen's handbills! Our modern handbills are coldly functional by comparison. Engraved pictures began to appear in newspapers at the beginning of last century, in both England and America, but the standard of artistry sank greatly during Victorian times, a standard which, in this writer's opinion, was not raised until times following the Second World War. I can speak only of Britain, but the same may be true elsewhere; the artistic standards of many of our placard advertisements today are high.

The attitudes of the citizens of N. America and of Britain, towards advertising and the respective advertisement pressures upon them may sometimes be very different. Britain spends about one per cent of her income upon advertising, whereas America spends about twice as much. In Britain many people may deplore advertising as somewhat vulgar, but a necessary curse. In America there is far more of it, both in print and on T.V. The reasons for this are not to be found in our national characters but rather in the distinct ways in which our industrial histories developed. Thus the history of advertising has been quite different in the two countries, from the early 18th century onwards. In England, a tax was placed upon newspapers in 1710 which was not removed until the year 1855; during this century and a half both the number of different papers and their total circulation became more than four times as great in the U.S.A.* There were several consequences of this Newspaper Tax; among other things 'popular' distribution of papers was held back and with it perhaps also literacy, among the poorer classes. However, the Tax was openly defied by working class newspapers in the North of England.[250, 355]

Why was this tax levied? The answer was 'to control seditious libel'. Now this fact is interesting, because similar paternal concern by the State for 'public protection' has been shown by authorities on the introduction of *all* new communication services. Anxiety had arisen in Cromwell's time, about abuse of the new Postal Service. Similar concern arose later, for example when the telephone was invented and, later still, radio and television. This point is taken up again on p. 118.

Whilst the Tax was in operation in England, newspaper circulation was naturally small, so that advertising would not have reached the bulk of the people. It is not surprising then that bill-stickers were to be found everywhere in London. Bills and posters were stuck on everything that would hold them, houses, shops, lamp-posts, walls; London in mid-19th century broke out into a pox of paper. If any readers feel that their environment today is spoiled by posters, or become annoyed at the constant interruption of their favourite T.V. programmes by commercial 'plugs', pray cast your minds back 100 years, for it was far worse then. Legislation was introduced in the 1860s to clear London of this mess and to confine advertisements to large hoardings where they could be seen in one place. Perhaps we shall find legislation coming soon to confine our T.V. advertisements to special times of the day.

Although newspaper advertising was invented in Britain it is in America that it has been developed into many forms. For one thing, no corresponding tax was levied there and perhaps it is fair to comment that advertising played a somewhat different rôle in America in the 1800s, as that country was expanding out into virgin lands and populations were fast moving into them.

---

* The populations of the United Kingdom and the U.S.A. were then nearly equal. See Figure 2.4.

New settlements, new towns, meant many new things were required. A whole new continent was being patriated.

If there is one single symbol that can be named of the American spirit of commercial energy in mid-19th century it would surely be that king oɪ showmanship, Phineas Taylor Barnum. No 'exquisite art' for him. Rather brass bands, circuses, coloured illuminations, banners . . . fakes, even a mermaid and a midget. He used showmanship to advertise show business. The extrovert showman of all time, the stuntsman, the joker. Surely the welter of monkey tricks he thought up to advertise his shows would put our T.V. advertisements today in the shade. His blare and extravaganza burst upon America in the 1830s and 40s, dinning into its citizens that show business is its own advertisement, and impressing upon their minds the moral that advertising of other things than entertainment, namely all commercial products, should, to be successful, be a form of show business. The lesson was learned.

Advertising, today, is far more than the presentation of true plain facts. Advertisements must entertain, use comic strip methods, funny cartoons, extravagant displays, meaningless pseudo-scientific patter, sex symbols . . . the lot. Advertising, T.V. advertising above all, has today become a branch of show business. Stand in the middle of Piccadilly or Times Square on any night and what do you see all round you? Gigantic structures of coloured lights, moving and flashing, huge cartoons in neon strips, a phantasmagoria of dazzling coloured comics fifty feet high. If you can't afford to enter the bright doors of the halls of entertainment nearby, the cinemas, theatres and music halls, then you may at least stand outside on the pavement and get your show there for nothing. In fact, hundreds of people do so, every night.

Much advertising of consumer goods today is, I submit, show business. Psychologists are employed by the hundred, computers too.[132] Intense research is carried out into the effects of sizes and shapes, of lettering, pictures[297] of readers' social status, of use of funnies and of sex symbols, nothing is spared in the search to find what grips the reader or viewer.[298] Indeed, commercial T.V. puts advertising and entertaining on a par; in this medium, advertising frankly confesses its true nature of show business.

Our newspapers today try to serve many different purposes. They provide news, political comment, articles on everything, crossword puzzles, the weather, horoscopes, comic strips, crime reports, sports, news, Stock Exchange prices, letters to the editor . . . what else? Advertisements, of course, which enable you to buy your paper for a few pence. What other single material object can we imagine, which serves more diverse a *range* of purposes: news from Vietnam on the front page, funnies printed on page two, and a crossword puzzle to end. The incongruity of it all! Let us confess it; newspapers are not solely bearers of news. They are entertainment too.[284] Stephenson refers to this view as the Ludenic Theory of Newsreading.[284] 'Ludenic' being taken from Latin *ludicrus* = done in sport, and *ludo* = to play, amuse, frisk, frolic.

A newspaper can serve ritualistic functions:[284] 'the morning paper' carried by suburbanites in trains, or 'the evening paper' (which most likely contains little real news). The very way it is carried; rolled, flat, or shambled, has significance. So can failure to get our familiar daily paper be significant to ourselves. We feel lost, ignorant, 'out of it', anxious and even ashamed.[15]

6. Mass-communication media. A new medium does not replace an older, but only some of its functions

The term 'mass-communication' is of fairly recent origin, being taken over, by analogy, from the earlier expression 'mass-production'. It is a false analogy and carries with itself the unfortunate suggestion that mass-communication means the mass-production of minds: the very word 'mass' comes from the Greek maza, meaning barley-meal! It can then be used as an emotional term, being convenient to use in argument as a broad generality and to avoid specificity. Thomas Carlyle was one of the first to use the expression in a way suggesting contempt and fear, when he spoke of 'the masses' as: 'Swarmery, Sons of the Devil, blockheadism, gullibility, bribeability, amenability to beer and balderdash.'[357] Barley-meal, porridge, is a poor epithet for people.

It might well be asked first: who are 'the masses'? Are you and I two of such people? Do you and I ever think of ourselves as such, or do we think of a grey amorphous lump, millions of others, 'out there'? What have the masses got in common that makes them a social group, to be referred to in this way?: reading the same newspaper? watching the same T.V. programme? voting for the same Party? having the same occupation? Clearly, such different groups would not comprise the same people. The term the masses is meaningless, unless it is qualified: 'the mass of people who do so-and-so'. It has degenerated into an emotional term which may conveniently be used in a contemptuous or pejorative way.

As S. Maclean Jr. has put it: 'There are some implications in the term "mass-communication" that there are scheming powers of evil that will influence and change many of us, and that somehow they are going to harm us—like evil gods or something'.[197] I agree. 'The Masses' form almost an existentialist idea, like 'The One' of Heidegger (*One ought to . . .*), an abstract 'They' ('*They say that it's going to rain*'). The Masses are never you nor me, only 'the others'.

The very words, the masses, convey a sense of contempt. Even today for us there still lingers around these words a feeling of fear, as there did for John Stuart Mill, a hundred years ago: fear of 'the mob'. But, strictly speaking, you cannot communicate with the masses; a better wording would be: you communicate with individual human beings, in massive numbers—a very different matter.

A common error in lay discussion of social questions is this lumping together, thus fogging the real questions with such terms as *the working class, the average man, the African* . . . the particular images of which will depend entirely upon who *you* are; there is no single objective reality.

It may be reasonable to apply the term 'the masses' to people in certain, very specialized, circumstances such as those in the Army, trained out of all personal opinions. Or, when with 100,000 other people at a football match I wear my funny hat, my striped scarf and huge coloured rosette, swinging my rattle, chanting in unison with all the others, roaring when a goal is scored, then indeed I am in 'the masses', behaving as one great single monster. But don't condemn me for that alone: I may be enjoying myself. On the other hand, when I sit with my family before our T.V. set and watch a football match, I am unaware of the millions of others doing the same, and we do not exhibit crowd behaviour in the sitting-room.

So much for the masses; now let us look at the word *communication*. There are so very many different media of communication and transport, newspapers, books, radio, aeroplanes, railways, T.V. . . . and they each have quite different characters and have enabled societies to change in different ways. Each has contributed what I shall call a different *quality*. It is incorrect to regard any one mode as wholly supplanting an earlier one, which thereby becomes 'old-fashioned'. Thus T.V. has not supplanted radio, nor has it totally replaced the cinema and film (Figure 2.1), nor has the telephone

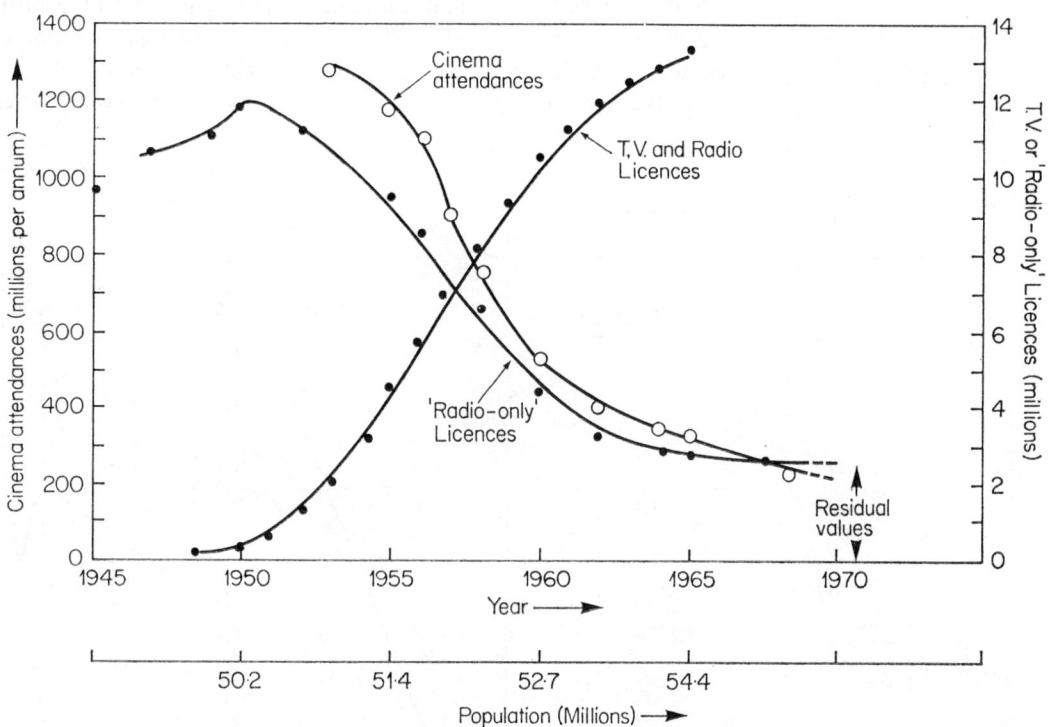

Figure 2.1. Television has not entirely replaced the cinema and sound radio. (Example relates to the U.K.)
(From the *U.K. Annual Abstract of Statistics*, by kind permission of H.M.S.O.)

supplanted the telegraph, nor have cars replaced railways (Figure 2.2). Another prognostication so often made today is that newspapers will soon be replaced by data links, in homes and offices, showing news printed on a T.V. screen. Such new techniques may indeed come (and our present T.V. news bulletins are a small step towards this) but, if they do, newspapers will still continue to be published; though their form and functions will change, as they have been doing for 350 years past. It is often said that books will soon be replaced by texts stored in computers, or by rolls of microfilm, but don't you believe it! Books can be used in so many different ways, not only read for factual information. They can be scribbled on in their margins, read outdoors or in the train, fondled. The demand for books and libraries is rising fast today, in countries rich and poor. The 'electronic media' do not replace them, quite the contrary. (See Chapter 6, Section 6.) Nevertheless, the introduction of any one new mode of communication certainly changes the values and uses of earlier ones.

Each mode has contributed something quite new, some additional quality, to the growing structure of communication. The way in which we regard one another in our various groups (families, social classes, nationalities . . .) and so, in turn, the way in which we each think about ourselves, depend upon which of these various modes of communication we possess. In the advanced countries we possess the lot; 30-odd years ago we did not have television, and we were changed by its coming; a hundred years ago we didn't have the telephone, and people had no conception of being free to do many things which they can do today.

The fact that any one new-introduced mode of communication does not wholly replace, or supplant, an earlier one is evidenced by a host of statistics.[80,123,312,325,330,332,333,334,337] A number of typical examples may be shown here, drawn from British[123] and U.S.A.* sources.[333,334] We see from the historical curves of Figures 2.2a and b that the motor car did not

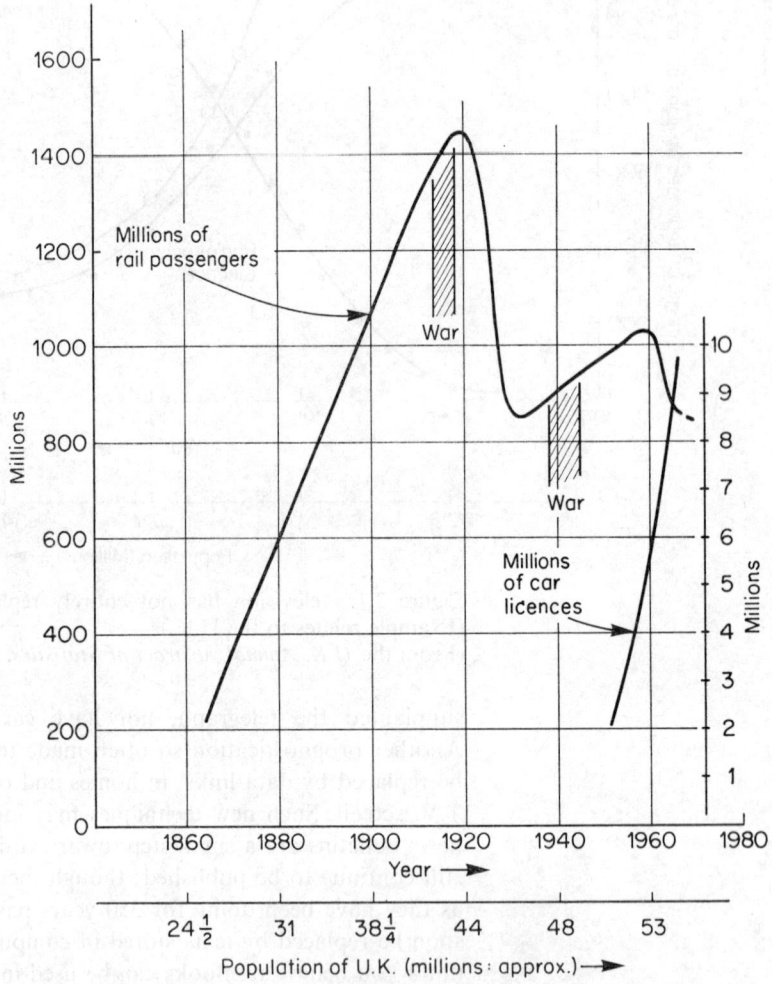

Figure 2.2a. Decline of rail passenger traffic in the United Kingdom.[123]

destroy the railways, though passengers rapidly *reduced* drastically, following the end of the First World War in 1918, to a new level which has changed more slowly during later years, as cars have increased in numbers.

The futility of trying to predict future demands solely by projecting curves of statistics skywards is well illustrated here. Thus the boosted rise, and subsequent reduction, of rail traffic (See Figures 2.2a and b) is coincident

* When U.S.A. growth statistics are referred to, due note should be taken of their very rapid population increase. (See Figure 2.4.)

with the First World War and its immense demands for transport. Major changes of demand are as likely to be the result of changing social circumstances as they are of technical innovation. Figures 6.6 and 6.7 show the effects of War upon newspaper circulations.

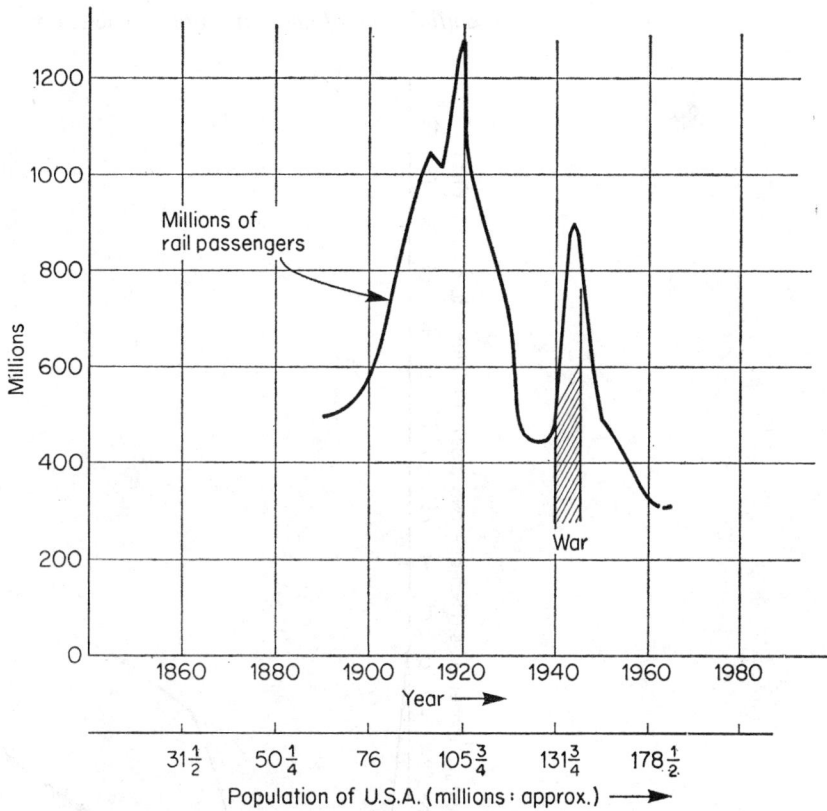

Figure 2.2b. Decline of rail passenger traffic in the United States of America.[333]

To take another instance, television has not destroyed the cinema (Figure 2.1) but has only taken over some of its values (and introduced its own).

Again, the very rapid growth of overseas air traffic[135] has not stopped the increase in sea passengers, though certain routes have grown to favour one or the other[3] (See Figure 2.3). Thus transatlantic air routes are relatively short, inexpensive and under very high demand,* whereas countries like Australia or New Zealand, being very remote places, favour sea travel. The traditional maritime countries, Britain,[123] Scandinavia and Holland, also maintain a heavy sea-traffic.[3] (Their combined sea passengers in 1965 were five times as many as air passengers; for South Africa too, the ratio was three to one.)

The postal service too is very old, but this also has not been made old-fashioned by electronic communication, and continues in increased and more varied use, in countries both rich and poor.

The lessons from statistics of this kind are clear. New methods of communication do not supplant old ones in all respects. They may improve certain social values, or introduce wholly new ones, but some values of the older modes still remain.

* Nevertheless, sea passage demand also still rises.

In the manufacturing industries many new machines do actually supplant older ones, which fall out of use. But it seems that in the field of human communication, this does not happen. We may ask: why?

The only answer can be that there is a continual demand for the old modes so that, as emphasized before, *these various modes, old and new, are essentially not of the same nature.* The telephone is not just a better telegraph;

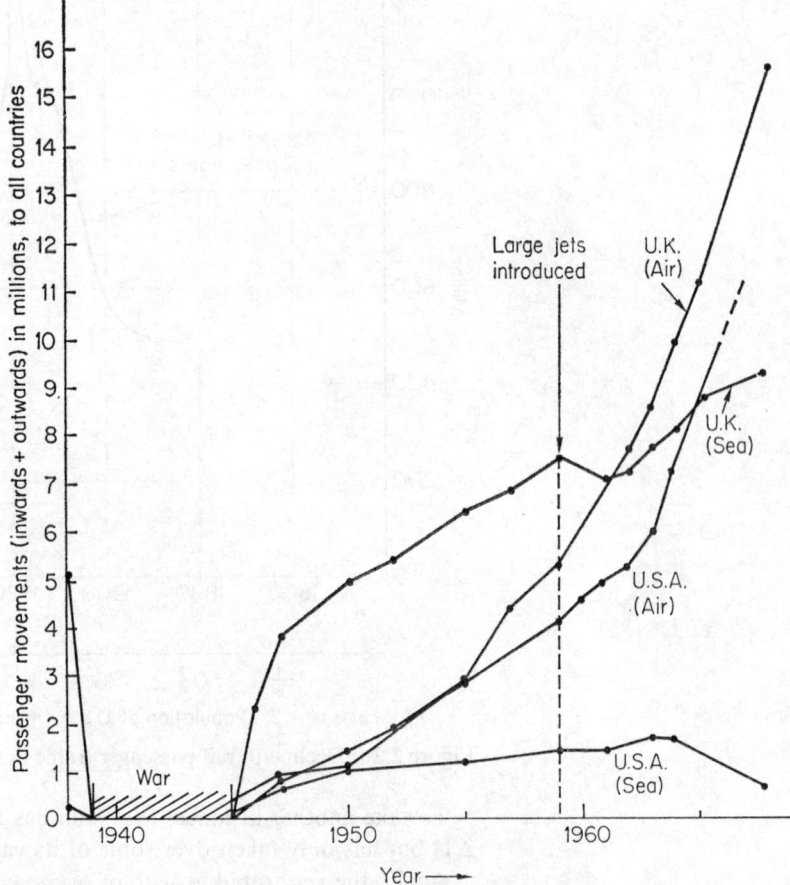

Figure 2.3. Postwar growths of both sea and air passenger traffic between (a) United Kingdom (b) United States of America and all other countries.
Figures from (a) *U.K. Annual Abstracts of Statistics*[123] and (b) *Statistical Abstracts of the U.S.A.,*[334] with grateful acknowledgments.

television is not just a better cinema or radio; they are categorically different, though each brings its own 'quality' to the whole structure of human communication. It is most deceptive and confusing to lump all together as mass-communication.

The various modes of communication which have been evolved or invented at different times in history have very varied significances and it is important to distinguish them. Thus a telephone call is quite different in its nature from a letter and both are different from telegrams; again, a radio broadcast differs in function from a newspaper report or a T.V. news bulletin, and so on. All are methods of communication, but quite distinct in character and in the ways they serve to change us. Only too frequently do we hear the expression mass-communication used to refer to all modern methods, both print and electronic, lumped together. Not only does confusion sometimes arise for this reason, but also because most members of the public think only of their use in the home, their *domestic* use, whereas so many of their uses are not private; these *public* uses remain so often unobtrusive or even out of sight. For example, their uses by the Police, by the Army, for aircraft navigation, and by Banks, businesses and other public authorities. It is worth considering their different social functions and characters, in turn and in historical order.

First, speech itself; this is what primarily distinguishes man from the animals; it is part of human nature.[175] To repeat from Chapter 1: speech is

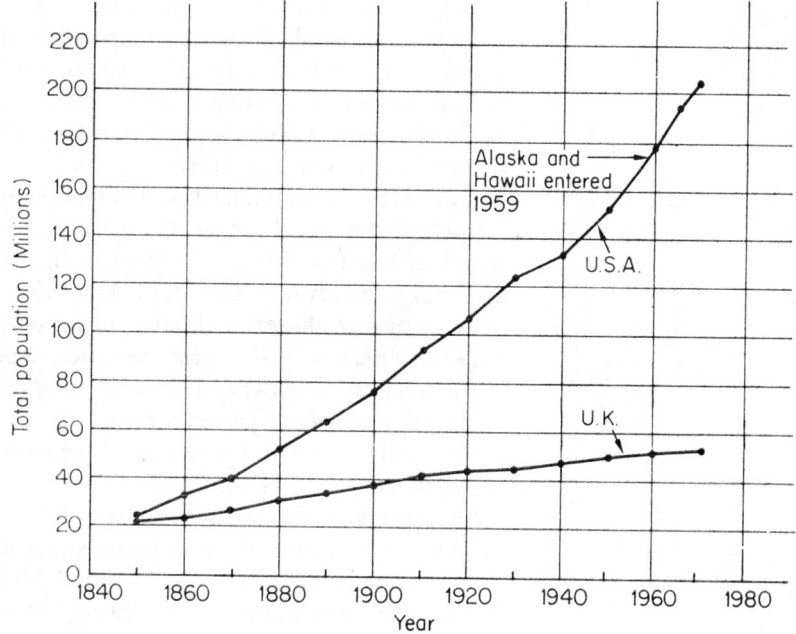

Figure 2.4. Growth of the populations of the United States and the United Kingdom, in the past century.

always *between* people (even 'we' with 'ourselves' when soliloquizing) giving us a sense of individuality and of sociability at one and the same time. Speech does many things to us and to our relationships; it signifies our cultural beliefs, our moods, our attitudes: many things. It essentially reveals our personal states and natures, both as unconscious and as thinking creatures.

Next, writing and all forms of scribing. These, from the earliest cave drawings onwards, are all deliberate, conscious, *intellectual* acts. I can babble nonsense with no effort whatever, even in my sleep; but I cannot write or draw by virtue of similar muscular habit; I must *think*, however little. Secondly, though related, writing connects past, present and future and enforces the concept of historic *time* upon us. Thus I wrote these words in this book in the past, for the purpose of your reading them in the future; we write *for* the future, but read *about* the past. Such connexion enables comparisons to be made, records, differences noted, and so *questionings* to be enforced upon us: deliberate, intellectualized questionings, the raising of doubts and their resolutions. There are endless examples of the lack of a sense of enquiry among illiterates. For example, Paul Foster refers, among other examples, to the case of an African student standing on the dam at

Lake Victoria, where the Nile emerges, and saying: 'How odd it is that during all these centuries my people have never wondered where this river went to!'[91]

Next, the invention of printing enabled these various questionings to be spread among large literate populations, thereby providing more sources of *group questionings*. New philosophies could be formed, discussed and widely criticized. Among these, the field of thought called *science* emerged. Science is possible only where records are made, and compared. Leonardo da Vinci achieved his remarkable results not only by virtue of being a remarkable thinker, but because he kept careful records, writings and drawings. Another well-known example is John Locke. Yet another is Jules Verne, whose remarkable predictions rested upon his file of 25,000 items. On a longer time scale, it is true to say that the whole historic movement called the Renaissance arose from a new examination of old Islamic, Hebrew and Greek scientific records when translated into Latin; the old theories could then be questioned and their *recorded* facts doubted, [111] new theories evolved and tested, whole cultural or national philosophies attacked.

Next, the postal service. As a means of communication this serves both private and public needs. In Roman times the *cursus publicus* (see Section 3) would primarily have been of public service, in the sense of use by the military or governing officials and, later, in Europe, of the ruling courts. Its private use emerged only in recent centuries, especially the 17th. As a mode of communication letters, of course, provide a person-to-person service, or else an authority-to-person service.

Broadly speaking, the postal service carries out both of these two distinct functions; either private and confidential, between friends, acquaintances (or would-be acquaintances), or else impersonal: orders, instructions, information, demands and acknowledgments. Such multiple use, or *diversity*, is found in all modern modes of communication: radio, T.V., telegraphs and even roads and railways. The reasons are economic and will be considered in Chapter 5.

Therefore, since the post facilitates both person-to-person and authority-to-person communication, the specific quality which postal services have contributed to civilization is their power to *organize*, whether personally or publicly; patterns of relationships could be set up, more complex business, industrial and national organizations created, operating over larger areas.

Historically, the next step in the evolution of communication has been the coming of electrical methods, the invention of the telegraph, closely followed by that of the telephone.[13,56,114] Technically speaking, the two are closely alike, but socially they are utterly different.

The chief quality newly introduced by the telegraph was that of speed. At one stroke, the speed of messages was raised some *ten million times* by the telegraph, from that of the horse to that of electricity. The implications of this vast increase of speed have been several-fold. Basically it implied that an institution or organization, say a business (the 'pattern of relationships'), could send far more messages and receive more replies per day than before; that is to say, more instructions, advices, decisions, etc. could be made per day. *Ceteris paribus* this would mean far higher costs per day. However, such increased message traffic and correspondingly increased costs mean only that these institutions were enabled *to grow in size*; larger economic organizations could exist, with the message traffic dispersed among more people and over greater areas of the world.[355] If messages are faster, then more 'elements' of an organization can be related per day or per week. In particular, world news services have developed; news agencies have followed wherever the telegraph has gone.

The function of the telephone is different. It is not only personal, in the sense that private letters are, but it has far greater significance, for the simple reason that human *conversations* are possible. As was argued in Chapter 1, conversation is an essential human relationship. When you speak to someone on the 'phone, even a stranger, you hear far more than factual premeditated messages; you respond to tones of voice, to moods; you may interject a remark; it is a person you are involved with, not a machine. Though unseen, you continue to gesture, to smile or frown, and move your hands; you are *conversing*, linked, 'involved' and 'committed'. (See Chapter 1, Section 5.) You can discuss, persuade, enquire, argue and perhaps reach agreement in a few minutes, in a personal way. Rapid converse, enquiry, resolution are the powers offered by telephones to organizations.

In private homes the telephone has added other qualities. It has enabled members of the family to travel, or even to emigrate, not only with increased security, but with less personal distress. It is the *availability* of the international telephone service which is of such significance to the common man today. He may not use it personally very often; but it is there. A telephone conversation means far more to, say, a mother, than any letter arriving after three days delay or even a telegram; a call can resolve uncertainties, doubts, or anxieties and give greater *assurance*; even if the news told is bad, the truth can be made known. The telephone has contributed to personal *mobility* in a way no other medium has because the traveller does not have to stay in one place, waiting for an answer, but may continue his journey and telephone later from a callbox or hotel.

All these various communication techniques so far referred to are seen to contribute quite distinct and various qualities to society: writing, printing, the post, telegraphs and telephones. No one technique has supplanted an earlier one, but rather changed the nature of communication and the structure and size of our organizations.

The story continues. The coming of radio at the turn of the century has been dramatic in its eventual social effects. Its immediate value was for ships at sea[277] which could, for the first time, keep in contact with one another or with shore bases, when out of sight.*[279] But, further still, it meant that they could all be contacted simultaneously. Radio changed the whole nature of warfare, first during the Russo-Japanese War of 1904–5. *Broadcast* communication had come, though public 'broadcasting' was delayed by the First World War. In a sense, radio today is most closely analogous to printing, which also is a broadcast system, but it has the speed of the telegraph, allied to some of the values of the human voice.

What other particular new quality can be said then to have been contributed by radio? I would say without hesitation that of *sociability*. Now I am aware that such a belief will be furiously contradicted by many readers, so please bear with me a moment, whilst I explain.

By sociability I do not mean that, because we have radio and T.V., we shall all come to love one another more. I mean only that radio has the power to affect our sociability, both for better and for worse because it is the first medium we have found for simultaneously speaking to virtually all

* Marconi[203] had carried out his early experiments, in spite of the advice of Heinrich Hertz (one of the greatest scientists of the day) that he was trying the impossible.[120]

the citizens of our already vast national populations. In the Greek city-states a single speaker could do this by oratory, but we cannot in the modern world, without radio. But whether or not radio is actually used wisely is another matter. It merely has this potential.

To hark back to a theme of Chapter 1: when I listen to a radio programme, say a play or a concert, I listen as an individual, alone in my room, or with my family. In no sense can I be said to be 'a mass'; the communication is personal: the performers performing solely for me and my family. At the same time I can be said to *know*, by a conscious effort, that millions of others are hearing the same programme, and I may discuss it next day with friends and colleagues. Radio, therefore, has enhanced both my sense of individuality and my group relations; hearing your local (or national) programme, like reading your own local newspaper, gives you part of your community sense.

Of course, a great number of the programmes broadcast may be regarded by some people as puerile, or rubbish, but which ones these are depends entirely upon the people concerned, for programme standards should be as varied as educational standards.

Perhaps it may be better to illustrate by example the great power that radio has for affecting our sociability, for better or worse. First, every American will remember his experience on the early afternoon of November 22nd 1963, whichever town or city he was in, when President Kennedy was assassinated.[105] The spread of the news and its social consequences that day have been fully recorded.[10, 260, 275] Within half an hour of the shooting *two out of every three people* in the U.S.A. knew. Within less than two hours, over 90 per cent knew.

The consequences of this rapid spread of the news showed sociability *in extremis*, comparable only to that experienced by civilians during or after air bombardment during the Second World War. They also illustrate the possible *stabilizing* effect of rapid news spread, mentioned earlier. Rumour and counter-rumour were prevented, for all knew at least the main events, virtually at the same time. About half the American population heard or saw the news on radio and T.V., whilst the other half learned by telephone calls from acquaintances and relatives, or by word of mouth.[260]

Similarly, during the Second World War the values of broadcasting for maintaining and raising civilian morale were clear to everybody. Radio could be used to combat the demoralizing effects of rumour and counter-rumour (see Chapter 6, Section 7, p. 199). It did much to maintain our sense of community.

An example of the way in which radio can be used in a socially *destructive* sense may be quoted.*[37] On the evening of 30th October 1938, a radio play was presented in the U.S.A. by Orson Welles, based upon the story by H. G. Wells, *The War of the Worlds*, but it was presented in such a manner and with such realism that terror overtook thousands of listeners, who became panicstricken. Many fled, using towels as improvised gasmasks. Many prayed and prepared for death, believing that Martians had landed near Trenton, New Jersey, and were wiping out the population with ray guns. It resulted in panic behaviour described as being 'of national proportions'. Such a type of broadcast will not be repeated; the authorities learned a lesson about that powerful new medium, radio, not easily forgotten.

At the beginning of this programme, the atmosphere was built up by mock

* Reported also in *The Times* (London) 1st November 1938.

weather forecasts and dance music from an imaginary hotel. Emergency interruptions were made, saying that astronomers had noticed something strange about Mars. An 'authoritative' astronomer came to the microphone and, eventually, a 'national emergency' was created, with soldiers, guns, monsters and other terror symbols. The broadcasting authorities *did* announce the whole affair as being a play but, however, thousands of listeners had switched on a while *after* the start of the programme. The *New York Times* wrote afterwards: 'Radio is new, but it has adult responsibilities. It has not mastered itself or the material it uses. It does many things which newspapers learned long ago not to do. . . .'

This frightening event provides a good example to illustrate my earlier argument that mass-communication is a misleading term. For here people listened to the radio play as *individuals* or families in homes and panicked as individuals. It was every man for himself. The ways in which different social organizations react to severe stress situations depends upon the nature of the group.[10] But here there was no group.

However, on the occasion of the assassination of President Kennedy the population of the U.S.A. was indeed grouped, in common bonds of emotion. But there is one great difference between these two disasters; Kennedy and his family had, through T.V., become 'well known in an unusually intimate way'.[260] He was, symbolically, *shared*. The group was already formed and people responded as a group to the news.

So much for radio, for the moment. Now, what specific qualities did television introduce?

Before deciding upon this, we should perhaps remind ourselves of one or two points. First, that the coming of television and its very rapid spread have occurred almost entirely since the end of the Second World War. It has spread in two ways: geographically, inasmuch as there is some television broadcasting done, or being planned, in almost every country of the world,[160,320]* and socially, because television has spread in depth, within the major industrial countries, and has entered nearly every home. It is also important that within these countries television has come upon a public already inured to the cinema, radio and the Press.

During this 'era of television', there has also been an educational revolution; many standards have greatly improved and, at least in industrial countries, universities have greatly expanded in proportion to population, young people travel more and class mobility has increased.

Television came during the post-War period of great social change. During this same period private wealth has increased† so that a great section of our population can now afford to possess, or rent, a T.V. set who, before the War, would not have conceived of having other comparable possessions of the time, such as a refrigerator or small car.

It is easy to explain this rapid and universal adoption of T.V. in the sort of terms so often heard: that people like it because it is a 'drug', or that it obviates the need to think or to *do* anything, or that it is forced upon people by commercial pressures of advertising, etc., etc. These are not real explanations, but only vague and emotional generalizations. The fact is that T.V. *has* come into nearly every home in the wealthier countries: and these homes are as varied as the winds, containing families of all kinds, all economic and educational levels, all interests.

---

* South Africa is the only industrial country which has no television whatever.[320]
† Not in all sections, e.g. the elderly.

At first sight television may seem to be nothing more than a cinema in the home, which may be switched on and off at will, so that we can get our entertainment without taking the bother to go out of the house and walk or drive to the cinema. But in some ways the two do not compare. The cinema is basically an extension of the live theatre, which itself developed from the mystery plays and masques of the 17th century (performed before audiences in church or in special tents outside). Both the theatre and the cinema give presentations before collective audiences. The cinema took over some of the traditions of the theatre, especially developing the cult of 'stars'. It could reach larger audiences, because the same film, with identical actors of star repute, could be shown concurrently in many towns. Children could afford to go to the cinema and the triviality of many of the plots and themes which satisfied them showed the great need for *sheer visual display*. Film themes did not need to be original or particularly deep; it was visual display, exotic, romantic, and *active* above all, that was so needed in the drab grey industrial cities of our advanced countries. It has also been found that audiences in some developing countries, to whom the cinema is a novelty, also perceive only the display and ignore the plot.[258]

Film can do many things which cannot appear on the stage with realism; it can continually change the scenery, show galloping horses, houses on fire, close views of beautiful women, mountain ranges, crashing aeroplanes, huge crowds and mobs . . . cataclysms and glories. The film developed an extravaganza of its own. It brought Aladdin's cave to the poorer man and to his children. It could give them deep, though temporary, emotional involvements, and the popularity of the cinema proved they needed them.

Television has brought visual displays into the home, but the showing of films by television may give no better, or even less, satisfaction than at the cinema. It is a medium which can be used for so many other different purposes and has at least two qualities which the cinema lacks: *immediacy* and *domesticity*. Television can show events whilst they are happening, though you may not deeply sense that fact; you are not really 'there', and it shows these to you privately, with only your family or friends around you, totally unconscious of millions of others outside. Again, going to the cinema or the theatre is an *occasion*; looking at a T.V. programme at home, is not.

In Table 2 an attempt has been made to distinguish some of the characteristic 'qualities' of the various media (or modes) of communication, as they have been discussed here, shown in historic order of their coming.* No suggestion is made that this list is complete, or widely accepted. It shows the opinions of the writer only, purely as a tentative schema.

Before closing this Section, perhaps mention should be made of another source of confusion arising in discussion of the evils or benefits of mass-communication. This is overgeneralization. Not only are the various modes quite different, telephones, radio, newspapers, etc., but any one of these serves many, quite different purposes. Thus the existence of the Press enables other and varied journals to be published also, from scientific papers to comics, whilst the whole printing industry also supports a very wide range of different kinds of book (see Chapter 6, Section 6).

It is confusing then to speak of *the* Press, or *the* television or *the* telephone, just as confusing as to speak about *the* wheel (for push-chairs? automobiles? clocks and watches?). The telephone, for example, is an instrument which

---

* For a list of dates of *Landmarks in the History of Telecommunication*, see Meynart in Vol. **32**, Dec., 1965 issue of Ref. 153.

serves an immense variety of purposes, industrial and domestic. Its value depends entirely upon where that particular telephone is (home, hospital, police station . . .) and, above all, upon who is using it and in what circumstances. It may be regarded as one of the most versatile instruments ever invented.

Table 2. Various modes of communication, in historical order, and some peculiar qualities contributed

Mode	Qualities or values
Speech	Thinking, knowing. Self-consciousness within society.
Writing and scribing	Intellectualization. Deepened sense of 'historic time' and of social change. Personal questionings.
Printing	Comparisons across time intervals. Group questionings.
Postal service	Organization of groups. Personal mobility with security.
Telegraph	Speed of organization. Larger groups in stable operation; aid to industrial activity.
Telephone	Speech; human personality. Conversation. Personal mobility, with security. Resolving and decision-making.
Cinema	Broadcast communication (i.e. in groups). Cult of stars. High emotional involvement. Education potential.
The modern Press	Broadcast communication. Increased political awareness. Advertising; enhanced industrial activity. The slogan.
Radio (sound only)	Broadcast communication over very wide areas; sociability. Immediacy. Domesticity. Education potential at higher levels.
Television	Cult of stars. Education potential. Wide social penetration. Social unity potential. Visual display in homes. News and public affairs *as* entertainment.[a]
Data links, computers	Growth of industrial and other economic groups. Larger social enterprises. Improved planning (national and international).

[a] The Ludenic Aspect. See Ref. 284.

A telephone can be most personal; you may whisper words of love and affection into its ear, whilst the law forbids you to swear at it. On the other hand it can be an arrogant master who can barge into your room or office at any moment, without even knocking on the door. Its bell stops conversation and *demands* attention; it shoves itself to the front of the queue.

7. Speed of communication and social stability

The means of communication possessed by a society may limit both its size and its 'organic' adaptability to change. If communications are non-existent, slow or unreliable, the alternative is a system of regional government, highly trained to strong central loyalties as in the case of, for example, the Roman Empire (military), the old British Empire (public schools) or the U.S.S.R. (the Communist Party).

Every American who knows his history will be aware that the 'Little War of 1812' need not have occurred at all were it not for the fact that the efforts of diplomats were frustrated by an unlucky series of events and slow communication. It is a classic story, which illustrates the great importance of *speed* of communication, and I will tell it here in potted form:

(1) Both England and Bonaparte's France were attacking American shipping, only England did the better job by seizing nearly 1000 ships and impressing the men for her own Navy. President Madison, being frustrated without an effective navy from making war against England, considered taking Canada instead.

(2) England added fuel to the flames by instituting an 'Order in Council' which legalized the setting up of a blockade to restrict American exports.

(3) This of course produced a trade depression in England because, in turn, manufacturers were frustrated from exporting to America. They pressed for repeal of the Order, a sensible thing to do. However, unfortunately what next happened was:

(4) King George III became temporarily deranged in mind, and there was delay in appointing a Regent, who could have acted for him.

(5) Furthermore, the Prime Minister, Spencer Perceval, was assassinated, an event which added further to the administrative chaos.

(6) Not until 23rd June 1812, was the Order in Council repealed, where-upon British traders and merchantmen rushed to re-establish trade relations with America.

(7) The situation might have been saved by this triumph of common sense, but it wasn't, because the news travelled by ship across the Atlantic too slowly. Two days *later*, on 25th June, the American Congress declared war!

In his *Diplomatic History of the American People*, T. A. Bailey writes of these events: 'Had there been a transatlantic cable to convey the glad tidings (the repeal of the Order in Council) the Senate probably would have mustered the necessary four votes to defeat the War Hawks'.[8]

The so-called Hot Line (a teleprinter link) between Moscow and Washington was set up after the Cuban crisis, for precisely this purpose of stabilizing global situations, by providing very rapid information. It consists of 18 teleprinter lines, and includes Press services. It is not specially set up but uses the ordinary commercial transatlantic channels (see map, Figure 3.1).* During the recent Arab-Israeli war . . . '. . . the Washington–Moscow Hot Line has been in action many times'. (B.B.C. News, Friday, 9th June 1967.) The world is a big place and, until the coming of electric communication, news took days or weeks to travel across the Atlantic. When situations of antagonism or hostility arose, ignorance of what the other side might be doing, or had intentions of doing, would be likely to aggravate hostilities: for reasons of sheer self-defence you had to act, 'just in case'.

The mere existence of means of communication of course does not guarantee the resolution of doubts, leading to stabilized situations. That would be putting the cart before the horse. Situations can become unstable by absence of communication, but if means are installed then peace is not automatically ensured, unfortunately! On the contrary, communication can produce very unstable results; in Section 6 an example was quoted, of a radio broadcast simulating an emergency (invasion from Mars) which was received simultaneously in thousands of homes, news which for certain reasons resulted in widespread panic. However, broadcasting is a one-way process, from

* See *Telecomm. Jour.* (I.T.U.) **30**, Sept. 1963, p. 269.

transmitting station to many homes; there are no ready means for thousands of people to enquire back to check the truth. No conversation or resolution of doubt is possible. If it had been possible to provide some adequate way for very great numbers of frightened people to *enquire back* quickly, then no panic might have ensued; that situation could have been stabilized. Unfortunately, with broadcasting this cannot be done, yet.

Other cases arise in which time delay may cause social instability, through the spread of *rumour*[4] which, being passed by word of mouth between persons, can sometimes be slow. If quick confirmation cannot be obtained, or *if beliefs have built up so strongly that people have no wish for confirmation* and desire the rumour to be true, then riots can occur.

In all cases, it is the time delay in making enquiry back which takes control, which must be less than the time taken for consequential actions, to ensure at least the *possibility* of stability.

To take an imaginary example, suppose there are two countries, Redland and Blueland, whose separate histories have led them to be mutually suspicious and ill-disposed towards one another. One day a false rumour is started in Blueland that Redland is going to launch an attack (which in fact it has no intention of doing); what could happen? First, Blueland might reach a critical degree of belief and, if it had no rapid means of checking, it might be forced to launch a 'defensive' attack on Redland; to prevent this, *news must travel far faster than weapons*.

On the other hand, if Blueland possessed really fast communication with Redland (say, through its agents) it could obtain confirmation or denial of the truth of the rumour, before taking action, and the situation might then be stabilized. But lack of very fast communication can lead to disaster for other reasons. For example, if news reached Redland that such rumour was building up in Blueland to a critical pitch, then they, Redland, might feel compelled to make the attack which they never intended: because of *their* belief about the other's belief. So the danger of precipitous actions extends, belief about belief about belief . . . owing to the time delay caused by lack of fast communication.

Numerous examples from real life could be cited. Thus the international airways today form the most widely dispersed industries of all time; at any moment, a number of aircraft may be leaving from various countries all over the world, all, say, with their destination London Airport, at different times of day or night. The stable operation of such services is made possible only by virtue of high-speed telegraphic information reaching this Airport, both from the other Airports and from the aircraft themselves, together with weather reports, etc. The planning of schedules for the aircraft to land can then be executed with the assistance of a computer (see Chapter 3, Section 5). For example, at London Airport, information about an aircraft destined for New York, concerning such things as take-off time, passenger and goods load, and other factors must be transmitted from London to New York within 25 per cent of the flight time, in order that New York can prepare landing schedules. This was one of the chief purposes for which the transatlantic telephone cable was laid between Britain, Iceland, Greenland and Canada (see Figure 3.1). Only by such rapid communication can any airways system operate with stability; otherwise there would be chaos.

It was not mere chance that one of the earliest international telegraph lines laid happened to be set up to connect two Stock Exchanges, London and Paris (see Section 4), which is another sphere in which rumour can be important. In modern times, one of the results following from the laying of the transatlantic telephone cables (starting in 1956) has been extension of international industries operating with branches on both sides of the Atlantic (see Figure 3.1). Many examples could be quoted, of large-scale international organizations which have come to grow in size and global dispersal only because very rapid communication is possible today. Modern communication has simply changed the geometry of the world, its size and shape. Of course, the mere increase of speed of communication, with its consequent reduction of time delays cannot guarantee stability, but only provide the mechanics to render it more possible. What actually *will* happen in future cannot be predicted on technical grounds alone. But without rapid communication, human wishes can be totally frustrated in an expanding world; it is an essential prerequisite, no more.

By 'increased stability' I mean only conditions which encourage trade, travel and other forms of exchange, agreements and treaties which discourage war; that is, it is a prerequisite for the expansion of International Organizations (see Chapter 4, Section 5). However, the *extent* of these faster communication services, their distribution, and who should own them to achieve this desirable objective raises other questions. It will be argued later, in Chapter 4, that social *instability* could alternatively result from a too hasty installation of international communication links, unless other conditions are fulfilled.

If I were pressed to give any formal definition of the expression 'social stability' then I would say this: a socially stable group (or community) is one in which *long-term plannings* may proceed, implying that *frustrations* are felt to be reduced by all concerned.*

It may seem obvious today that the mere existence of fast communication services cannot itself guarantee greater world stability; but we today have had long experience of global communication. It was different for people 50 years ago. Thus when broadcasting first came many people hoped that here at last was a means whereby 'Nation shall speak peace unto Nation' (the inscription carved over the doors of B.B.C. Broadcasting House, London). The history of the past 50 years has taught us otherwise.

If stable world development is a thinkable process, based on constructive interrelations of our several socio-political systems and our highly unbalanced distribution of resources, then fast international communication is an essential prerequisite, no more. It will be argued here that its values lie not in its apparent powers to attack one another's national or cultural images, but first and foremost by its known powers to assist the many International Organizations[82, 86] to carry out their practical tasks of smoothing the flow of trade, of transport, of monetary arrangements, of health and scientific knowledge and many others; that is, for practical organization against frustrations of practical life.

Positive achievements, unfortunately, are less newsworthy than failures and, so often, less dramatic, besides which failures throw up problems for our further attention and for our energy and action; these demand urgent attention, achievements are things of the past, finished, done, achieved and filed away in our minds.

---

* There is a certain rough analogy between 'social systems' and 'physical systems'. For example, concerning physical models of organisms, Ross Ashby has remarked that, in order to survive, systems must have an 'alerting' mechanism that activates attempts at adaptive behaviour. See his *Design for a Brain*, John Wiley, New York, 1952.

3

The Communication Explosion

'So far as human foresight can judge, the Old and the New World will be in telegraphic communication before tomorrow night . . . Indeed, now that the great enterprise is completed, there can be no doubt that in a few years the entire globe will be spanned by the telegraph wires, and the news of the planet will be given every morning in the London papers.'

The Times,
London, 27th July 1866.

1. Post-War expansion of world communication
It could be only too easy, for the subject of this book, to lapse into the broadest generalities and to seek protection in grand expressions like 'World Society', 'World Integration', 'The Desires of Mankind . . . etc.', and yet fail to expose any real practical points of interest. At this point in the book, therefore, I should like again to emphasize that the idea which is central to my theme is the idea which I have called human *involvement*. Human involvements are quite different in idea from 'integration'; perhaps they can even be measured or assessed. Involvement, as the idea is used here, may be regarded either from personal points of view or equally well from national or cultural, or political and other views on the *grand* scale. The link between these two dual aspects is of course an old philosophical question, that of the individual and society, but all that I wish to do here is to regard both personal and public aspects of our expanding human involvements in the light of *communication*.

The explosive growth of our various means of communication, which concerns us in this Chapter, is almost wholly a post-War phenomenon. In its mass-communication form it involves the individual; what distinguishes mass-communication today from earlier modes is its universal application to all classes and conditions of people, its relevance to all, not only to a highly literate aristocracy.

On the public side, today's communication explosion takes the form of a sudden increase in our powers of *organizing*: trade, business, industry, travel, transport, news services, a host of institutional affairs both national and international, particularly those termed the International Organizations (see Chapter 4, Section 5). The facts about the post-War growths of these various public services are probably less well known to most readers; for one thing they may appear to be less personal to many and more 'technical'; for another, such public services tend to become taken for granted, like sun and rain, and are only noticed when they go wrong. It is easy to become emotionally involved in mass-communication and interested in any facts and figures reported about it (right or wrong), whereas the public services arouse interest only when individual people fail to get the service which they feel is their due.

In this Chapter we shall examine in more detail the growths of various public communication services. Only a sketch can be presented here, but it is aimed particularly at bringing out the great differences between the nations.*

For two thousand years and more the only means of distant communication were various postal services, derived from the Roman *cursus publicus*,[243] working at the speed of the horse: and then the 'explosion' hit us, not immediately upon the invention of the telegraph, but nearly a century later. It is the sheer suddenness of the expansion which is of such profound social importance, principally following the Second World War.

Consider for a moment. There are still some people alive today who saw the introduction of the telephone in the 1870s and these same people are seeing pictures sent back from Mars by satellite television. Their children were raised through the period we called 'wireless', which was a movement of amateur scientific interest and amateur construction, for which I know no parallel in history unless it be the early stages of the Industrial Revolution; it was a brief period of a few years, a period of great public excitement when whole populations hopefully saw the world begin to shrink. (The space-cult today is very different, for it is run by authorities and experts, not by amateurs.) From crystal sets in 1920 to a television service in 1937 was only 17 years!

Yet it is only since the Second World War that the communications revolution has become truly 'explosive'. Thus the first transistor appeared in 1948 and the first Sputnik followed only nine years later. During this same brief period computers have emerged of ever increasing size and speed; the public has become aware too of so-called 'automation', either as a technical marvel or as a threat to our social order.

The 18th century concept of robots was revived in those same nine or ten years, in the form called 'cybernetics' (a word first used by André Ampere in 1834 in his *Essai sur le Philosophie des Sciences*[50]), but with the reality of electronics this time, to give them substance.[351] Nevertheless, little practical application has yet been found and cybernetics still remains rather a theoretical, though realistic, study. It is the *idea*, the theory, of cybernetics which is important, for it has changed our concept of what machines are and what they can do. In order to explain their possibilities today it seems natural, if not unavoidable even, to use such words as *artificial intelligence, learning, dummy neurons*, etc. For sheer inventiveness electronics has no equal in history. It is a field of invention whose flowering has excelled all others, unless it be synthetic chemistry, both in its variety and in its suddenness, and it shows no sign of withering.

Nevertheless, this explosive growth has, as yet, appeared wholly within and between the advanced industrial countries. These few technical wonders to which I refer are also their creations and may seem to many people to be nothing more than rich men's toys. They are nothing of the kind, for their influences will be as deep, though in some ways very different, upon the poorer countries. There are already millions of transistor radio sets in Africa and the Middle East;[26,180] South American countries are planning to establish world communication links by satellites (see Section 4); closed-circuit television and films are in use for teaching both children and adults in Delhi and Samoa (where approximately two-thirds of Government Schools are equipped with television receivers, see Singapura, E.T.V., Vol. 1, No. 1, Sept. 1966), Israel, and many other places.

* This Chapter draws upon material presented in my Third Cantor Lecture to the Royal Society of Arts, London, 1966, with kind permission of the Society.[52]

Unesco places great emphasis upon the needs of developing countries for improved communication,* to help 'translate human rights into effective reality' and fully recognizes 'that expansion of the information media, press, radio, film, television (is) closely linked to economic and social development.' Surveys of the needs of the continents of Asia, Latin America and Africa have been undertaken and . . . 'has already had widespread effects'.* Mass-communication can only come to these nations as life-blood by virtue of modern electronics, and the transfusion is already started.[180] The U.N. Conference on Trade and Development, Geneva, May 1964, well recognized this.

Thus, although the major investment in communication equipment has been made in the advanced countries, and although the majority of the world's message traffic at present passes within and between those countries, the effects upon the others are already, or will be, profound. For the whole elaborate and costly technology, costly in research, in development and manufacture, is *potentially* available and the poorer countries may ultimately benefit. Equipment may be purchased or received under economic aid programmes, and people may be trained to operate and maintain it. In other words, the *means* of communication have been created, well suited to the difficult terrains of many poor countries, and their existence and values will not be ignored by these countries when making their development plans. The introduction of communication techniques, radio, film, mobile television, print and others, on even a very modest scale, may breed revolutionary changes, and equally well constitute an 'explosion' in the lives of our poorer brothers, of a nature quite different in significance to our own communication explosion. But the first should not be regarded as only a pale shadow of the other. If you have nothing but a pigeon post (valuable though this can be[285, 320]) a telephone is a revolution.

Nevertheless, much of our Western technology may not be suitable for application in developing countries, without considerable modification to suit local needs. Only the inhabitants themselves can advise on the matter, though they may require help in formulating their particular difficulties and needs.

Examples of growth of communication traffic are shown here to illustrate the expansion so characteristic of post-War times. It may be felt that the figures involved are all very small to make a fuss about on a world scale, and that the only explosion worthy of serious attention is the so-called 'population explosion'.[239] The real significance of these growths, however, is that the numbers of people really involved in the expansions they signify are out of all proportion to the numbers shown on the curves; for example, a single telephone or high-speed telegraph connexion with some distant News Agency may carry news concerning millions, just as one single intercontinental connexion with a developing country may be vital for its security or economy.

We cannot pretend that every figure contributing to these curves is equally important. Some messages are personal, though vital for that person perhaps, whereas some concern industries or Governments. In this Chapter we shall be concerned with the growth curves themselves, leaving discussion of their significance to later Chapters. It must suffice here rather to show some of these data as curves and maps, and those readers who may wish to examine the facts in more detail are referred to the original sources.

* See Ref. 320 and others under *Unesco*.

The communication explosion has a three-fold nature:

(1) *Geographical*, the rapid spread over countries, continents and the globe.

(2) *In its traffic*, the rapid growth of messages carried (or goods and people, in the case of transport).

(3) *Technical complexity*, partly through increased variety, technical equipment has become increasingly complex and costly, requiring an increasingly high level of technical training and specialism to design and to maintain.

The spread and growth of world communication is not casual, but is determined by geography, population, language, economics, cultural relations or history, traditions and other determinants of human involvements. These various factors will be considered more closely in later Chapters.

2. World news. The spread of News Agencies

There may be no better example of the explosion which results when the spark of technology touches the tinder of social readiness, than the sudden spread of world news since the end of the Second World War.[263] Certainly, news from many foreign countries has arrived in past times, but much more slowly, from far fewer places and, in particular, in far smaller amounts. Before reliable intercontinental telegraphs were installed last century news reached us mainly through the overseas agents of the Merchant Banks. Today, every form of communication is used, telegrams, telephones, Press, radio broadcasts and modern high-speed telegraph systems such as the Telex, which uses unattended receiving teleprinters directly between offices and which can work all night if necessary to beat the clock. Already by 1950 the transmission and reception of news through the News Agencies was beginning to be automated.

Not only this, but, since all countries are now broadcasting news to their own people or to foreign ears, a great deal of such material may be overheard in listening stations, set up specially for the purpose.*[44] The news overheard may then be abstracted and sent to the broadcasting authorities for use in their own news bulletins, or to national News Agencies, Government Departments and other contributing authorities.

In brief, it is only in very recent times that news on a massive scale has been received, with very little delay and with great precision of recording. It is the *mechanization* of today's news services which does this, whilst in pre-War days all efforts were directed more to increasing the *volume* of news traffic.

Most News Agencies are established in capital cities around the world and their locations naturally follow the news. 'News', of course, is not synonymous with 'events'; events only become news if people are interested, concerned or in some way involved, however remotely.[264] I am sure there have been millions of appalling happenings in the world in the past, which you and I do not know about, could not and never shall.

News, especially foreign news, is something which costs money; the richer you and your country are, the wider your horizons of interest and influence, and the more reasons you may have for needing that news. The poorer countries are handicapped today by their lack of news services, partly because they may not be able to afford subscriptions to News Agencies; this applies

* The British Broadcasting Corporation maintain a radio monitoring station at Caversham and Reuters have one in Hertfordshire, England. Other nations have their monitoring stations.

particularly to South East Asia and the Middle East; they are handicapped too by their lack of telecommunication facilities and by the fact that they cannot, as yet, readily and *cheaply* connect on to the world intercontinental network, neither to its telephone cables nor its satellites.[320] It may be of interest to glance at Figure 3.1 showing the intercontinental submarine telephone cables and compare it to the map in Figure 3.2 which identifies the poorer countries.[140] The entire 'belt of poverty' shown black on Figure 3.2 contains little more than 5 per cent of the world's telephone instruments. Note particularly the situation of the African continent (see Chapter 4, Section 7). A great part of these poorer regions (marked black) lie within, or close to, the tropical zone where communication in East and West directions by radio is also unreliable, being disturbed by various ionospheric effects caused by the sun. For example, radio communication between Britain and Pakistan is often near-impossible, owing to radio 'fading'; it is also a fact that the neighbouring tropical countries of East and West Africa may have to communicate with one another via London! The coming of satellites has changed all this,[42] to the benefit of the poorer, tropical, countries (see Chapter 3, Section 4).

News is gathered by correspondents and bureaux in most areas of the world and sent to their nearest News Agencies, which act as central collecting points and from which abstracted versions are transmitted not only to newspaper offices all over the world, but also to broadcasting authorities and to various authorities, such as Lloyds, Embassies and of course other News Agencies under bilateral agreements. These News Agency messages differ in certain ways from ordinary private telegrams or even from the telegraph messages sent between business offices, airports and other major users of intercontinental communication links. Thus news messages can be very lengthy and they must reach deadlines of time; further, they do not need replies. News is gathered in the Agencies and is usually delivered within a few hours, whether by day or night, either to a single destination office or to several simultaneously (by radio).

For these reasons, and others, special communication services are set up for the Press, as they are for airways also, by international agreements, although they use the public networks as well.* Special conditions of use are imposed and special tariffs apply. All modern techniques are now being introduced to help speed up the message flow (e.g. international dialling) and, as the volume of message traffic steadily increases so the existing channels of communication are strained to their limits and new channels are introduced. These new channels naturally employ more modern techniques and so are faster and more reliable. Today high-speed telegraphy such as offered by the Telex service has so many advantages over early forms of telegraph that its traffic is expanding explosively (see Figure 3.3) for it combines the speed and dialling facilities of the telephone with the advantages of printed message *records*.

Language differences present difficulties and add to the cost and complication of international news services. The Arabic countries are fortunate, within their own area, and so is the English speaking community, but in many areas of the world, news must be sent in several languages. However, the English language is being increasingly used as a *lingua franca* for news transmission, for example, in India, Pakistan and Africa, where there is

---

* See note in Vol. **31**, Jan. 1966 issue of Ref. 153, on the *International Press Telecommunication Committee*.

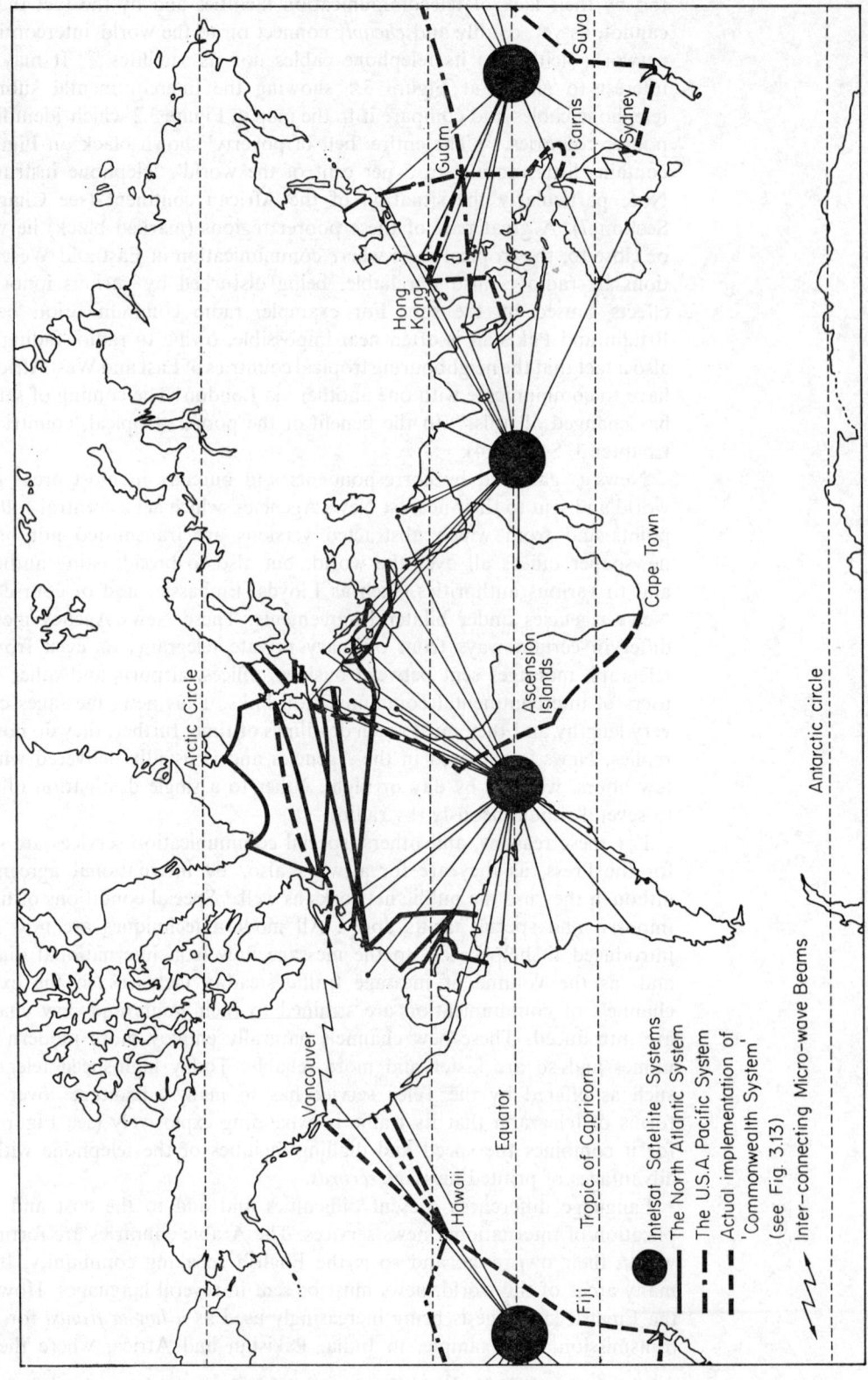

Figure 3.1. The world's principal intercontinental trunk routes (cable and satellite) for telecommunication (telephony, Telex, etc.) as at April, 1970.

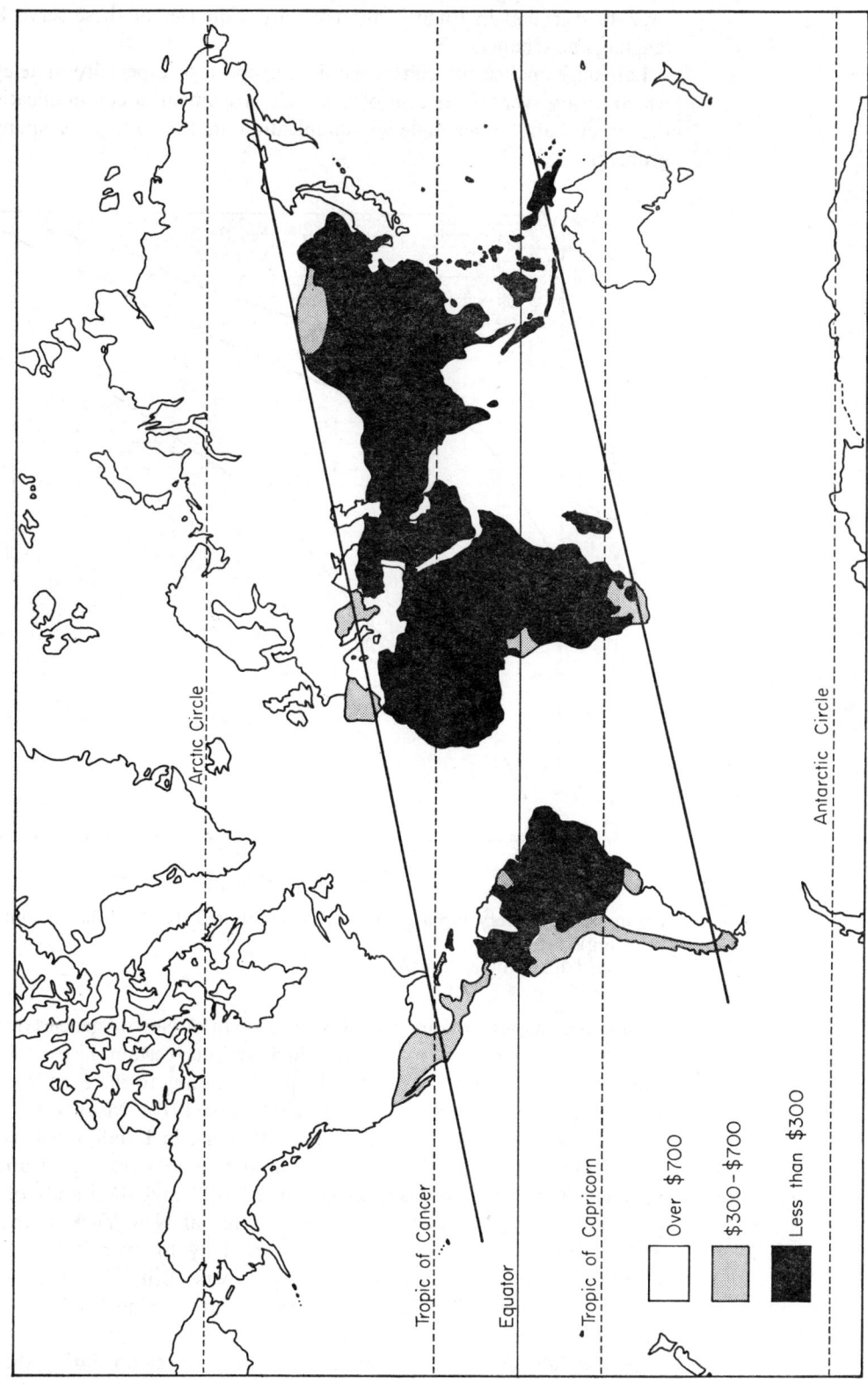

Figure 3.2. The belt of poverty. Gross national product, per capita, 1967. See *World Bank Atlas*, 1969.

such a wide range of native languages. For instance, Pakistan sends news to over 40 Agencies in English, though only a quarter of these serve English language newspapers.[320]

Language makes difficulties within Europe too, especially in telephony, which forms over 90 per cent of Europe's investment in communication; on the other hand, inter-State communication in the U.S.A. is spared this problem.

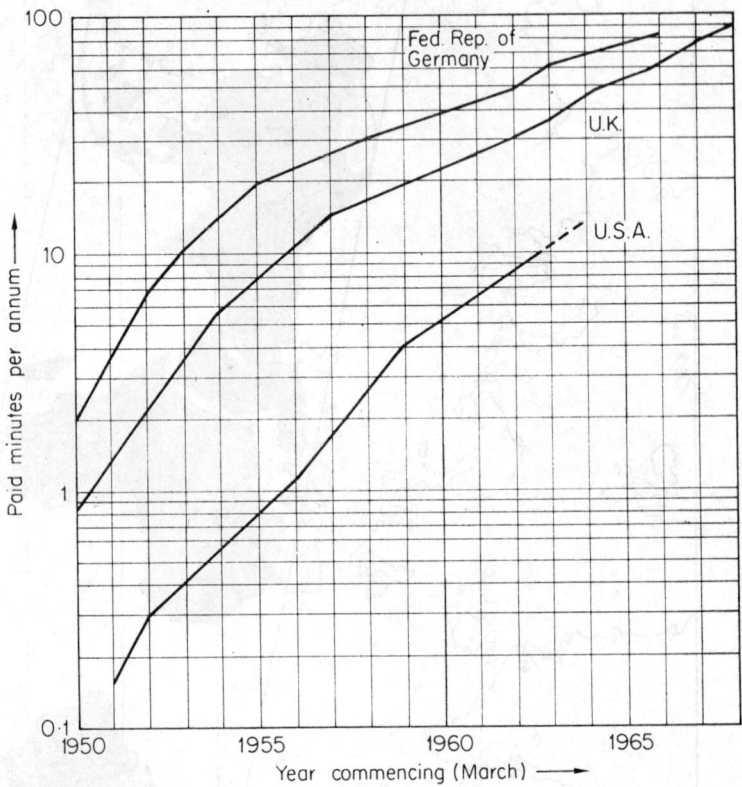

Figure 3.3. The very rapid growth of international Telex traffic (incoming plus outgoing).
(Source: I.T.U. Publications.)

The four maps in Figure 3.4 show the growth of News Agencies during the past century, arranged in a way which reflects certain historical trends. The first map (Figure 3.4a) covers the period leading to the First World War (no agencies were established between 1905 and 1917). Most of these are in Europe, including some in the Balkans. Reuters, in London, was set up in 1851,* the year of the Great Exhibition, and its massive organization now includes 60 or more bureaux around the world and thousands of correspondents.[285, 320] The Associated Press, centred at New York, is the largest and is slightly older. Reuters sends news daily to over 100 foreign and Commonwealth country and territory subscribers; Britain's massive overseas news connexions today are to be expected, considering her long maritime history and Commonwealth connexions.

Figure 3.4b shows the Agencies which became set up during the period

---

* Prior to this date, Paul Reuter had been operating on the Continent of Europe.

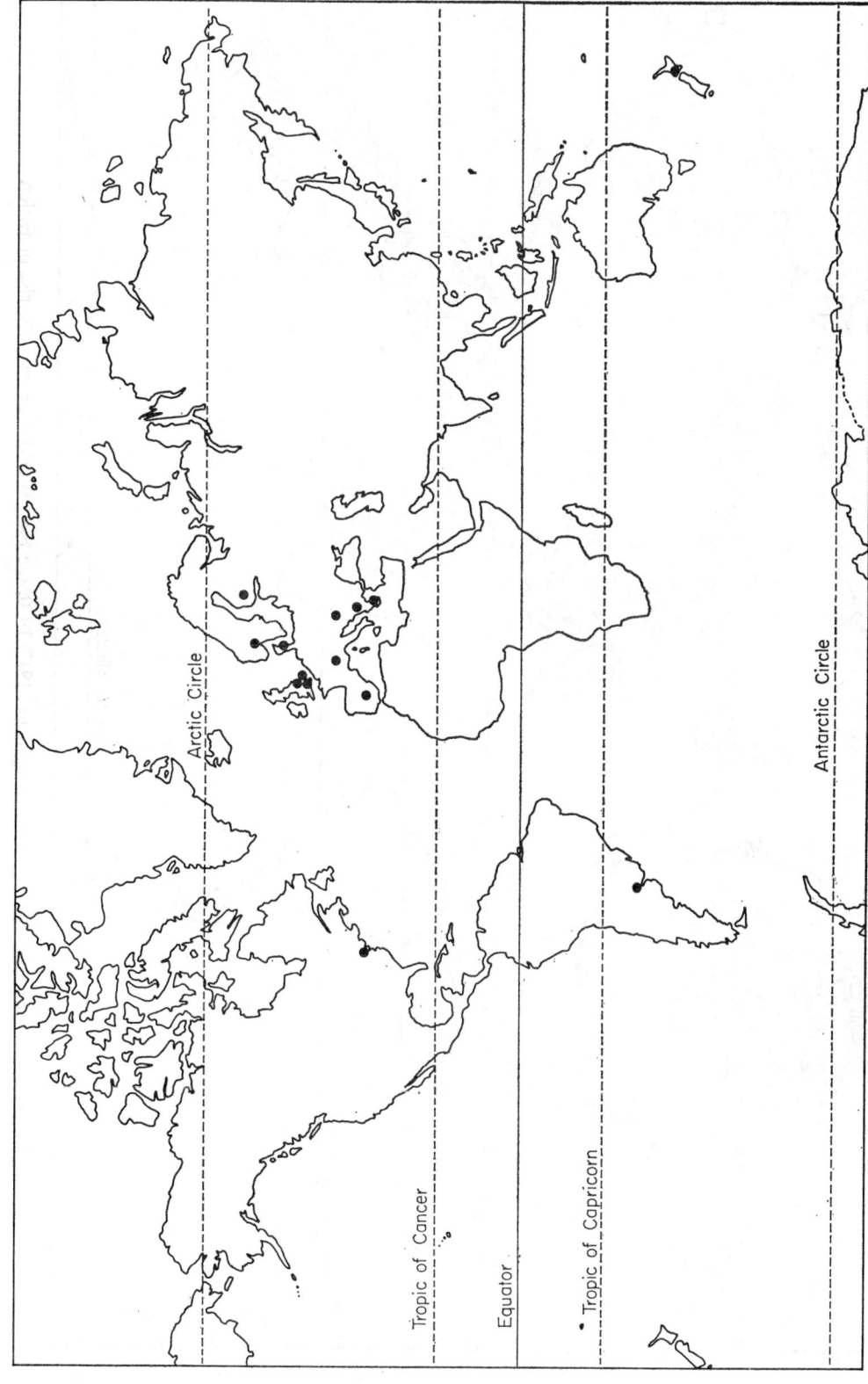

Figure 3.4a. The global spread of News Agencies. News Agencies established before 1905. Approximate locations only: exact locations for Figures 3.4a–d are listed under cities in Reference 320.

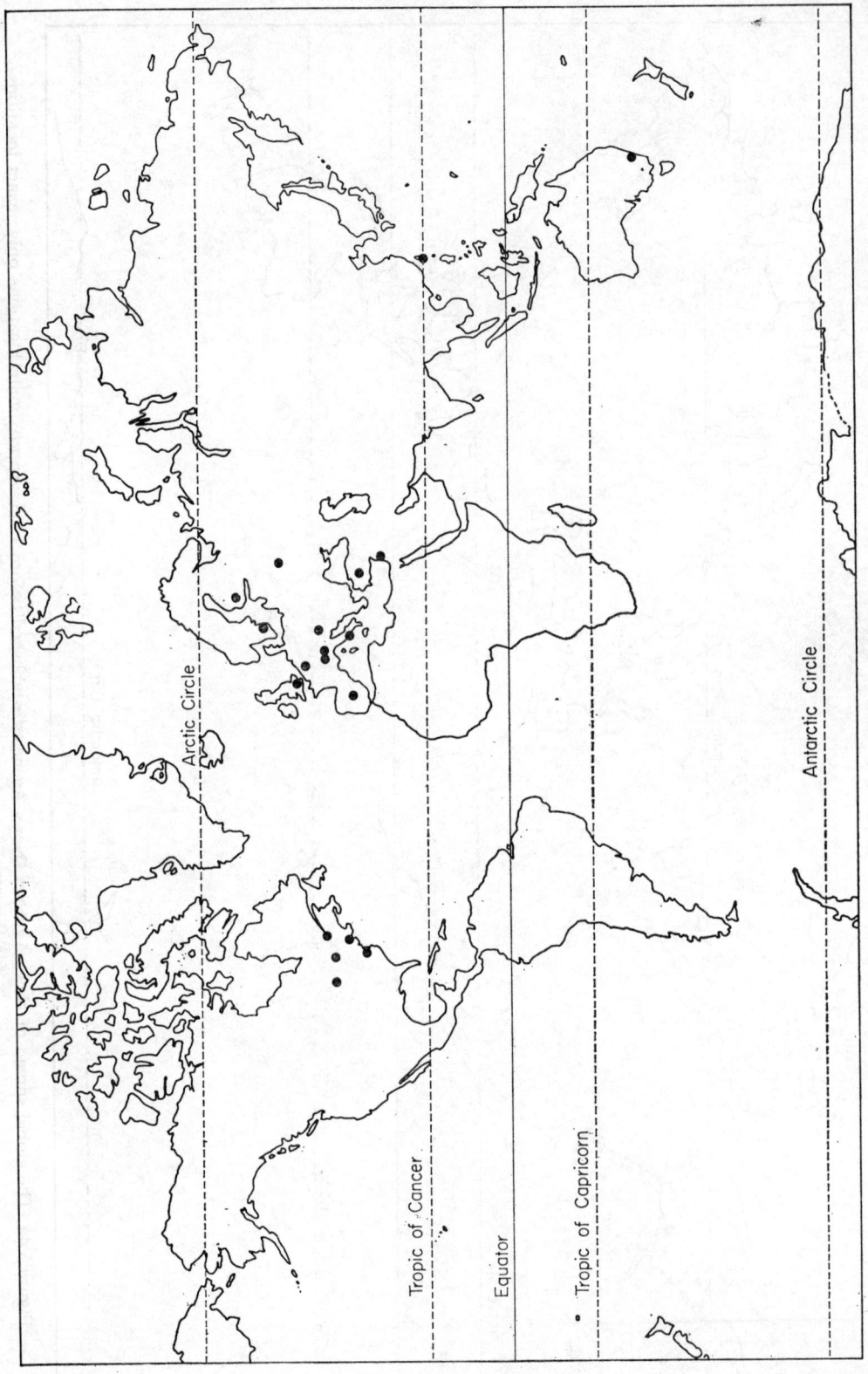

Figure 3.4b. The global spread of News Agencies. 1917–1930, the First World War until the rise of Hitler.

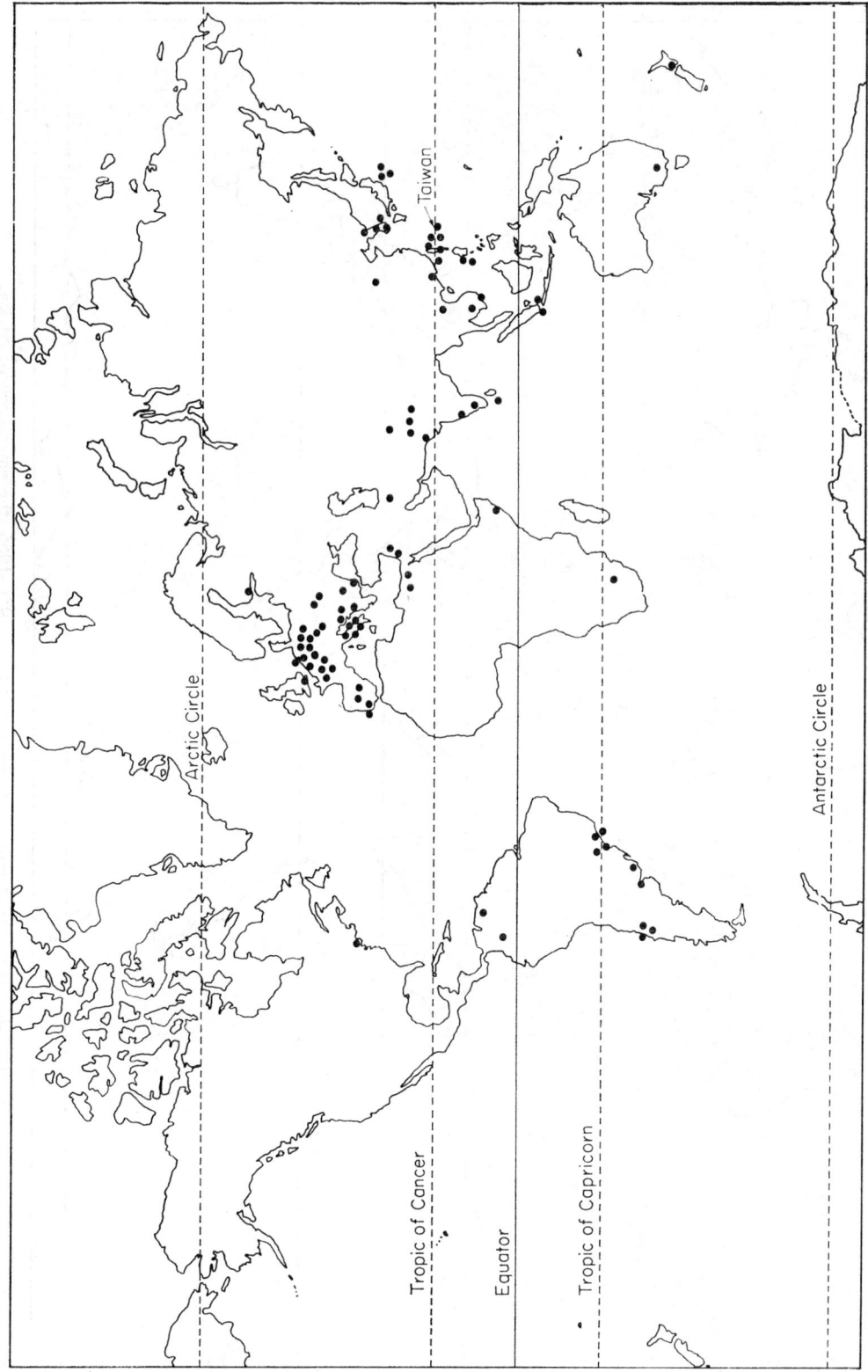

Figure 3.4c. The global spread of News Agencies. 1931–1955, the engulfment of Europe and the aftermath.

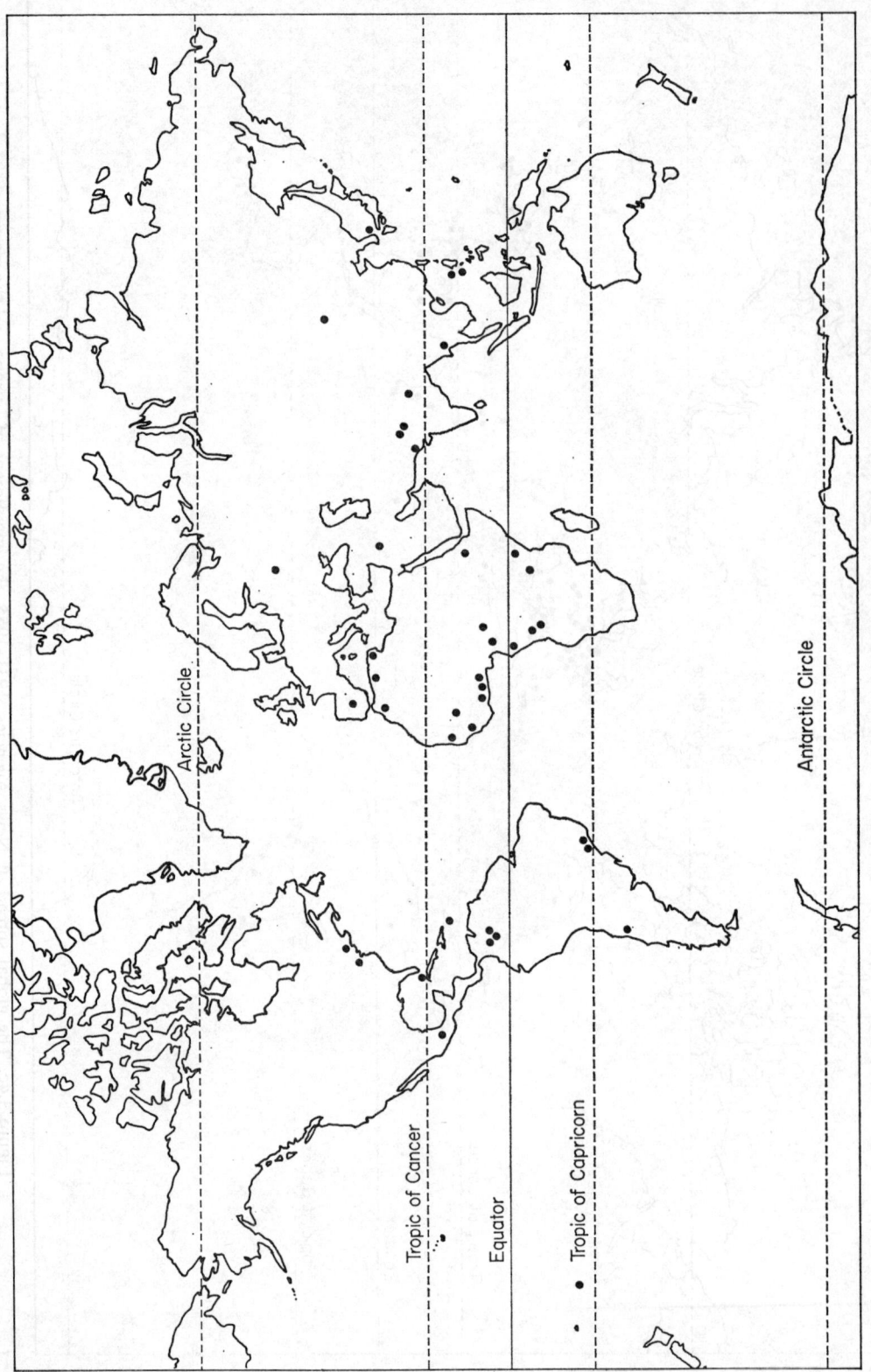

Figure 3.4d. The global spread of News Agencies. 1956–1965, the emergence of Africa.

between the First World War and before the rise of Hitler (1917–1930); the growth of North American Agencies is to be noted, all set up during or shortly after that War; Moscow established its Agency. 'World News' now involved both sides of the Atlantic, but the whole of Asia, Africa, South and Central America, the whole of the 'poor countries', yet contained but one, in Taiwan.

It was during the rise of Hitler and the steady engulfment of Europe that news of other countries really forced itself upon the attentions of millions. The global nature of the Second World War ended parochialism and the Agencies spread like a pox across the Middle East, India and South East Asia. The international concern of our newspapers and news bulletins developed further during the aftermath of the War, with all its various settlements, new national groupings and alignments, and above all with the Korean War and the Chinese Revolution, (the New China Agency (Hsin–Hua) is in Pekin)[211]. The map (Figure 3.4c), shows this expansion of world news between 1931 and 1951, and the continent of Africa is seen as almost blank.

Africa has well been called the Dark Continent. It was not until 1961 that there were any serious numbers of Agencies set up; Africa emerged late as a world centre of news, as State after State of that complex continent sought and achieved independence. Figure 3.4d shows this very sudden change; most of these Agencies appeared during the year 1961.

These four simple maps of Figure 3.4 give but one illustration of 'world expansion', so characteristic of this century, though in a way which represents not only the great change of international involvements but also our personal interests; for all the Agencies shown report *news* and, as stressed before, news requires *people* to be interested, to want to know it and, particularly, not to mind paying for it. The News services have not spread casually around the globe, but have grown as countries have been able to afford them and so acquired the power both to enquire what is happening elsewhere and to inform others about themselves.

These global news services have developed alongside the development of telecommunication techniques and services of all kinds, telegraphs, telephones, radio, Telex and others. It is then relevant to extend our picture of world expansion by looking now at some examples of these technical systems and of their phenomenal growth.

3. 'Inland' (or national) communication. Comparison of countries

Let us now compare the different countries of the world with regard both to their *possession* of telephones, teleprinters, etc., and to the *use* which their people make of them. We shall find that such comparison is not so simple as may seem at first and, to make any sense, must be done with regard to certain distinctions of usage. In particular, we must distinguish between *domestic* uses (homes) and *economic* uses (offices, bureaux, Government, News Agencies, etc.). These are usually referred to as *residence* and *business* uses, in published statistics, terms which are felt to be too restricted for this book. Most telephone authorities distinguish these spheres of use by different tariffs. We must also distinguish between *inland* or *national* and *overseas* or *international* uses. We shall examine the national sphere of usage in this Section and the international sphere in the next.

These two classes of usage and two forms of traffic have developed to different patterns and distinctions must be drawn if any meaning is to be extracted from the statistics relating to different countries.

Such statistics are published regularly by different authorities[5,85,98,149] but, as with many other national statistics, they should be treated with caution for several reasons, including these:

(1) Some terms used may be ambiguous or used in different ways by different countries (e.g. whether *traffic* includes *through traffic*, i.e. traffic which arrives in *transit* to another country, or not.

(2) Although every country knows the figures for its own outgoing traffic, its incoming traffic from other countries may perhaps be available only by enquiry from all those countries.[45]

(3) Some countries may not have gathered accurate statistics nor even been able to.

(4) There are always the dangers of prestige values overriding clarity of expression or accuracy when comparative figures for different countries are published.

(5) Gross statistical figures, representing averages for whole countries, may conceal great variations within each country. It is just such variations which can be important and some will be illustrated in this Section.

One danger from the use of the published statistics of communication lies in the temptation to compare countries medium by medium; that is to say, to compare the high number of telephones in one country with the low number in another and to draw conclusions, or to compare their number or circulation of newspapers, or of radio and T.V. licences, etc., separately. There are many reasons why a country may put different weightings upon the values of each, among which are factors of geography, population distribution, levels of literacy, age distribution, history and other determinants of human involvements. *It is totally misleading to expect all the countries of the world to use precisely the same media of communication and to the same extent*, even those countries of comparable economic levels.

Figures 3.5 a and b show how the number of telephones in the world has been growing since the Second World War.[5,149] These are instruments,* on people's desks or in their homes. In all the various countries, rich and poor, they are used with very varying frequencies and for very different purposes. These curves alone are of little significance, except perhaps to tell us that most of the people who have access to these 'phones can speak to most of the others if they have the need to, have the money and can speak the language. The mere presence of this rapidly growing number of instruments represents a *potential*, an investment. What they are used for, and how often, depends very much upon where they are, in which country and whether in the metropolis or not, or whether they are in homes, in offices, airports, Government bureaux or bookmakers' homes. Unfortunately such detailed figures are not available, except by sample questionnaires made by various authorities. The only details to go on are the figures published by each separate country, together with certain accounting data, though even these have some interest, but only to the extent that their accuracy can be trusted.

About one half of the world's telephones are within the U.S.A., but herein lies the first deception! To explain, let us compare the figures for the U.S.A. and for the United Kingdom in 1966. In total, there were 94 million

* In Britain these are known technically as telephone *stations*, as distinct from subscriber *lines* connecting to exchanges: i.e. *stations* includes all extensions.

telephones in the U.S.A.,[334] with its population of 194·6 millions[334] and 10·7 million in Britain[98] with a 54·7 million population.[123] That is, the ratio was:

$$\frac{\text{Telephones per 100 population in U.S.A.}}{\text{Telephones per 100 population in U.K.}} = 2\cdot47$$

a fact which has often caused comment, even in Parliamentary circles. However, it is more meaningful to separate each country's 'phones into two classes: (a) *Domestic*, being those in private homes, used by the family, and

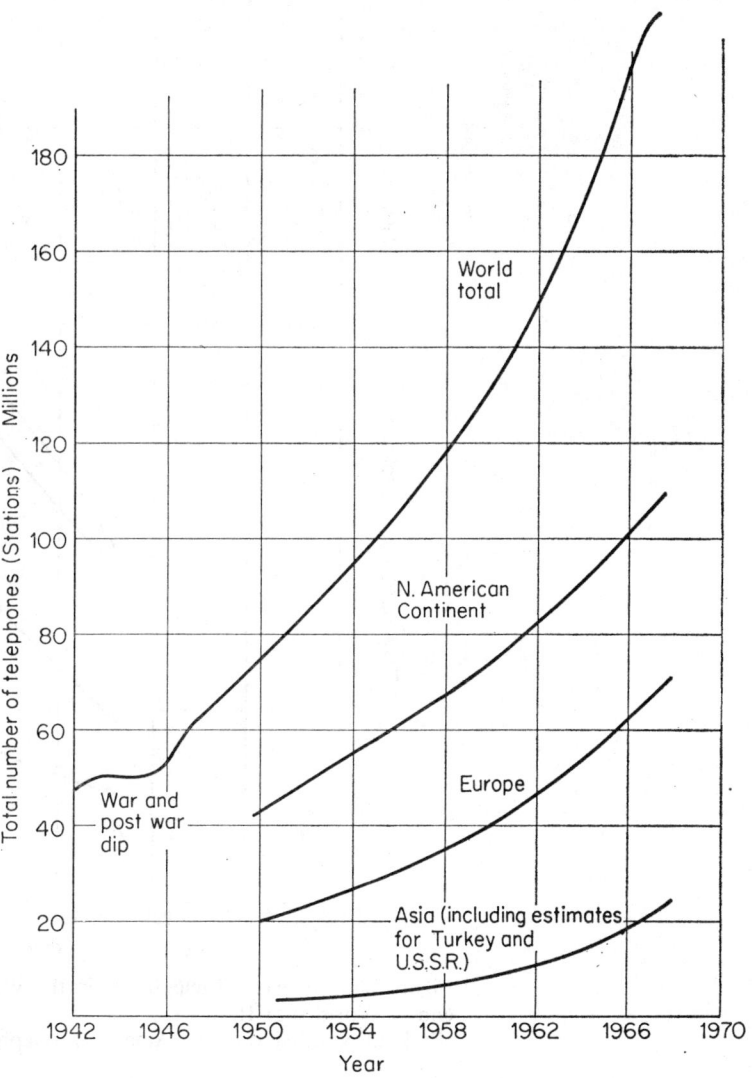

Figure 3.5a. Increase of telephones in the world and in various continents since the end of World War II.
(By kind permission of the American Telephone and Telegraph Co.)

paid for by individuals and (b) *Economic*, being those in offices, businesses, bureaux, etc., and paid for by these institutions, though this sharp division introduces small errors, because there are certain one-man businesses, such as authors and bookmakers, who operate from their homes. Separating these two spheres discloses a surprising fact, that most telephones in the

U.S.A. are in private homes (2½ times as many as there are in the economic sphere) whilst most of those in the U.K. are in the economic sphere. Table 3 shows the figures for 1966, given to the first decimal place.

The figures in the right hand column (b) Economic Sphere, in Table 3 have been calculated by dividing the 'economic sphere telephones' by the 'working population', on the assumption that this ratio represents their

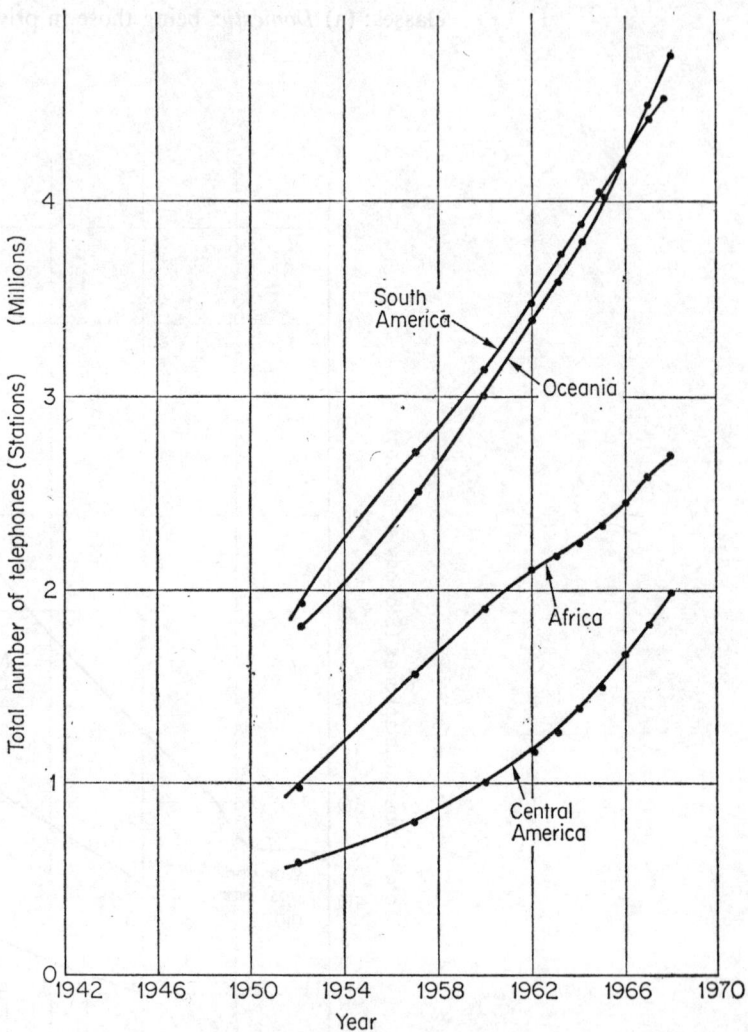

Figure 3.5b. Increase of telephones in the world and in various continents since the end of World War II.
(By kind permission of the American Telephone and Telegraph Co.)

contributions to the countries' economies. Alternatively the total population figures could have been used; this would reduce the relative difference between the U.K. and the U.S.A. in column (b),* to 10·6 and 12·6 respectively (see Table 4, also). Note that column (a) in Table 3 has been based on *total* populations and column (b) on the *working* population. Such calculations are clearly over-simple but, whatever reasonable allowance is made for this,

* Because total labour force in U.K.[325] was 25·6 million and in U.S.A.[335] was 77·6 million; the total populations were 54·7 and 194·6 million respectively.

it is clear that the great difference between telephone usage in our two countries is in the domestic sphere.

Table 3

	Working population (millions)	Telephones (Economic sphere) (millions)	Telephones (Domestic sphere) (millions)	Telephones per 100 people		Economic telephones per 100 *total* population
				(a) Domestic sphere	(b) Economic sphere	
United Kingdom	25·6[325]	5·9	4·8	8·9	23·0	10·6
U.S.A.	77·6[335]	26·0	67·6	35·0	33·5	12·6

Classification of telephone *calls* between the economic and domestic spheres is less easy. How should we classify telephone calls made say by a housewife (domestic sphere) to a shop, or her doctor, or Council Offices (economic sphere)? Or calls made *to* her by such institutions? We might regard a subdivision of the two spheres in this way:

Serve personal (domestic) use $\left\{ \begin{array}{l} \text{Person-to-person} \\ \text{Person-to-institution} \\ \text{Institution-to-person} \\ \text{Institution-to-institution} \end{array} \right\}$ Serve institutional (economic) use.

Such classification is not restricted to telephones, but applies generally to other forms of communication, the post, rail and air travel, telegrams, etc. But it does not apply to the various *broadcast* services, radio, T.V. and newspapers. However, calculations of the kind we have made in Table 3 now become complicated, because several different statistics are relevant. For example, how should we assess the number of telephones per 100 people in the case of 'person-to-institution' communication? Should we take the figure for *all* telephones, domestic and economic together, or that for domestic telephones only? The latter might be more valid, provided we assume that all institutions, or nearly all, possess a telephone.

There are several ways of computing the statistics for these four categories of communication. When it comes to placing *values* upon each of them we are in even deeper water, and we shall not enter it here. Such values rest partly upon one's political views, or feelings about individual and social values. Not only do telephones arouse strong feelings and arguments at times, but so do roads, railways, T.V. and all forms of communication. We must expect to find, as we do, great variations between the statistics for different countries, especially those relating to personal uses of communication media. The variation is least, not surprisingly, in the fourth category, institution-to-institution—the wholly 'economic' sphere.

The important segregation is that between (a) domestic and (b) institutional or economic spheres of communication. They serve quite distinct social purposes and the efficiencies of services are judged by different criteria. Personal satisfaction in the home is very important; but the efficiency of industries and other social institutions is quite different. Unfortunately, a telephone network has to provide both private and public services. So do other modes of communication, for example roads, for both *sport* and *transport*.

In the private, or domestic, sphere the great differences between people of different countries show up in the statistics of *usage*.[20] Thus even those people in Britain who possess a home telephone and are prepared to pay its quarterly rental, very seldom use it! The average calling rate in Britain is little over 1 call per day;* in Canada they make an average of 6·3 calls per day (more than in the U.S.A.).[5] On the other hand, we in Britain buy more newspapers, per head, than do any other people in the world.[320] In Europe, especially Eastern Europe, newspaper circulation steadily increases.[320]

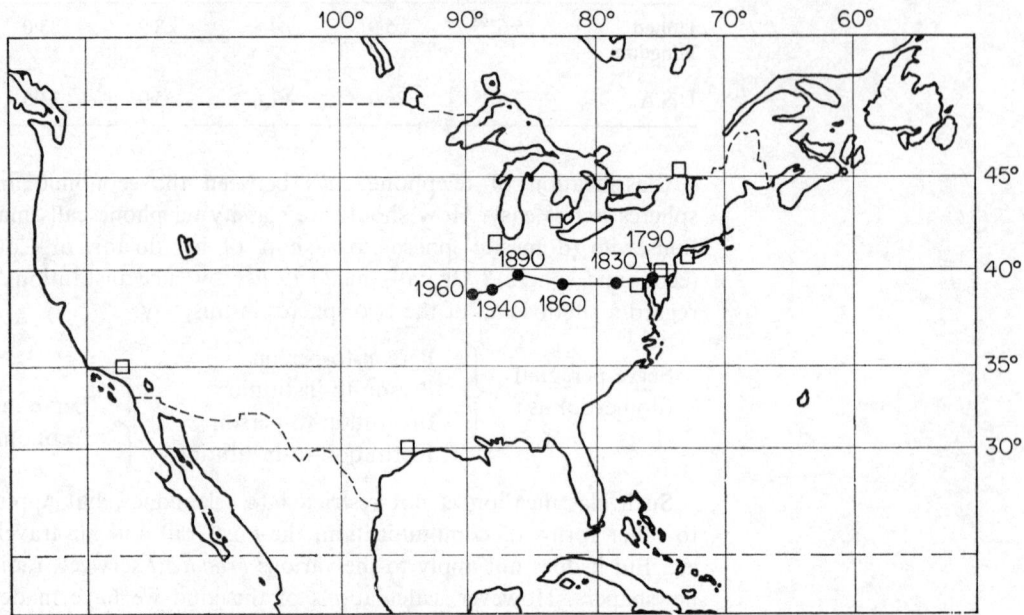

Figure 3.6. Westward migration in the U.S.A. since 1790. The spots show 'centres of gravity' of population, as though every person had equal weight.[333]

There are many reasons why telephones are used to very different extents in different countries; personal wealth is only one. First, geography and population distribution. The population of the U.S.A. is more dispersed among small towns and villages than Britain's;[21, 334, 344] Britain is more urban and has more large cities, close together,† with 10 per cent of its land area built up and 80 per cent of people living in towns and cities,[205] (nearly a fifth of the British people live in the London counties alone) and the post is therefore quick. Second, the population of the U.S.A. has itself grown explosively during the same period of time that the telephone network grew and spread,[333] and when the railway was thrown across the continent and millions migrated Westwards. There were about 40 million people in the U.S.A. in 1870, 76 million in 1900, 123 million in 1930 and 195 million in 1966.[334] (See Figure 2.4.) The U.S.A. has also expanded its boundaries since World War II.

The map (Figure 3.6) shows how much the centre of population of the U.S.A. has moved Westward over the years, almost exactly Westward, in fact, along the 39° parallel.‡[234, 333]

---

* In 1966, private subscribers made 2030 million calls, local and trunk, whilst there were 4·84 million domestic 'phones. That is, 1·13 calls per telephone per day, average.

† See General Tables, under Ref. 124.

‡ For a study of the social effects upon the emigrants of the 'moving frontier', especially relating to education, books and 'progressiveness', see Wright, L. B.[359]

America is a very youthful country today, due to her very high birthrate in the early 1950s, when it exceeded even that of India.[21,172,234] I am conjecturing that their use of telephones in *homes* may partly depend upon their number of teenagers; if there is anything in this belief, it may be noted that only 38 per cent of Britain's population is under 25 years of age,[124] whilst over 46 per cent of America's is so young,[172,334] and likely to be

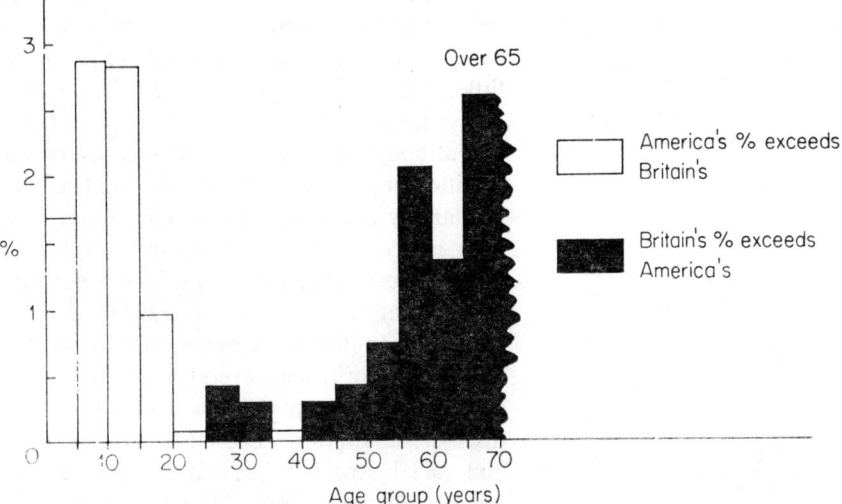

Figure 3.7. Britain's population is older than America's. The percentage quoted here is the difference between the percentage of American and British populations within each successive age group of five years.

50 per cent by 1970. It is worth comparing the age distributions of our two countries (see Figure 3.7) for their difference may account partly for other distinctions in social habits. Age alone cannot account for the extremely different habits of *private* telephone usage, nor does wealth. These other

Table 4. *Economic and domestic usages of telephones in a variety of countries*

Country	Telephones in economic sphere per 100 population (in 1966)		Telephones in domestic sphere per 100 population (in 1966)	Conversations[a] made on each telephone (average, per annum, for year 1965)	Conversations per person per annum in year 1965
Argentina	2·9		3·8	2840	187·4
Brazil	—	1·6[b]	—	5400	85·4
Canada	10·8		26·8	1780	635·6
Czechoslovakia	8·1		2·4	750	74·5
Germany, East	—	9·7[b]	—	686	63·9
Germany, West	—	14·8[b]	—	775	107·2
Italy	5·1		6·5	1350	145·5
Japan	9·8		4·3	2520	313·9
Spain	5·9		2·9	—[c]	—[c]
Sweden	13·2		32·8	1240	541·4
Switzerland	20·2		17·6	795	285·1
United Kingdom	10·6[d]		8·9	700	127·1
United States	12·6[d]		35·0	1360	620

[a]Total; local and long-distance added.
[b]Combined; no separate figures available.
[c]No data on conversations available.
[d]Figures shown on Table 3 are per 100 *working* population.

factors, geographical, traditional and demographic all bear upon such national customs.

Table 4 lists a few countries, for which statistics happen to be readily available,[5] but the countries differ widely in politics, geography and population, history and technical development. In most cases the figures are shown separately for the economic sphere (column 2) and for the domestic sphere (column 3); in these cases what is most striking is to *compare* these two columns. Thus we find that, whereas the density of telephones in the domestic spheres (private homes) varies very widely indeed between countries, their densities within the economic sphere (business, industry, etc.) vary relatively little. The evidence given by this Table is intended here not for detailed analysis, but merely to illustrate a point made several times before, namely, that although telephone densities vary very much between industrial countries of different geography, population and economic conditions, these variations are largely accounted for by telephones in private homes. Some countries have many 'phones in their homes, others very few, and there are several valid reasons why. But in business, industry and other institutions within the economic spheres, these 'major' countries vary far less among themselves. Further examination of these figures is made in Chapter 5.

Table 4 illustrates several other points concerning national differences, some contrary to popular belief, but it may be more appropriate to defer discussion until the next Chapter, where we shall be concerned with economic and social aspects of communication. However, it is appropriate here to notice that the countries listed in Table 4 are among those considered as major. There are a host of other developing countries which certainly *are* economically handicapped by lack, not only of telephones, but of other modern modes of communication too.

The telephone is only one mode of communication, though one of special value to industrial societies. Its use depends upon many things, including the existence and efficiency of other modes. Though the poorer countries may be handicapped industrially by lack of internal telephones, they may nevertheless have organized themselves around the pigeon post, or the talking drum or other non-electronic modes. Such ancient methods are not to be despised as primitive. On the contrary there are situations in which the pigeon post may provide the only reliable means of communication, even in advanced countries.[78, 285, 320] It was regularly used in Europe and elsewhere until radio came,[78] and it has been used in wartime since. The talking drum[49] may be a fast and useful means of telecommunication when a traditional set of messages are being communicated. It does not merely send out messages in a code. It is used like a musical instrument to simulate the rhythm, the rise and fall of pitch and other characteristics, simulating the human voice. It literally 'talks'. But we Britons must admit it as a sad criticism of our colonial rule that, when the independence of Botswana was proclaimed in 1966, the news was flashed from the capital Gaberones to Mafeking by pigeon post . . . By whom? By the special correspondent of London's *Financial Times*. He had no alternative.*

The authorities within any one country, or area, who are responsible for communication services must naturally predict, as accurately as possible, the likely future demand for those services, in order that they may be installed. How can this be done?

---

* See *The Guardian* editorial, 4th October 1966.

Such installations are very expensive (e.g. an intercity trunk telephone cable) and will be in service for many years, during which time many things may happen which can change the expected demand. It would help the authorities and the economy of a country if long-term forecasting were possible, say 20 years ahead, but unfortunately little guidance is afforded by

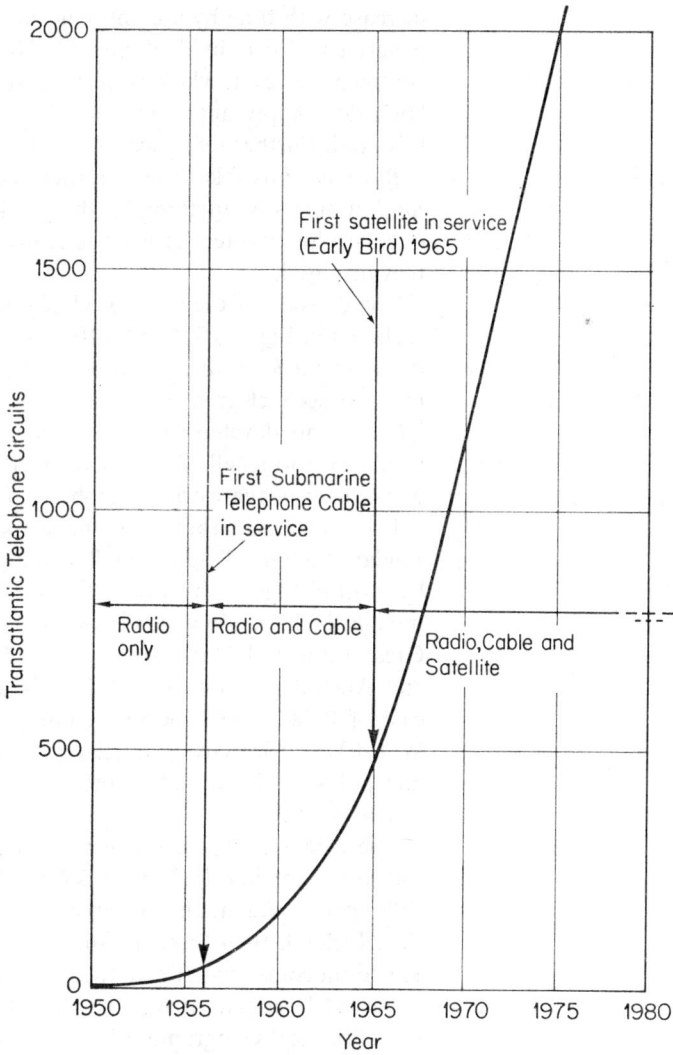

Figure 3.8. Official prediction of telephone circuits on the North Atlantic (the 'Rome Plan').

corresponding predicted growths in any other sphere: consumer goods, employment figures, wages, building society loans, etc.[214] Predictions for a whole country or very large area may reasonably be expected to be more accurate, more, perhaps, than for a single city (technically speaking: 'exchange areas'). As one expert has said: 'there is no simple method which will give (estimates of) long-term growth for individual (telephone) exchanges'.[214]

One difficulty may be that a telephone trunk line is usually used for both *domestic* and *economic* purposes, homes and offices as well, and the factors which control the growth of each may possibly be totally different.

A comment made earlier in this Chapter was to the effect that a telephone trunk line or for that matter any communication service, national or international, is an investment, a potential. Telephones and teleprinters, etc., are not consumer goods but capital ones, 'utilities'. This is most obvious in the case of those in offices and elsewhere in the economic sphere. Consequently it might be expected that their numbers within any area would increase with time by a compound interest law. Alas! Even this is not completely true for individual cities.[214] However, for the whole world, or whole continents or even whole countries, the compound interest law ('logarithmic law') does apply approximately; Figure 3.5 and Figure 3.8 show curves of this kind. Further reference to such laws of growth will be made in Section 7.

But what possible value can there be in knowing such data as these? The *total* numbers of anything 'in the whole world' may be of fireside facts-you-ought-to-know interest; what is really important is *where* they are and how they are used.

The division of the world's telephones among various industrial countries is shown in Figures 3.9 and 3.10 in a way which illustrates their growth over the years; a *logarithmic* scale has been used in order that the early growth may be seen clearly. These are the countries which possess most of the 'phones; no developing country can be shown here because their figures would be too small. Between them, the countries shown here possess about 95 per cent of the world's telephones today.[5]

It is worth remarking that the shapes of most of these curves are grossly similar, though all have small variations here and there, probably caused by tariff changes (which have temporary effects of two or three years only), though the large dip which is seen to occur just after 1930 is the result of the Great Industrial Depression which affected the U.S.A., Canada, Germany and Australia particularly.[20] The flattening between 1939 and 1955 in the case of Poland is of course a consequence of her destruction in the Second World War. (See Group B.) Experts have noted that crises, economic, social and political, do not affect the telephone statistics of different countries in similar ways.[20]

The extent to which various countries *use* their telephones seems also to follow no simple rule. Thus it is Canada whose people make more telephone calls, per capita, than any other country, closely followed by the U.S.A., then Iceland, then Sweden, an order which may surprise you. The United Kingdom comes right down the list; for every call a Briton makes, a Canadian makes at least six.[5] It may be that Britain suffers from having too good a postal service! Geographically she is a small country, with a highly urbanized and concentrated population (see Ref. 124, General Tables); the post is quick and very reliable by international standards. For private use the post is very cheap,* but few industries seem to have examined in detail the relative costs of letters (including secretaries, typists and filing, etc.) and those of the cheap telephone (for the sort of messages which require no written record). Some estimates have, however, been published. In one case[30] (in 1957) the cost of a single sheet quarto letter (typing, paper, carbon, envelope, etc.) taken in shorthand came to 15 pence; however, if the dictator's salary be taken at the modest figure of £3300 and postage, filing, handling, messenger service, etc., be included, the cost of a letter becomes nearer to 55 to 60 p., or say $1·50. Business letters are more expensive than they may seem.

---

* Compared to real value of money.

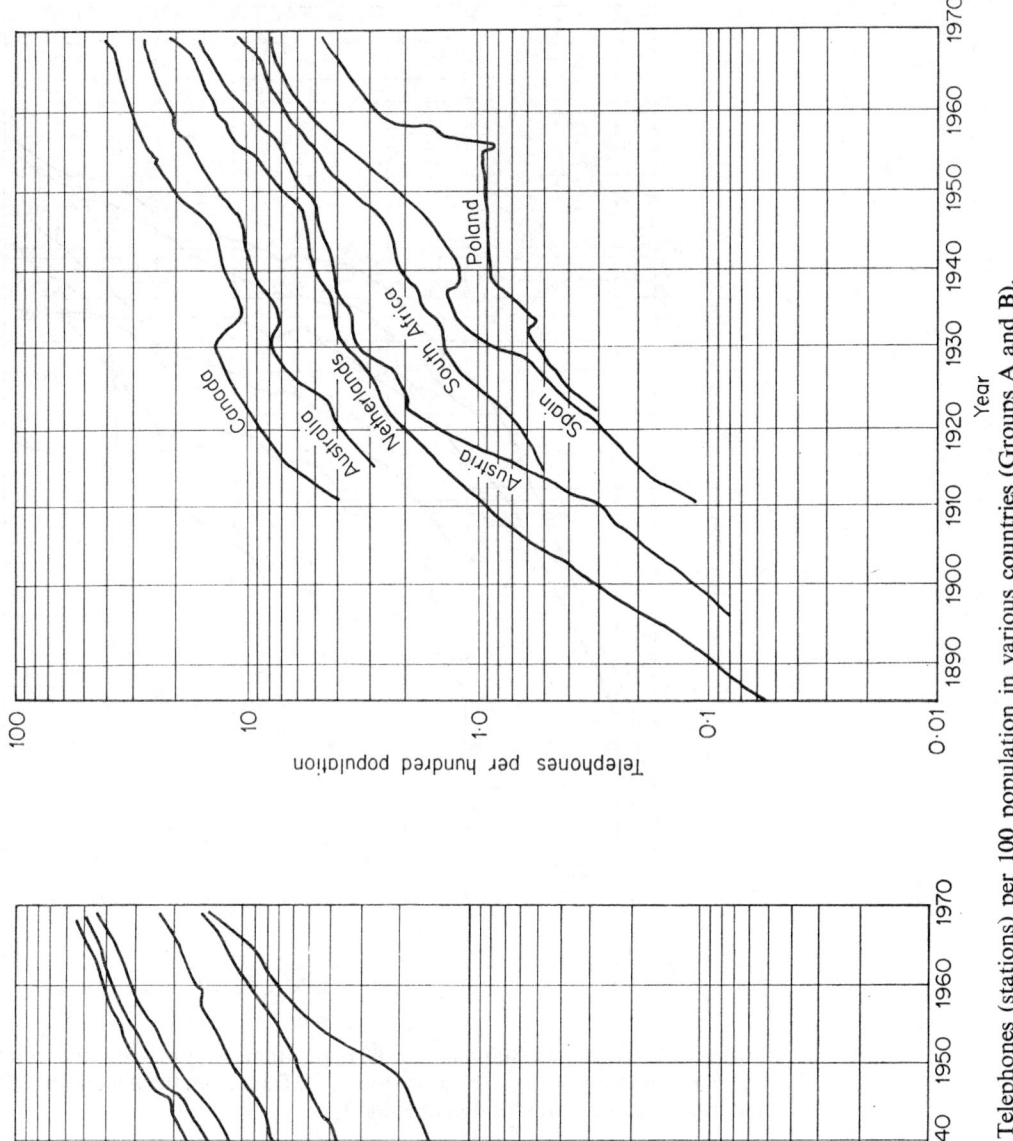

Figures 3.9a and b. Telephones (stations) per 100 population in various countries (Groups A and B).
(With acknowledgements to N. J. H. Jones.[162] Data from the American Telephone and Telegraph Co.,[5] with kind permission.)

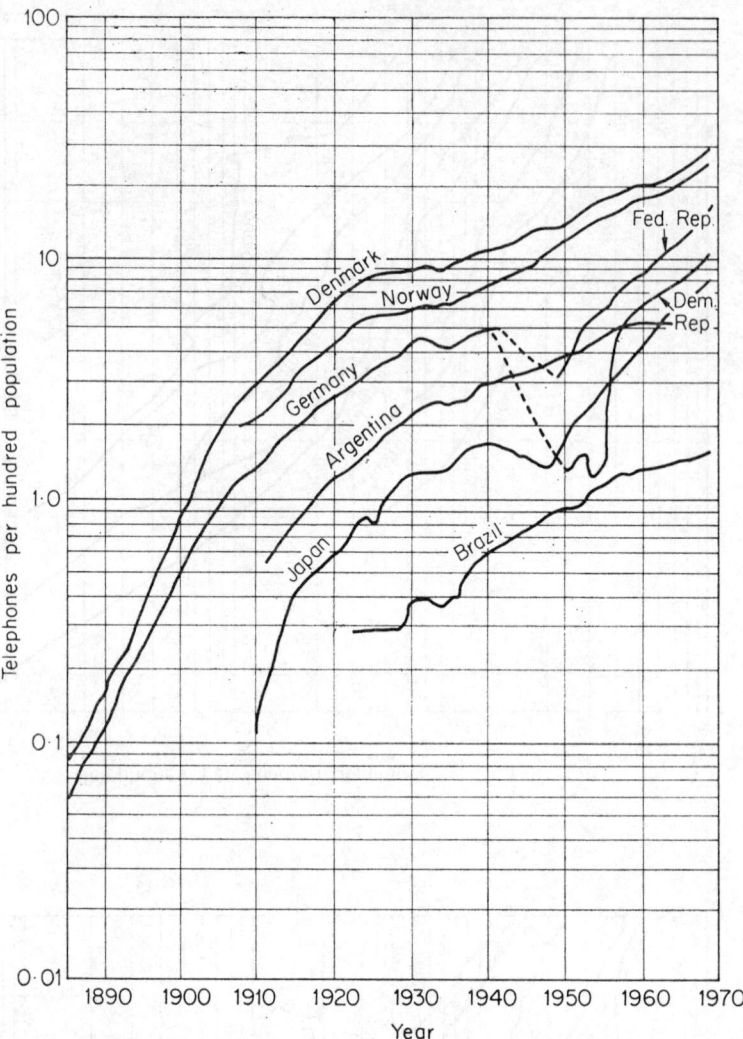

Figure 3.10. Telephones (stations) per 100 population in various countries (Group C). (With acknowledgements to N. J. H. Jones.[162]. Data from the American Telephone and Telegraph Co. with kind permission.)

4. International, intercontinental and overseas communication

When it comes to overseas, long distance, international forms of communication, the story is quite different, if only for the obvious reason that countries must share compatible techniques, similiar standards and conventions of operation. The distinction between the economic and domestic spheres of use is greater too because, at present, the bulk of such traffic is conducted by institutions of many kinds rather than by private persons: probably less than 10 per cent of international telephone traffic is private.[287] Intercontinental traffic thus represents relations between institutions to a major extent, Government Departments, Press Agencies, businesses, airways, etc., and so may be regarded as being executed *on behalf of* people, rather than *by* individual people, a fact which may have certain social implications which will be discussed later in Sections 3 and 4 of Chapter 6.

It is difficult for us today to imagine the world as it was little more than a century ago, when all foreign news was several weeks old, for there was no method of high-speed overseas communication before telegraphy. If there can be said to be any one hub of international telegraphy today that hub would be London. Overseas telegraphs have been of singular importance to Britain from their beginning in mid-19th century because the countries of her Empire were widely scattered and separated by oceans.

This statement should not be read to imply that Britain's communication links with her overseas interests were strong ones. Far from it. They were not and never have been. Although our overseas communication links then were the best in the world, they were nevertheless very slender ones.

In the 19th century, telegraphs and ships were the only means of intercontinental communication and Britain, with supremacy in both, was therefore the hub of world communication. This is still true today, for telegraphs; in particular, Britain is the busiest world centre for Press telegrams. It was Reuter's 'Press Telegrams' that made the first public use oɪ telegraphs for the Press, in 1850, for sending political, financial and economic news between Berlin and Paris.[146,285] The early history of the telegraph centred within Europe rather than the United States because 'the telegraph services were in the hands of National Governments'.

The coming of radio changed this situation by providing more flexible, movable and even portable means of communication; other countries adopted the techniques. Nevertheless Britain still held most of the world's telegraph cables until after the First World War, say 1920. The world's main telegraph routes had already been laid by 1905; up to this time it had been almost entirely commercial traffic which paid for this network, the first high-speed means that had ever been created for international communication.

Telegraphs are still of growing importance today for long-distance *international* communication and will continue to be so, though their techniques are changing to use high-speed automatic means of sending and receiving. Unlike telephone conversation, they present no *immediate* language problem; they are economic, they also provide a printed record of the message. The system called Telex,[146] which originated in Europe in the 1930s, is a modern high-speed form of dialled international (and national) telegraphy which uses special automatic teleprinter receivers: these need not be attended and so they may operate night and day, thereby beating the clock. For intercontinental communication this obviously is an immense advantage, and it is not surprising that, following the Second World War, the system was adopted by one country after another and grew more explosively than any other international communication medium, both in its global scale and in its traffic (see Figure 3.3).[67] Germany (Federal Republic) is a particularly heavy user of Telex[146] and it was from Europe that the system spread outwards to other countries and continents, to cover most of the globe, in little more than 10 years following the War. Curiously, perhaps, the U.S.A. comes well down on the list of Telex users, at present.

Another form of telegraphy is that which is nowadays called *data-transmission*[110] and its adoption shows the beginnings of yet another 'explosion', arising from the increasing use of digital computers in industry, business, government and other spheres of social life. Uses by the world's airways alone already place heavy and rapidly growing demands upon intercontinental datachannels. For example, the cable shown on the map, Figure 3.1, connecting Scotland, Iceland, Greenland and Newfoundland provides means of communication to assist the passage of our aircraft traffic over the North Atlantic.

Reliable *telephony* (speech communication) of really good quality between the continents has become possible only during the last 10 years or so.

Though speech does not give the advantage of recording messages, nor does it 'beat the clock', it has one overwhelming benefit to give, it provides means for *discussion*. The human significance of conversation has already been stressed in Chapter 1; it establishes *personal* relations and may lead to decisions (even the decision 'not to decide' or to disagree).

Short-wave radio was for a long time the only medium for intercontinental speech. When it was introduced in the early 1920s the demands for traffic slowly grew and realization of its values spread through the 'economic sphere'. Figure 3.11 and Figure 3.12 show two growth curves (a) for the United

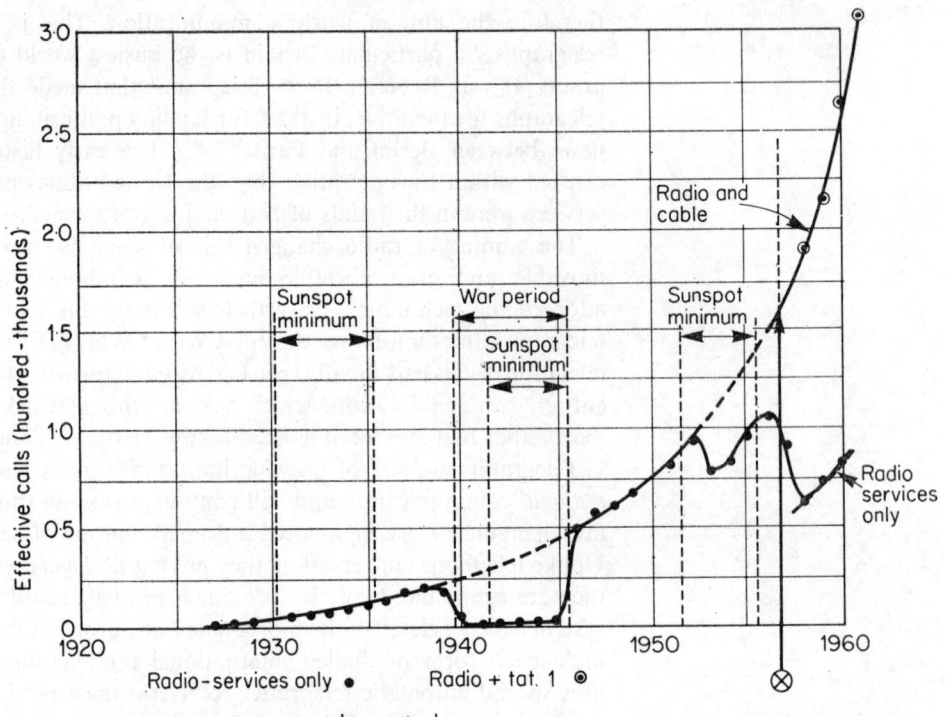

Figure 3.11. Intercontinental telephone traffic. U.K.-originated effective extra-European calls (British G.P.O. data). Takeover of failing radio-telephone traffic by transatlantic cable in 1956. Note: sunspot minimum periods arbitrarily defined by a value of the Zurich relative sunspot number (annual mean) of less than 50. (From Telford and Isted,[287] with kind permission.)

Kingdom, (b) for the United States, the two then most industrialized countries. (Note that the curves do not strictly compare[287].) As the demands grew, made by all countries and by ships at sea, a difficult situation began to develop called *congestion*, meaning that these demands, for overseas traffic especially, began to exceed the number of wavelengths available,* even though several users might be operating on the same wavelength. The consequence was (and often still is) excessive message interference. Furthermore, the situation may be aggravated by such adverse effects of Nature as sunspots, causing 'fading' and total 'blackouts', etc. The effects of such disturbances upon telephone traffic may be seen on Figure 3.11 during the years 1951 to 1956 when they were particularly serious for the United Kingdom.

* These are agreed upon internationally, and recorded by the International Frequency Registration Board. (See Chapter 4, Section 6.)

After the Second World War, world expansion increased rapidly; News Agencies spread, industries became more international; intergovernmental, United Nations and other International Organizations' affairs extended (see Chapter 4, Section 5), air passenger traffic itself 'exploded' (Figure 3.16) and many other social pressures built up and pressed upon the limited communication services of the world.

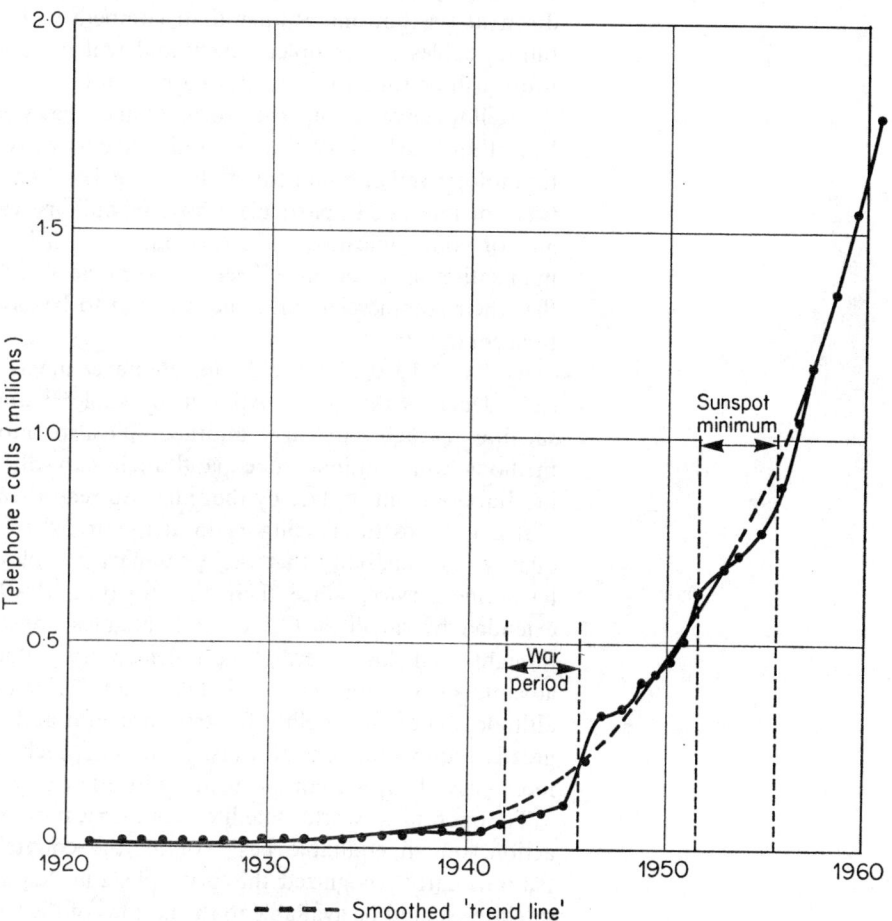

Figure 3.12. Intercontinental telephone traffic. U.S. overseas telephone calls. (A.T. & T. Co. data.)
Note: the data from which this Figure was derived gave totals of outgoing and incoming calls—these have been halved before plotting. The expression 'overseas' is used here to include Hawaii, Puerto Rico and Alaska. Calls to these U.S. territories, with calls to Cuba added, accounted for 60% of total calls in 1959.
(From Telford and Isted,[287] with kind permission.)

Something had to be done about it and two solutions emerged, each based upon Wartime technology: cables and satellites. The first of these developments had already started before the War and its subsequent evolution has depended very much upon the great flowering of electronics (Figure 3.1). The method consists of so improving upon the older idea of telegraph cables that they may carry speech: not one, but many simultaneous conversations. Though the image they create is possibly of less popular appeal than is provided by the science fiction image of satellites, (giving a picture of space-travel) these deep-sea intercontinental telephone cables are remarkable enough, each carrying as it does a sequence of electronic amplifiers of great complexity inserted at regular intervals of twenty or thirty miles in the cable, lying on the sea-bed. Their spacing differs somewhat, on different routes. Figure 3.1 shows a map of these submarine cables as they exist today. Hundreds of these amplifiers have been operating at the bottom of the Atlantic and the Pacific Oceans, many for over 10 years. They are supplied with electric power from the shore ends and have been operating faultlessly, miles down at sea bottom. Rather than compete with satellites now and in the future, cables are complementary and will be used together *with* satellites. More will be said about them in a moment.

Satellites have a complex history,[336] since they were predicted and described by Arthur Clarke in 1945.[55] Not only have they had to await another wartime technology (missile launching) but they have entered into several distinct fields of interest, in particular those of military value, of scientific research and of communication. The economics of their use for global civil communication have therefore been far from clear and it is only in recent years that their commercial values have begun to be assessable with any pretence to accuracy.[251]

By April 1970 about 1322 telephone channels (or equivalent) could be carried across the North Atlantic by cable[291] and about 600 or more by satellites (which can carry another 400 also into other continents). *Both* methods will continue to expand their capacities, and these figures will inevitably be out of date by the time you read them.

It is now worth glancing again at Figure 3.8 to observe the effects of high quality and reliability that these submarine cables have had upon overseas telephone services since their introduction in 1956, an effect now being extended by satellites. Cables and satellites are not rivals, as at one time thought, but have several complementary values[45] and there are even advantages in using them in combination.* For example, by using a high-altitude stationary satellite for one direction and cable for the other; this greatly reduces the time of transmission of speech and can make conversation more easy. They are complementary in other ways too.

To operate a world satellite communication system requires the joint action, on an equitable basis, of all the countries involved. The United Nations early recognized this principle, that 'communications by means of satellites should be available to the nations of the world as soon as practicable on a global and non-discriminatory basis'.† This principle has been acted upon reasonably well with the result that an international body of a unique character has been set up, called Intelsat: i.e. International Telecommunications Satellite Consortium. (See Chapter 5, Section 7.) This body is unique because satellite communication presents unique problems. 'A communications satellite system, if it is to perform its function, must of necessity be international in character' said Joseph V. Charyk, first president of the U.S.A. Communications Satellite Corporation, in 1963, and he went on: 'The Corporation is convinced that only a single system serving all users and handling all traffic throughout the world makes sense from technical, economic, and other considerations'.[46]

A conference of representatives of British Commonwealth Governments

---

* E.g. see B. M. Dawidzuik and H. F. Preston, *Comparative Evaluation of Modern Transmission Media for Global Communications*, American Inst. Aeronautics and Astronautics, 3rd Communications Satellite Systems Conference, Los Angeles, 6–8th April 1970.

† Resolution No. 1721 (XVI) of the General Assembly.

held in 1962, led to discussions between the U.K., Canada, the U.S.A., Australia and European countries. In 1963 the European Conference on

International Telecommunications Satellite Consortium (Intelsat)

(a) *Original signatories, 1964 Country*	*% Share quota (December 1969)*	*Original signatories, 1964 Country*	*% Share quota (December 1969)*
Australia	2·38	Norway	0·35
Canada	3·25	Spain	0·95
German Fed. Republic	5·28	Switzerland	1·73
Ireland	0·30	United Kingdom	7·27
Japan	1·73	United States	52·8
The Netherlands	0·87	Vatican City	0·04

(b) *Later signatories Country*	*% Share quota (December 1969)*	*Later Signatories Country*	*% Share quota (December 1969)*
Algeria	0·54	Liechtenstein	0·05
Argentine	1·41	Luxembourg	0·05
Austria	0·17	Malaysia	0·24
Belgium	0·95	Mexico	1·46
Brazil	1·41	Monaco	0·005
Cameroon	0·05	Morocco	0·29
Ceylon	0·05	New Zealand	0·41
Chili	0·28	Nicaragua	0·05
China (Taiwan)	0·09	Nigeria	0·33
Colombia	0·54	Pakistan	0·24
Denmark	0·35	Panama	0·04
Ethiopia	0·07	Peru	0·50
France	5·28	Philippines	0·50
Greece	0·09	Portugal	0·35
Guatemala	0·05	Saudi Arabia	0·05
India	0·47	Singapore	0·10
Indonesia	0·27	South Africa	0·27
Iran	0·25	Sudan	0·01
Iraq	0·009	Sweden	0·61
Israel	0·57	Syria	0·04
Italy	1·9	Tanzania	0·05
Ivory Coast	0·10	Thailand	0·10
Jamaica	0·05	Tunisia	0·18
Jordan	0·05	Turkey	0·50
Kenya	0·05	Uganda	0·05
Korea	0·05	United Arab Republic	0·32
Kuwait	0·05	Venezuela	1·00
Lebanon	0·07	Vietnam (South)	0·05
Libya	0·03	Yemen	0·03

(c) *Countries allocated quotas, but which have not yet acceded to the interim agreement*

Country	*% Share quota (December 1969)*	*Country*	*% Share quota (December 1969)*
Bolivia	0·05	Honduras	0·05
Congo Dem. Republic	0·05	Paraguay	0·05
Costa Rica	0·01	Trinidad and Tobago	0·05
Dominican Republic	0·05	Senegal	0·05
Ecuador	0·05	Zambia	0·05

Figures here are given to an accuracy of 2 decimal places. For full details, refer to: *Report to the President and the Congress*, 20th April 1970, Communications Satellite Corporation, 950 L'Enfant Plaza, S.W., Washington, D.C. 20024, U.S.A.

Satellite Communications was held (in association with Australia) at which the U.S.A. accepted the principle of international ownership, management and participation in design of a world satellite system. Intelsat was the result.

The needs of the various countries for international telephones and other message traffic are very varied. The U.S.A. and other highly industrial countries had immediate needs for many channels, whilst many 'developing' countries yet require only very few. (Their *internal* needs are another matter.) This is a situation which it is to be hoped will progressively change and improve. Consequently the sharing among the various countries, of both their investments in their ground stations and of the available satellite channels, must be subject to regular revision.

The list of countries having Intelsat membership is listed on p. 85, together with their quotas, as they stand at the present day (December, 1969).

A satellite system of international communication has two parts; first there are the satellites themselves, used in common by all parties and not standing on any nation's territory, and second, the ground stations which are owned and controlled separately by the various nations who are sharing in the use of the system. The satellites are thus 'shared' whilst the ground stations are national (or perhaps held for use by neighbouring countries under bilateral agreements) and are operated under national laws. *Ownership* of the satellites is then not to be confused with *administration* of the whole system.

For some years the ability to construct and to launch satellites lay within the power and economic range of one country, the U.S.A., but their value for overseas communication depends entirely upon their being adopted for use by other nations, and satellites are now being designed and constructed in several countries. The U.S.A. Authority initially set up by Congress in 1963 for attending to their satellite interests was called Comsat: Communication Satellite Corporation. Fear that their technical prerogatives would lead to control of overseas communication by this one country has not proved to be too well founded. A satellite is one thing, but an operating system is another, for systems cannot be operated without the agreement of all interested national authorities. Other and preferable forms of satellite ownership may perhaps eventually appear, for example, through the U.N.

The organization called Intelsat, which has been set up by international agreements is thus, principally, an administrative one. It is formed by representatives of the national communication authorities in a consortium of countries, and membership is not closed. New member countries may wish to join, from time to time, in which case a resharing of *all* countries' quotas is arranged. In view of the great range of these quotas, a special voting system has been devised with the object of guarding against dominance of control by any of the richer countries.*[127]

The real uniqueness of this whole international organization, Intelsat, arises from the fact that this international Consortium *employs* Comsat (the United States Communications Satellite Corporation) as a Manager for all matters concerning the satellites themselves (the 'space segment'). Ground stations are the responsibilities of each member country.

This American body Comsat was initially conceived by the U.S. Congress, in their Communications Satellite Act of 1962 and the body was created in

---

* The effective 'Board' of this organization consists of one representative of each of the signatory countries' authorities whose quota is not less than 1·5 per cent and of any group of countries having common spheres of interest whose combined quota is such. This controlling Board is called the Interim Communications Satellite Committee (I.C.S.C.).

1963 'to plan, initiate, construct, own, manage and operate, either by itself or in conjunction with foreign governments or business entities, a commercial communications satellite system'.[127] It was set up, not as an establishment of the U.S.A. government but as a company financed by public subscription, 50 per cent of the shares being reserved for U.S. 'common carriers' (i.e. their telephone and telegraph authorities). Comsat is centred in Washington. The turn of events has changed this conception somewhat; it is now employed as Manager by Intelsat to act for all member countries, though it still forms the central authority for satellite communication within the borders of the U.S.A. itself.

It is Intelsat which was responsible, in 1965, for setting up the first geostationary satellite popularly known as Early Bird (at 22,300 miles altitude and more correctly called Intelsat I) which now carries part of the intercontinental telephone and Telex traffic. It is capable of carrying up to 240 simultaneous telephone conversations. Other satellites have since been launched, including the latest design (called Intelsat III) which carry 1200 conversations each. These satellites are situated in groups, equally spaced around the equator and at about 22,300 miles altitude (see Figure 3.1). New satellites are being developed now which will carry 6000 channels.

These and other so-called 'second generation satellites' will need to carry such a greatly increased quantity of traffic, in order to keep pace with the explosive demand predicted. (See Figure 3.8 for example, for the transatlantic route). But it is well worth noting that telephone cable technique is improving equally fast; both cables and satellites will be used in future, especially cables for connecting highly concentrated industrial areas of the world.

The international planning for the global cable system of telephony (and other services) has proceeded differently. There have been three major spheres of interest (see Figure 3.1); first, the North Atlantic for common American, Canadian, British, European and Middle Eastern connexion; second, the British Commonwealth system linking continental areas of common trading and political interests;[116,136] third, the system serving the United States' interests in the Pacific sphere.

The first of these cables was laid across the North Atlantic in 1956, by joint U.K. and U.S.A. enterprise and its message capacity was taken up very quickly, because the need for high-quality, reliable speech communication had long been urgent. The North Atlantic route is by far the busiest in the world, for both message and aircraft traffic. (Telephone traffic alone is growing at the rate of 15 per cent per annum.)[127] A second and similar cable was laid in 1959, this time to Paris and Frankfurt, and a third in 1961 from Britain to Canada,[136] followed by others. Each cable laying has been paced by a subsequent rise of traffic demand. The situation in 1970 is shown on the map, Figure 3.1.

The growth of North Atlantic traffic channels since 1950 may be seen from Figure 3.8, which shows also an official prediction of the channels then thought likely to be needed up to 1975.[45] Such predictions, made in situations of such rapid change as today's, must always be regarded as liable to revision; there is reason to believe that, these predictions are underestimates,[45] probably large underestimates.

The second sphere of overseas cable development serves in the first place the needs of the British Commonwealth,[112] where good quality overseas speech communication has always been lacking. Responsibility for promoting telecommunication services within the British Commonwealth has, since 1949, been vested in the Commonwealth Telecommunication Board.

In July 1958 the Commonwealth Communications Conference was held in London, at which it was recommended that a 'round-the-world' submarine telephone cable should be provided; the map Figure 3.13 shows the original plan of routes, linking the major Commonwealth countries (and making overland or short sea connexions possible for others) forming a complete girdle round the earth.

Political happenings have forced changes upon this original tentative plan and the cable sytem which has actually been laid, at the date of writing, is that shown in the composite map Figure 3.1.

If we look at this simple map and consider the millions of human beings living on each continent and then at these scarce and slender lines of communication, carrying but a few persons' conversations at any one moment, and if we then glance at the few growth curves which have been illustrated in this Chapter to show the rapid response to each new installation, a curious picture may appear. It is a picture of isolated nation islands, some intensely busy with their own internal affairs and some much less so, carrying on mutual trading in conditions of the greatest difficulty, each knowing little of the others in any depth, perhaps frightened of each other, with nearly all their social attitudes and relations decided for them by various official institutions. Even if we regard all the other forms of world communications, telegraphs, radio, ships and air travel, tourism, satellite television and all else, the picture seems little different. The *rates* of growth of all these media may have been truly explosive since the last War, but their magnitudes are small; the facilities they offer are still comparatively slender, though some will undoubtedly continue to grow even faster. But it is the very suddenness with which these facilities for world communication have appeared, and been used especially by institutions and organizations, which suggests a desperate act to overcome the effects of past restrictions.

From such considerations of the world picture of intercontinental communication, we can draw one conclusion of major importance: *all the signs indicate that the nations of the world have been socially deprived in the past through lack of means of communication*; their means, such as have existed, have been utterly inadequate to assist them to resolve their mutual involvements in stable ways, *however much they may have wished to do so.*

I should hasten to add that this is far from saying that now, when our means of communication are beginning to expand at last, we are using them for their best purposes or in the wisest ways. This would be expecting too much of technology!

This is a question of great importance: are international relations, at all the various levels, trade, diplomacy, personal attitudes and education, and others, seriously handicapped by inadequate means of communication, even *today*? Suppose that a fairy-tale wish could be fulfilled by some miracle of economy and these means be increased tenfold overnight; would it be for the better or worse? It will be argued in the next Chapter (Section 2) that the explosion *could*, in theory, proceed too fast and be disastrous. There may be some optimum rate of expansion, but there is no doubt that we have been, and still are, far below this ideal.

Writing in 1961, Telford and Isted commented, after surveying the U.K. and the U.S.A. and other intercontinental traffic: 'To the authors the most striking lesson is that present facilities for long-distance telephone

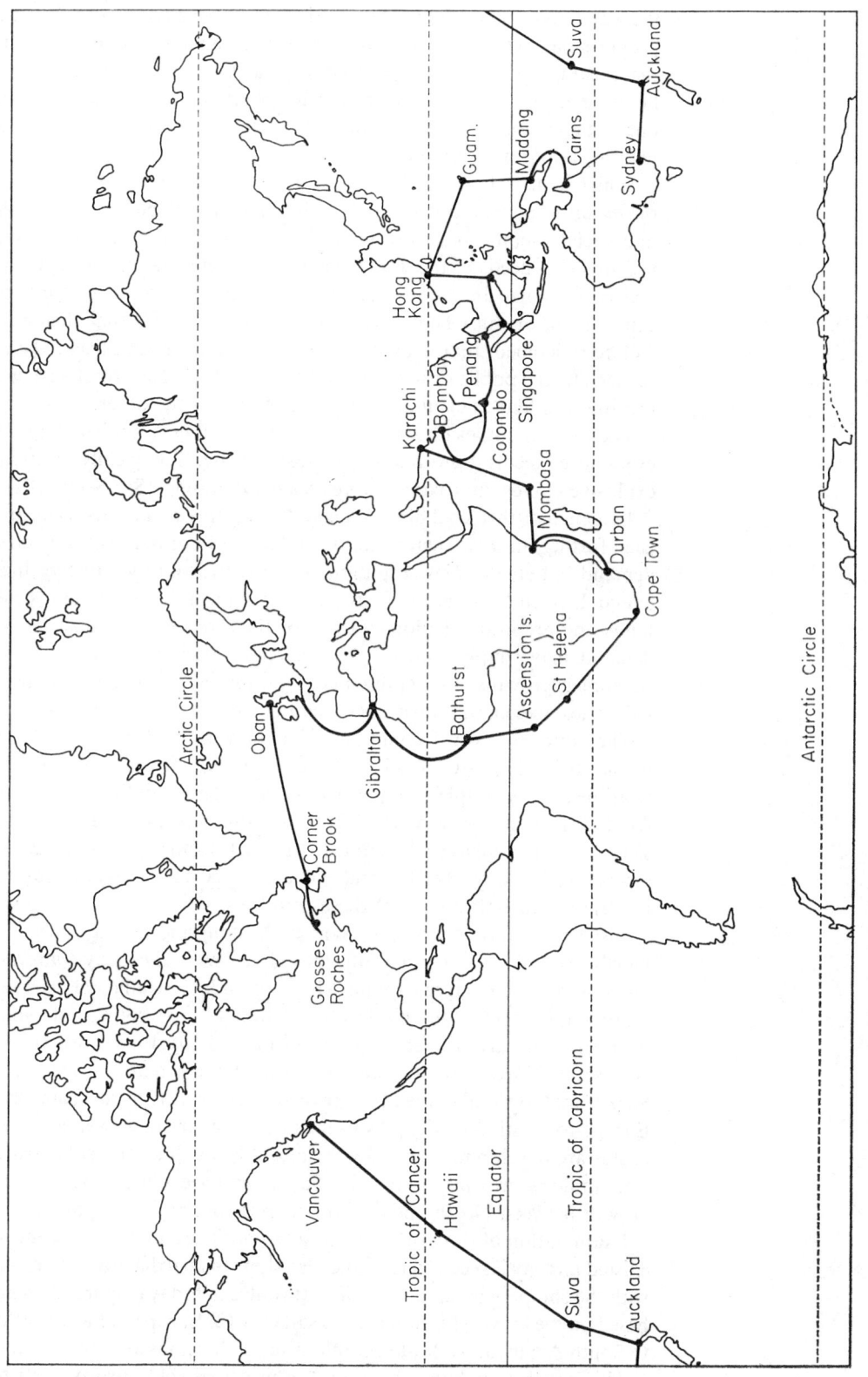

Figure 3.13. 'Round-the-World' telephone cable system, as conceived at the Commonwealth Communications Conference, 1958.

communication are, in the majority of cases, utterly inadequate for the needs of the world today and tomorrow'.[287] Six years have passed since then and great progress has been made, but the conclusion remains true, namely, that both the existing facilities for world communication and their rates of growth, however rapid, can scarcely be said to reflect the more explosive growth of our detailed international involvements and suggest still a preoccupation with local, national affairs.

Which comes first, the *demand* for communication (the social need) or the *means* to make it possible (the technical facility)? No technology develops in a social vacuum but to some extent, greater or less, is created out of the urgent social needs of the day; sometimes it is created far too early in history and is still-born. Inventors must to some extent be motivated by their past experiences, or must believe that there is some *chance* that their inventions will be welcomed, that is to say, believe that some need exists (whether it be realized by the public or not) which they can satisfy. Nevertheless demand and facilities are like chicken and egg;[262] one creates the other.

The various curves illustrating this Chapter all have similar shape, bending ever more steeply upwards as the years go by. Technically speaking, such explosive curves approximate to *exponential* graphs. (See Section 7.)

Evidence of this kind always suggests a *regenerative* growth, meaning that each further improvement in technical facilities not only satisfies an existing demand but creates new conditions which give rise to yet further increase in demand. Such 'regenerative' growths are typical of *service* industries of all kinds and are in distinction to the growths of *consumer* industries, in which demand may simply increase with increased wealth merely to be satisfied; consumer growths are represented typically by straighter graphs. Service industries, like capital investment, can be creators of new wealth.

The routes of world communication of various kinds have not evolved haphazardly but are closely related to international trade and political relations. For example, Timmerman *et al.*[291] have published the noteworthy fact that Britain's gross revenue from her communication services (telephony, Telex and telegraphs combined) with, at least, France, Netherlands, Belgium, Germany, Norway, Sweden and the U.S.A. bears a fairly constant ratio to her trade values with each of these countries.

Just as the early telegraphs were built alongside railway lines,[146] so our North Atlantic telephone traffic correlates with the heavy aircraft traffic on that busiest overseas route. Much of today's traffic, of various kinds, follows the general directions of traditional trade routes, of which three form the main arteries (see Figures 3.14 and 3.15). First, and busiest today, across the North Atlantic; second, from Britain and Europe through the Suez Canal to the Far East (i.e. prior to its closure); third, from Britain and Europe to South America. As well as these, other and newer communication routes are developing especially for aircraft, satellites and submarine cables: e.g. traffic is growing across the Pacific and we must expect a very rapid growth between North and South America too.[147] (See Figure 4.2.)

Examination of the world's main intercontinental telegraph routes, as they existed already last century, would also show them to have a certain correlation with the shipping and even the aircraft routes of today (Figures 3.14 and 3.15), based on the tripod skeleton (1) transatlantic (2) Europe to Far East (3) Europe to South America. Radio-telegraph traffic connexions are not shown here.

This rough correlation between the principal ship, airways and telegraph traffic routes held until very recent years, the routes being determined mainly

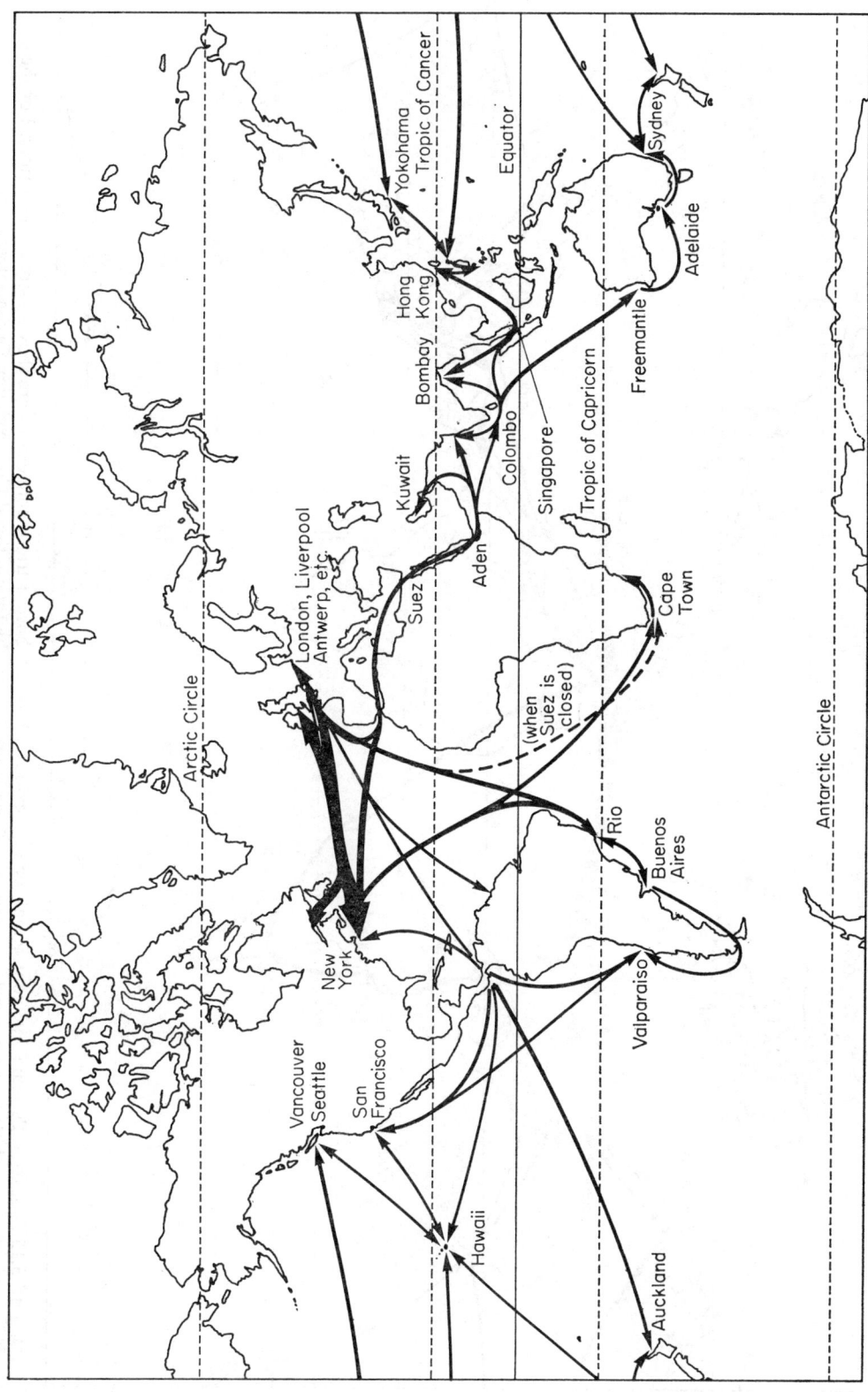

Figure 3.14. The world's main shipping lanes (when Suez is open). The thicker the line, the heavier the total tonnage. (For details see any good commercial atlas.)

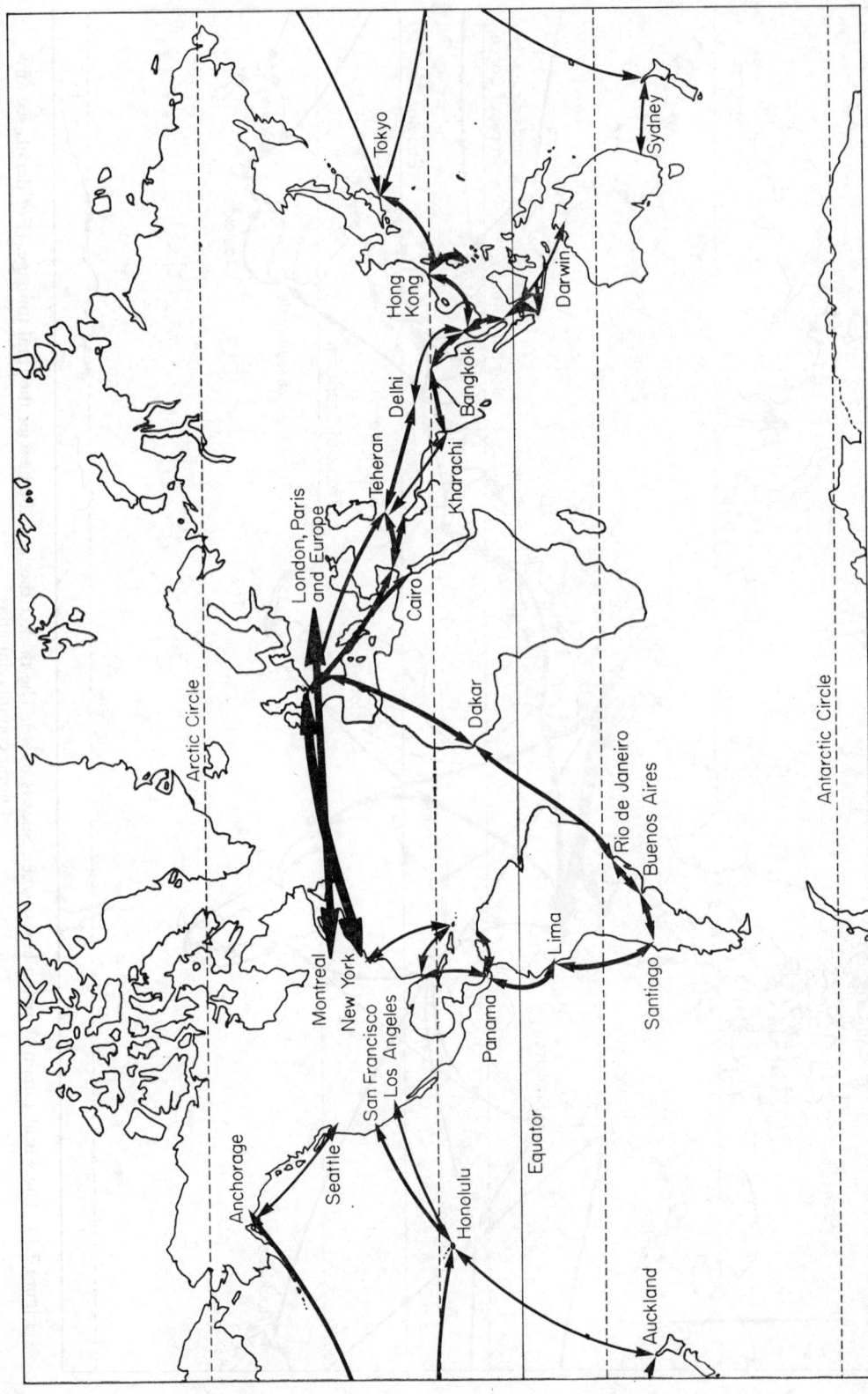

Figure 3.15. The world's main intercontinental air connexions. Only the busiest traffic connexions are shown—not actual routes. For the whole world network, see *Regional Plans*, published by the International Civil Aviation Organization.

by trade and political relations, coupled of course with geography, rather than by technology. Thus aircraft, in theory unconfined by sea coasts, nevertheless have their most dense traffic following the *general* routes of shipping, and message traffic naturally follows.

Thus these same three 'legs' of world traffic form the basic skeleton of global telephony and Telex traffic too. Figure 3.1 shows how the very busy North Atlantic traffic is carried by both cables and the mid-Atlantic satellite system; this same satellite system carries the Europe/South America traffic also. The satellite system over the Indian Ocean carries the Europe/Far East traffic. However, the Pacific satellite system represents a more recent strengthening of global communication—a fourth leg.

The expected traffic growths along these principal world routes of communication are shown in Figure 4.2 which is based upon the official International Telecommunication Union predictions.*[45,147] The absence of any direct Europe–Far East traffic route is very obvious in this diagram (what has been called the 'second leg' here); however, these I.T.U. predictions were made in 1963, before the possibilities of satellites were at all clear.

I have been using the word *traffic* a good deal, without making much distinction between its use to mean *transport* (aircraft, ships . . .) and to mean *message traffic* (telegraphs, telephones . . .). It is a convenient word to use to mean 'communication activity', without specificity.

As the quantity of message traffic grows, in ways such as those illustrated by graphs here, so it becomes less possible, in general, to distinguish between the various forms, because any one technical system, whether cable, satellite, microwave beam, or other, may be used for carrying several forms of traffic: e.g. telephone messages, Telex traffic, television, data . . . . Systems of communication like satellites and intercontinental cables are of a global scale of size and so costly that the economics of their use demand this *traffic diversity*. That is to say, they must be designed to carry various different kinds of message traffic so as to increase the chance that they are used 24 hours in the day, by planned allocation.[45]

It is this diversity of present day traffic needs of the industrialized countries, leading to the design of these gigantic global systems, having flexibility of usage, that has made at all possible the likelihood that poorer countries may share these services. Their traffic demands are at present small and more specialized, but under such planning as that of Intelsat, sharing does become a theoretical possibility.

In the meanwhile, the overseas communication needs of these poorer areas have most economically been met by using short-wave radio, as all countries did before 1956, but this situation cannot be expected to persist.[291] Satellites do indeed offer hope to such areas,[45] a fact which was recognized early in the history of experimental satellites. Small, transportable, satellite ground receiving stations were already made and being tested in 1962 using the experimental satellites Telstar and Relay.[154] Small satellite ground stations may be designed to suit the limited traffic needs of the developing countries, operating with internationally owned satellites[45] though, unfortunately, as we shall see in Chapter 5, such stations may be far less economical to use than large ones.[154] Similar remarks might be applied to the possible use of satellites for communication with aircraft and ships, a technical possibility, but expensive.

* Called the 'Rome Plan'. See Chapter 4, Section 7.

Since the Commonwealth telephone cable (Figure 3.1) now connects mainly those areas of the world which already had some forms of communication before, because of their past political and trade relations, satellites will have special value to the non-Commonwealth developing areas of Africa, the Middle East and South America; to these we might add the Commonwealth countries, Pakistan and India, whose overseas radio-telephone and telegraph communications are often unreliable, because of atmospheric radio conditions in the tropical belt.

As can well be imagined from a glance at the various explosive growth curves of international traffic, illustrated in this Chapter, very careful and elaborate forecasting is needed in order to predict future needs as accurately as possible.[25,45,67,168,214,287,364,365] Modern overseas communication systems are very expensive, whether for message traffic, or aircraft transport. The large capital should not be laid down too early by installing systems before there is enough traffic demand to make some use of them, nor should traffic growth be inhibited by lack of new systems. Prediction of future traffic is a very important matter therefore but, unfortunately, it is singularly difficult to do with any accuracy, partly because owing to the unprecedented rates of growth there have been inadequate experiences to call upon. As already mentioned there is a further reason that the growths of demand for each specific form of traffic (i.e. telephones, telegraphs, aircraft, post . . .) *within* each country seem not to be correlated with identical social factors within the various countries.[20] The habits and environment of each are varied. Predictions of international traffic growth must be made, for simple economic reasons, but they cannot be made with accuracy for more than a few, say five, years ahead whereas the operating lifetime of a new system may be expected to be 20 years or more. The International Telecommunication Union's appropriate body, the Comité Consultatif International de Telephonie et Telegraphie, recommends 3–7 years for 'short-term forecasts' and 15–20 for 'long-term,' in their *Manual on National Telephone Networks.* For certain aspects of planning fifty year forecasts are recommended! (Geneva, 1964.)

There is a third difficulty in the way of accurate prediction. In our present industrial stage, with its proliferation of new ideas, new methods, new materials and inventiveness, especially in electronics, there is no feeling of certainty that a newly designed system will not be out-of-date and uneconomic to use before it has paid for itself. Some new types of aircraft are well known to be in this situation. Neither is it known beforehand just what stimulus may be given to traffic demands by the introduction of a new system.

Such difficulties as these of course face any industrialist of today, in most fields of technology; the important point about communication being that each system newly introduced is both enormously expensive and essentially international in its function.

5. Airways traffic, air mail and tourism—post-War phenomena

Brief reference to international airways traffic has already been made (see map, Figure 3.15), and to its complete dependence upon electronic communication. Popular air transport is very much a post-War phenomenon, part of the 'opening-up' of people's vision caused by that War and by the increased personal wealth of large sections of our industrial populations. Like other means of communication, telephones, telegraphs, cars, etc., the airways serve dual purposes, that is social and private, for both business (economic sphere) transport and private (domestic) tourism.

Few of the passengers when in flight, strapped to their seats in rows, like parcels on a rack, trying to glimpse something of interest through tiny portholes, can have any idea whatever of the abundance of electronics and communication apparatus needed to keep them safe and to ensure that they arrive at their correct destination, on time and unharmed. Those who may accept the stewardess's invitation to go forward and visit the captain in his cabin may be most impressed by the hundreds of dials, meters and knobs which cover the cabin walls, the lights and the switches; an impressive sight. But what our travellers do not see at all is the far greater mass of electronic equipment on the ground. They see nothing of the global trunk networks covering Europe and connecting with Africa, or Australia, or the Americas, sending by radio-teleprinter and land line information about weather, traffic movements, and warnings to pilots, to ensure safety and regularity of flight. They accept as natural their 600 m.p.h. without realizing that such high speed requires messages to be sent at least four times as quickly, ahead of them, to prepare the airport at their destination; little do they know that weather data is being transmitted automatically, at regular intervals of time, between established centres in all the continents they cross and re-transmitted automatically to warn their pilot. Neither do they know much of the radio-telephone network which links all the main airports of a continent for controlling their 'plane during flight (telephones ensuring *conversation*, for decisions must be made quickly and with confidence), and for obtaining landing permission, emergency services and other help. As they cross the coast into another country our passengers are too interested in trying to identify places on the ground, cities, rivers or mountains, to care about the fact that they have entered a Control Zone and are being guided into a 'lane' by long-range radars, perhaps 200 miles away, to be handed over later to a short-range radar, some 20 miles from home, and gently conducted by further radio guidance systems into a glide-path for landing. Impatient passengers may sometimes wonder what is causing the hold-up before landing, having no idea that, together with other aircraft, they are being 'stacked', one above the other at intervals of 1000 feet (perhaps ten deep above a really large airport) whilst they are sorted out and called down safely by radio. Even as they step out of the 'plane, they may give no thought to the great organization in the airport all around them, for refuelling, police, Customs and Excise, health, immigration, luggage and bus transport, services dependent upon telephones, radio-interception of messages, and perhaps a computer. All this massive complex of communication and signalling, exceeded nowhere outside the military sphere, is unseen and unheeded. Our travellers step out, fiddle with their watches, and go about their business.*

Not only do modern electronics and telecommunications serve the airways and, in fact, make it possible for them to operate at all but, conversely, the airways have come to serve the international message communication needs of the general public too, in the form of *air mail*.

Air mail, although it is an extension of the familiar and ancient Postal Service, came to be seen by the public as a new mode of communication, a new kind of service.† Letters were sent overseas to relatives and friends by the pre-War mail using ships, of course, but air mail provides very cheap

* The international organization of air traffic, and its relevant body, are described in Chapter 4, Section 6.

† For statistics of international mail, see *U.N. Statistical Yearbook* 1966.[330]

and *rapid* means for ordinary people. Rather than the telephone, it is at present the air mail which is the major overseas means of private communication, used by masses of people and helping to maintain international friendships and make emigration more endurable. I say here 'at present' because the intercontinental telephone is becoming relatively cheaper as time passes, and as its increasing use by business, industry and other official bodies makes it increasingly economic; its use by private people may also 'explode' before very long.

The North Atlantic is the busiest air route in the world today, also with 'exploding' traffic (see Figure 3.15) as it is the busiest for message traffic too. In 1965 some $4\frac{1}{4}$ million passengers were carried across, and the expectations are nearly 10 million by 1970 and 15 million by 1975.[87] Cargo may increase at a faster rate. The signs are much the same with regard to air traffic as they are for message traffic; the demand is rising so steeply that facilities are never adequate, in many parts of the world: a world which has been 'under-communicated' for so long. Such signs are not confined to the wealthier countries either, for airlines are also developing fast in India, South East Asia and Central and South America.

The explosive growth of international air traffic is something for which no country's authorities have ever been fully prepared; nor can they be expected to be, for prediction of future needs is more hazardous and may involve greater steps in financial outlay than any other system of communication.[227] In Britain there is the added problem of land shortage and the noise disturbance to large populations of residents (as we know from the controversies over new London airports).

The traffic growth curve for the British Airport Authority's London airports is shown in Figure 3.16. London has been selected here for illustration because it highlights the problems which may soon face many other airports in the world. Thus London is the busiest airport in the world for international traffic. Britain, being a small island country, situated nearly centrally in the world's land mass, has a relatively small domestic, inland air traffic, whilst the major proportion of its air traffic is international and includes a great deal of through traffic to other countries. However, curves for other large airports could equally well have been shown and they would be found to be similar. Figure 3.16 shows that the London traffic started on its 'straight-line' growth at about 1958–59, climbing at the rate of about a million extra passengers a year ever since. During the 'regenerative phase', prior to this time, people were becoming accustomed to this new form of world transport and to the possibilities it offered, not only to business men but to steadily growing masses of people to whom holidays abroad became a genuine reality.

At this point it would make me happy if I felt able to say with confidence that these growing millions of holidaymakers were 'bringing the nations closer together' or serving the interests of 'world peace and understanding', as they fly abroad to spend their one, two or three weeks in foreign countries; but, alas, I have grave doubts about this, though it will be more appropriate to discuss these doubts in Chapter 6 (Section 2).

6. Technology both satisfies and creates demand

The launching of communication satellites may have done more than anything else to focus attention of the public on 'the communication explosion', which has hit us since the last World War, and which has been illustrated in preceding Sections by several graphs.

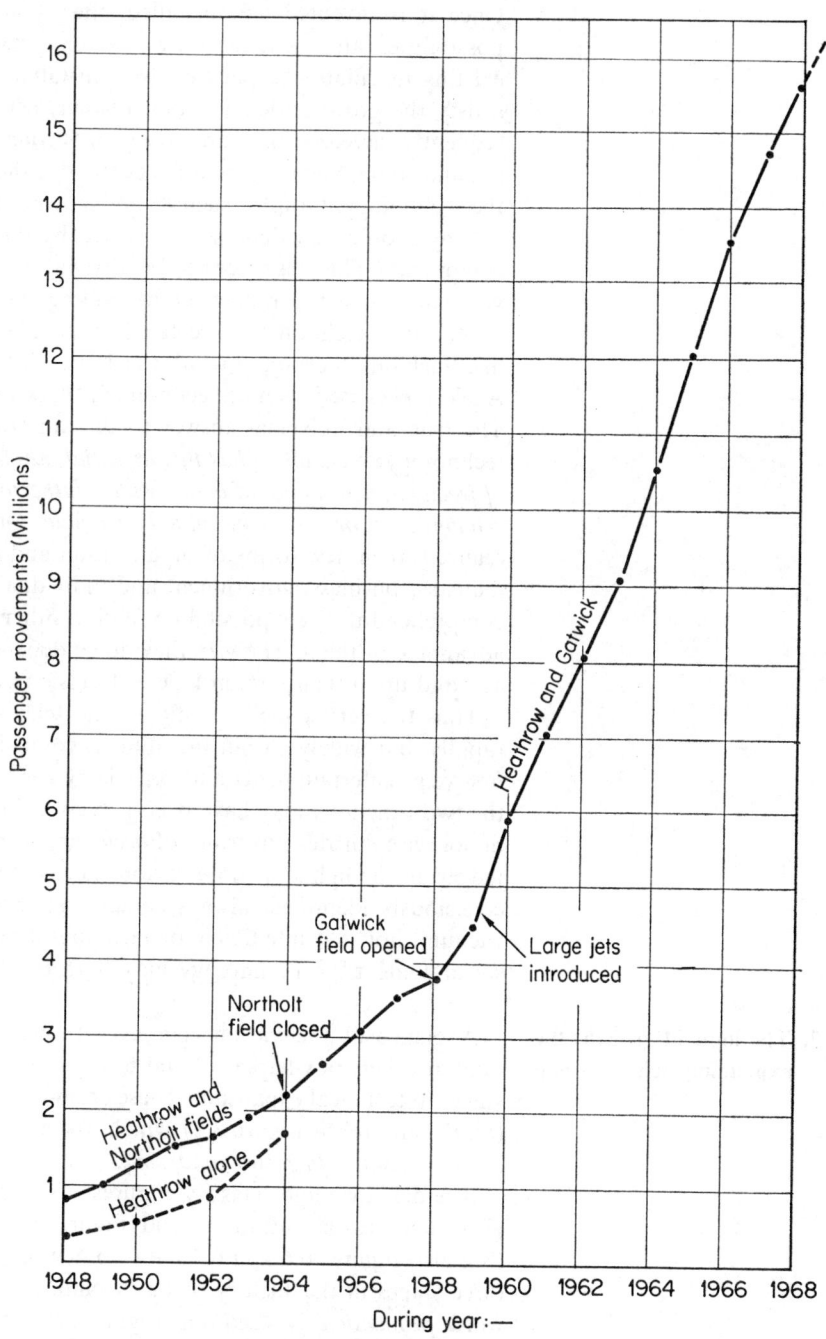

Figure 3.16. Civilian air passenger movements in London. 1946, Heathrow and Northolt opened: 1954, Northolt closed: 1958, Gatwick opened.
(Figures kindly supplied by the British Airports Authority.)

Such explosive growths of demand represent the interaction of technology and society. A new technology of communication is not usually invented as a result of public demand, but in the creation of far-sighted individuals. Once it is invented and installed, the public becomes aware of the new possibilities and demand arises, which grows eventually to outstrip the existing installation capacities. New installations are made, which not only satisfy the growing demand but, further, usually *create* new demand; consequently increased pressure arises for further new services to be introduced . . . and so on. Such regenerative demand is then both *satisfied* and *created* by the technology. Graphs, such as are shown here, are the result.*

Why should new demand be created by the mere installation of technical equipment? This may seem to be a trivial question with an obvious answer, yet many answers can be given depending very much upon who you are and upon which technology is referred to. It might be answered by expressions like 'fashion', 'keeping up with the Joneses', 'because this is a Technological Age'(!) 'because it is more economic', 'Parkinson's Law': a host of answers. The true and universal answer to this question exposes the real nature of technology: *technology has this essential nature, that it opens up new degrees of freedom, new modes of action which, hitherto, may not have been physically, economically or even conceptually possible*. Once these new possibilities are realized, then new forms of organization and operation become possible for industry, business, government and individuals, who are sometimes slow to comprehend the new possibilities and at other times are not, but rush to take advantage of them. The way they do so depends much upon who the people are, and upon their circumstances. Decisions are always human.

Thus the very same technology (e.g. television) may have been accepted rapidly and widely within the affluent countries for a particular purpose at first (e.g. entertainment) and only later for another (e.g. education) whilst the two functions may have been perceived in the opposite order of priority in poorer countries. Priorities of *need* vary so much and technologies become judged in the lights of those various needs. Need of some kind, perhaps not consciously identified, always comes first; no technology arises in a social vacuum, nor is it intelligible or meaningful at all in isolation, but only in a social context.[262] Technology may both create and reveal need.

7. The logic of growth: the expanding rich–poor gap

A glance at the various curves with which this Chapter is illustrated, (and at others in Chapters 2 and 6) may suggest that there are three distinct stages in technical expansion. These are brought together for clarity as curves (a), (b) and (c) in Figure 3.17 which, for apparent reasons, have been called *explosive, saturating* and *collapsing*.

Broadly, we might classify Figures 3.8 and 3.11 as explosive, Figure 2.1 (T.V. licences) as saturating and Figure 2.1 (radio licences) as collapsing. (See also Figures 6.6 and 6.7 showing newspaper circulations. They represent three stages in the history of any technical expansion, (a), (b) and (c). The word *production* is used on Figure 3.17 here to represent whatever is expanding (e.g. numbers of telephones, air transport, etc. . . . any service). All three curves start off as explosive, the production increasing at an ever-growing rate; such a growth of production resembles, at least approximately, a *compound interest law*, by analogy to economics. Thus, when money is invested and the interest accruing is continually reinvested the 'production'

* The same was true of Public Lending Libraries, see Chapter 6, Section 6.

(money) increases in this way*: or would do so if certain checks were not applied, such as taxation! By analogy, we may use such words when considering the effects of introducing a new technology. There is the 'take-off' period during which the values of the new service are becoming appreciated, leading to a straighter 'climb' period with no apparent limit: the 'explosive' (compound interest) growth. Such *growth curves* are typical of many situations in which the increase in production p in one year is proportional to

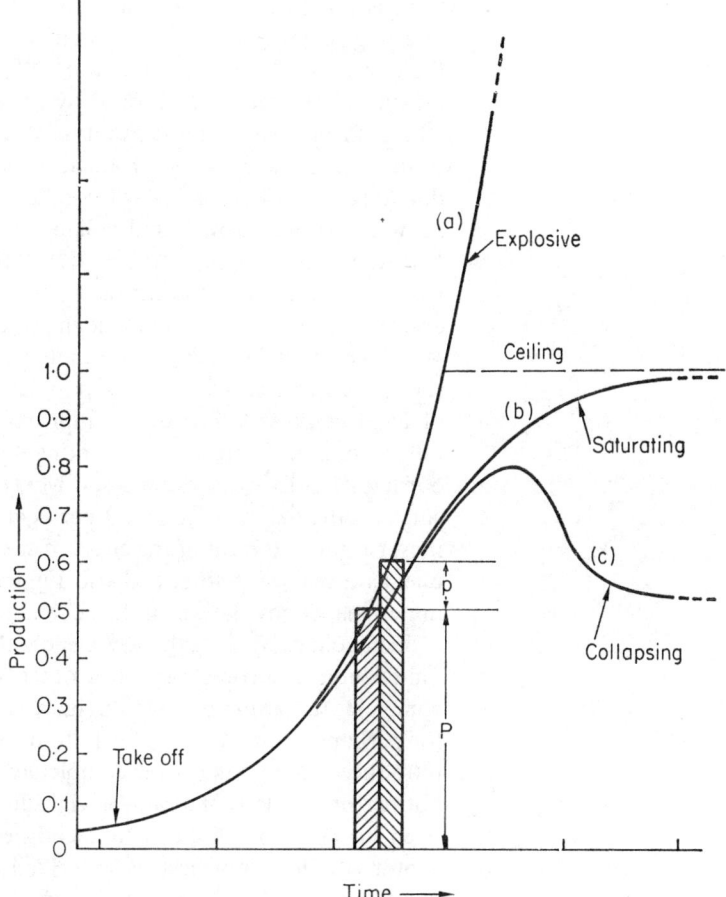

Figure 3.17. The logic of growth (three broad classes).

the whole production P made in the year before (i.e. demand *created* by production).

However, there are certain forms of 'production' which become seen as threats, not as blessings, when higher regions of the curve are reached. The example which first springs to mind is of course the so-called *population explosion*,[282, 331] (see also p. 47) about which so much has been heard since the end of the 1939–45 War. Another post-War example commonly discussed is the *document explosion*,[61] which signifies the alarm aroused in many people's minds (especially scientists) by the ever-growing flood of documents which 'have to be read', otherwise one's knowledge soon becomes 'out of date', or else one may carry out work already done by others and so become inefficient.

* Known in mathematics as an *exponential* curve. In practice the various growths do not follow such curves exactly, of course, they indicate only general classes.

Explosions cannot go on forever though, and curves such as those in Figure 3.17(a) will, at some time or other, begin to turn and very often become flat or *saturated* as in Figure 3.17(b) which shows a type of *logistic* growth curve. Such a growth corresponds to a steadily reducing rate of interest $p/P \times 100$ per cent. For example, even the population explosion cannot continue for ever;[327] it is stupid to argue that 'if the present birth and death rates continue unchanged there will soon not be enough land for us all to put both feet on the ground'. What can really happen is that various *checks* to growth will become felt, forces either to reduce the birth rate (e.g. contraception,[239] malnutrition) or to increase the death rate by the disasters of war and starvation;[280] checks can be voluntary, enforced, taught or imposed by Nature or by economics.

But all explosions must eventually come to a peak and flatten off. The third stage in the curve of 'production', shown as (c) in Figure 3.17, is always due to some sudden change of conditions. For example Figures 2.2a and b show the steady growth and collapse of railway traffic in Britain and the U.S.A. around the year 1919;[123,333,334] the railways had caused the same fate to their predecessors, the canals, by buying them up after the 1840s, but not destroying them. (They continued in use, but with greatly reduced traffic.)[78,295] What destiny is in store for the motor car remains to be seen; but there are signs, such as redistribution of populations, shops, offices, etc., and growth of local centres, by virtue of improved telecommunication and computer links; congested streets and parking lots will eventually force changes in our habits of living, shopping and working. Similarly, television has reduced cinema attendance to some 30 per cent (Figure 2.1). Such collapse, seldom if ever total, is typical of the effect of some new technology upon a previous one, as discussed before. See also Figure 6.6, which shows the sudden drop in newspaper circulations in the U.K., after 1957, due to several causes.

Such collapsing growth curves show the fates of inventions which become old-fashioned in some respect or other though the collapse is rarely total and complete; rather the production figures fall to some lower level and stay there (or perhaps continue very slowly to decline). To repeat: an invention newly introduced rarely takes over completely from an earlier one, because it does not perform exactly the same social function; new inventions tend rather to open up new possibilities and social needs and priorities become changed. Motor cars have not destroyed the railways (Figure 2.2), nor has the radio destroyed reading (Figure 6.5 and Chapter 6, Section 6), nor aircraft destroyed shipping (Figure 2.3). To regard invention as a taking-over process rather than an opening-up process is to mistake the nature of technology.

The pessimistic view is often expressed today that, in spite of economic aid being offered to the poorer countries, the gap between rich and poor is still increasing. It may be worth noting here that this frightening truth is an inevitable consequence of the fact that the richer industrialized countries expect to *preserve* any growth rates at all let alone raise them. It inevitably follows from the very idea of economic growth, in a world where countries start industrializing at different times in history: it is the result of the 'compound interest' law. A simple diagram can illustrate this.

The simple diagram of Figure 3.18 shows (a) the increasing wealth of some hypothetical country, having a *constant* growth rate of 5 per cent per annum; the curve (b) is identical, representing the wealth of another country which started industrialization only 30 years later. These are identical 'compound interest' curves. Because of the increasing steepness of such curves the gap must increase with time. These figures are arbitrary; the same principle applies whether the growth rates are 2 per cent, 10 per cent or any other, provided they are held constant.

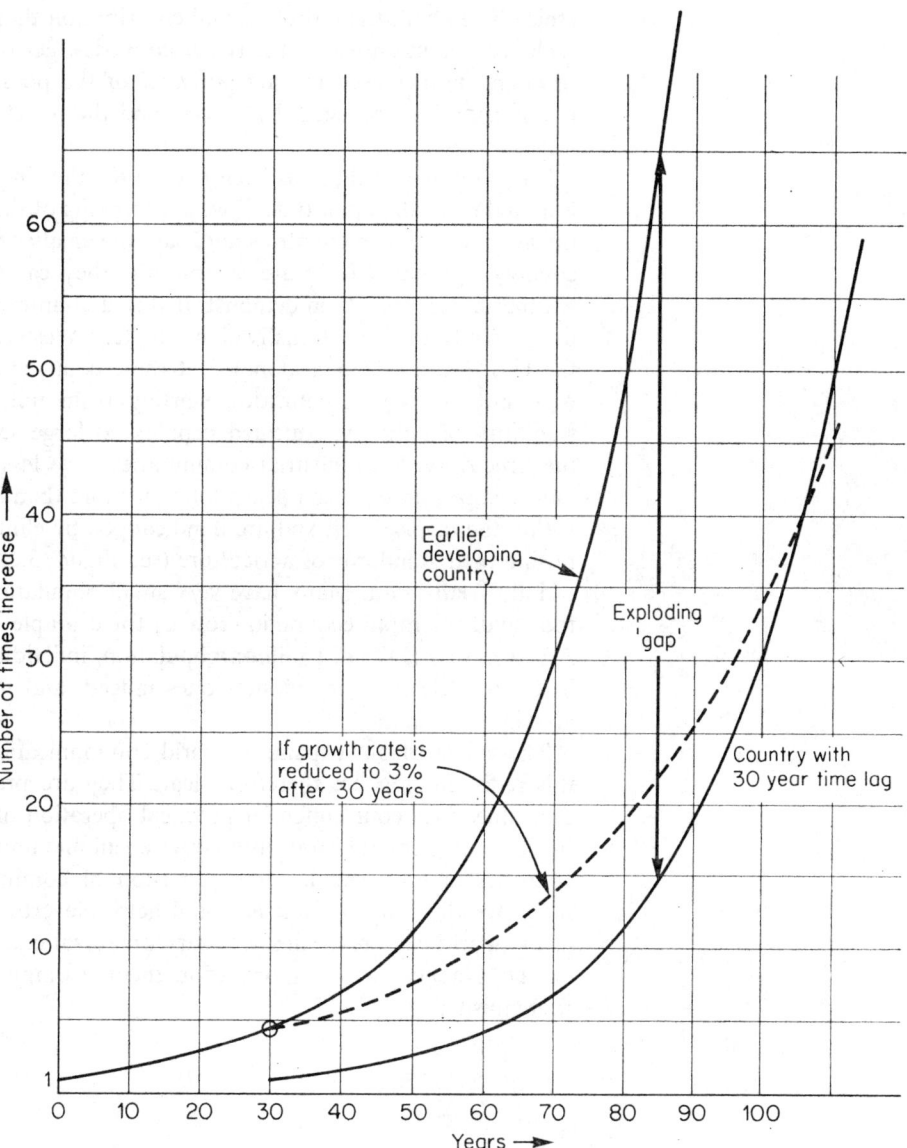

Figure 3.18. The exploding economic gap. (Two hypothetical countries, each having 5 per cent growth rates, but having a 30 year time gap.)

The only ways for the gap to be narrowed are either (1) for the richer country to reduce its growth rate drastically or (2) for the poorer country to raise its growth rate far above that which the richer one has ever been able to achieve. For example, Figure 3.18 shows the result of the richer country reducing its rate from 5 per cent to 3 per cent, and who ever heard of any country choosing that policy? Perhaps we should not put the blame upon the greed of the rich, for we have all felt need to climb out of the mud, nor upon the laziness of the poor, but rather upon the historical time gap itself. But in an industrializing world the battle cry: 'We must keep our growth rate up!'

must ensure that the national rat race can never be won; it is a handicap race, with the contestants starting at different times.

Such a 'closing of the gap' would imply an immense redistribution of the world's productive resources with an equally immense change of political ethics. Even with the pitifully small contribution that we now make towards such redistribution we, in the richer countries, get back more than we give, through the increased trading potential of the poor. Our growth rates are not substantially reduced, by choice, and the mans gap grow increasingly large.

The 30 year gap that has been chosen for the simple diagram Figure 3.18 is a mighty small gap of time, if we are thinking of the economic gap between the affluent Western countries and, say, the smaller States of Africa. But no country's growth curves are as smooth; they can be very erratic indeed. Furthermore, it has been demonstrated that countries devastated by war can indeed recover at exceptionally high rates (e.g. Western and Eastern Germany, the U.S.S.R. and Japan alone). But these countries, after war devastation, were not developing countries, starting from nothing; they already had traditions of industry, educated people and large scale organization to aid their recovery. Pre-industrial communities have less advantage, whilst their industrialization has been delayed by far more than 30 years. All of them lie within the tropical belt and are handicapped by climate and environment in raising their standards of agriculture (see Figure 3.2), an essential precursor of industrialization. Many have very small populations and are individually too small for rapid economic growth; for example half of the countries of Africa have less then $3\frac{1}{2}$ million population, individually.[140] Thus the curves in Figure 3.18 are very modest ones indeed, and merely indicate how the growing gap arises.

The values of our expanding world communication network for assisting this redistribution are therefore clear. They are practical values; they are the values they could offer for practical operation of *federations* of national bodies both rich and poor, into larger economic units. Too many individual countries are too small. Mere provision of communication channels will not solve the problem, but it would help. Nevertheless, no amount of will in the world can create the necessary organizations and institutions if there are no practical ways of operating them. Communication is an essential prerequisite.

4

Communication, Politics and Pleasure*

'They eat with their fingers instead of chopsticks. . . . They show their feelings without any self control. They cannot understand the meaning of written characters (i.e. Chinese script). They spend their lives roaming about without any fixed abode, and barter what they have for what they have not. They are, however, a harmless sort of people.'

From a 16th century record of the first Portuguese to reach Japan. (Quoted by Dr. Raghavan Iyer†.)

1. A vision of world communication in the year 1866

On July 27th, 1866, *The Times* of London published an article headed 'Shrinking World', in which these sentences appeared:‡ 'So far as human foresight can judge, the Old and the New World will be in telegraphic communication before tomorrow night. The prospect opened to the world by this achievement is so marvellous that any attempt to describe it must give only a faint and feeble picture. The two most active and energetic nations of the globe are placed in hourly communication. The Governments of England and the United States will be able to converse rapidly and freely, removing misconceptions should they arise, and transacting their affairs without the delay of a voyage during which the face of events may be changed. To the mercantile interests of both countries the gain must be immense . . . also for corresponding with British North America§. . . . Indeed, now that the great enterprise is completed, there can be no doubt that in a few years the entire globe will be spanned by the telegraph wires, and the news of the planet will be given every morning in the London papers. The Atlantic makes the only great break in the continuity of the land of the globe. The three old Continents are a single mass. . . . By bridging the Atlantic these two great systems are brought into connexion. It is a great work, a glory to our age and nation, and the men who have achieved it deserve to be honoured among the benefactors of their race.'

If theirs was 'only a faint and feeble picture' of the future, ours today of what their world was like a century ago can be little better. We can scarcely imagine the full drama of this announcement and can have little feeling for what life was like for men of responsibility, who had national decisions to make and information weeks old upon which to make them. (See Chapter 2, Section 7.) I do not believe that the announcement of the first Sputnik, or of communication satellites in modern times made any comparable impact. The most important and immediate implications of the *instantaneous* property of telegraphs were clear and obvious to industrialists and Governments in

---

* Certain items in this Chapter draw upon the author's article in the volume *Communication* (Ed. Lee Thayer), Charles Thomas, Illinois, 1967.[48]

† From Dr. Iyer's Introduction to: *The Glass Curtain between Asia and Europe*, Oxford Univ. Press, London (with kind permission).

‡ Reproduced with kind permission. Report abbreviated here.

§ i.e. Canada.

1866—the result of removal of very long frustrating delays—but those of the first commercial communication satellite, in 1965, were not. Again, though computers are now seen to have the power to transform the world as much as telegraphs did, it has taken several years for the picture to become clear. At first, computers were conceived and constructed as simple hand operated arithmetic machines; then as automatic (programmed) calculators. Later, their powers to assist business, accountancy, record offices, banks, etc., as 'automatic filing cabinets' were realized. Only subsequently were their values appreciated for automatic control of industrial processes (automation) and for assisting with decision making in Government, business, and other complex organizations. E.g. see G. A. Miller, *Advancement of Science*, **XXI** Jan. 1965, p. 417.

It is noteworthy that, in the article quoted above, *The Times'* first thoughts regarding the new telegraphs were upon their value to *Governments* by the removal of the dangers inherent in the time delay caused by the slow speed of ships, 'during which the face of events may be changed' (see Chapter 2, Section 7 on this topic). Furthermore, only the modest claim was made of 'removing misconceptions should they arise'. No sweeping claims were put forward nor rosy visions of 'contributing to world peace and understanding'; such noble words and sentiments are more 20th century in tone.

The Times article gave as its second thoughts the immense gain likely to be offered to mercantile interests by the telegraph, the first instantaneous mode of communication. The first long-haul overseas telegraph opened up, at last, the possibility of organized international industries. *The Times* next gave as its third opinion that the new Atlantic telegraph would have great value for news reporting; weeks would be lopped off delays in reporting world events in newspapers, thereby creating a totally new situation, the likely consequences of which were, we notice, not guessed at.

It should be remembered that, in that year 1866, *news* and *newspapers* reached only a relatively small fraction of the population, although circulations in Britain at that date were growing at their fastest rate; from 1856 (after Repeal of the Stamp Tax) to 1882 circulations increased several hundred per cent.[44,252,346,356] (Raymond Williams gives the figure of 600 per cent, saying that, by 1850, daily papers in Britain were read by about 1 adult in 80, and by the end of the 19th century, some circulations were measured in hundreds of thousands.[44,355]) In Britain the penalizing Stamp Tax had held back the spread of newspaper buying, although illicit, duty-avoiding papers were circulating among the working class in the industrial North of England in tens of thousands during the 1830s, stimulated by the Chartist Movement.[295,346] (In 1839 the *Northern Star*, which was such a paper, sold 50,000 copies per week.)[250,355]

At the date of this *Times* article, 1866, newspapers were just entering the period of mass-reading; the 'Golden Age of Journalism' had begun.[252]

2. Modern communication media and our personal attitudes

The century-old *Times* report, quoted at the beginning of this Chapter, has not been shamed by history. It was down-to-earth, modest and practical. It basically predicted what has come to pass; the great world networks of today, stemming from the telegraph, most successfully serve practical, day-to-day operations of various *institutions*. However, the public today, after two World Wars, revolutions, popular education, newspaper expansion, radio, colonial independencies, and a host of other forces upon them for 'world awareness' may often expect far more. This world awareness today, when and where it exists, has been instilled in us almost entirely *through* the various technical media of world communication, e.g. news reports in newspapers, or by radio, films, books, tourism, television documentaries, etc., and the major institutions operating thereby, Government agencies, schools, broadcasting authorities, etc. These media may then give an illusion of having great power, and the more they expand the more power they seem to have. Perhaps this illusion is one source of today's concern, so often heard expressed, that the world does not seem to be getting much better, but *ought* to.

Communication media have, of course, no power whatever in themselves. They are dead, inanimate things. The power resides in the people who use them. They may serve to *multiply* the power of these people of course. They have no more power themselves than flags have, pieces of coloured cloth. The power of flags arises from people's *beliefs* in them. One flag waved in the street might arouse little interest, but increase them to a thousand and you may be swept up in patriotic fervour.

Similarly the power of communication media resides in people. One telegraph line could not be expected to do much towards world unity; but now that we have thousands of opportunities for speaking to and seeing one another across the world we might expect the net to draw us ever closer together and be disappointed that it doesn't seem to do so. The fault does not lie in the media, however, but in people and their circumstances, attitudes, emotions and beliefs. And these are not so readily and quickly changed by mere installation of technical apparatus. After all, a broadcasting station is nothing more than a big megaphone.

Such positive powers for national, or world, constructiveness which all our communication media give to us are therefore not exposed by studying them as technical *things*, any more than a study of flags would help us understand patriotism or national relations. We should rather try to examine what among the specific powers which we various peoples possess are, or could be, multiplied or enhanced by our various different communication media. We must not generalize about all, or any, of them as being 'good' or 'bad' but we should be specific, saying to *whom*, on *what* occasion, *how* used, etc. Nor would a study of politics be of value if no references were made to the technologies which various nations possess to press their policies with: types of armaments, ships, machines, communication, transport, etc. It is the relation between the two, policies and technologies, that is significant, the uses made of these physical means. With regard to the very varied uses of communication media in politics, the expressive term 'political articulation' has been coined[248] to denote the effectiveness with which various media, such as radio, press, film, etc., are used by countries in different stages of development, to change the attitudes and behaviour of others within a polity and also to communicate across the boundaries of other cultures: the essential elements of politics.[177]

Over and over again, in newspaper reports and in technical literature, the idea is voiced that the installation of some new communication link between countries or the continents 'will help towards peace and international understanding'. In other contexts, on other occasions, other people will insist that: 'It will only be used for propaganda'. What is the truth; do expanding world communications help or hinder? Certainly, the absence of communication media in the past has been a source of troublesome frustrations, but whether or not any particular new link, an airway, an overseas broadcasting station, a film sent abroad, actually does help or not depends wholly upon the people involved in its use.

I should like to be able to decide in my own mind a simple answer to this question for, as one who has spent a lifetime in the field of telecommunications, I should be easier in my conscience. But there is no single and simple answer. Rather we have to ask first: what *sort* of communication? News reporting? Telephones? Airways? Books? Eurovision? Telegrams? A host of different media are subsumed under the blanket term 'communication'.

In my own view some meaningful answer is found if we remind ourselves that the rapid expansion of world communication has not progressed equally in all media; some have been developed far ahead of others and have produced an imbalance, with the result that we, in different countries, with different languages, customs, histories and traditions are today trying to operate with a superabundance of some media and with inadequacy of others.

Furthermore, we cannot judge this imbalance of the media as they exist at the present day solely in terms of their statistics, their economics or their technical efficiencies. We should also consider their very different *significances* to different peoples. For example, in Western industrial countries more faith may be placed upon news reported in print than upon the same news received verbally (i.e. by radio, or word of mouth); spoken reports may, after all, be 'rumours', to *us*.[4] It must be different in illiterate societies,[253] and the trustworthiness of news to them may depend upon other criteria: *who* it is that is telling the story perhaps.[4] In the Second World War, for example, people in Britain changed their criteria in just that way; the B.B.C. News Bulletins assumed great importance here (and, it is said, in the Occupied Countries too) because the confidence they inspired was strengthened by the fact that they were verbal, and the Announcer was identified by giving his name in his familiar voice. Trust then necessarily depended more upon the source (the speaker, the voice, the B.B.C.) than upon the medium, *per se*.

The different *significances* which one and the same medium may have to countries in various stages of development can be very varied and surprising. Who would have thought, before the Second World War, that cheap radio sets would have spread through the Middle East and African countries like wildfire, to play a major part in political change?[248] Western films have long been seen by African and Asian audiences, and many of us have felt anxiety about the impressions of Western life which some of them may have left. Herbert Hyman's findings may comfort us perhaps; for what might we think would be the effect upon Burmese audiences of films with such titles as: 'Loving You', 'Rock Baby Rock', 'She Demons'? Hyman found that 'the impression was predominantly favourable'.[248] It is more likely *we* who may be shocked. Such a visual medium must have quite different significance to them and, rather than be impressed by what we would call 'the story', they may be more impressed by sheer visual display, the pictures as pictures, like being more impressed by the coloured wrapping of a chocolate than by the chocolate itself.[248]

Leonard Doob has shown how we in the West may be equally well deceived in our interpretations of rituals, symbols, family and tribal customs of other peoples, quoting many examples.[71] As technical means of communication spread among countries, rich and poor, to magnify their powers of expression, in their own symbols, so may the dangers of misinterpretation be magnified. Mere increase of these technical means (radio, film, documentaries, T.V. and even tourism) may possibly drive us farther apart rather than draw us together, *internationally*, that is. Within a country or a developing area, on the other hand, communication media are urgently needed, especially the mass media, as Unesco has pointed out[301, 302, 307, 320] and many sociologists have emphasized.[248, 262, 265, 266]

The most clearly constructive contributions to 'world peace and understanding' which modern international media of communication will make are in those fields of international relations where the needs are held more in common; food, health, trade and all the various essential mechanics of living which, though they are of course exploited by politicians, do not themselves form the symbols whereby national, political, religious, and other cultural beliefs are *expressed*, at least not directly. If we listened only to the political affairs of the U.N. we might well despair at much of the debate. Unfortunately, it is these debates which reach the headlines most readily. If more publicity could be given to the enormous body of constructive work done by Unesco and other special agencies[82, 200, 309, 318] (which deal with the mechanics of living, through international technical committees) it might put better perspective on the world scene today (see Section 5 of this Chapter). Unfortunately, technical matters are not regarded as being of much interest by the 'popular' press in the West; they are insufficiently Ludenic (see Chapter 2, Section 5, p. 41),[284] another example of the importance of *significance* of media. Nevertheless, it is first and foremost through their practical contribution to international organization that the media are today of such value to 'world peace and understanding'.

The very rapid increase in the number and variety of International Organizations[82, 200, 323, 324] since the 1939–45 World War is one of the characteristic 'explosions' of these times which was not described in the previous Chapter; a brief account will be given in the next Section.

We have already made a brief examination of the various technical media available to us today and of the very different qualities that each contributes to human communication (Chapter 2, Section 6). They have both organizational and emotional powers. It is through these various and different media that we not only report our news, execute our business, conduct our trade, travel, but we also learn about one another with varied accuracy and build our mental images of other peoples, etc. And according to the media used so our images will vary. This is true even in the simple case of transport. For example, visiting a foreign country by air is quite a different experience from going by sea and overland routes; in one case you merely arrive with great efficiency and with no knowledge of the intervening gap (except the weather) whilst in the latter case you have been impressed by great distances and times, by conversations with fellow travellers, perhaps by the appalling conditions of roads, by foreign food, and many things. Unfortunately the increasing use of air travel, which varies in extent in different countries (Chapter 3, Section 5), may conceivably lead us or our children to develop too rosy a picture of the world; but tourism is a topic I should like to raise again later, in Chapter 6, Section 2.

I have referred earlier (Chapter 1, Section 7) to the great scientist Schrödinger as saying that the mental picture of the world we each have is not of the world 'as it is', but as we have been *taught* to see it by our parents and others, and by our predecessors through literature in our own language.[268] If this be true of the physical world, how much truer must it be of our mental pictures, our imaginings, of other peoples and their doings and sayings! For none of us can experience more than a very minute part of the world, nor encounter more than a few of its people in a lifetime;[193] virtually the whole of our knowledge and beliefs about other peoples are constructed from reports, spoken, written, painted, photographed. . . . We read their literature, where it exists (in translation), or newspapers based upon 'on the spot' reports and journalist's interpretations. We may see films, giving vivid glimpses of happenings torn from their context; we may travel as tourists, preconditioned by our own history books. However we construct our pictures, they must depend upon the various media of communication we happen to possess and upon the ways we have habitually come to use them. We do not need to look beyond the shores of our own country to see the truth of this. Thus many young people drop the reading of literature after leaving school, having had a bellyful of it there; 'books' are what have to be studied and analysed for 'exams'. Nevertheless they may watch a T.V. serial based upon one of the same schoolbooks with great interest and, visually stimulated and refreshed, be moved to read it for pleasure.* Library book lending has rapidly increased since television started, at least in Britain (see p. 188). This of course does not imply that television is the direct *cause*. (See the lines on p. 187 concerning educational T.V. programmes and library books.) It is not a simple matter of intelligence either, for in early childhood television viewing is, on the whole, more prevalent among those of higher intelligence.[267]

Again, at least within the Western countries and those which have grown under their influence, newspapers serve several different functions apart from news reporting (see Chapter 2, Section 5, p. 36). The fact that world news, however tragic, is read within a context 'surrounded by the women's page, the sports page and the comics, and an accent of a few violent accidents' (see p. 39) may leave us with the impression that the world can't be so badly off, after all (Herbert Hyman, Ref. 248). L. W. Pye poses the hypothetical question: why shouldn't newly literate people see news this same way? Because they are likely to have learned their politics before, in a more stark context.[248] Our personal conditions will determine *how* we read, or hear, or see, the news. 'Propaganda may work with everyone else but never with the refugees themselves', wrote Martha Gellhorn.†

3. Overseas and international broadcasting

Clearly, any attempt to examine the influence of communication technology upon international relations must take into account broadcasts made in foreign languages.

The term 'propaganda broadcasts' is one which I should like to avoid for a moment, for it prejudges both the purposes of the broadcasting countries and the effects of their broadcasts. Furthermore, a great part of overseas broadcasting is not of *direct* political interest, but could equally well be considered as educational. We must expect different uses of radio to be made by different countries, according to their conditions of development, their feelings of security, the numbers of broadcasting stations they can afford, their expanding trade interests, even their growing sense of self-respect and pride in their own internal economic growth, their sense of importance in the world and political independence.

Overseas broadcasting is not lightly, frivolously or casually done. It is expensive. It is a thing which each country takes very seriously. They each

---

* Frank Stenton has made the comment that T.V. does this, whereas the cheap literature of the past did not.[283]

† In 'The Uprooted', in *The Guardian*, 26th September 1966.

possess only a limited number of suitable broadcasting stations and funds, so they can broadcast only a limited number of programmes during each 24 hours. Consequently, one of the first things they each have to decide is the *languages* in which they will speak, which is not necessarily determined by the countries covered because so many countries are multilingual and multiracial (especially some of the newly established ones). Broadcasting essentially addresses a person in his own *language*, and appeals directly to his linguistic loyalties, with their religious, cultural, historical overtones, and through those to his national and other group loyalties. We in Britain have to look no further than our own shores to see this, with the B.B.C. broadcasts in Welsh and our various Regional announcers chosen because they have the accents of their regions.

In this Section, the expression 'overseas broadcasting' will be used, without discrimination, and in a neutral way, confined entirely to facts and figures.[27,28,156] (The *World Radio and T.V. Handbook* publishes details of foreign language broadcasts, with times, wavelengths, etc., from most of the world's broadcasting stations.[160])

The first country in the world to broadcast in foreign languages was the U.S.S.R., who transmitted in both English and German in the mid-twenties; by 1930 they were broadcasting in some fifty languages and dialects.[57] Lenin himself in 1917 spoke of broadcasting as an 'international newspaper'.[109,180] The significance of this is difficult for us to appreciate, we who have never known a world without broadcasting; to feel just how slender were the threads of human connexion between nations until the coming of radio. Few of the population had travelled, except for diplomacy, emigration, war and trade; foreign books, even in translation, required literacy (and money); more contacts were made under conditions of war, invasion and occupation than any other way. Perhaps we should not try to comfort ourselves, even today, with the thought that international broadcasting is a great liberating force, that 'our voices can now span oceans'; because the great bulk of listeners in this world are still listening to the radio programmes of their own countries for most of the time.

This last statement is undoubtedly true, but I can offer no statistics to support it, for it is a fact that no broadcasting authority in the world knows with precision just how many foreign people listen to their broadcasts, particularly in less developed areas or in countries with whom they have few formal relations. They know even less about the effects of their programmes. Sample surveys are difficult enough to carry out in one's own country, but in other people's the difficulties are greatly magnified. Not only may the terrain and the low literacy rate be great barriers but, what is more important, in many areas the peasants may very naturally misunderstand the motives of questioners (even though they are local nationals); they may be suspicious or frightened. Furthermore, much listening is casual and people's memories are short. After all, carrying out a population census is hazardous enough in many parts of the world, so how can we reasonably expect to measure by census such a subjective matter as the effects of foreign language broadcasting, either in quantity or in nature? Broadcasting authorities have to make many guesses, and millions of pounds, dollars, roubles, yuan, and all other monies are spent according to this shaky accountancy. Broadcasting, although a form of international exchange, is quite different from trade in this respect; its effects and values cannot be judged by any simple form of economic measure.

It is true that, for example, the British Broadcasting Corporation, like other authorities, receives thousands of letters annually from listeners all over the world*; but such letters do not constitute a census sample, for several reasons. Thus, to write a letter you must be literate and, even then, you must have some strong motive for writing it and for paying the postage and taking the trouble. Such letters may be more of *qualitative* value, giving some evidence of the relative audience sizes for different types of programme and subject.

The facts about overseas broadcasting are known to a limited extent within areas where countries are closely related politically or where agreements exist for exchange of information.[28] Within Europe, for example, the amount of listening to foreign broadcasts is certainly high; probably a third of the people who have radio sets listen to foreign broadcasts in their own languages, 'at some time or other'; this is admittedly a vague statement, but such facts are necessarily vague, for no-one really knows precisely.† Listening to foreign broadcasts, within Europe at least, probably depends very much upon individuals, their interests, where they have travelled, their knowledge of language, what they have read and other factors. The same thing is likely to be true of people in other countries, at least with regard to technical, literary, language teaching, and similar programmes.

Language teaching is a specialized use of radio which has flourished in recent years.[27] Many countries are now teaching their own languages to foreign listeners both by radio and by T.V. film recordings sold, loaned or exchanged abroad for retransmission. The response is high and increasing. One of the most popular for English teaching is the series of B.B.C. film recordings called 'Walter and Connie' which are sent abroad for retransmission by T.V.; they are followed by some 20 million viewers and two series have now been issued; they 'have now been screened in forty-five countries in Eastern and Western Europe, Africa, Latin America, and Asia . . .'[27] (B.B.C. information.) The B.B.C. provides over 230 English teaching transmissions a week on sound radio too and sends recorded versions of these to 90 countries, free of charge,[27] including all countries of South America and many in Africa, Asia and Europe. English is fast becoming the world's *lingua franca*, among those people who have the need (see Chapter 6, Sections 5 and 6).

Radio and television can provide a very valuable service today for teaching *immigrants* and for helping them to settle down in the strangeness of their new host country. For example, the B.B.C. is doing this for Indian and Pakistani immigrants in Britain.[27]

Audiences measured in millions suggest that broadcasting has become a significant international force.[109] Outside West Europe, both Egypt and the U.S.S.R. are particularly active in teaching their languages to millions of listeners in other countries. The U.S.S.R. transmits in 72 foreign languages, whilst Egyptian activity is confined mainly to African languages. With regard to the amount and effect of *listening* to foreign countries' programmes, within the U.S.S.R. and other Communist countries, little is known.

The learning of foreign languages by listening to overseas programmes, especially those designed for teaching, is certainly increasing today and the numbers of 'students' are measured in millions. It is a mistake however, to regard these language programmes as actually doing the *whole* teaching, for learning requires activity on the part of the student. They may stimulate him,

---

* E.g. for some figures, see *B.B.C. Handbook*, 1967, p. 98.[27]
† Opinions expressed privately by members of the External Services Audience Research Department of the B.B.C. See also Refs. 27, 28, 29.

arouse his interest, challenge him, and so encourage him to do something about it. He may decide to attend classes or to join language clubs, buy books and language records, or take up pen friends abroad, or travel. Radio can be an effective teacher only if followed up by activity. On the other hand, radio can be of direct value to those people who are already well versed in a foreign language, but get inadequate opportunity to listen to it. Many people in Europe, for example, regularly listen to radio to 'keep up with their English': that most widespread *lingua franca* (see Chapter 6, Sections 5 and 6).

I have referred much to English! There is a traditional belief among those Englishmen who have never travelled farther than Calais or, if they have, have encountered only literate and educated people there like Travel Agents, Couriers, Head Waiters (but never a peasant), that 'everybody abroad speaks English'. This is, of course, rubbish. English may be the most wide-spread second *language* of any, used by foreigners, but it is spoken only by a minority of *people*. On the score of numbers of people, Chinese certainly wins. Spoken Chinese divides into distinct, but related dialects. Of these, Mandarin is the most common (about 70 per cent) of Mainland China's population, Wu dialects (about $8\frac{1}{2}$ per cent), Cantonese and Hunan (about 5 per cent) and Hokkien (about 4 per cent). Nevertheless, as a *lingua franca* for the purposes of international relations, of trade, of conferences and of travel, the English language is in widespread use around the globe.

This spreading of the English (spoken) language has been greatly en-couraged by broadcasting, for both the U.K. and the U.S.A., the major English speaking countries, were among the first to develop broadcasting. These, with Australian radio, are today still great forces for the spreading of spoken English abroad. This is not to say that English is spreading at the expense of other languages, nor that broadcasting will lead to the eventual extinction of minority languages. It will be argued later, in Chapter 6, Section 5, that broadcasting is most likely to be a force for *preserving* much of the world's language variety, not for reducing us all to one tongue. Polylingualism is more likely.

There are, then, two forces acting upon the principal broadcasting countries. In the first place there is the desire to *teach* others their languages by special teaching programmes, etc., partly for their own subsequent advantage and, in the second place, there is the desire to *reach* audiences in many countries who understand no second language; political forces for presenting their national and cultural images, ranging from pure slogan propaganda to scientific, cultural, scholarly programmes. The way in which these two forces balance and determine how any country shall distribute its available broadcasting resources, bearing in mind its own urgent domestic needs, will certainly vary greatly between the countries.

International broadcasting has been sullied from time to time by the practice called *radio jamming*, an attempt by one country to prevent its people from hearing the broadcasts of another, by diverting some of its own transmitters from their normal use to that of making a noise. It is rarely completely effective, except in areas close to the transmitters. The most wholesale experience of this has been within the U.S.S.R., during the post-War period when Stalin was trying to isolate his country and people from all contact with the world outside. By 1952 the whole of Eastern Europe except Yugoslavia was blanketed in an attempt to prevent the people from listening (an estimate has been made, that some 2000 transmitters were used for jamming in the U.S.S.R. alone[178]), but its ineffectiveness has been demonstrated on very many occasions of crisis. For example, during the Hungarian rising of 1956, 'Moscow University students had been pinning up bulletins of B.B.C. news . . . on their notice boards'.[178]

Poland was the first Communist country to cease jamming foreign broadcasts, in that critical year 1956, when her spokesman stated that 'the ideological battle could not be won by a refusal to listen to the other side of the argument'. It was then disclosed that jamming activities had cost Poland £500,000 per annum, 'enough to supply electric power for a medium sized town.'[212]

If broadcasting is an expensive business, so is jamming, for this also uses transmitting stations of high power. It is entirely negative and can be politically unwise, or self defeating, for it may serve as an advertisement for the competitor's goods while concealing what they are. It can arouse interest, as an unwrapped parcel does. To forbid is to raise desire. It is like refusing to tell your children 'where baby came from', which only makes them more determined to find out.

Jamming is quite the opposite to censorship. Censorship, as that word is commonly used, means action taken by governments or other authorities to prevent information being given, wittingly or in innocence, by its own people *to* some enemy. Jamming, on the other hand, is action taken to prevent an enemy communicating *with* those people. Letters are censored in wartime to prevent people from giving away information which might fall into enemy hands, or which might cause alarm and despondency among the home population or its troops in the field. Censorship unduly prolonged may be self defeating, by arousing suspicion or alarm. Jamming however makes a confession that there is an enemy within the gates who must be prevented from hearing and using the information, like a Trojan horse. It can be justified and of value only in just such circumstances, when a country's people are immature, or in a state of *internal* conflict and insecurity.

For a long time after the Second World War, the rift in Europe which Churchill called 'the Iron Curtain' was encouraged by radio jamming, by the U.S.S.R. and her satellites, but the political unwisdom of this was recognized when, on June 10th 1963, the Russians ceased the practice. Their jamming had already been greatly reduced in 1959 after the Anglo–Soviet Cultural Agreement,[212] and they have not resumed jamming against the West since, although jamming between Russia and China still continues. Certainly, it could be said that there was little purpose in continuing it because about half of the 70–80 million radio receivers in the U.S.S.R. are 'wired receivers'* and not radio; these receivers are anyway incapable of receiving overseas radio broadcasts. This would be somewhat of an uncharitable view though, because the geography and population distribution of the U.S.S.R. are well suited to wired receivers, and also to short-wave radio. In 1963, the year when the jamming stopped, there may have been up to 20 million short-wave receivers used in the U.S.S.R.[212] Furthermore, the proportion of *radio* receivers in the U.S.S.R. is rapidly increasing (ref: Unesco, *Statistical Yearbook*. Their figures are 'declared figures').

Improvement of our international radio relationships has steadily continued in recent years, at least within Europe, East and West, as shown by the rising statistics of programme exchange. Television shows the same trend.

---

* Ref: Unesco, *Statistical Yearbook*. These are 'declared figures'.[212]

Within Western Europe the various countries' T.V. services may be linked as the organized continent-wide network called Eurovision whilst Eastern European countries may be similarly connected into the network called Intervision. These two, Eurovision and Intervision, may on special occasions be connected together, thereby enabling common programmes to be seen throughout Europe, from Moscow to Madrid. The concept of Eurovision started to grow in 1950; Intervision came a little later.

These Eastern and Western groups of European countries have an organized system of exchange of T.V. programmes. For example, by 1963 Eurovision had already transmitted 49 T.V. programmes made available by Intervision countries, and in 1965 over 100 (see April 1966 edition of Ref. 144). Organized arrangements for exchange of television programmes, including news items, now exist on a global basis and the numbers exchanged between all countries are measured in tens of thousands. The problem of language is dealt with by 'dubbing' new sound tracks, especially for the Middle East, Latin America and the Far East.[27]

Such *organized* arrangements for exchanges between countries, planned by agreement, are of growing importance. There are the two ways of doing it: (a) by shared programmes, broadcast simultaneously (e.g. Eurovision) and (b) by direct exchange or sale of recorded programmes. Books have been doing a similar thing for the printed word (and for literate people) for very many years through the publication of translations (see Chapter 6, Section 6 and Figures). Anyone who has access to a T.V. receiver today is familiar with the idea of watching foreign programmes, or of participation in joint programmes, but he may not be aware of the great organization needed for doing this, which involves far more than programme exchange. The responsible bodies are known as the Broadcasting Unions (see Section 5, on the International Organizations), of which there are at present some half a dozen, all having as their principal aim the *promotion* of international broadcasting projects,[83] while the programme exchanges, etc., are actually *effected* by the various national broadcasting authorities. (They are referred to again in Section 6.) The European Broadcasting Union (E.B.U.) publishes a monthly *Review*.[83] The Communist countries of Europe are united under another organization, called The International Radio and Television Organization (O.I.R.T.) which publishes a quarterly journal *Radio and Television*.[144, 145] There are also the Asian Broadcasting Union[6] (A.B.U.), the Asociacion Interamericana de Radiodiffusion (A.I.R.), and the Union of National Radio and T.V. of Africa (U.R.T.N.A.).[340] All these Unions are concerned with promotion of international programme exchange.[160]

4. On propaganda The word *propaganda* was used first as an ecclesiastical term, being the name given to the Committee of Cardinals in the Roman curia, *Congregatio de propaganda fides*. This 'congregation for the propagation of the faith' was a committee 'having the care and oversight of foreign missions'; it was founded by Pope Gregory XV in the year 1622.* Since that day the word *propaganda* has come to be applied within many spheres of life, to mean 'an association, organized scheme, for the propagation of a doctrine or practice'.†

The word is bandied about today very freely, in conversation and in popular journalism, as a highly emotional term of abuse, and is frequently

---

* *Oxford English Dictionary* and *Encyclopedia Britannica* (11th Ed.)
† See *Concise Oxford Dictionary* and *Oxford English Dictionary*.

associated with that other misused term, mass-communication (see Chapter 2, Section 6). It is a word used in clichés and slogans, often in a mindless way, and it has served as a weapon for those people who believe that our modern mass-communication systems, radio, T.V., newspapers, cinemas, comics, 'cheap' books (though not, for some reason, expensive ones) are corrupting influences today, which the world would be better without. It is associated most often with other people's politics and with advertising; rarely do we hear the word used in connexion with education (not one's own, that is).

It is important to notice that there is nothing modern about the word *propaganda* and that these emotional and pejorative uses of the word are not the creation of the 20th century. In fact, such uses first appeared within the sphere of religion, round about the end of the 18th century (when religion and politics were less distinct than today), references being made to Catholics and Jesuits as *propagandists*. Thus, Southey in 1829: 'The propagandist of Atheism and the Jesuit both find facile converts'. The *Oxford Dictionary* quotes this and several such examples showing early uses of the word in both the religio–political and the politico–military spheres. Even the words 'propaganda war' appear in a quotation dated 1854,* whilst another, even earlier in date,† might well have been written in the mid-20th century: 'Derived from this celebrated society (i.e. the Committee of Cardinals), the name *propaganda* is applied in modern political language as a term of reproach to secret associations for the spread of opinions and principles which are viewed by most governments with horror and aversion.' (*O.E.D.*) Notice: *governments*, not people, whilst 'modern' meant 1842.

Propaganda has been going on since man first spoke. Man has always sought to persuade his fellows, to change their ideas, to assert himself, for without such desires and powers no change, no progress would have been possible. Propaganda, *per se*, stripped of all emotional prejudice, is not sinful, but is an essential tool of social evolution. Propaganda, as such, cannot be said to be 'good' or 'bad', neither can it be 'true' nor 'false'. It is morally neutral, and many serious writers on propaganda have stated this. See, for example, Ref. 92. Such qualities depend wholly upon the motives of the propagandist and upon his doctrines, or those of the missionary and his missions; a teacher can be sincere and altruistic or he can aim to corrupt; an advertiser may aim to sell a genuine product or rubbish. Proselytizing, teaching, advertising and all forms of propaganda, as such, are morally neutral and we should not condemn them, but rather judge the ways in which they are conducted in every case and the ends to which they are directed.[73]

Propaganda fides: propagation of the faith. Genuine and effective propaganda needs a faith, a firmly held set of beliefs; it does not consist of casual, wicked statements, conforming to no long-term policy except opportunism, changing with the winds. It was in this that the propaganda of Goebbels eventually turned against him and became his own undoing, for Nazism gave him no consistent philosophy for guidance, no real aims or positive policy.[31, 361] A good propagandist must be a zealot and not a cynic,[92] just as any good teacher must be in love with his subject. He must also have a real and genuine cause. He must be filled with desire to convert unbelievers whether religious or political, whether he is conducting a

---

* Abbott, J. S. C. *Life of Napoleon*, 1854. (*Oxford English Dictionary*.)
  † Brande, W. T. *A Dictionary of Science, Literature and Art*, 1842. (*Oxford English Dictionary*.)

campaign for literacy, for better hygiene or for uses of fertilizers in backward areas, or whether an anti-litter or anti-smoking campaign in an 'advanced' country. Whatever he is propaganding he must himself believe in and he must have a genuine desire to convert others to those beliefs, for their *own* good. Goebbels was perhaps the greatest zealot of them all, but he had nothing to be zealous about and no really consistent faith to offer.[72]

If we wish to search out the sin in political propaganda, if and where it exists, it is into the propagandist's beliefs that we should look, so far as we can infer these from our own interpretations of the jargon and language he is using; we should not question the fact that he is doing it at all. We can only then judge what he is saying in the light of what we know of the historical origins of those beliefs and try to understand why he holds them. The words we hear uttered may seem to us to be nonsense, or plain malicious lies, or a distorted half-truth, but the person who speaks them may see good reason to do so and may feel a burning sense of mission in so doing. The sin (if there be any sin) surely lies not in the ravings of that one solitary maniac, but in the whole circumstances that have produced him and led him to think, or forced him to think, and speak in the way he does and to have the support of his people.

I do not think it an over-charitable assumption to make that, if 'all men are born equal' then all are born equally reasonable. That is, that all men are made reasonable by Nature but can be made unreasonable by circumstances. Reasonableness is not a matter of racial genetics, but is determined by social conditions and experiences. A man may seem to us to be reasonable when he is in happy circumstances, but put him behind bars, or half starve him, or insult him, or *frustrate* him, and his attitudes to *us* seem to change. We are all reasonable people to ourselves, even in those moods when we know that we are behaving unreasonably, for even then we *know* that fact and feel it reasonable to be that way.

If you ask me now, was Hitler a reasonable man, the answer is clearly: no. He may have been reasonable as a baby and, had the European situation of the 1920s been otherwise, he might have grown to be a happy painter. Unfortunately it was not. His emotional tirades and mock-heroics had such great effect upon his young countrymen, not because he had a brilliant mind or because they were born stupid, but because the whole political situation of the day made it easy for him,[73] (e.g. see p. 110 of Ref. 31). Any fool can fan a fire. As Lindley Fraser has said: 'Propaganda can do no more than activate emotions which are already existent, if dormant, and bring them into full play and vigour';[92] hence National Socialism propaganda, though for long highly successful in Germany and among Germans living abroad, failed outside Germany and Communist propaganda has failed throughout the English-speaking world.[92]

What is the source of the strong feelings of 'horror and aversion' which can often be aroused by simple mention of the word *propaganda* today? The word has a sinister ring, setting up thoughts of evil, scheming people aiming to wear us down with words, for no positive purpose or justification. Such feelings have long existed, as quotations have shown, but they are especially strong and widespread among educated people today.

There are several reasons but, above all, there is the memory of the particular uses of propaganda made by Goebbels under the Hitler regime in the 1930s.[72, 361] Goebbels set up a radio propaganda machine of unprecedented size and one came to see vividly at that time (and really it was seen for the first time) the immense power which radio offered to the bloody-minded. He also used the cinema for propaganda, a particularly suitable medium for playing upon the emotions.[169,361] It was only in hindsight that the ineffectiveness of the German foreign propaganda *in the long run and outside Germany*, became apparent. At the time, in the 1930s, it was something new. Although radio had been harnessed to war long before, first being used for naval communication in the 1904–5 Russo–Japanese War, it had been mainly confined within the military sphere; but now the public saw *broadcasting* itself as a weapon. Something which had evolved until then as a thoroughly domestic institution, something for home entertainment, as domestic and personal as the Edwardian piano, was being used as a weapon. It was perversion.

Regarding Nazi Germany's radio propaganda in the 1930s, one thing should not be forgotten, namely, that foreign language broadcasting services in Britain, which might have been a counter force, were not started until shortly before the 1939–45 war began.* Germany's short-wave broadcasts to European countries were solely in German, aimed at Germans in the Saar, Austria and elsewhere, for there were 27 million people of German origin then living outside Germany.[361] Other countries broadcast in their own languages but did not answer, or attack them, in German, although, at the outbreak of War, some 25 countries were broadcasting in foreign languages to some extent (e.g. Vatican, France, Italy. . . .)[361] Public opinion in Britain, particularly, was against any such 'vulgar' forms of publicity and, until 1938, the British Council was our only major mouthpiece beyond Commonwealth countries.[92] Once war started, in September 1939, the B.B.C. rapidly built up its German and European Services (Figure 6.4) upon the principles of objective truth and consistency, not on moral grounds alone (for we were at war) but simply for practical reasons, because no propaganda can be effective *in the long run* if it is appreciably untrue or inconsistent.[92,180] The stupidity of departing from this policy was made very clear during the Suez crisis, when the Anthony Eden Government set up a short-lived propaganda station in Cyprus, which was quite independent of the B.B.C. Slanging matches serve no purpose and are not private if conducted by radio, for the whole world can either hear them or read of them in their Press.[345] The full story of this immense radio-war effort, of its part in confounding the enemy, of succouring occupied Europe and of preparing its Underground Forces for the Allied landings has not yet all been written, though the first part of it has.[181,254] This wartime investment in the B.B.C. External (overseas) Services provided Britain, after the Armistice, with the largest overseas broadcasting organization in the world (see Figure 6.3).[180]

There have been three basic philosophies of radio propaganda developed in Europe. First, that of Nazi Germany based on short-term expediency and taking no cognizance of truth in any sense, nor morals; a *short-term* policy which led to its own undoing.[72,254] Second, that of wartime Britain, joined by the U.S.A. in 1942, based on the assumption that the War would *not* be a short one, so that truth and consistency needed to be regarded, as essentials.†[180] Third, that of post-War Communist practice,[134] which does

---

* The B.B.C. started theirs in January 1938, in Arabic, with German following in September. See also Chapter 6, Section 5.

† Lindley Fraser, Chief Commentator of the B.B.C. German Service during the 1939–45 War, refers to situations in which lies can make effective propaganda, though only on a short-term.[92]

not necessarily interpret the word 'truth' in the sense of logic or of factual truth, nor does 'falsity' necessarily mean plain lies; 'true' and 'false' are what 'support' or 'contradict' the epistemological system of Marxism–Leninism. No questions of logical or factual consistency of statements arise, nor moral questions of 'lying' as we would interpret that word in the West. Within their system of thought, words are defined and used consistently, but they do not translate into the same words as used within the system of Western thought:[66,129] in Lenin's words: 'Our philosophy is not a dogma but a guide to action'. *Collected Works*, **XXI**. (1), p. 133.[134] Such *doubletalk*[92,129] is then not a short-term policy of expediency, as it often seems to us, but is propaganda guided by definite political principles. (See Barghoorn: *Soviet Doctrine on the Role of Propaganda* in Ref. 16.) Soviet political language distinguishes between *propaganda* and *agitation*. The first term is applied to the spreading of ideas and theories which require detailed explanation, locally and to small groups; the second, to political activity for influencing the 'consciousness and mood' of the masses, by spreading ideas and slogans.[66,90,134] Thus, in the Soviet view, our Western churches, schools, advertising, broadcasting, etc., are *agitators*, not propagandists.

Who tells lies? Peter Ouspensky sharply reminds us that we all do:

'What is lying?

As it is understood in ordinary language, lying means distorting or even in some cases hiding the truth, or what people believe to be the truth. This lying plays a very important part in life, but there are much worse forms of lying, when people do not know that they lie. . . . We cannot know the truth but we can pretend that we know. *And this is lying*. Lying fills all our life. People pretend that they know all sorts of things: about God, about the future life, about the universe, about the origin of man, about evolution, about everything; but in reality they do not know anything, even about themselves. And every time they speak about something they do not know *as though they knew it, they lie*.'*[233]

Many clichés and slogans fall under Ouspensky's definition of lying; so does much commercial pseudo-scientific advertising jargon,[183,281] so do most political speeches. We all lie in support of our deepest beliefs, or our national loyalties, not in any scheming, deliberate sense of the 'bloody lie', but because we cannot bear (or bother) to do otherwise. This is firmly brought home to any traveller on foreign soil, when he is challenged upon some doings or sayings of his own Government; he may find himself trying to justify, or to excuse, whereas he speaks out loud against them when back home. But he has not travelled there like Sir Henry Wotton's ambassador, . . . 'an honest man sent to lie abroad for the good of his country'.†

To return to our present discussion: a second reason why many people fear propaganda in its modern forms may be due to their gross overestimation of the powers of radio, T.V. and the Press. Such fears are nothing new, and have been aroused several times in history, at the introduction of any new mode of communication.

Thus, I need hardly remind readers of all the book-burnings that have taken place in history, in the name of religion, or morals, or politics,[75,236] from Biblical times (e.g. St. Paul in Acts XIX, 19) to the Nazi book-burnings of the 1930s, all done in 'the public interest', nor of the Roman Church's

---

* With kind permission of the publishers, Hodder and Stoughton, London.

† Written in 1604. For discussion of this 'merriment' and of James the First's displeasure see *The Guardian* (Miscellany, Aug. 10; Correspondence Aug. 14 and 17, 1967).

Index Librorium Prohibitorum, nor of the continued censorships today,[75, 88] made for reasons of State security, or education, or subversion or protection of the morals of the young and on other grounds of 'public protection', in all countries.

In Oliver Cromwell's day the new postal service (see Chapter 2, Section 4) caused alarm in the breasts of the government; why? Because letters might be opened by the ill-intentioned; Cromwell was frightened of spies, *and he was Public Protector*. Two hundred years later the new telephone was considered likely to lay people open to blackmail, because conversations might be overheard. Broadcasting too: even the great reformer Beatrice Webb, and others, realized the immense *potential* for corruption and control of whole populations, before a public broadcasting service was even set up, in 1922.[24] Authorities are always paternal: *the public must be protected.* Of the fears aroused by television, I need say no more here (see Chapter 2, Section 5) but refer to the findings of serious enquiries into these.[121, 267] So with all new modes of communication; libraries are watched over by those officials responsible for public morals; films, T.V. plays, advertisements and 'cheap' literature are censored or criticized for their content of horror, violence and sex, two hundred years after Dr. Johnson first sounded a note of anxiety (see Chapter 2, Section 5). Yet if you want to read anything really disgusting, written by imaginations which have deliberately searched out every sickening image of horror they could conjure up, you need read nothing more modern than some of the medieval and premedieval descriptions of purgatory. There was propaganda for you! Hell was no simple clean fire to burn the souls everlastingly but its meaning was rubbed home in vivid, mind-searing language which makes our horror comics pale by comparison.[182] Or you may contemplate the fearful penances of the early Saints, no doubt willingly adopted, or the sickening tortures of the 17th century Jesuits, inflicted upon sinners *for their own good* and *accepted* by them as right and just, and from which their eventual burning to death was not a merciful release but an entry into a purgatory far worse*[131] The Europe of the 17th century could tell us all about 'brain-washing', and more.[31]

Nor were the children spared such propaganda,[182] for the same principle applied then, as today, that propaganda of all kinds plays most effectively upon the young. Minds are formed early in life into moulds which are not readily reshaped in adulthood.[31, 92] Re-education of adults is far from easy, whether into new ways of thinking, or new habits of living, or buying, even of using new household equipment, or into new political, religious, philosophical, social attitudes and beliefs. Our basic selves are formed early. The great historical examples of adult conversion are rare; there have been few Sauls, few Donnes and, today, few political 'defectors'. The *masses* are not converted by propaganda, though their children may be.

It is a false notion that man is a helpless being, who is manipulated by individual schemers, by advertisers, by propagandists armed with the mass-media: by Them.†[261] Manipulators can only manipulate those who are prepared to be manipulated, and children have little alternative though, as Schramm and others have emphasized, even our children are not helpless,

---

* Thus, Thomas à Kempis (*Of the Imitation of Christ*, Chap. XXIV, paras 2, 4): 'There is no sin but shall have its own proper torment. . . . One hour of pain there shall be more bitter than a thousand years of the sharpest penance here! There is no quiet, no comfort for the damned there . . .'.

† See Schils and Janowitz: *Cohesion and Disintegration in the Wehrmacht in World War II* in Ref. 16.

silent, stupid puppets but can indeed be critical and choosey of what they read or see on the T.V.[121,267] They can also be damning about their teachers on occasions! The facts about persuasion by the mass-media have been greatly exaggerated into fiction;[11,65] it is an example, as I have said already, of the fear that all our media of communication have aroused in past history, since man first learned to write.

This concern about 'manipulators' today is undoubtedly connected with the power apparently possessed by the owners of newspapers and their Editors;[77] but the power of such people is restricted in many ways. The 1949 Report of the Royal Commission on the Press[125] showed that in Britain, (whose newspapers have the highest circulations in the world*)[44,320,355] the ownership and control of newspapers was very varied, and included joint stock companies (the most common), trusts, co-operatives and private individuals; further, that the motives of different papers varied greatly, including politics, profit, causes, tradition maintenance, pride of good publishing, and others.[355] 'There (was) nothing approaching monopoly in the Press'; the main national newspapers had a circulation which, in total, hovered round about 20 per cent of total circulations. The Report's conclusions expressed no concern at all. The Report of a second Royal Commission, 1961–62,[126] was set up specifically to examine the economic and financial aspects of publishing, following upon public concern arising from a rather sudden reduction in the numbers of British newspapers. This, too, expressed no anxiety, though it made some recommendations.[44] Walter Lippmann has pointed out that there are relatively few journalists and reporters to do the job of reporting upon the vast canvas of daily world events;[193] they each can only be in one place at once and, by telephone, Telex and other means gather such news as they can, and report it to Agencies and offices. There it is sifted by *different* people and so, through a whole sequence of selections by 'copy tasters', sub-editors and editors it eventually reaches the Chief Editor's desk.[44] No one man selects that news, but many.[197] Those who have financial control may try to exert a general policy, but their readers are not their helpless prey. Neither do they necessarily know what their readers want and are prepared to pay for.[197]

The notion of mass-communication being a modern institution through which 'they' (the manipulators) control 'us' (the helpless public) is nonsense. Communication is, as I emphasized in Chapter 1, not a thing which proceeds *from* any one sender *to* a receiver: it is a net of mutual involvement, a sharing. Most simply put, any individual is subject to influences, not from one, but from many different sources, not only those of newspapers and other mass-media, but those of his friends, his family, his colleagues; he is under the influence of his own education and his whole life experience. He has a host of loyalties to different groups pulling upon him. And, unless there is some World Conspiracy of which I am unaware, all these manipulators are not acting in concert, but are playing upon his interests and loyalties in a variety of ways.[11,163]

There are more subtle and important forms of propaganda than those of mass-communication, which are also less conspicuous. There is propaganda by omission and propaganda through censorship, which may be quite well-meaning in some cases; for instance, by virtue of the fears of teachers and librarians that controversial books on their shelves could be embarrassing.[88]

---

* Ref. Unesco *Statistical Yearbook*.[312]

Above all, there is the propaganda written into school history textbooks, not only the deliberately 'rewritten' history books of totalitarian States, but that unconsciously written through inheritance of national traditions, legends, heroics and hatreds.[128] Unesco has been actively concerned with this source of international strain.[1] Although it may be considered that objective writing of history, devoid of racial, national, class and other bias, is not possible, because writers are themselves involved in the historical processes described, nevertheless many of the worst excesses of nationalisms might well be avoided. For example, see *Cyprus School History Textbooks*[179] which gives extracts of literal translations from books written in Greek for Greek Cypriots and in Turkish for Turkish Cypriots showing how old feuds are kept alive. As the Introduction says, '. . . let us be clear: the Cypriots are certainly no worse than others. . . .' The language of many history books extracts out of reality, which may for ever remain concealed. Our beliefs and imaginings of 'great' events may be pure fiction created to support our beliefs today. Television and film may yet knock out some of the glory and heroics of war that history books and narrative verse have written into it.

At the time of writing, much news is heard and seen daily about the doings of the young Chinese Red Guards, waving their little red books, *The Thoughts of Chairman Mao* and chanting extracts.[202] Do they chant them because many cannot *read*? Within our early Medieval churches, many peasants too were illiterate and could not read Latin or English.[2] But they could learn the services by heart and chant them. But what exactly *is* a Red Guard and what does it feel like to be one? The truth is that we can have very little idea at all. All we know about is what they are reported as doing; interpretation is hardly possible, for most of us, in terms of our own European experiences. We are in little better position to understand than would be a Martian watching an American football game. The words Red Guards and *Thoughts of Chairman Mao* are used by us as symbols. Have you ever read this little red book, for instance?—an English translation has been published in London.[202]

What may be even more important than the growth of our own knowledge of events in 'the mysterious Orient' in modern times, is the fact that the countries East of Suez now know much more about us, and through the very same media of communication which Western technology has created: radio, film, T.V. and newspapers. Our increased knowledge, such as we have, may be enlightenment to us; theirs may seem quite different, for they may increasingly see us as 'the inscrutable West'. The East and many uncommitted nations have so far built their images of us, the Western industrial countries, not so much through propaganda which we may have pumped at them, but more through plain brute facts.

It is we in the industrial countries who had a monopoly of communication until the end of the Second World War, with our newspapers, radio, films and books. This situation has been changing rapidly within the past decade or so.[320] It has been we who have owned the greater part of the world communication network and who have been presenting our own images to *them*, with the implication that it is our industrial cultures which they should imitate. We in the West have been obsessed with words, surrounded by a great sea of print, talk, advertisement, instructions and advice to others. We should now *listen* more, and listen to the sort of questions which other people in the world would like to ask us. So far, they've had little chance to get a word in edgeways. We should stop sending out questionnaires to other people, with our own presumed questions and sent out blank sheets instead, for *their* own questions.

Propaganda, in the proper sense of that word, can be a vital factor in human emancipation. Without it we shall neither learn about one another, nor about ourselves, but shall remain for ever ignorant. Propaganda, one day, may perhaps come to be used in the way that Matthew Arnold defined 'criticism': as 'a disinterested endeavour to learn and propagate the best that is known and thought in the world'.

5. The growth of International Organizations

Within the Western industrial countries our daily news has a major content of tragedies and disasters, of rifts and strifes. Success is less commonly news. It is as though we are unduly conscious, even obsessed, by the possibility of things not going right: we feel they *ought* to in the 20th century and, when they don't, it's worth reporting (see Chapter 2, Section 2). In Communist countries, newspapers publish lists of production statistics and 'economic achievements', etc. which, to us, would make dreary reading in our daily newspapers. It is not our custom; such data are to be found more in technical journals, in government and other special publications. They are not *news*; except the Stock Exchange price lists! It is natural too that in developing countries every positive achievement is newsworthy.

One consequence of our Western concentration upon negatives, read as *news*, may be to inhibit our attention from seeing the vast number of positives being achieved today, many of them small by themselves, but jointly of great importance in the way in which they contribute to the expanding world of international relations. To a Western reader, a reported speech made by some minor politician may be more newsworthy than some minor treaty or trade agreement made that same day. The debates and arguments within the General Assembly of the U.N. take precedence over the practical achievements of Unesco and other specialized agencies. Political affairs provide drama; economic, social, legal ones may seem mundane by comparison, to the non-specialist general reader. Perhaps our traditions of news reporting contribute no small amount to Western gloom.

It was Jawaharlal Nehru, President of India, who said in his Address to the U.N. General Assembly on 10th November, 1961, that he thought it might be helpful if more attention were directed to the co-operative activities being pursued by the nations of the world, 'even between countries which are opposed to each other in the political and other fields'.*

Such co-operative activities on a truly global scale have become practically possible only in mid-20th century, by virtue of the growth of international communication and transport. These technologies are of course not their *cause*; but, without them, human will is frustrated. What does 'frustration' mean, except 'a will without a way'?

There has been a very great and fast-growing number of practical successes in international relations, since the end of the Second World War, whilst that same period has of course been overshadowed by very major political problems. However, whereas major political problems have always existed, it is the steadily mounting list of international agreements which is something totally new: technical agreements, agreements on trade, exchange and travel, legal agreements, cultural agreements, control of pests and epidemics, social service bilateral agreements, the I.M.F., trusteeship of non self-governing

* See Enckell, R. (Chairman, Comm. for Int. Co-operation Year) in *U.N. Monthly Chronicle*, **1**, No. 7, Dec. 1964.

areas, the International Court, and a host of other international operations. Our world is a world of separate and noncontemporaneous states, and states-in-the-making, with no supranational government. International politics will go on, for a very long time, controlling the general directions of change, of progress or recession but, in the meantime, these practical 'mechanics of living' are developing to provide a base on which to build. Without them politics are powerless to remove international frustrations and frictions; they have neither the detailed social facts to argue with, nor the specialized expertise to reason about and with them. International relationships cannot develop and improve by politics alone, for the problems could not be formulated with any clarity in such terms. The International Organizations, with their expertise and professionalism, are beginning to introduce *precision* into international law.[22, 200]

Here surely lies the great difference between today's United Nations Organization and the pre-War League of Nations. Whereas the League, founded on 13th January, 1920,[200, 343] was almost wholly a political talking shop and, as such, could only fail to bring 'peace and understanding', the U.N. *operates* in the economic and social fields and, most important, has made provisions for co-operating with the various international specialized Agencies. These Agencies, including Unesco, are autonomous bodies, not member bodies *of* the U.N. Their work is co-ordinated by the U.N. organ called the Economic and Social Council.[22, 286, 332]

It is then the genius of the U.N. Agencies and of the other International Organizations that they separate the political and the operational (in the field) spheres, at least to a very great extent; national sovereignties are not infringed. The individuals who constitute the Heads of the delegations of the various countries which are members of these Agencies are people accredited by their own national Governments and, only to that extent, they are political 'representatives'; of the many delegates some are civil servants, some represent Governments, some are members of private firms or of professional bodies. Each person acts as a professional specialist, as a scientist, an engineer, a medical man, an economist, etc., with all the integrity of his profession and loyalty to it, though naturally within the political traditions and ideologies of his own country, for no practical successes would be achieved if abandonment of national identities was laid down as essential.

Because of this partial political/operational separation it is possible for countries who are not members of the U.N. to receive help and advice from the specialized Agencies and even to be Associate Members. Thus, the German Federal Republic is a member of all of them, whilst Switzerland is a member of most, though neither are Members of the United Nations Organization itself.[286, 332]

Today about twenty-eight Agencies, with related Bodies, deal with educational, scientific, cultural, sociological, economic, health, mass-communication, agricultural, aviation, postal, maritime and many other essentially *practical* bases of international existence.[82, 332] It has often been said that the fact that they operate amicably and successfully at all, should not bring their delegates much credit or national glory, because they deal with comprehensible problems which are clearly in everybody's interest to be solved. Exactly; that is the point and part reason for their success: they increasingly *define* these problems and thereby bring greater precision to international law.[22, 200]

Of these various Agencies, no less than four are concerned directly with world communication planning,[200] namely (a) the Universal Postal Union, (U.P.U.) dealing with the world's international postal services (see p. 129),[58, 338, 339] (b) The International Telecommunication Union (I.T.U.) dealing with telephones, telegraphs, and radio (see p. 129),[59, 153] (c) the International Civil Aviation Organization (I.C.A.O.), dealing with the international aspects of civil airways, navigation, safety, etc. (see p. 130),[141, 142, 143] (d) the Intergovernmental Maritime Consultative Organization (I.M.C.O.),[137, 138, 139] dealing with shipping engaged in international trade.[286, 332] (See p. 130.)

In a sense, all the Agencies of the U.N., together with the various Commissions and Committees, are concerned with communication, for they are all set up to improve international *organization*, and organization inherently requires communication, the gathering, collating and dissemination of information.[50] Unesco especially is concerned with the uses of many modern communication techniques, with books for schools, with literacy teaching, with films and travelling exhibitions, with mass-communication, with collection and analysis of many sociological statistics, with exchange of cultural information between countries, with museums, journalism, translations, the arts . . . a host of aspects of human communication.[286, 317, 318] Unesco has a Department of Mass-Communication, for its Constitution (Article 1) refers to 'advancing the mutual understanding of peoples through all means of mass-communication'. And the four specialized Agencies handle the world's communication *services*, which provide the necessary means; they will be described a little more closely in the next Section.

The various member countries of the U.N. are not each necessarily members of all the specialized Agencies, for various reasons.[332] For example, the Communist countries would not be expected to be members of the World Bank (I.B.R.D.), the International Monetary Fund (FUND), nor of the International Finance Corporation (I.M.F.), with the exception of Yugoslavia, a member of I.B.R.D. and FUND (see p. 102 of Ref. 22), whilst countries without sea coasts (and many others) are not members of the Intergovernmental Maritime Consultative Organization, etc. However, all the Communist countries do belong to the Universal Postal Union (U.P.U.), the International Telecommunication Union (I.T.U.) and Unesco, with the obvious exceptions of China and the German Democratic Republic which are not yet members of any Agencies.

Although they are most well known to the general public, these specialized Agencies of the U.N. constitute only a small section of the whole list of the world's International Organizations. They are of course very significant, inasmuch as they have been set up for advising Member (or non-Member) countries on matters which, *by their very nature, cannot possibly be national responsibilities, confined to the geographical boundaries of each country.* At present, together with their various associated Bodies they are equipped for dealing mainly with questions of (1) Labour (2) Food and Agriculture (3) Education, science and culture (Unesco and others) (4) Civil Aviation (5) Banking and international trade (6) Monetary co-operation (7) Health (8) Postal services (9) Telecommunication (10) Meteorology (11) Financial aid (12) Maritime (civil) affairs and (13) Atomic Energy. (Strictly speaking, the International Atomic Energy Agency is more autonomous than the specialized Agencies, being associated directly with the General Assembly and Security Council and not with the Economic and Social Council.[22]) Agencies clearly must work together a great deal and they naturally fall into the three categories: (a) Social (b) Technical (c) Financial. Some Commissions and Committees deal with legal questions, with trusteeships of special areas and administrative matters.[332]

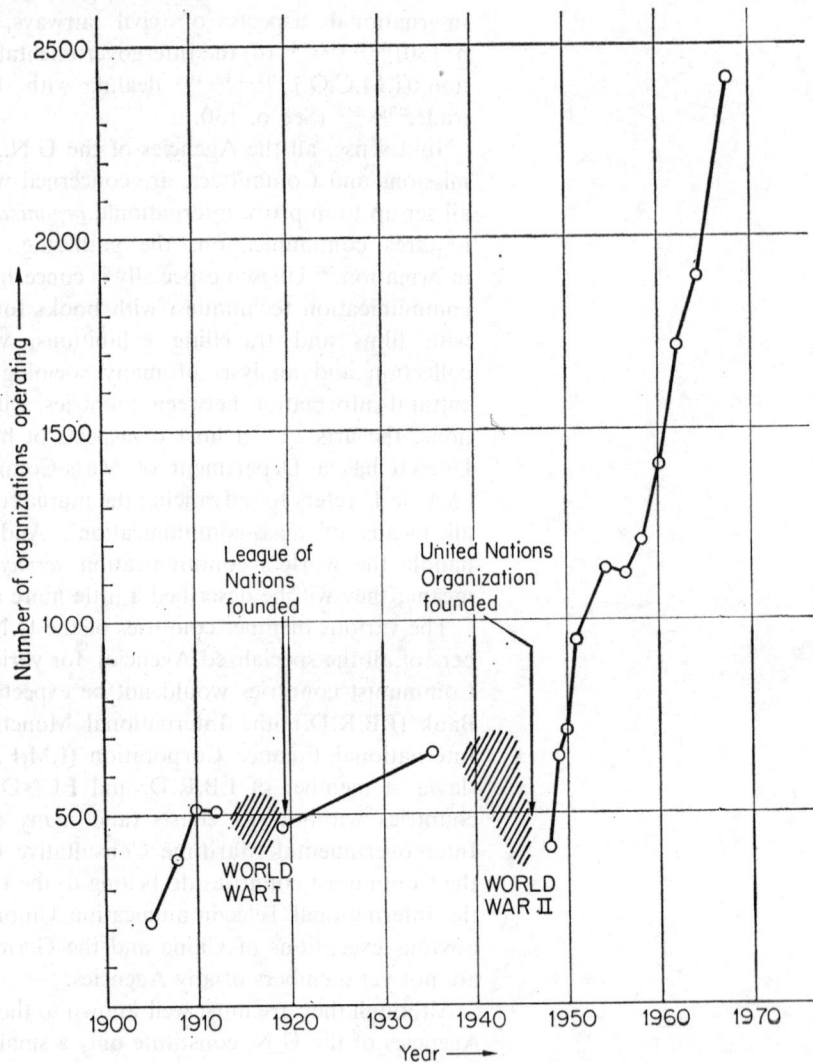

Figure 4.1. Growth of the listed International Organizations, both Governmental and non-Governmental, since the turn of the century.

Apart from these various organs of the United Nations, there are today (1970) some 3000 other listed International Organizations,[82, 86, 278, 323, 324] many of which are not fully worldwide, but confined to specific groups of countries having specific common interests. Figure 4.1 shows how rapidly their numbers have increased during the post-War period; those included in this count are listed and described in the *Yearbook of International Organizations*,[324] published by the Union of International Associations (which also publishes a monthly journal in English and French)[323] and they form a very wide variety of working organizations, large and small, covering many aspects of life: politics, trade, travel, Trade Unions, science, religion, sport, the arts, the professions, and hosts of others.[82]

Of the 2500 or so Organizations existing in 1967, and included in this count (Figure 4.1), 230 were intergovernmental institutions, 126 falling within the United Nations sphere, with 10 from the European Community and 191 others. There were 2188 other non-Governmental bodies, about 250 being professional, and business groups of the Common Market and the European Free Trade Association. The Charter of the U.N. provides for its co-operation with these non-Governmental bodies.[22, 328] These figures all relate to the year 1968/9.

To quote from a publication of the Union*: 'It is becoming increasingly obvious to those who like to look reality in the face that the destiny of each one of us and of each social or economic enterprise is coming to depend more and more on decisions taken by international organizations. Yet the extent to which the network of these international organizations stretches, what they do, how they operate, and what they offer to the countries participating in their activities, is still little known, except to a few specialists.

'The undeniable fact is that the development of international relations is one of the most remarkable characteristics of the modern world. This is no mere ideological conception; it is based on a multitude of facts, numerous aspects of which could unquestionably be studied further to great advantage.'

The idea of co-operation between States, to provide peace, prosperity and common good, is of course older then the Greeks, e.g. the Federation of 10 city–states in the 3rd century B.C., called the Aechaian League, having an elected general, magistrates and assembly. The ancient Greeks founded several political Leagues,[200] e.g. see Polybius. There have been several proposals for union between European countries and others during the past few centuries.

Although the concept of an international society consisting of sovereign and equal States had begun to emerge in Europe during the 16th and 17th centuries, it was ultimately the ending of the Napoleonic Wars which led to action being taken when in 1815 the Congress of Vienna opened up a new era of international co-operation.[200, 278] The Congress,[22] attended by all the crowned heads of Europe and over 200 national delegations, did not meet to settle the Peace Treaty, which had already been done (Treaty of Paris, 1814), but to deal with both political *and* socio–economic problems involved in the remaking of Europe. It could well be regarded as the fore-runner of the League of Nations and the United Nations Organization. It led to the proclamation of freedom of navigation of international rivers and of the abolition of the slave trade. Various International Organizations were set up; some lasted, some failed, and their numbers slowly grew. At the beginning of the 20th century their numbers increased very rapidly (see Figure 4.1), but the dream was shattered by the 1914–18 Great War. As Figure 4.1 shows, the period between the two World Wars was stagnant; dominated by the Versailles Treaty, the League of Nations could do little, whilst economic paralysis and the cloud of Nazism in the 1930s scarcely favoured international planning. The world that emerged from the Second World War was a very different one, with a very different outlook, in which the interdependences of the sovereign States in a thousand different ways have never been more clear, though the political forms for rationalizing them

* With kind permission of the Secretary-General, Mr. G. P. Speeckaert.

may yet be far from being found. The explosive growth of the International Organizations since 1945 is one of the most important and hopeful signs of today. In particular, the post-War world has been characterized by an enormous number of so-called *Regional* Organizations, to deal with specific interests of groups of politically related countries.[22, 82, 86] In spite of any will that may have existed in the past three centuries of nationalism, for better co-operation between States and whatever proposals were made (e.g. by Rousseau), there did not exist the physical means to carry out the necessary organization. Treaties may be made and political agreements reached yet, if the day-by-day channels of communication are not there, no action can be taken without risk of error, no corrective acts made, no orders passed, no checking done; policies are empty things, if means are absent.

The kinds of planning and organizing that are needed to produce any really effective co-operation between nations involve many people. They must travel to conferences, return for consultation with their Governments; there must be multilateral consulting; they must gather their facts and seek expert advice. Co-operation is not just a matter of Heads of States signing pieces of paper. It involves hundreds of people, separated by hundreds of miles and millions of words.

It has been the 'communication explosion' of the post-World War II era (see Chapter 3) that has made at all practicable the elaborate system of international co-operation, at practical level, which we are witnessing today, being carried out despite all the political argument and haranguing that we read about. 'International law looks . . . more and more towards treaty agreements rather than towards foggy custom'.*

The dual consequence of the communication explosion has been to keep informed, in all countries, those people who are fortunate enough to have newspapers and radios. No major events, and few aggressive acts, can take place anywhere today, without millions of eyes being turned upon them within a matter of days or hours. And the number of referees is increasing fast.

The grand dream we call 'world peace' may be so complex as to be incomprehensible; it is a very easy phrase, convenient to use like a slogan. To speak of such grand concepts as world peace is to invoke an imaginary structure, a vision, for the words convey nothing about the *form* of that structure; what sort of world would it be? Who runs it? Would it permit change? Revolutionary change? How would that peace be maintained? The architecture of the structure depends not only upon the architects but upon the materials available to them and, as world involvements become increasingly complex, so expertise is increasingly needed. Whether the structure we design stands up or falls down does not, of course, depend upon expertise alone. Nor can all those experts working today in the various fields of international co-operation be said to have the noble aim of 'working for world peace'; but each is doing his own professional job well, whether this be in medicine, science, agriculture, law, transport or other fields in which he is truly competent. And without these foundations nothing can be built.

6. The planning of world communication

How is world communication organized and operated? By its very nature it is international: the post, telephones and telegraphs, airways, connect together countries which have different political and economic systems,

* From G. J. Mangone, *A Short History of International Organizations*,[200] McGraw-Hill, New York, 1954. Used by permission of McGraw-Hill Book Company.

which are in different states of social development, have different standards of operation and facilities, different monies and totally different traffic needs and demands. Traffic also needs to be passed through other people's territory, so transit arrangements must be agreed upon. Furthermore, all these forms of traffic, and others, not only connect the countries but pass *into* those countries to continue their journeys as part of each nation's own internal systems; thus, a telephone call coming in from overseas must be routed into a country's own telephone network, etc.

World communication has essentially forced the various governments to get together and agree upon how it shall be done, whether they like each other or not. It has had to be done by mutual compromise and agreement, for there has been no supranational authority which could lay down the law.[22, 108] It is fair to say that the organization of world communication has been a triumph of common sense. It is so efficient today that you and I gladly write letters to others overseas, or catch a 'plane to fly there or, over a great part of the world, put in a telephone call or send a telegram; we expect to read the news from all corners of the globe. We assume these rights without much question; we may at times marvel at the technical wonders involved, but rarely at the political and organizational complexities.

Although agreements between countries for exchange of mail, for international telephony, etc., have existed for a century, traffic on any really large scale is a post-War phenomenon: the Communication Explosion, which was described in Chapter 3. The global planning of all its modes (post, telephones, telegraphs, airways, etc.) is today the business of the special Agencies of the United Nations, which were referred to in Section 5. At the same time, certain aspects which concern only single continents or groups of related countries are the concern of other so-called Regional Organizations,[200] formed by member countries of those local areas (e.g. as Eurovision is the concern of the European Broadcasting Union;[83] there are the Arab Postal Union, the Asian Broadcasting Union,[6] the Commonwealth Press Union, the African Telecommunication Union,[340] and many other Regional bodies).[22]

Thus there are three principal levels at which planning must proceed: Global, Regional and National; arrangements for day-by-day operation, for collaboration, for incorporating the advantages of new techniques and research, for advising the less technically advanced countries; for tariff agreements and a host of others must be made, or the world would be paralysed.

All modes of communication are forms of *sharing*. There is no advantage to one particular country in owning, say, a fleet of long-range civil aircraft, or launching a communications satellite*, both intended to improve communication with other countries, unless those other countries are willing to use the things too and they will not use them unless it is to their own advantage, economic or other, directly or indirectly. This is, of course, not to say that the richer of the countries, which may have constructed or may own these facilities, does not have the higher economic advantage; only that *both* ends of a communication link, of any kind, must have some degree of benefit, even though the benefit is greater to one than to the other. The advantage usually lies with the richer countries, for they have needs for heavier traffic and, as will be explained in Chapter 5 (Section 4), the heavier

---

* Except for internal communication in cases of countries large enough to need them, which few are (e.g. the U.S.S.R. and the U.S.A. see p. 164).

the traffic on any communication route, whether message or transport, the cheaper, in general, it becomes.

World communication is something which continually changes, and the various bodies which are set up, and the plans which they make, must be highly flexible and regularly reviewed. There is no question of plans being made by agreements between the world's countries and settled once and for all. The need for such changes arises from several causes, of which the two most prominent are, first, scientific and technical progress which provide a cornucopia of new methods in electronics, new types of aircraft, etc. and, second, the changing economic and social needs of the different countries, with their corresponding effects upon traffic demands. Those who plan national, regional, or global communication systems today are continually trying to predict, to anticipate, and even to make judicious guesses; and yet they can have only partial information to go upon. The installation of any large communication link may involve very large capital outlay, whether it be a transoceanic telephone cable, a satellite or a new airport or aircraft; furthermore the design and installation of such things today takes a very long time, time which may be comparable to their useful operational lifetime. Long-term planning in the various fields of communication today, may be interpreted as meaning, 'roughly, 10 years'. Beyond this, prediction and planning are hazardous and decisions only tentative. Nevertheless, certain such plans must be made (see remarks on p. 162). It is a common jibe at military aircraft designers that their machines are out-of-date as soon as built, but those concerned with civil communication of all kinds have other difficulties and dilemmas—for they are involved with all the lengthy paraphernalia of international planning and agreements and they cannot be wholly indifferent to the laws of economics.

The three specialized Agencies of the U.N. which have shouldered these responsibilities since the end of the Second World War are (1) The Universal Postal Union,[82, 200, 286, 332, 338, 339] (2) The International Telecommunication Union[82, 146, 153, 189, 286, 332] and (3) The International Civil Aviation Organization,[82, 142, 286, 332] but their histories extend further back;[200] in the case of the U.P.U. and the I.T.U., by about a century. These three organizations clearly must have close liaison, because their spheres of interest overlap to a considerable extent; thus the intercontinental postal service depends upon air transport, whilst air transport depends upon radio communication, Telex, radio navigation,[36] meteorological information, etc., and it will be making increasing use of satellites.*

In addition to these Agencies, there is the Intergovernmental Maritime Consultative Organization (I.M.C.O.)[137, 138, 139] which was set up in 1959 'to facilitate co-operation among governments and to achieve safety and efficient navigation (and) seeks to remove restrictions on the movement of international shipping'. Its interests include radio communication, from the viewpoints of safety at sea and navigation.[82, 286]

These are the Agencies which are directly concerned with the organizing of world communication today; the one common factor between them all is telecommunication, in all its various forms, without which none could operate on today's global scale.

---

* E.g. See historical articles by P. Oomen in *Telecommunication Journal* (I.T.U.)[153] **31**, March and April 1966. Also, in same Journal, other articles; **31**, March (Aeronautical Radio Conf.); Feb. 1964; **32**, Feb. (refers to U.S.S.R.); May; July 1965; **33**, Sept. 1966 (satellites).

The Agencies have varied histories. The first formal agreements for regularized communication between neighbouring countries were made in Europe not, as may be thought, in relation to the postal services, but as the result of the invention of the telegraph. As was noted in Chapter 2 Section 4 the telegraph was the first instantaneous means which, at one stroke, changed the whole nature of communication. Its coming forced governments into action, for the enormous economic advantages of international working, with common technical standards and arrangements for charges, etc., were obvious. It was in Paris, in 1865, that the various existing bilateral agreements between European countries were rationalized, when the International Telegraphic Convention met, under the initiative of Napoleon III, to set up the International Telegraphic Union, an organization which was opened to all countries in the world (for the global implications were already foreseen, see Section 1).[22] The first world authority for communication was thereby established, only half a century after the Congress of Vienna. It became a permanent body in 1868, with Headquarters and Secretariat in Berne, Switzerland, and took over similar responsibilities for international telephones in 1885: private telegraph companies were admitted, without right to vote.[22] Telephones and telegraphs have been closely related throughout their history, both in their administrative arrangements and in their industrial traditions and standards of manufacture.

When radio first came, it broke away from these traditions in several ways and it has developed ever since rather apart, as a new industry closely conditioned by the early great wave of popular enthusiasm for 'wireless' and home entertainment, with the corresponding need to manufacture cheap, mass-produced, radio, gramophones and T.V. sets. Telegraphy and telephony have always been bound by more 'professional' standards of manufacture.

The organizing and regulating of radio, on a world basis, was started by the International Radio-telegraph Convention in 1906, at Berlin, which was attended by 27 maritime states: the immediate value of radio was to ships at sea (see Chapter 2, Section 6).[59,286] It set up the Radiotelegraphic Union, also in Berne.

Two Unions thus existed to serve world electrical communication, the first for Telegraphy and Telephony and the second for Radio-telegraphy. Both were concerned with public services and, furthermore, the scientific bases of their technologies came to overlap more and more as time passed. It was natural that the Unions should be merged, as was done in 1932, at the International Telecommunication Convention in Madrid, when they were replaced by a single body, called the International Telecommunication Union,[59,82,286,332] which remains the world authority today.

Following the Second World War, a plenipotentiary conference was held at Atlantic City in 1947, when the I.T.U. became a specialized Agency of the U.N., with new headquarters in Geneva; it was radically reorganized, with a permanent Secretariat, Administration and technical Boards[59,74,82,200,286,332] capable of dealing with the immensely complex technical and administrative problems of communication in the new and rapidly changing post-War world. The Communist countries are members.

The postal service has had a more simple history.[58,339] As we have already noted, there were many attempts made in earlier centuries to establish national postal services (see Chapter 2, Section 4) and by the first half of the 19th century the several countries of Europe and various States and districts of America had a very mixed bag of local services operating, each with their own system of charges and regulations, with different time delays and losses of mail; virtually no organized system for wide international exchange existed in workable form.[200] Initiative towards establishing a worldwide postal service was first taken by a German Authority in 1868,* when their Director-General of Posts proposed a Congress which, delayed by the Franco–Prussian War and other causes, eventually led to the historic Postal Congress of Berne, 1874.[200, 339] This Congress rationalized the postal services, introduced a unified system of charges based on weights, made arrangements for handling of accounts, transit of mails between countries, settling disputes, and all the essentials of an international service which could operate within 'a single world postal territory'. At the same time a permanent organ was established in Berne, the International Bureau, to serve as the central office of the new Universal Postal Union. Membership was open to the Postal Administrations of all countries of the world, and expenses were to be shared equitably among countries according to the volume of their business.[339]

In 1948 the Universal Postal Union became a specialized Agency of the U.N., with the International Bureau at Berne serving as Secretariat.[58, 339] This Bureau takes under its wing not only letter mails, but also insured packages, money orders, C.O.D. items, International Savings Bank, subscriptions to periodicals, and other services. A new constitution came into force in 1966 as the legal and diplomatic instrument binding on member countries. Practically all countries of the world are members.

The other two specialized Agencies, namely I.C.A.O. (for airways) and I.M.C.O. (for shipping), both deal with world transport rather than message traffic and constitutionally they are rather similar,[22] though their histories are very different. Again, both are primarily concerned with safety, with efficient navigation and with ensuring co-operation between nations for the smooth running of services. Not all Communist countries are members.[60, 286]

Legislation concerning air travel was set up long before aircraft existed; it was balloons which first required regulation, shortly after the French Revolution.[200] During the later years of the 19th century and the early days of flying machines it was again legal questions which concerned a series of international conferences in France and Italy, occasioned partly by the uncertainty of whether an aircraft was anybody's national 'territory' or not, with questions of 'sovereignty' of airspace, etc.[60, 200] The 1914–18 Great War saw tremendous development of military aircraft and, at its conclusion, the first international air treaty was drafted, which included sections on technical matters of airworthiness and rules of take-off, flying and landing. The International Commission for Air Navigation was set up and there was further development of 'aerial law' made later.[60] In the 1920s Europe led the world in development of air passenger services.[256]

In the meanwhile the U.S.A. had pursued their own path, leading to the Havana Convention of 1928. It was, however, the Second World War which ensured the coming of a truly global organization, able to handle the immense growth of civil aviation that later emerged. That War not only greatly developed aircraft themselves, producing jet propulsion, but it forced countries to ally with one another so as to produce concerted plans and agreements; the ground was laid for the post-War setting up of the International Civil Aviation Organization (I.C.A.O.) as a specialized Agency.[22] Created in 1944, it was formally established in 1947, the Convention being

* The North German Confederation. An Austro–German Postal Union had been operating since 1850.

adopted by 52 nations.[22, 142, 286] I.C.A.O. is today the world organ (that is, excluding Communist countries) for civil aviation; it is an intergovernmental body, whose Council adopts necessary international standards, recommends advisable practices and acts as arbiter between nations; its permanent Secretariat is in Montreal.[87]

Most air lines are not Government owned, but are commercial Companies operating under Governmental authority in various ways. The Organization called the International Air Transport Association is the commercial consortium which deals with flying agreements, tariffs, etc.

Now, aircraft are fairly modern things, whereas there have been ships of all kinds for thousands of years. Fleets have sailed between and around continents since recorded history: the early Norsemen, the Greeks, the Arabs and others. Yet maritime history is more a tale of invasion, war and piracy than of international accord until near modern times. (There have of course been some notable examples of peaceful maritime trading peoples, e.g. the Phoenecians.) Seaborne traffic is rapidly increasing today; by 1956 the world tonnage of international trade had doubled in 10 years (see Figure 2.3). The Intergovernmental Maritime Consultative Organization (I.M.C.O.), the youngest specialized Agency of U.N., was created without any antecedents, long after the end of the Second World War. There had been long delay since its initial conception, when a Provisional Consultative Council was established in 1946. (For maps and details of intercontinental shipping and trade see Ref. 3.) It first assembled in 1959, its Articles referring to the 'provision of machinery for co-operation among governments' in relation to regulations and practices for efficient navigation, radio-communication, safety, removal of restrictions, etc. (reference *I.M.C.O. Basic Documents*). Most maritime Communist countries are members.

These are the four U.N. specialized Agencies which are specifically concerned with *global* communication, I.T.U. and U.P.U., concerned with message traffic; I.C.A.O. and I.M.C.O., concerned with transport communication. Their constitutions and methods of operation are varied, with different state memberships, different forms of representation (i.e. drawn from national Administrations, as in the case of U.P.U., or from both these and private industry, as for I.T.U., etc.) different voting procedures, intervals of meetings, budgets, procedures, etc.[22, 286]

Working through their permanent Secretariats, these Organizations hold meetings of their highest administrative bodies ('Conference', 'Congress' or 'Assembly') who deal with general policy, and of administrative or executive Councils, Boards and Consultative Committees. These latter bodies, the Committees, deal with the complex and changing technical problems of world communication; they may set up Study Groups and Working Parties. Scientific and technical progress, upon which their decisions and recommendations are based, is the workaday business of thousands of people, all over the world, in both private industries and government institutions. Co-ordination and direction are given to such work by earlier decisions of the Committees who may have identified specific problems requiring study and, by agreement among the representatives, allocated them to various study groups and working parties distributed among countries with the required research facilities, expertise and experience. In this way, the various countries' experts pool a great deal of their own, or their company's, experience, without at the same time shedding their commercial independence. The Secretariats receive, translate as necessary, and re-issue Reports prepared by these experts so that they are kept informed of each other's progress, in order that, when they eventually meet in Study Groups or in Committee, their business may proceed smoothly and quickly. These Committees come to their conclusions, and issue their Recommendations. They are essentially *advisory* bodies, with no powers to enforce action by countries upon their recommendations. The 'force' of such international law arises out of 'common agreement', consent or sanction; no country can afford to be the odd man out.[22]

Of these four Agencies, the I.T.U. has the most complex organization.[59] It has three permanent organs other than its Secretariat, namely: (1) The International Telegraph and Telephone Consultative Committee (C.C.I.T.T.),*[74] (2) The International Radio Consultative Committee (C.C.I.R.)* and (3) the International Frequency Registration Board (I.F.R.B.). Each of these committees works through the Plenary Assembly, which meets every three years. The whole I.T.U. organization is a form of 'technical assistance' available to any of its members and its interests include training: so important to new and developing countries.[198,259]

Jointly, the two Consultative Committees, C.C.I.T.T. and C.C.I.R., operate what is called the Plan Committee. This Committee was originally formed to consider telecommunication in the continent of Europe, but the rapid march of events and technical progress have forced telecommunication to be planned on a global basis. As a consequence Regional Plan Sub-Committees were constituted for Africa,[148] Asia and Latin America, each of which studied the special needs of those developing, continental areas. In 1963 the proposed plans of these three Sub-Committees were considered together, leading to the publication of the first co-ordinated plan for world telecommunication: the so-called Rome Plan.[45,147,152]

7. Worldwide telecommunication. The Rome Plan and the Mexico City Plan

The first international committee to be set up to consider advance plans for a worldwide telephone, telegraph and high-speed telegraph network met in Rome in November–December 1963 under the authority of the International Telecommunication Union. Representatives of more than 70 countries attended, with the aim of co-ordinating work already carried out by three Regional Sub-Committees who had studied the needs of the three developing areas of Africa, Asia and Latin America. Furthermore, the Rome meeting aimed to relate the needs of these areas to the existing and projected networks of Europe and North America.[45,147,152]

This committee was specifically concerned with *traffic flow* between continents and smaller areas of the world, in order to estimate how many telephone channels (or their equivalents for telegraph) would be needed to link the various countries, as assessed by the authorities within those countries. The meeting was not so much concerned with techniques nor with geographical routes; for one reason, satellites at that time were hardly out of the experimental stage and neither their possibilities nor their economics could be judged. Such technical planning was the business of a subsequent Conference held in Mexico City, November 1967. The Report[151] was published in 1969.

For this purpose the map of the world had been divided up into 34 zones, some being single large countries (e.g. the U.S.A., European U.S.S.R., Brazil . . .) and some being areas containing several countries related politically

---

* These are initials of the Committee titles in French.

and geographically (e.g. S.E. Asia, East Africa, the West Indies . . .). Europe, that hornet's nest of nations, was divided into no less than 10 zones, perhaps a sad reflexion on the historical and linguistic division of that tiny continent. The fact that these 34 zones were agreed upon 'without comment' by the Plan Committee[45] lends support to the idea that these zones of 'mutual interest', or 'spheres of interest', which are so much fewer in number than the total of the world's nations, are widely recognized as alike, by all the various nations (see Section 5).

The countries had each previously been asked, through their various communication authorities, to assess the traffic which they exchanged with the other countries in the year 1962 and also to estimate their needs for 1968 and 1975. The result of all this data was the construction of a matrix showing how communication traffic flowed between each of the 34 zones at the time, and how these flows were expected to change in the future. From this matrix[45] a simplified map has been constructed here, Figure 4.2, which indicates the principal traffic flows in a way which gives some indication of expected future changes by the years 1968 and 1975.

The eventual accuracy of these predictions is not of great importance here. The figures represent the various authorities' expectations, however these may have been founded. A great deal of guesswork must have been used in some cases. Nevertheless, the diagram shows a number of interesting points.

Most obvious of these is the very rapid increase in the expected traffic between the U.S.A. and South America; with Central America and the Caribbean too. We notice also the U.S.A.'s rapidly expanding interest in the whole continent of Africa. Australia's demands for connexion with Britain and Canada indicate how that continent has been isolated hitherto (when the Commonwealth telephone route between Britain, Canada and Australia was opened in 1963, telephone messages over it from Britain soon doubled in number: but *from* Australia *to* Britain, their numbers trebled (see Figure 3.1).) The North Atlantic routes, connecting the two major industrial areas of Europe and the U.S.A., were expected to expand to about 2000 telephone channels by the year 1975; it remains by far the busiest route in the world. (See map, Figure 3.1). Also surprising may be the proposals for connecting France, Spain and Italy with the developing areas of North Africa and the Near East by no less than 900 channels, nearly half the North Atlantic number. The surprise is heightened by the fact that, within their own borders, France, Spain and Italy have fewer telephones per 100 population than any of the other industrial countries of Europe (see Table D and Figure 3.9).[20]*

Detailed analysis could not possibly be made upon such reduced data as Figure 4.2 presents. The intention here is no more than to call attention to this example of international planning, upon which trade, world airways, news reporting and other international dealings depend.

Such long-term planning as this is a hazardous business for many reasons. In particular, the development of some new technique of communication can offer such a radically improved service that the volume of message traffic becomes increased beyond expectation; for as was shown in Chapter 3, demand rises if business, industry, news services, etc., find that they can operate in new and perhaps cheaper ways. Again, message traffic between countries can receive major stimulus or setback owing to unforeseen political

* See Table 4, on p. 75 and also Figure (3.9).

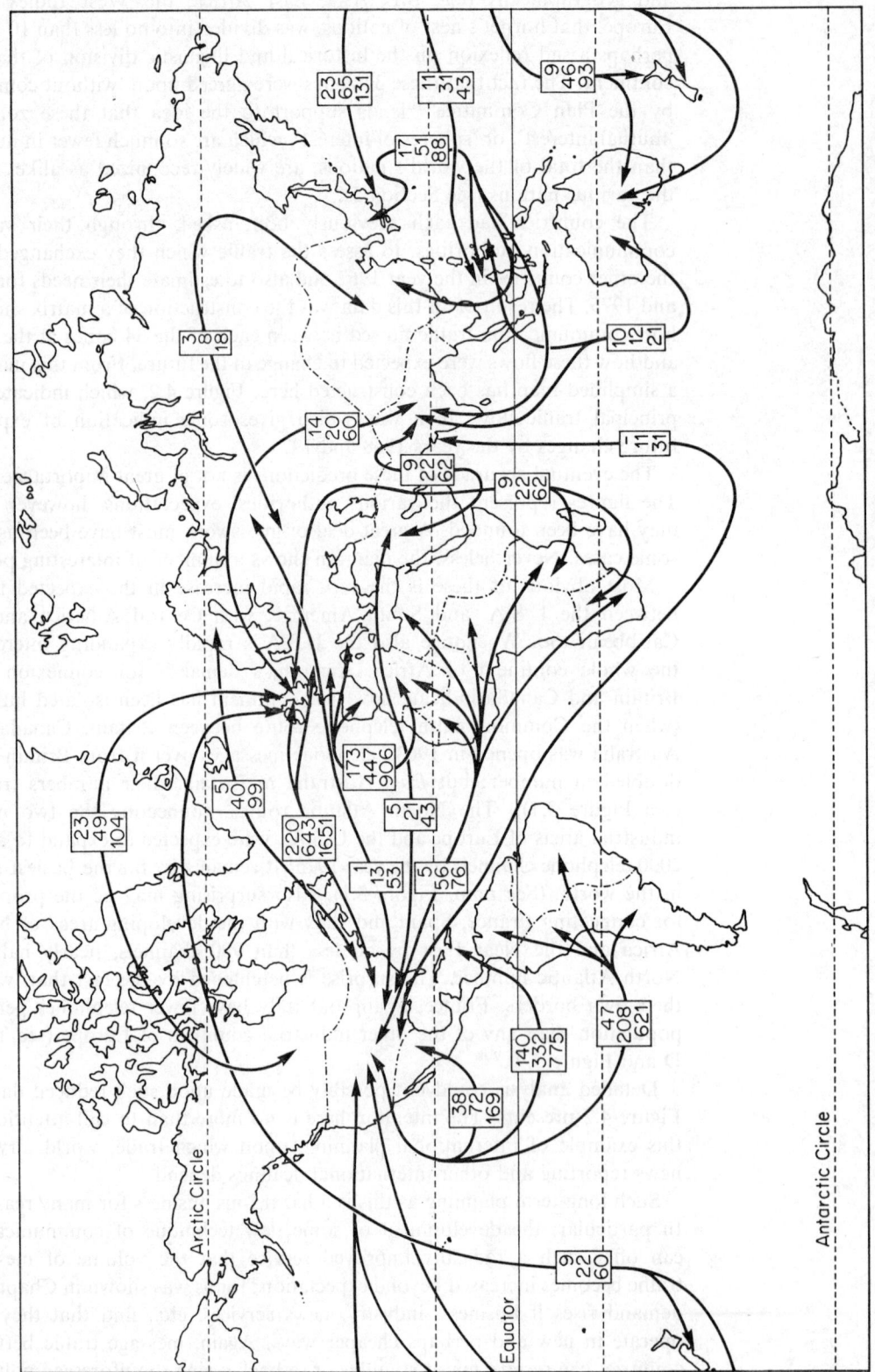

Figure 4.2. 'The Rome Plan', 1963. The principal intercontinental flows of telephone traffic, or equivalent Telex and telegraphy traffic. Figures indicate telephone channels in years 1962, 1968, 1975.

or other changes in international relations. Traffic prediction must therefore be continually revised.

Consequently, it is not surprising that the 'Rome Plan' of 1963 did not remain a fixture. The authorities in the various countries were continually reconsidering their likely needs and, after further meetings of the continental Regional Sub-Committees,[148] a second Plan for world telecommunication was drawn up by representatives of all I.T.U. countries, at Mexico City in October 1967.

The mandates of the Rome Plan and the Mexico City Plan Committees were strictly limited to work of general planning, which was intended to serve only as a guide to countries. The actual preparation of detailed projects, financing and construction came under the jurisdiction of the various countries themselves. At the Mexico City 1967 meeting, however, the Committee not only revised their ideas of the message traffic which each country would need but made preliminary study of the geographical routing of the traffic between countries and continents. By this time, satellites had proved themselves as economic propositions for international telephones, telegraphs and television, thereby introducing new problems of routing, international connexion, and switching. Five techniques of communication were considered (1) Cable (2) Radio-relay (3) H.F. radio (4) Submarine cable (5) Satellites.

As stressed before, in Section 5, international relations are more and more coming to be interpretable as facts and figures, e.g., facts of economic geography; as time goes on these are made increasingly precise by agreements, treaties and *operable* international law. It is commonly said that today we live in 'a shrinking world' (so far as the clock goes). Figure 4.2 is evidence of this; it also shows one important fact, namely, that the world is not shrinking everywhere like a deflated balloon but very irregularly, more like a dried apple, furrowed and distorted.

5

Communication and Wealth

'All progress is based upon a universal innate desire on the part of every organism to live beyond its income'.

Samuel Butler (1835–1902)
Note Books. Life, XVI.

1. Communication and wealth: the advanced countries

To what extent are our various technical communication services luxuries or necessities: the telephone, radio, T.V., airways, cinema, print, etc?

There is no simple answer to this question for, as stressed before, the values of these various media depend upon so many factors, particularly economic, social and political standards. Nor should we assume that each medium has similar value to different countries, even after industrialization. Unesco publishes a volume at intervals giving details of Press, Radio, Film and Television services in most of the world's countries,[320] from which one can quickly make (approximate) comparisons of the extent to which each medium exists there; the variations between countries are enormous. The relative developments of each medium are also very uneven among the countries and it is not possible to quote one single statistic for each, defining the total 'communication services' of that country. Any attempt to assess the relative values of the different media immediately leads one into a morass of value judgements and speculations. For how should we compare, in economic terms, the relative values of radio and telephones, or newspapers and television? All the media are, as argued earlier, quite different in their natures; no one of them can be simply regarded as a 'better' version of another (see Chapter 2, Section 6 and Chapter 3, Sections 6 and 7). There is no simple value measure.

In economic terms, it might be argued that the values of each medium to any particular country could be simply assessed by the capital investment in each. But this would not be a complete story. For one thing, capital can be sunk either in the consumer sense or in the investment sense; for example, we have already distinguished two classes of telephone, (a) the domestic 'phone, in homes, and (b) the economic 'phone, in business, industry, etc., though this distinction is far from sharp (see Chapter 3, Section 3). Again, some uses of communication may have immediate economic values (e.g. a business call or a telegram) whereas others have delayed values (e.g. the educational values of radio, T.V. and films). Attempts to explain *why* any country invests the way it does, in the various media, must be based to a great extent on speculation. Thus, why does Britain place so much value on print: books[312] and newspapers? (See Chapter 2, Section 5, Chapter 6, Section 7 and Figure 6.6).[320] Why does America so value the telephone but not the Telex Service? Why does Japan produce far more feature films than any other country in the world?[320] Or why does Germany so favour the Telex? (See Chapter 3, Section 4 and Figure 3.3.) Answers might be offered in terms of geography, history, traditions, literacy rates, and many social factors; but no one simple economic explanation can account for the great differences between countries, whilst explanations based upon 'national characteristics' can only be based on prejudice and speculation (see Chapter 3, Section 3).

Nevertheless, certain generalities can safely be made. First, however, I would offer my opinion that the various communication media are not correctly to be regarded as commodities, as things, worth 'so much'. They are more like *potentials* or powers. In many respects, communication media are closely analogous to money itself, media of exchange, an analogy which will be pursued in Chapter 6.

Next, with regard to the question: to what extent should we regard the various communication services, national or international, as being necessities or luxuries? The answer depends wholly upon the particular countries one has in mind, upon their economic conditions, educational standards and many other factors. Wilbur Schramm has argued, very rightly, that communication investment in general should be slightly ahead, and never far behind, investment in the other institutions of the developing countries.[188] For communication is basic to any organized changes. But to ask how far any one medium should be developed before it becomes a 'luxury' is another thing; no general answer can be given to such an all embracing value question. Luxury is only the extension of necessity, as standards rise and become taken for granted.

Nevertheless, the direct economic values of certain media are more obvious than those of others. Telephones, telegraphs, railways, roads have perhaps the most direct values; the Press is less direct and must await the coming of a sizeable literate population; the values of radio, T.V. and cinema depend upon educational standards. In many poor countries newspapers and wall sheets reach far more than the literate population. Thus the published statistics of newspaper circulations may give little indication of the actual number of people they reach. Further, they reach the illiterates too, frequently, by being read aloud to them, e.g. in China, special people are appointed to chalk up news on blackboards in the villages and to read it aloud for the sake of illiterates.[188] It would be futile to try to put all the various media precisely on any imagined scale of values.

A more meaningful question might be: does investment in the more direct communication services, such as telephones, precede or follow industrial and economic progress? Or, again, to what extent is a country's telephone system a producer of wealth and to what extent a consumer? There are many ways in which one might try to approach the same question but all are blocked by lack of adequately detailed statistics.[161,162,166] All communication services operate the two classes of traffic; in the economic sphere and in the domestic sphere. As observed before, in Chapter 3, Section 3, the same roads are used for both sport and transport, the same telephones for business calls as for gossip, the same telegraphs for urgent business as for birthday telegrams, and separate statistics are not commonly recorded.

A real question which administrations have to answer is: how much money should we invest in extending our services? What fraction of the country's resources should be devoted to the telephone system, to roads, and other services? Under-investment seems to have been more common during the current explosive phase in telecommunication (see Chapter 3, Section 4), whilst over-investment has been made in other fields at other times. For example, the U.S.A. appears to have over-invested in railways during the explosive phase of their development in the 1880s: see under *Railways*, in Ref. 78.

A country's communication services and its economic development are again like chicken and egg; we cannot say which comes first. Better services make administration and industry more efficient and, in turn, the economy can then afford to invest in extending or improving those services. One thing is certain however, the two are closely *correlated*; this word may need explaining.

Correlation is a term used in Mathematical Statistics merely to indicate that two quantities depend upon one another, on an *average*. As a simple example, we can say that in a population of people their heights and weights will be correlated; that is, on an average, the taller any person is, the heavier he is likely to be. The simplest way of showing correlation is by constructing a 'Scatter Diagram', which has been done in Figure 5.1 for this example of

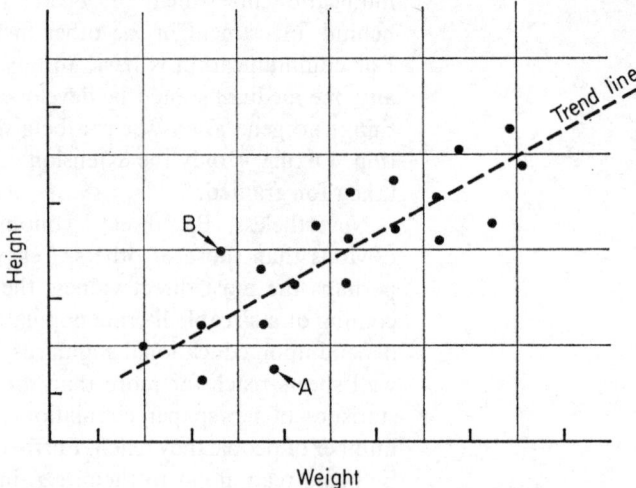

Figure 5.1. A Scatter Diagram, showing the heights and weights of 20 people of a population.

people's heights and weights. Here, each spot represents one person, showing his height and weight; the 'population' here is a mere 20 people. Not surprisingly, the spots do not all lie exactly along a straight line, because some people are fatter than others (i.e. another cause is at work!). However, the spots are scattered about a line, shown dashed, which is called the Trend Line (technically known as a Regression Line); there are precise rules in Statistics for finding this best Trend Line, but they do not concern us here.

The closer the spots lie to this Trend Line, the more correct we would be in saying that, *on an average*, the people's weights depend upon their heights (i.e. that fatness, etc., could be ignored). That is to say, 'the more closely are their heights and weights correlated'. If height and weight had absolutely nothing to do with one another, the spots would be scattered widely all over the page. The extent of correlation can be calculated from such a diagram and quoted by a number called the Correlation Coefficient. When this turns out to be 1·0 the two quantities are completely correlated and the spots would lie along a line, with no scatter; but when they are scattered so widely that the Coefficient is zero, the two quantities have no relation to one another at all.

Notice, now, that such correlation measures the dependence (of weight and height here) only *on an average*. The people (spots) vary among themselves a good deal. Thus, in Figure 5.1 person A is considerably heavier for his height than is person B. So, too, we could say that all other persons lying *below* the Trend Line are heavier than those of equal height lying above the Trend Line.

Such a Scatter Diagram tells us, at a glance, at least two things: (a) how closely two properties of a population are related to one another on the *average*, and (b) how much each individual differs from the trend of the population, or from all the others.

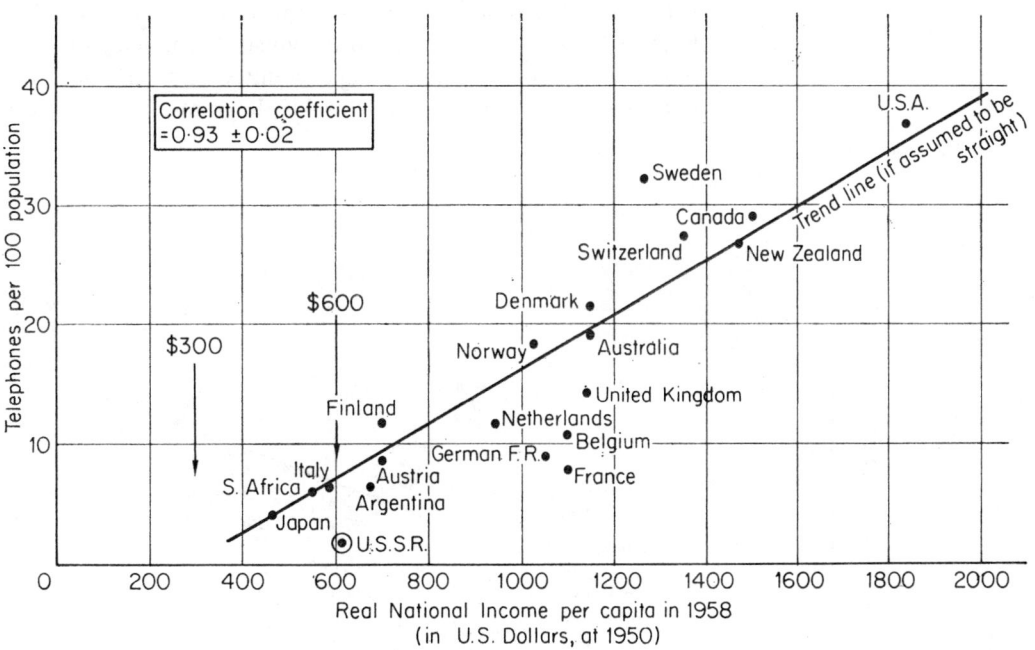

⊙   denotes a Communist country

Figure 5.2. Correlation between wealth and possession of telephones in the industrially advanced countries (in 1958). After N. J. H. Jones.[162]

Using such Scatter Diagrams, we may study the correlation between wealth and possession of various communication media (telephones, radio, newspapers, etc.) among the populations of nations, so as to see how they are related to one another on an average and, again, how the nations vary among themselves.

Let us first consider telephones as an example. It can be shown that, among the industrial countries at least, the number of telephones per 100 population is very closely correlated with wealth, on an average, though countries vary much among themselves. One early demonstration of this was by N. J. H. Jones,[161, 162] in a diagram reproduced here as Figure 5.2, which shows the telephones per 100 population in the major industrial countries[5] and their per capita incomes for the year 1958. See Ref. 140 for more recent G.N.P. figures for countries of the world, also p. 146. In this case, *all* telephone instruments were counted, in homes as well as offices, etc. We see here that the points representing countries lie fairly close to the Trend Line, which has been approximately fitted on the diagram. Other authors have shown very similar diagrams, for later dates.[20, 67, 159, 162] In this example, the correlation coefficient turns out to be 0·9 ± 0·02, which is very high indeed.*

Such a diagram merely shows the existence of a high correlation between telephones and wealth among countries, but does not pretend to be numerically precise. Two sources of uncertainty exist. One lies in the methods used for assessing the wealth of countries, which may conveniently be based upon figures for industrial and other production. In the introduction to the *World Bank Atlas* of per capita Production and Population, the Editor states some of the difficulties of assessment, saying that ' . . . the figures must be taken with some reserve'.[140] The other is the changeable exchange rates between the nations' different currencies. Jones has sought to overcome both of these difficulties and to demonstrate the telephones/wealth correlation law by considering a single country and currency, the U.S.A. and dollars. Figures 5.3 and 5.4 show his diagrams.[162] Here the two classes of

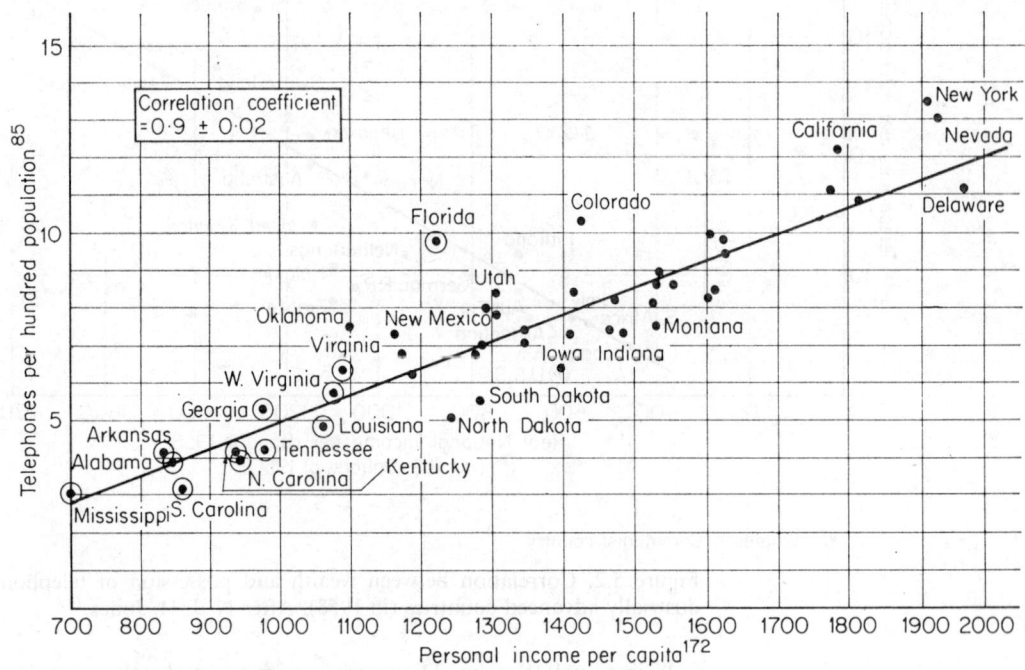

Figure 5.3. United States of America, 1951. Relationship between personal income and telephones for each of the States, in business, industry, etc. 'Economic sphere' (after N. J. H. Jones[162]). See also 'Federal Communications Commission,[85] and Kuznets and Thomas.[172]

telephone have been distinguished (those in the economic and domestic spheres)† and the spots represent different States of the U.S.A. Only those States lying farthest from the Trend Lines have been named, as apparently valuing the telephone either substantially more or less, than the average

---

* Spearman's Coefficient of Rank Correlation has been used on all these diagrams.
† Note. The correlation laws for these two diagrams differ, the 'personal income' axes being linear and logarithmic, respectively.

for the whole Union, together with the poorer Southern States. Again the correlations are very high (shown on the Figures).

Such diagrams apply to the stated years only. However, Jipp has shown that, over a succession of years as countries grow richer, the Trend Line of Figure 5.2 remains virtually unchanged, whilst the spots representing countries merely climb higher along it.[159]

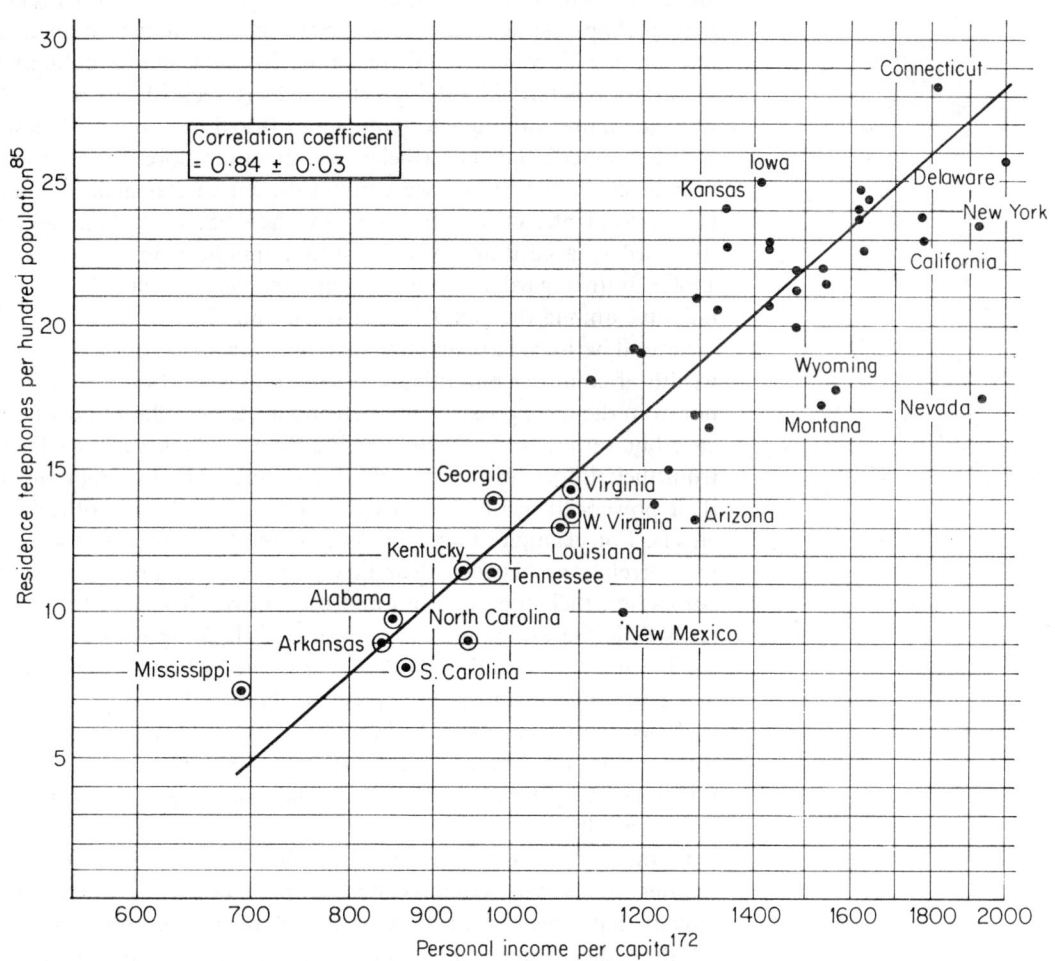

Figure 5.4. United States of America, 1951. Relationship between personal income and telephones for each of the States, in private homes. 'Domestic sphere' (after N. J. H. Jones[162]). See also 'Federal Communications Commission',[85] and Kuznets and Thomas.[172]

The countries represented on the diagram Figure 5.2 are all of the so-called industrially advanced group, in the Western pattern. Nevertheless, the range of wealth shown is nearly ten to one, and these countries vary much also in geography, politics, in extent and types of industry, and in their population distributions. But there are no 'developing' countries appearing on this Figure, either in Africa or Asia, whilst few from South America either are represented; they would all fall too low on the diagram to be seen clearly.

Some comment has already been made, in Chapter 3, Section 3, upon the fact that, although the telephone densities (per 100 population) vary so much among the advanced countries, these differences are accounted for largely by home telephones; the telephone densities in the economic sphere vary far less among the countries. Table 4 on page 75, relating to the years 1965 and 1966, shows this for countries whose statistics are available. Thus, notice that with the exception of the South American countries (Argentina, Brazil) the figures in column 2 vary only between 5·1 (Italy) and 20·2 (Switzerland) in the economic sphere; Switzerland's very high figure may perhaps be accounted for by the great number of international administrative offices centred there. In the domestic sphere (column 3) the range of variation is far wider, lying between 2·4 (Czechoslovakia) and 35 (U.S.A.).

Incidentally, although Argentina and Brazil have relatively few telephones in either sphere, they nevertheless use them far more than do the other countries listed in the Table (see column 4). Japan too makes a high usage of her instruments, closely followed by the U.S.A., Iceland and Sweden, in that order, according to one official publication, *World's Telephones*, 1966.[5] With regard to conversations per *person*, Canada[5] seems the most talkative among the countries listed (column 5)!

Several writers have commented on such close correlation between the wealth of countries and other types of communication media*[262,307] arising, not from the mere possession of telephones, telegraphs, radio sets, newspapers, etc., but rather from the organizing power which such media donate and from their informational powers, their effects upon literacy or desire for it, their powers to instil the concept of change, and from other psychological effects. For example, Fagen has considered 93 countries, and has computed the correlations between their newspaper circulations, their radio receivers per capita, their literacy rates and their Gross National Products (G.N.P.). (G.N.P. is the estimated market value of the output of goods and services produced by a nation's economy, before deduction of depreciation charges and costs of consumed capital assets. 'National Income' is the value *after* such deductions are made.) These correlations are all high.[84] He also shows that, on the contrary, as time passes the *growth* rates of these two media are little related to literacy or G.N.P.: in the case of newspaper growth, scarcely related at all.

In the writer's opinion this latter finding is to be expected for several reasons. Thus, the economically advanced countries, having high literacy, already have near saturation of newspapers and radio (or T.V.) sets;[320] on the other hand, many poorer countries (including Communist ones) encourage literacy programmes, radio, communal T.V. viewing, newspapers, wall sheets, film and other mass-media, as part of their policy for catching up.[188,262]

Some Unesco Reports have also drawn attention to the correlation between these same variables (per capita income, literacy, cinema seats, radio sets and newspapers per 100 population) and also with urbanization (percentage of population in localities of 2000 or more persons) and industrialization (percentage of gainfully employed males in non-agricultural work) indicating that, even in the poorer countries, 'there is a very high correlation of the mass media with economic factors in general development, particularly income'.[307] In the author's opinion this statement needs some qualification for, as will be shown in the next Section, 5(b), if we take as the 'poorer countries' those whose G.N.P. falls below $300 per capita per annum,

---

* See numerous Reports, under Unesco in Bibliography.

then some correlations fall well below those of the industrial countries. (See Figures 5.10, 5.12 and 5.13.)

However, Unesco has been concerned mainly with that class of mass-media which it calls the *information media*; these are newspapers, radio, T.V. and cinema, in particular.[320] On the other hand, telephones, telegraphs and the like are not *sources* of mass-communication; they connect specific persons or institutions. We shall be referring to such media here as *organizational* media, in so far as they have direct values in the economic sphere. In the economically advanced countries, at least, the informational media are mostly bought and paid for privately, and have much more the nature of private consumer products; we might expect to find their statistics closely correlated with per capita incomes. But in the poorer and developing countries these informational media are of more immediate, urgent and direct value to economic progress if on a long-term basis and they are, to a greater extent, the responsibility of governments, of external aid programmes, and other non-private sources; they have also a very much lower penetration among the populations.[320] In other words, the richer the people of a country the more money they can *afford* to spend on informational media, newspapers, radios, T.V., films, etc., whereas the poorer they are the more their governments and other authorities *need* to spend on them. The conditions under which the media operate may be totally different.

Consequently, it may be better to consider the values and significances of both the informational media and the organizational media to the developing countries, in a separate Section.

It has already been suggested that we should not expect the different countries of the world to use the various communication media, telephones, newspapers, radio, etc., in the same proportions, but that many social factors other than wealth will decide their use, including tradition. Thus merely to state that use of the various media is 'closely correlated with wealth of countries' is telling only half the story. The variations between countries are also interesting, though it may be hazardous to cite the causes!

Figure 5.5 and Figure 5.6 have been constructed using the most recent data available at the time of writing.*[140] They relate only to the industrial countries of Europe and to Canada, Australia, New Zealand and the U.S.A., showing how (a) telephones per 100 population (total: business and domestic)[5] and (b) daily newspapers (not Sundays) per 100 population[330] vary among these countries according to their wealth, as measured by their Gross National Products.[140] In both these cases, the correlations are extremely high (see the values, stated on the Figures), though countries vary much among themselves.

It is worth noting, at this point, that the scattering of the spots on these and the other Scatter Diagrams may be due to two causes. First, because countries vary in their adoption and use of the various media; this is the real interest. Second, it may be due to inaccuracy of the data for, as already noted, national statistics of this kind should 'be taken with some reserve' (see Foreword, Ref. 140) for their estimation can be very difficult, as can other census data, especially for less developed countries. However, it is unlikely that the various sources of inaccuracy will *reduce* the amount of scattering; they are more likely to increase it. Consequently, from such

* The figures for the Gross National Products (G.N.P.) of various countries, used in these and other diagrams, have been taken from the *World Bank Atlas*, by kind permission of the International Bank for Reconstruction and Development.[140]

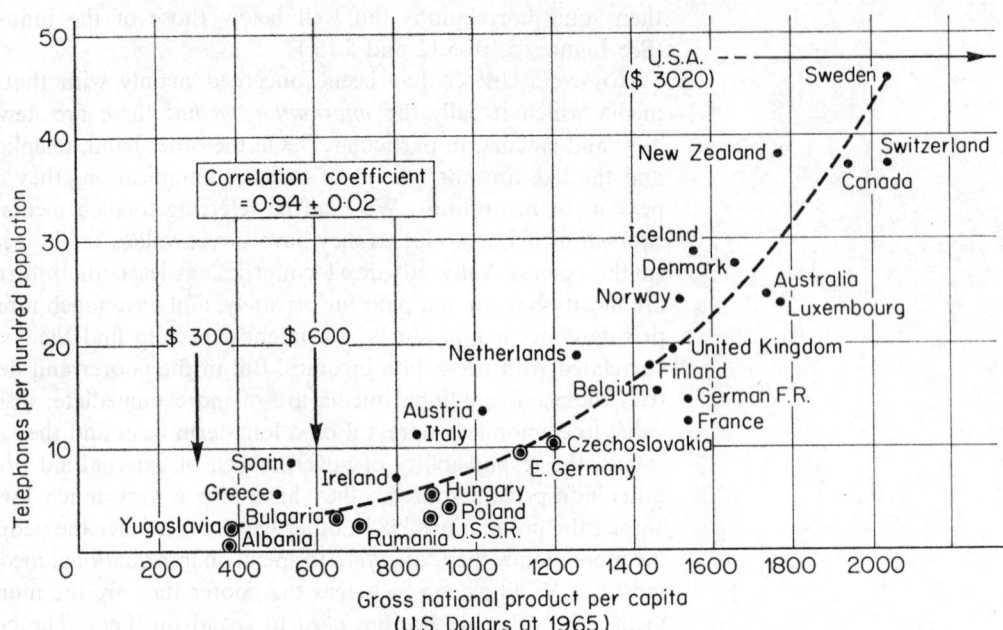

Figure 5.5. Correlation between wealth and telephones in the industrially advanced countries of Europe, Canada, Australia, New Zealand and U.S.A., in 1966.

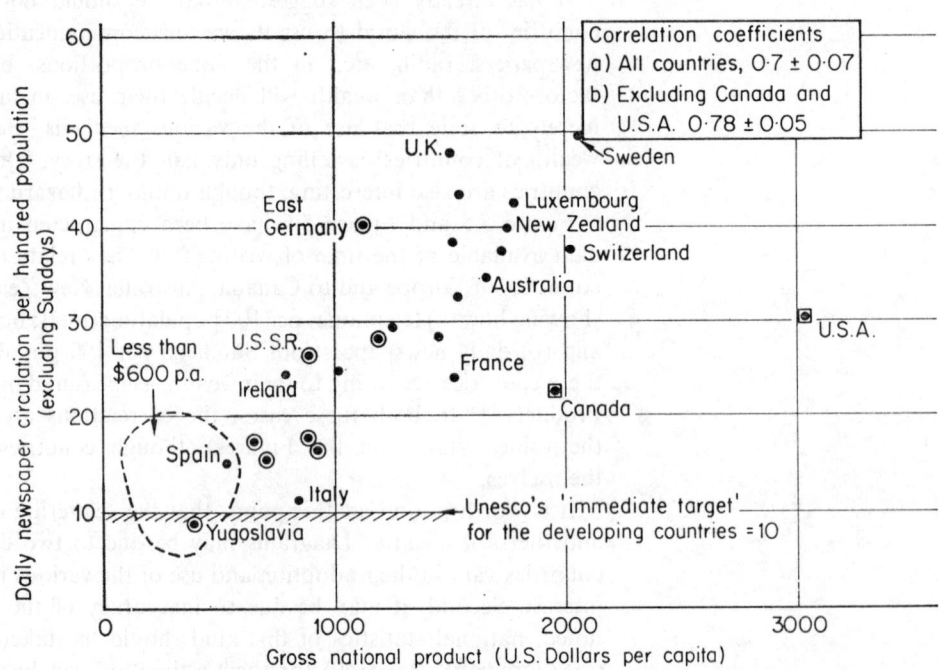

Figure 5.6. Correlation between wealth and daily newspaper circulation in the industrialized countries of Europe, Canada, Australia, New Zealand and U.S.A., in 1966.

From newspaper circulation data, copyright United Nations (*Statistical Yearbook*, 1966). Reproduced by permission.

diagrams we can reasonably assess at a glance which countries value the media more or less than others, considering their relative wealths.

For example, Figure 5.5 shows that Sweden, Switzerland and New Zealand, in particular, invest in far more telephones (in relation to their wealth) than do France, the German Federal Republic or Belgium. Again, in relation to its *wealth* ($3020 per capita) the U.S.A. possesses relatively *few* telephones (47·8 per 100 population). All the Communist countries shown have fewer telephones than the others; it is in newspapers that they excel.

It may be of interest to compare Figure 5.5 with the earlier Figure 5.2 to see how the various industrial countries have changed their relative positions, with regard to their adoption of telephones as they have got richer over the eight years, 1958–1966. Notice too that the Correlation Coefficient has scarcely changed over that time. (It should also be noted that in Jones' Figure 5.2 wealth is measured as Income per capita and not as Gross National Product (see p. 142 for the distinction).

The Trend Line in Figure 5.2 has been drawn *straight*; the only justification for this is simplicity. Actually, a curved line would be rather better and such a line has been drawn on Figure 5.5, around which the spots cluster most closely.* They cluster around the line very closely indeed and the correlation between telephones and wealth (G.N.P.), in this case of the industrial countries has the very high value shown (0·94 ± 0·02). There is one remarkable exception to this clustering, the United States of America. The spot representing the U.S.A. falls very far *under* the Trend Line, to the right, as was noted before.

This Trend Line curves *upward*; consequently we may conclude that, as countries get richer, they invest in proportionally *more* telephones, though the U.S.A. is the one great exception. It is, perhaps, approaching saturation.

Turning now to newspaper circulations, Figure 5.6 shows the relation between *daily* newspaper circulations per 100 people and the G.N.P.s of the industrial countries. In this case, correlation is not particularly high (0·7 ± 0·07), partly due to the two remarkable exceptions of Canada and the U.S.A., both of which appear to have far lower *daily* (not Sunday) newspaper circulations than other countries. If these two be separated off, the correlation rises to 0·78 ± 0·05, which is considerably higher.

There is some suggestion shown by this same Figure that the Communist countries (ringed spots) increase their newspaper circulations proportionally more, in relation to wealth, than non-Communist countries, though the small amount of data gives nothing more than a suggestion.

We see also from this diagram that, in proportion to their G.N.P.s, East Germany and Britain circulate most newspapers per 100 population, and Yugoslavia and Italy least. If Sunday newspapers be added to each country's totals, the spots redistribute, putting Britain ahead as the country with the highest total newspaper circulation per head in the world.[320, 330]

2. Communication and wealth: the developing countries

Popular use of the terms 'advanced' and 'developing' countries may suggest that the world is divided sharply and clearly into two separate camps, separated by an ever-widening gap in all aspects of life: in incomes, birthrates, education, political development, etc. This is not strictly correct; the United Nations definition of a developing country is based solely upon

* There are precise rules in Mathematical Statistics for drawing such curved Trend Lines, but they do not concern us here.

economics; it is a country whose Gross National Product is estimated as being less than 300 U.S. dollars per capita, per annum.[140]

The map in Figure 3.2 shows these countries, marked in appropriate black and others, in grey, whose Gross National Products in 1967 lay between

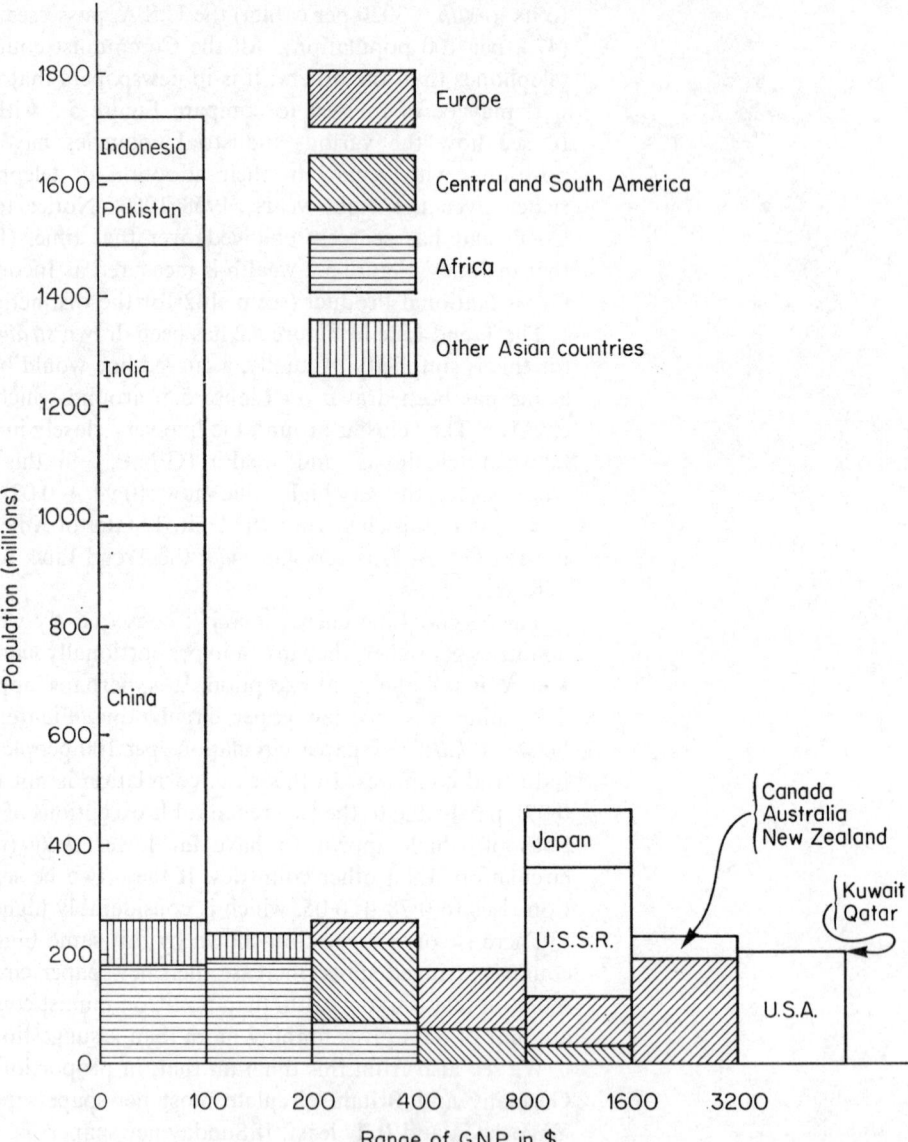

Figure 5.7. 'The Gap' between the poor and the rich countries, as at 1967. This diagram is based upon averages for whole countries and gives no indication of the great variations that may exist within each country.

(G.N.P. and population figures taken from the *World Bank Atlas*, published by the International Bank for Reconstruction and Development,[140] with kind permission.)

$300 and $600. Such a picture is based upon *averages* and gives no indication whatever of the immense variations of income that can exist among the inhabitants of each country.

Use of the term 'the gap' also suggests that there are no middling peoples, which is also not correct. Figure 5.7 has been based upon G.N.P. figures for most countries of the world, assessed for 1967, by the International Bank for Reconstruction and Development[140] and it shows the real nature of the economic gap. Most countries are included, with a total population of 3350 million. The horizontal scale has been divided into 6 intervals, each successive one representing a doubling of income (i.e. a logarithmic scale); within each interval the height of the block indicates the number of people living in those countries whose G.N.P. falls within that interval. (For example, 265 million people live in countries of G.N.P. between $200–400.) Furthermore, each block has been divided up, so as to show the continents and certain major countries making up these populations. This diagram illustrates a number of aspects of the gap. This diagram too is based upon average incomes in whole countries and gives no indication at all of the great variations among people within each country which, for many purposes, can be misleading. Thus, on this average *per capita* basis, Kuwait is the richest country in the world ($3490 in 1967).

The poorest section, having a G.N.P. less than $100, is made up almost entirely of the people of China, India, Pakistan, many African countries and Indonesia: over half the world's people. Other Asian and African countries comprise between them the populations lying in the next block $100–200. Most Central and South American countries lie within the third and fourth blocks, $200–800. Europe, the U.S.S.R. and Japan take up the whole of the fifth block, $800–1600, and the U.S.A. and parts of Europe most of the final block, $1600–3200 and more. The 'gap' then is not an empty gulf between rich and poor; rather it means that, as time passes, the *range* of incomes widens, still leaving nearly half the world's population at the bottom end, below $100.[362]

This diagram reduces the poverty of some 2000 million people to the neatness of geometry.

All these countries marked black on the map on p. 63 have one thing in common, that their average economies are so small that they have too little, without aid, to invest in agricultural improvement, industry, communication and education, except perhaps locally, but not in a way which involves the mass of their population on an organized basis.

Such a simple map as Figure 3.2 does indicate a few relevant facts. For example, the fractions of the earth's land surface marked white, grey or black, though the population densities vary so much within each. Thus within both black and white regions there are areas where people are packed like sardines (e.g. Calcutta, Hong Kong, London, New York, Tokyo) and areas which are virtually void (e.g. the Sahara, the Arabian and American deserts, the Himalaya, both Mongolias and central Australia). The map also indicates that the poor countries are not randomly scattered, but form one continuous belt, lying substantially between the 40th parallel North and the Tropic of Capricorn; or, to be more geometric, within the sloping belt shown on the map, with the one remarkable exception of Japan, with its 100 million people. This belt lies over the tropical and sub-tropical zones; geography, terrain and climate, as well as history, provide most of the seeds of difficulty, mountain ranges, monsoons and droughts, with wide seasonal variations, poor soils and other unkindnesses of nature.[282] These countries are poor only in certain respects, mainly economic, but what potentials they may have in both human and untapped material resources, what mental powers, what special abilities, have not everywhere had a chance to come to light.

Although these countries of low income may be lumped together under the title 'developing countries', they differ widely among themselves in many respects.[329,330] They are not 'a special sort of people'. As one U.N. Report emphasizes, widespread beliefs about differences between the mental and physical characteristics of people of different races are based upon literary accounts and not upon facts and statistics; the innate variations among the individuals of any one race are considered by some to be as great if not greater than the differences between racial averages.[213] The developing countries vary widely in ways other than income. They vary in their population growth-rates: for example population growths also vary much among the economically advanced countries. Over large regions of the world the statistics may have doubtful accuracies (e.g. Africa and Asia). The 'population explosion everywhere, however, is due primarily to reduced mortality rather than to increased birthrates'.[329] They vary too in climates, in their mineral resources, in having rivers suitable for irrigation or for hydro-electric power stations. They vary in disease, in land fertility, etc. On the social side, they vary in their political development, or in the degree to which they possess the concept of change, or in their traditions of land tenure, etc., or, in the cases of ex-colonial territories, in their inheritances of social institutions suited to the development of industry (e.g. newspapers, Trade Unions, schools). Economic progress does not depend solely upon possession of capital and material resources, but equally upon mental attitudes; for example it has been pointed out that, among many pre-industrial people, only *personal* relationships are understood and the remote, abstract bureaucrat may be quite incomprehensible or, again, that the abstract idea of 'the job', which can be filled by any suitable applicant, has not evolved as something separate from the person.[7] Even less can 'social progress' be measured in economic terms alone.[329]

The sociologist, Daniel Lerner, questions the use of such terms as 'backward' or 'underdeveloped' areas, as being Western in concept. He says:

'These were *our* words. *They* never thought of themselves as "areas" at all. . . . Now that they can throw out the imperialists, they are no longer "colonial". Now that they can articulate contempt for our civilization, they are no longer "backward". Now that they can reject our aid and advice, they may no longer be treated as "underdeveloped". . . . Since World War II, the global quest for new ways has been coupled with a repudiation of the Western aegis. . . . Any label that today localizes the fount of innovation in the West is bound to seem parochial. . . . Accordingly, we speak nowadays simply of "modernization".' He continues:

'The desire to do it oneself, the belief (whether true or false) that one *can* do it oneself, is a long first step along the psychic course of modernization. It carries people from the constrictive traditional universe of fatalism, ignorance, and apathy to the modern world of self-reliance, learning, and participation.'*[185,186]

Lerner distinguishes four essential processes towards modernization; one being *communication*, the other three being urbanization, industrialization, secularization, arguing that societies 'go modern' only to the degree that their people individually do so and, in an exploratory study, suggests that 'modernization', and 'rate of modernization' of countries, could be measured in terms of the correlations of their statistics on literacy, urbanization,

* With very kind permission.

communication media consumption, and voting.[184,185] No doubt other statistics on socio–economic–technological categories could be added, for such statistics are published extensively today by U.N. and its Agencies and by Government departments in the form of Yearbooks, etc., such as have been referred to so frequently in this book. (See Bibliography; for example, under United Nations, Unesco, United Kingdom, United States, and individual's names.)

As regards the values of the many forms of communication media available today, we have here broadly distinguished two classes (see Section 1); namely (a) their direct economic values (most clearly seen in the cases of telephones, telegraphs, postal services, etc.) and (b) their educational values (most obvious in the cases of radio, T.V., newspapers, books, cinema, etc.) though of course any of the media can have degrees of both values. We here refer to these two classes as, respectively, the *organizational* values and (following Unesco) the *informational* values. They are, of course, closely dependent. Furthermore, both values apply to the advanced as well as to the developing countries, though for different reasons. It is popular to sneer at the trivia in our own newspapers, in the cinema and on T.V. and easy to overlook the indirect or hidden ways in which they inform us, help to combat rumour, stimulate our criticism and in many ways educate us (see Chapter 6, Section 7). It is also easy to forget the immense range of intelligence, interests and knowledge of affairs which exists among any country's people, however economically advanced they may be.

Industrialization depends utterly upon the organizing powers of modern communication and transport and, furthermore, an industrial and stable society can evolve only alongside the psychological, educational values of the so-called mass-media, for it is only via the Press and radio, or wall sheets and other informational-media that large populations of people can be informed and can develop a sense of common living and purpose, or even a sense of nationhood: *whilst the conditions under which they live are changing rapidly.*[188] And change, rapid change, is one of the hall-marks of the world today, both in industrial and in many developing countries.

Professor Lucian Pye,* writing of the 'long slow process of institution building' in the new countries, refers to the values of the mass-media and other modes of communication for providing a basis of shared 'perceptions, cognitions, and emotional sentiments' (what he calls 'social communication') upon which understanding of political institutions can grow and trust develop. The roles of the Press, radio and other media differ in different countries, he argues, according to the degrees of development of their other institutions (e.g. Civil Service, Education . . .) and so does the 'freedom' which they should responsibly assume, or their 'rights' of criticism; we can be wrong in judging the Press and radio of developing countries, if we apply the standards of the Western stable democracies, whilst they are still struggling to develop their institutions and to relate them together. The freedom which the Press and radio of a new country can assume derives from the need to balance their two functions: (a) to act as 'inspector general' of government and other developing institutions and to criticize responsibly and (b) to 'inspire people to a vision of the new political world'. A developing Press (or radio), as an

---

* Passages used here are quoted from Lucian W. Pye, 'Communication, Institution Building, and the Reach of Authority', in *Communication and Change in the Developing Countries* (Ed. D. Lerner and W. Schramm) East–West Corner Press, Honolulu, 1967 with kind permission. (Ref. 188.)

institution, should itself try to understand the problems of the other various developing institutions and, Professor Pye observes, that ability does not always exist.[188]

One of the numerous handicaps under which the Press and radio of developing countries may have to operate is the difficulty of recruiting staff of adequately high calibre, for they have to compete with all the other institutions among the currently *limited pool* of educated and talented people.[164,307]

This difficulty is not of recent origin. As early as 1926, the Press Congress of the World, an international body of newspaper editors and journalists founded in 1915, urged the study of the problems of training journalists and recommended an increase in the number of training schools, or raising of standards and wider international exchange of both journalists and technicians.[307] Various other international professional bodies also took action. After the Second World War, the newly founded Unesco started a survey, first in Latin America and later extended to the other continents, to discover the deficiencies and the needs, including training needs, of the developing countries in order to raise the standards of their Press (and radio and other media). The War itself had aggravated the situation, because many countries of Asia, Africa and Europe had also suffered great losses of equipment and staff in their News Agencies, press, radio and film enterprises. The U.N. Conference on Freedom of Information considered remedies and encouraged the development of News Agencies, an increased production of low-cost radio receivers and production and distribution of newspapers (Geneva 1948). The U.N. and its specialized Agencies have continually sought to persuade governments of the great social importance of having adequate mass-communication media, especially in the new and poorer countries, as a basis for building both their economies and their politics, for raising standards of literacy and education, for training in agriculture, health, industry and all fields of social life.*[262,266,301,302,307,310,315,319,320]

As a result of an enquiry from the U.N., made to the world's governments in 1955, it appeared that they had many common problems and needs in regional areas; following this enquiry, a series of Regional Conferences were organized in S.E. Asia, Latin America, Africa and the Middle East which were specially concerned with problems of training for journalism and press in these developing areas.† Unesco has given extensive assistance to improve their news services and radio broadcasting, by helping to set up training centres for journalists, through improvement of printing techniques, by educational films, audio–visual aids, educational T.V., documentary films, experiments in community T.V. viewing, by development of special equipment suited to tropical countries without electricity, and in many technical ways. The abundance of technique which has poured from the cornucopia of Western technology during the post-War years not only provides more toys for the affluent, but offers great assistance to the others in their race to 'catch up'. However, the technology often requires both adaptation and cheapening to serve their individual conditions, needs and wishes; fortunately, both seem to be happening in certain fields of communication technology.

* See the numerous *Reports and Papers on Mass Communication*, published by Unesco. Specific ones are here referred to in the Bibliography; there are many others.
† See *Unesco Reports and Papers on Mass Communications*, No. 45, 'Professional Training for Mass Communication', 1965.

Other difficulties which bear upon the various media of communication in developing countries arise from the fact that the media are closely dependent upon one another. For example, before a newspaper can be printed locally, roads must be built in order that paper can be transported and the printed papers distributed.[71] Before news can be received locally, without days or weeks of delay, telephones and telegraphs must be working efficiently. Before telephones and telegraphs can be operated and receive the necessary maintenance, technicians must be trained, and their training and primary education requires text books or other printed material. So we might go on. Yet the various media of communication and transport often develop unequally for several reasons. Thus aid programmes, both technical and financial, may contribute more to one medium than to another, according to the specific manufacturing interests of the donor countries; or governments may not fully appreciate the full values of the various media. Again, colonial histories and highly specialized economies may have left countries after independence with the various media unsuited to the development of education, or of more varied industries and other new institutions. In the new countries, the various institutions of government, education, commerce, law, communication and others, tend to develop more independently of one another than do those of the economically advanced nations, whose long history of development has evolved more closely-knit and balanced sets of institutions.[188] The consequence is that we might expect to find the various media of communication in developing countries to be far less closely correlated with their economic product than they are in the industrially advanced nations.

Indeed, there is evidence that this is true. Among the many distinctions between the developing countries there lies their very varied possession of different communication media.[5, 149, 320, 330] From the published statistics it is possible, in principle, to study the correlation (or rather lack of it) between the various media and the economic states of the various developing countries. Unfortunately there are several sources of inaccuracy and doubt concerning many of the published statistics, which may tend to reduce the correlations and so obscure the results.

However, let us look at the same two correlations as were examined in the last Section in relation to the industrial countries (Figures 5.5 and 5.6).

Figures 5.8, 5.9 and 5.10, show Scatter Diagrams for the countries of Central and South America, Asia and Africa, relating their wealths (Gross National Products) and their possession of telephones.[5] Again, Figures 5.11, 5.12 and 5.13 relate to circulations of newspapers. It is worth comparing these diagrams with Figures 5.5 and 5.6 for the industrial countries.

In the case of the Central and South American countries, both their telephones and their newspaper circulations are well correlated with their respective G.N.P.s (see Figures 5.8 and 5.11). Haiti seems to be the worst served and Uruguay the best. Only those countries are shown which have G.N.P.s less than $600, which excludes the Argentine, Venezuela and Puerto Rico (see Table 5). South America is a continent of very varied economic conditions and possession of communication media.

Figures 5.9 and 5.12 show the corresponding Scatter Diagrams for Asia, and include only those countries having, in this case, less than $300 per capita per annum. This excludes a number of countries (see Table 5). In the case of telephones (Figure 5.9) the correlation is seen to be high (0·81) which testifies, among other things, to reasonable accuracy of the published statistics

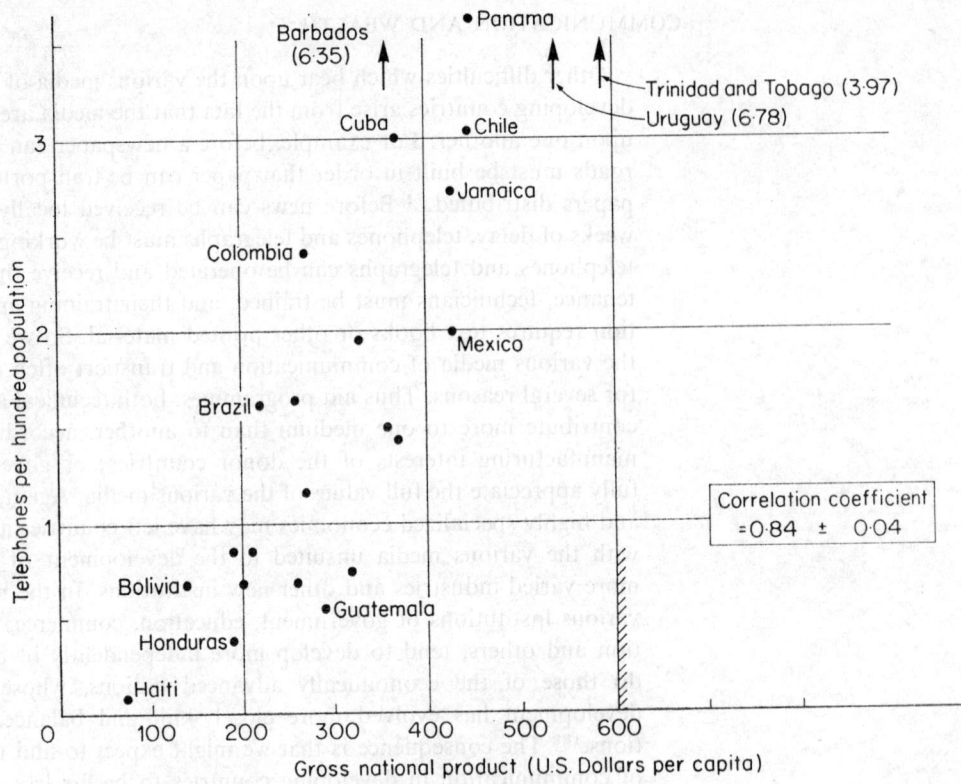

Figure 5.8. Correlation between wealth and telephones in countries of South and Central America (in 1966) with per capita income of less than $600.

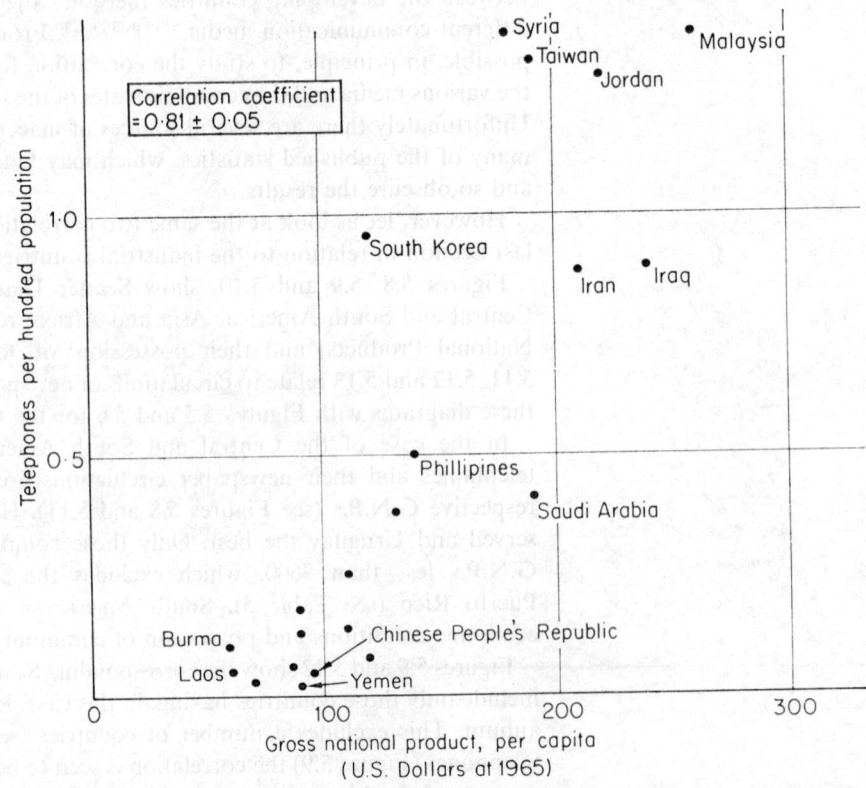

Figure 5.9. Correlation between wealth and telephones in developing countries. (a) Asian countries (1966) with less than $300 per capita per annum.

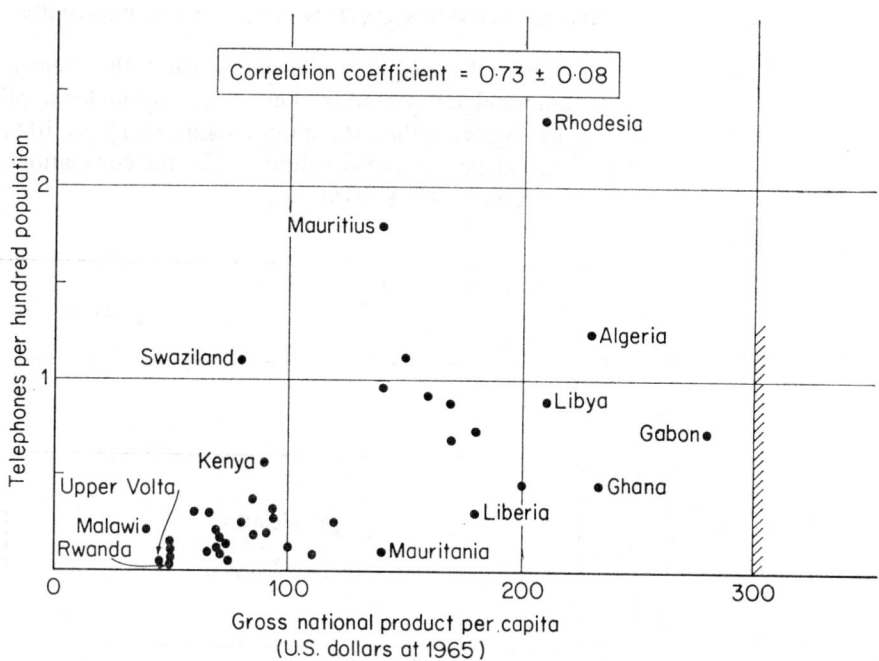

Figure 5.10. Correlation between wealth and telephones in developing countries. (b) African countries (1966) with less than $300 per capita per annum.

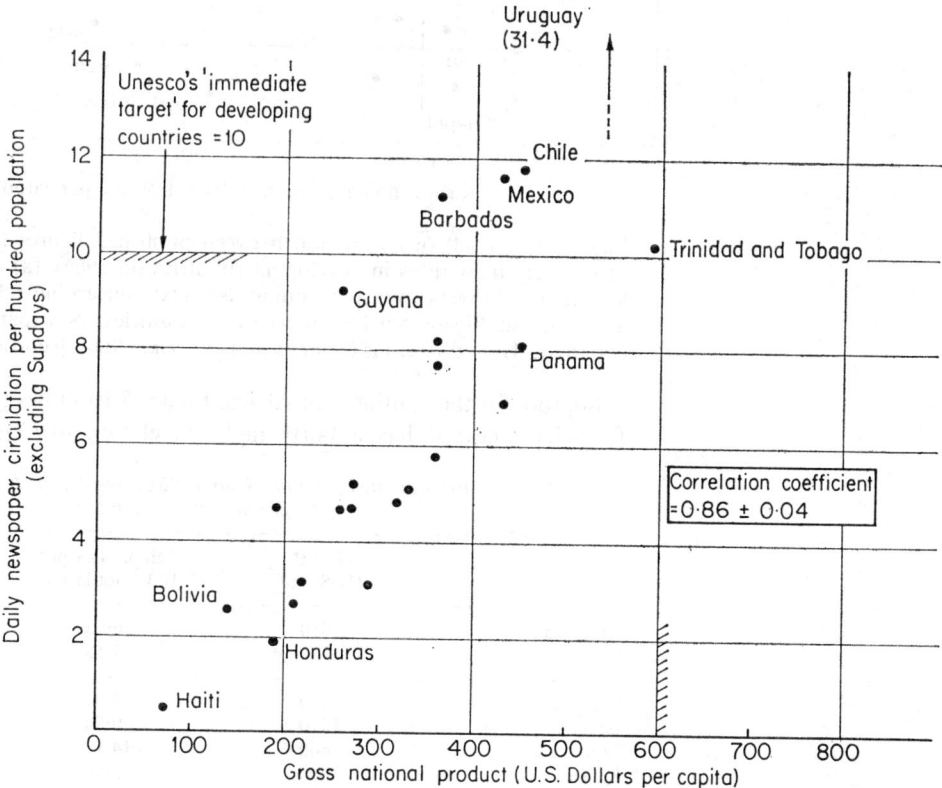

Figure 5.11. Correlation between wealth and daily newspaper circulation in countries of South and Central America (1966) with per capita income less than $600. Newspaper circulation data, copyright United Nations (*Statistical Yearbook*, 1966). Reproduced by permission.

Again the range is enormous, from the Yemen to Syria and Malaysia, although every country here is grossly undersupplied with telephones, none having more than the minute figure of 1½ per 100 population. In the case of newspapers however (Figure 5.12), the correlation is both very low and very uncertain (0·3 ± 0·16).

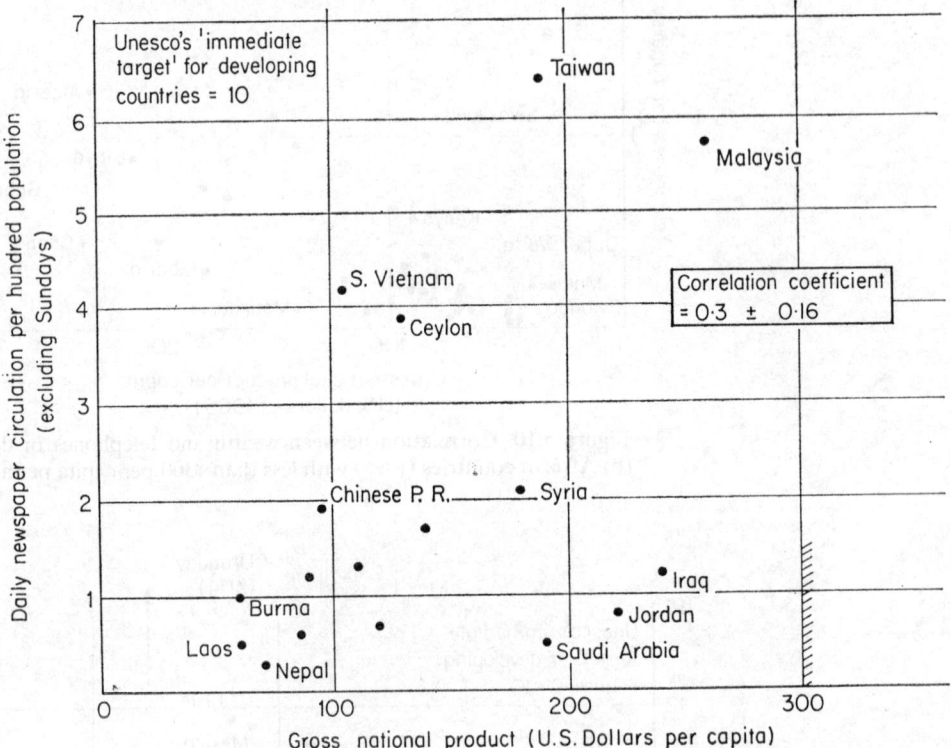

Figure 5.12. Lack of correlation between published figures for wealth and daily newspaper circulations in developing countries (in 1966). (a) Asian countries with less than $300 per capita per annum. See text concerning reliability of this data, and data on Figere 5.9 re other Asian countries. Newspaper circulation data, copyright, United Nations (*Statistical Yearbook*, 1966). Reproduced by permission.

So, too, for the continent of Africa. Figure 5.10 shows the Scatter Diagram for telephones; it has a fairly high correlation (0·73 ± 0·08) although a

Table 5. *Countries omitted from the Scatter Diagrams, having G.N.P.s greater than*
$300 per annum (year: 1966)

	G.N.P. (U.S.: $)	Telephones per 100 Population	Daily Newspapers per 100 Population
Argentine	650	6·65	14·8
Venezuela	780	3·18	7·0
Hong Kong	320	6·84	34·9
Israel	1070	9·84	14·3
Japan	660	14·18	45·1
Kuwait	3290	5·56	2·8
Lebanon	390	4·43	—
Mongolia	480	1·24	8·8
Singapore	460	4·6	26·8
South Africa	530	6·64	5·7

number of countries seem to be remarkably divergent, e.g. Swaziland, Gabon, Ghana. However, as with Asian countries, the newspaper circulations in Africa are very poorly correlated with G.N.P.; the Scatter Diagram (Figure 5.13) has a correlation coefficient of only 0·48 ± 0·11.

The broad result therefore is that telephones, which are essentially economic and organizational instruments, are closely correlated with wealth, whereas newspapers are so only in Central and South America, as well as in the industrialized countries.

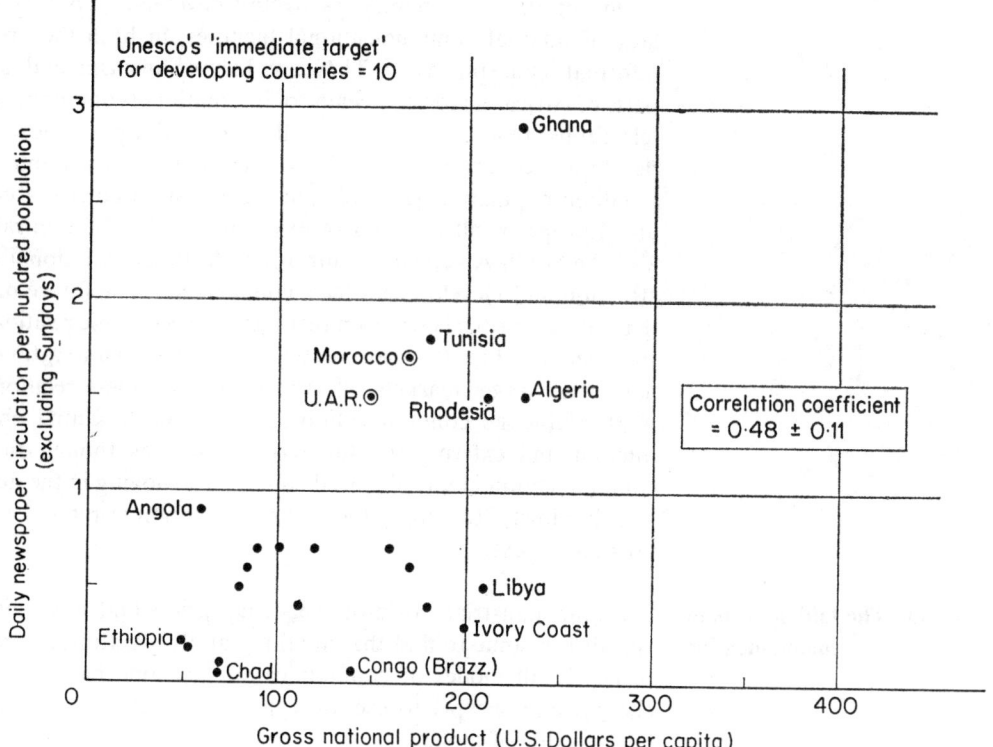

Figure 5.13. Lack of correlation between published figures for wealth and daily newspaper circulation in developing countries (in 1966). (b) African countries with less than $300 per capita per annum. See text concerning reliability of this information and data on Figure 5.10 relating to Africa.
Newspaper circulation data, copyright, United Nations (*Statistical Yearbook*, 1966). Reproduced by permission.

It must be admitted immediately that one plausible explanation could be the questionable accuracy of the statistical data for Africa and Asia. Such national statistics are notoriously difficult to collect and it is fairly certain that far better figures are known for telephones (which usually come under one reporting authority, which keeps records) than for newspapers (which do not). There are also other reasons, viz:

(a) The term 'newspaper' may mean anything from a single sheet to a journal of 50 or more pages.[330]

(b) Each copy may be read by (or read aloud to, in a meeting) many people collected together, especially in poorer countries. (There is a

Swahili newspaper published in Nairobi, East Africa, called *Baraza* which literally means *The Meeting*.) Thus the paper circulation figure does not measure the 'news circulation', by a long chalk.

(c) In the case of some countries, mostly poor ones, the statistics returned were based on a restricted number of their newspapers.[330]

(d) Newspaper statistics are not collected very frequently from some countries, so that some of the figures used to construct the Scatter Diagrams are out-of-date (e.g. China's figures relate to 1955).[330]

One of the great handicaps to any developing country's progress is its lack of internal communicational facilities, in both the organizational and informational spheres.[320] They are lacking in Asia and even more so in parts of Africa. So too are means for international communication: telephones, telegraphs, roads, railways . . . all means. Many, or most, of the new and developing countries are small; over half the world's countries have less than 5 million population. [In 1966, $\frac{2}{3}$ of the African countries, about $\frac{1}{4}$ of the Asian and European, all but two (Mexico and Cuba) of Central American and $\frac{1}{2}$ of the South American countries.][140] As the International Bank for Reconstruction and Development have commented: 'The future of small countries depends to a critical degree on their external economic relationships, including the extent to which they can combine with each other to rationalize production and create larger markets.'[140] And to develop these relationships they need vastly improved communication services, that 'essential prerequisite', both internal and external. Fortunately it looks as though the technology of communication in the advanced countries is moving in the direction required, if only slowly, to supply the means at economic rates. Let us look at this possibility next.

3. The falling costs of communication

In our industrial world of ever-rising prices and wages, it may come as a surprise to some to find that anything at all is getting cheaper. Yet it is true of nearly all modes of communication; as time has passed they have got cheaper and cheaper to use, though only if these costs are corrected for the falling value of money.

There are several reasons for this economic blessing. First, because the degree of organization that is possible for an industrial society, and its economic progress, *ceteris paribus*, is out of proportion to the communication means it possesses. For example, a new telephone trunk line, once installed, is available for the varied uses of thousands of people; and it can be used, not for one, but for a multitude of purposes. So too with a new airline, or trunk road, or Telex route. Such things enable many people and institutions in the economy to reorganize their affairs, both personally and in relation to one another. Basically, this is because communication is not a consumer commodity but a service.[215] Second, the falling costs of communication are due to a principle referred to often as *trunking* (as in trunk roads or trunk telephone lines). Briefly, this means that the more traffic that can be carried at a time over a single route or system the cheaper it becomes for any one user. For example, the more telephone circuits that can be packed into a single trunk cable, by improved techniques, the cheaper it becomes to use *per circuit*. Or again, as passenger aircraft have got larger and larger, carrying more and more people, so each person's fare per mile can be reduced; hence Jumbo Jets; so also has the cost of airmail fallen, and of other means.

There are several other reasons for these falling costs, including the rapid growth of traffic demands, i.e. the 'explosion' described in Chapter 3, the trends of research and design which are bound up with the search for new markets and, in certain cases, with policy relating to the developing countries. But, before referring to these reasons, let us take a few concrete examples which may be more convincing.

(a) *Newspapers*. The cost of newspapers fell dramatically during the 19th century, apart from a temporary rise caused by the notorious Stamp Tax, which was removed in 1855. (See Chapter 2, Section 5 and Chapter 3, Section 2 for some historical notes.)

In 1790 an English provincial newspaper cost $3\frac{1}{2}$d,[250] but no circulation exceeded 5000.[355] By 1815 the price had doubled, partly due to the Stamp Tax, though circulations were increasing. By 1850, no daily paper had more than 50,000 circulation but, by the end of the 19th century, at least one had a circulation of 750,000. The age of popular newspapers was well established. By 1955 there was one in Britain with a circulation of about 5,000,000.[355]

With these increasing circulations, prices fell. In the 1860s the London *Times* cost only 3d, for example; today the prices of our dailies range between $2\frac{1}{2}$p and 5p. However, the value of the £ has fallen by the ratio of 5 to 1 during that past century;[76] thus 3d then was about equivalent to 6p today (or, in U.S. currency, from 3 cents to 15 cents, very roughly). In spite of rising *nominal* prices, far more people can now afford to buy them.

(b) *Postal Service*. Perhaps one of the causes of the common illusion that 'prices are always rising' is the obvious fact that prices can rise only by jumps. This is well illustrated by the cost of stamps; for example, when the British letter post rose from 3d to 4d, many people grumbled, not realizing that the post was still cheaper than ever, except for the time *just prior to that rise*. If the price could have risen in infinitesimal steps, they would scarcely have noticed; but prices cannot rise by units smaller than the smallest coinage. It may not escape our memories that a letter in Britain, *before* the last War, cost $1\frac{1}{2}$d which at today's money values is about 2p (see Ref. 76); but our money values are still falling.

The cost of letter postage has, in fact, fallen considerably during the past century. Thus, in 1840 a letter from New York to Boston cost $18\frac{3}{4}$ cents, a very high price, even before allowing for falling money values.[200] It was the rationalization of mail charges and postal organization, both within countries and internationally, consequent upon the setting up of the Universal Postal Union in 1874 (see Chapter 4, Section 6), that was partly responsible for reducing these prices enormously.

(c) *Telephones and Telegraphs, etc*. In the telecommunication field it is not only the explosive demand for traffic which has led to reduced costs, but the corresponding spectacular technical developments in electronics. As time has passed, newer techniques have evolved suited to carrying ever greater volumes of message traffic on a single route.

This is no place for a technical discussion of these techniques, but the facts are exampled by Figure 5.14, which shows how the relative capital costs of installing 100 miles of trunk line have fallen over 50 years, as new types of line have been introduced carrying progressively more conversations (or their equivalent in telegraph traffic*). Notice the effect of falling money values on the rate of cost reduction. Even more modern techniques, like the

---

* From Sir Albert Mumford (Ref. 218). With kind permission.

'laser', offer, if only as yet in *principle*, the possibility of sending more messages at once, over the same route, than will be needed in the foreseeable
future; electronic techniques have outstripped our social needs and research
is now concentrating on practicability, reliability and cost reduction. As
these principles are brought into practice, so costs of operation will continue

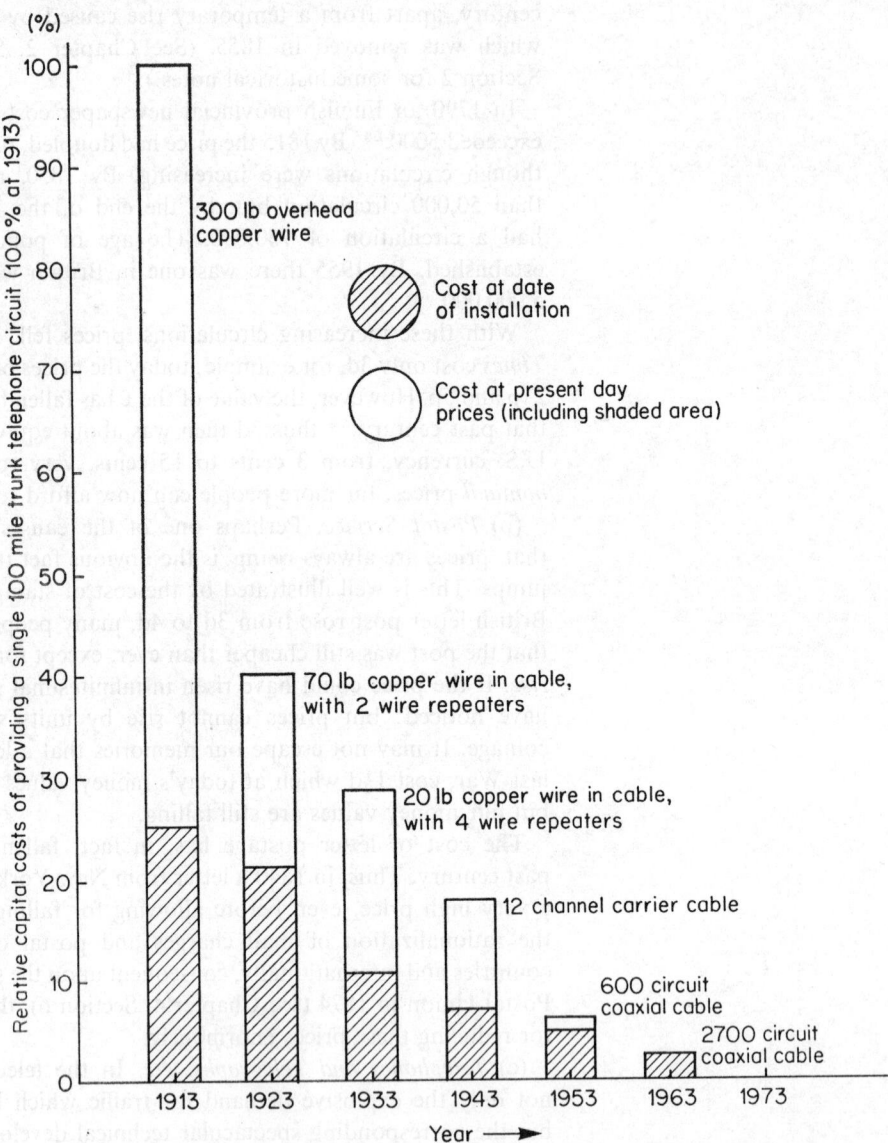

Figure 5.14. The falling costs of telephone trunk lines over the past 50 years,
accentuated by the falling value of money.
(After Sir Albert Mumford,[218] with kind permission.)

to fall. For example, waveguide and multiple coaxial cable methods are
now under consideration which may carry up to 100,000 messages simultaneously across continents. For long distance communication, satellites
will continue the same story for, now that really large and reliable ones have
been launched, they will *increase* the rate of cost reduction per message
channel. The present day satellites can carry twelve hundred telephone

conversations simultaneously, if needed. Soon, new models will go into commercial operation capable of carrying several thousands, and costs should fall dramatically (see Figure 5.15).

The essential price to gain all this cost reduction by using more modern techniques of communication, is to have the *need* to send thousands of simultaneous messages over the same route. Clearly, then, the advantage lies with those countries who have this need; that is, with the more highly industrialized countries. This important point will be taken up again in the next Section.

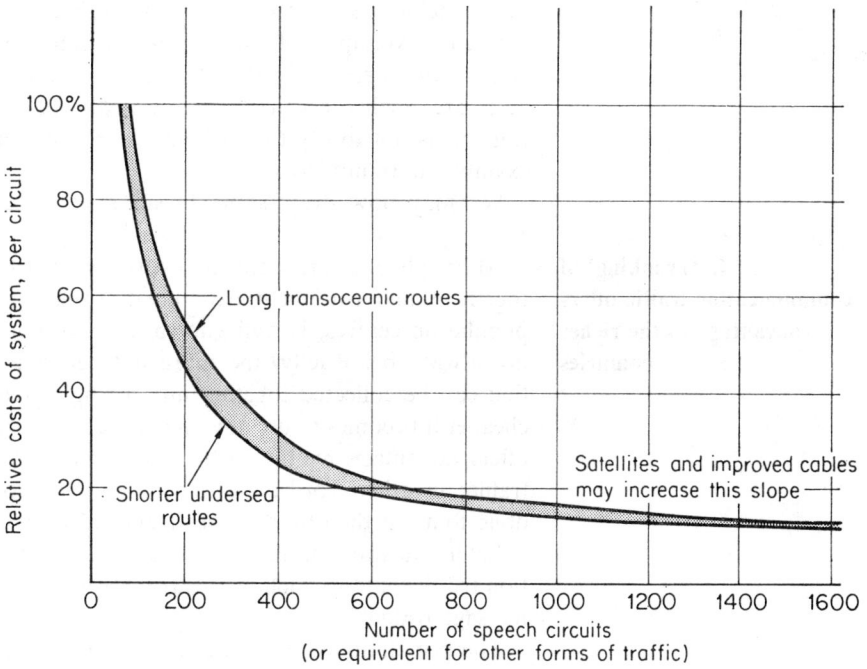

Figure 5.15. The economic advantage to the industrial countries of their heavy telecommunication traffic demands—overseas routes. This diagram merely indicates trends, and should not be interpreted with great precision.

If the falling value of money be allowed for, then it is true to say that telegraphs too have reduced their costs over their long history. When the first transatlantic telegraph cable was opened in 1866 (see Chapter 4, Section 1), one of the first messages to be sent was the news of the signing of the Treaty of Prague, and it cost Julius Reuter no less than £2 *per word*.[285] Inland telegraphy was of course far cheaper than that. Thus, for example, the cost of sending 10 words or less between New York and Philadelphia (and elsewhere) slowly rose from $0·25 to $0·95 between 1850 and 1956[334] but, over that century, the value of the $ fell by a far greater ratio.

At the present moment, some 80 per cent of the world's intercontinental telephone traffic is across the North Atlantic, connecting the industrial complexes of Europe and North America (see map, Figure 3.1). The cost of a three minute telephone call over this route has fallen greatly, from £15 in 1927 (when the first radio-telephone was introduced), to £9 the following year, to £4.4.0. in 1936, to £3 after the War, in 1945; today (1970) it is £1.13.9.[98] These figures are actual costs, *not* corrected for the falling value of money.[76]

It is worth noting too, that the capital cost of a satellite ground station suited to the traffic needs of developing countries is now only about $1·5 million to $2·5 million.

(d) *Air travel*. During its relatively short history, passenger air travel has become steadily cheaper, per passenger mile. Not only have technical developments assisted this economy, but aircraft have got larger, and, of course, the total passenger traffic has increased explosively (e.g. see the graphs Figure 2.3 and Figure 3.16). One published estimate states that the cost of passenger travel steadily reduced after the War, settling down to about 3d per mile by about 1955.[256]

Other examples of cheapening communication could be cited, where the reducing costs are due partly to technical efficiency, but mainly to the increasing volumes of traffic carried simultaneously (whether messages, persons or things) over the same route: i.e. to 'canalization'. These falling costs are further accentuated if we allow for the falling value of money. But this is not to say that *all* modes have become cheaper. Motor cars, for example, have not.

We may now draw some broad general conclusions from these facts.

4. 'Trunking' of communication traffic offers advantage to the richer countries

Although the practical necessity of collecting communication traffic together* and routing it over great trunk routes, between cities or other population centres, is well known, its enormous economic advantages may not always be. Briefly, the more independent channels of communication that can be collected together into a single great artery or trunk route, the cheaper it becomes to use any one of them. Clearly then, this general principle offers advantage mainly to those countries which have heavy demands for traffic; in other words, the richer industrial countries, unless something is done to assist the others, either technically or financially.

Let us illustrate this economic principle with the example of telecommunication trunk routes (which may carry telephone, telegraph, Telex, data or other message traffic).

The population of a country, or a continent, is geographically dispersed, with concentrations in cities and conurbations which vary much in size and dispersal. Message traffic is collected over local areas and routed together over trunk routes to distant points and there branched out to other areas, just as the twigs and branches of a tree send sap up and down the trunk to the roots. These trunk routes take many practical forms, the oldest being open wires slung on telephone poles, which were superseded by cables having higher message capacities; more modern techniques, e.g. coaxial cables, microwave beams, and others, have been evolved, as the years have gone by, which are able to carry ever increasing volumes of message traffic. Figure 5.16 shows the resulting steady fall of costs *per message channel* per mile. (A special scale has been used for this graphical diagram, called a logarithmic scale, but non-technical readers should have no difficulty in reading it.) This diagram does not take the form of an ordinary graph, but shows a wide, shaded band. The reason for this is that there are many different examples in use of each technical method; some, for example, use better materials than others, or are of higher efficiency for other reasons. However, broadly speaking, this band indicates how the costs have steadily fallen over the past decades, as new techniques have been introduced to carry the ever mounting volumes of traffic. We see from the downward slope of this band,

---

* 'Traffic' has been technically defined by the mathematical idea of 'information'.[50, 273] We shall not use the idea here.

that a ten-fold increase in the number of speech circuits may reduce the costs per circuit no less than five times. As indicated on this diagram, the same trend will continue into the future as trunk systems are introduced to carry 10,000, 100,000 and more simultaneous messages. This diagram relates only to overland systems.

It can be seen at a glance that, since the poorer nations at present do not have high traffic demands, the costs to them may be greater. However, it should not be thought that these nations are all confined to using open wire,

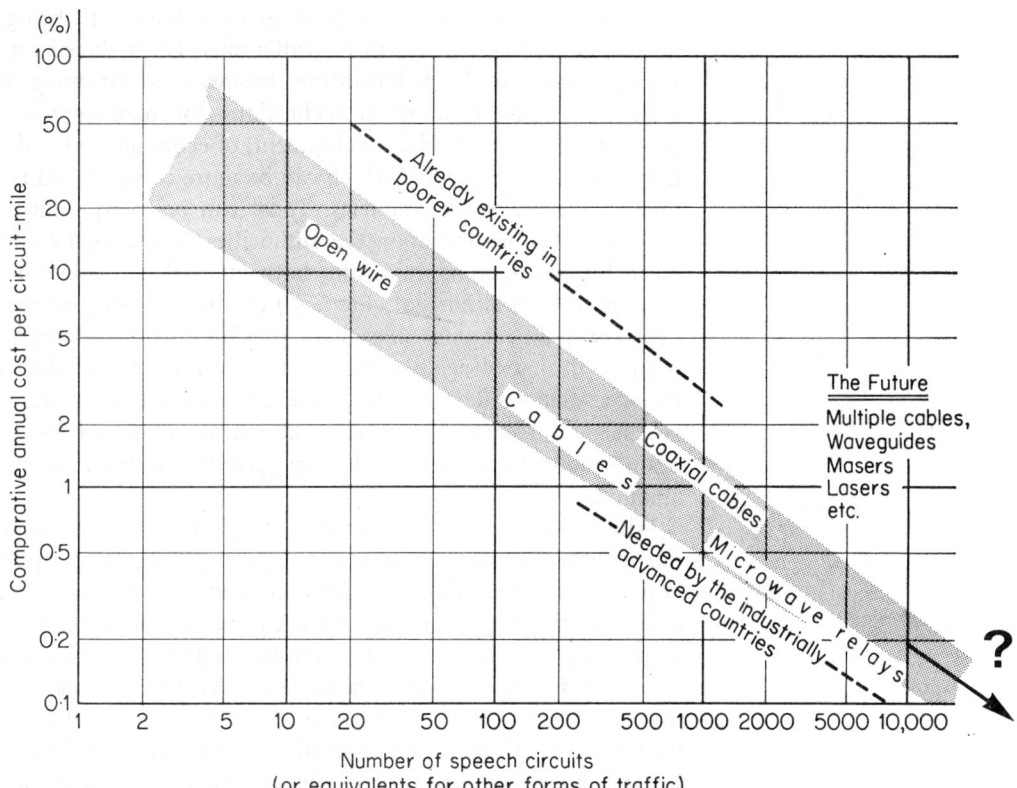

Figure 5.16. The economic advantage to the industrial countries of their heavy telecommunication demands—overland routes.

cable and the earlier techniques, for many of them are installing, or planning to install, microwave-relay trunk systems in anticipation of rapidly growing traffic (e.g. Mexico has done so, starting in 1962;[39] so have Peru and other Latin American countries; African countries are also anxious to improve their intercity communication, using modern techniques.[122,148,150]

Neither is it correct to assume that economic criteria alone determine the communication policies of developing countries; such things as terrain difficulties, security, dispersal of population, lack of trained personnel, etc., must also be considered. Nevertheless, broadly speaking, it is true to say that communication is more costly for the poorer countries, owing to their relatively small message traffic. In general, it is also more costly to them in capital investment, for the cost of, say, a long distance intercity link (which is measured in millions of dollars, and may be the first they possess) will be a disproportionately large fraction of their national income, unless aid is forthcoming.

One sometimes hears the charge that the powers-that-be in some developing countries want to have the latest technical equipment only for prestige purposes. There may be examples of this, just as there are also examples of unscrupulous salesmanship being foisted on the poor. Such squander or exploitation can arise not only from the desire to possess the technical facilities, but from wanting the wrong *kind*. Among all the plethora of techniques for national communication which are available today, it is not always easy for prospective buyers to choose, and expert advice is called for, but it must come from those who really understand on-the-spot conditions, physical and social. If expensive and large scale systems are being planned (say microwave relay) the growth of traffic must be predicted for the next 5–10 years, which can be a hazardous business, whilst programmes of road building, of the training of technicians for maintenance and operating personnel,[307] of industrial development, of economic aid and a host of other things must be considered which can be more complex and risky procedures than in the industrial countries. There can be many difficulties other than financial ones bearing upon the authorities in developing countries in their seach for better communication, both internal and external.[301,307] Populations may be multilingual; literacy may be low; electric supplies may not exist; or political difficulties may prevent their combining their message traffic with that of neighbouring countries in order to reduce costs. Even in Europe some similar difficulties exist; the various countries speak different languages, for example, whereas the various States of the U.S.A. do not; again, political difficulties in Europe have hardly been conspicuous by their absence.

Within the industrial countries the ever mounting demand for communication traffic has led to the evolution of techniques capable of handling hundreds of thousands of messages simultaneously; these, if only in principle, have outstripped our present day social needs. Of one technique (the laser) it has been said that it is 'a solution looking for a problem', so great are its potential message handling capabilities. As research and design introduce these new methods, so we move further down the trend line in Figure 5.16 towards ever cheaper communication in the future. Effort is now directed towards making these new possibilities practical, economic and reliable.

Reliability becomes increasingly important as the message capacities of systems increase. If a communication link carries only 5 or 10 messages at once, then a breakdown may not be too serious, at least within industrial areas where alternative modes of communication may exist. But if 10,000 are carried, then the disruption caused by a breakdown might be disastrous. So, as systems get larger, an increasing fraction of their cost is taken up to ensure reliability: in purity of materials, precision of manufacture, long life components, etc. The same principle applies to other modes of communication: to aircraft for example. Reliability and safety become increasingly important.

Again, as the message capacities of communication links get larger and larger, so they become of increasing value for connecting larger centres of population. Consequently, *ceteris paribus*, these links will become longer; but, at the same time the demands from the population of each centre will also continue to grow. This tendency has shown itself most markedly in the U.S.A. where proposals have been made to connect the great industrial complexes on the East and West sides by a link of 96,000 telephone channels (able, of course, to carry other forms of message traffic, as required).

5. Satellites and the poorer countries

It was explained in Chapter 3, Section 4, how communications satellites are not rivals to cables for intercontinental telephone and other traffic. Rather, the two are complementary in certain important ways. We shall see both techniques continuing in development and message capacity. Cables are 'point-to-point' in nature and serve particularly well to connect together industrially developed areas of high population density; for example, North Europe and North America. Satellites are more like broadcasting stations, inasmuch as they can 'beam' on to several different ground stations, in different parts of the world (see Figure 3.1).

Satellites which operate this way today are called 'multi-access' satellites and may be used, at different times of day for example, to connect those countries which have small traffic demands and do not need permanent connexion.

The primary purpose of communication satellites is to help with the rapidly growing international telephone traffic (see Figure 3.8 and others of Chapter 3) together with Telex and other telegraph traffic, and data etc. (e.g. related to the safe operation of the international airways*), and *not*, as often heard said, 'for worldwide television'. For television, films or tape records can be sent by fast aircraft more cheaply than direct transmission of programmes via satellites; only for certain important international events, when simultaneity of viewing is really meaningful, is direct transmission of T.V. by satellites economically justified.

Although the economics of satellites depend upon different principles from those of cables,[25] the same broad implications apply, namely that the heavier the volume of message traffic they carry the cheaper they are to use, per message channel. Consequently, they also offer economic advantage to the industrial countries, whose traffic demands are high, unless something is done to assist the others. The costs of a satellite communication system divide into two parts: (a) the capital cost of a country's ground stations, with maintenance and depreciation costs, and (b) the rental of the required number of channels in the satellite itself (e.g. payable to Intelsat: see Chapter 3, Section 4). A country which requires only a few overseas channels may decide on a small ground station, which will be cheaper in capital cost than a large one (a standard ground station may cost about £1½ million, say $4 million); however, such small stations make far less efficient use of the satellites, as a result of which their rental costs may be very much greater. It is these channel rentals which render the operation of small systems so much more costly. Figure 5.15 shows how costs rise with lower numbers of channels. Again, this curve has been drawn as a wide band to cover different systems and applies directly to transoceanic *cable* systems, whereas satellite systems are likely to slope downwards slightly more, at the right hand end. (The upper curve corresponds to long transoceanic systems, having channels spaced 3 kilocycles per second and the lower to shorter systems, having channels spaced 4 kilocycles per second.)

It is not only economics that determines the choice between cables and satellites for long distance communication; politics and geography also play a part. In fact one of the countries which may be among the first really to benefit by the use of a satellite for overseas civil communication is not an industrial but a developing country: East Africa. At present, East Africa is far removed from the nearest point of connexion to the world's telephone

---

* Ships too. See *Telecommunication Journal*, 33 No. 2, Feb. 1966, for several articles on the varied uses of world communication networks, including satellites.

cable system (see map, Figure 3.1) and cannot throw out its own to the
Western world without going through either the Suez canal or South Africa;
politics and geography together invite them to use the satellite which stands
over the Indian Ocean (see same Figure).

It may sometimes be the distribution of population which favours one
method or another. Thus the population of Canada is much concentrated
in cities which are spread out along an extensive line from Montreal in the
East to Vancouver on the Pacific coast, which invites a microwave link. On
the other hand the population of the U.S.S.R. is widely distributed over a
sub-continent 8000 miles long and 4000 miles wide, making satellites attractive.
The Russian satellite called Molnya uses an extremely eccentric orbit, as
shown in Figure 5.17, which circles the earth in 12 hours, exactly half a day;

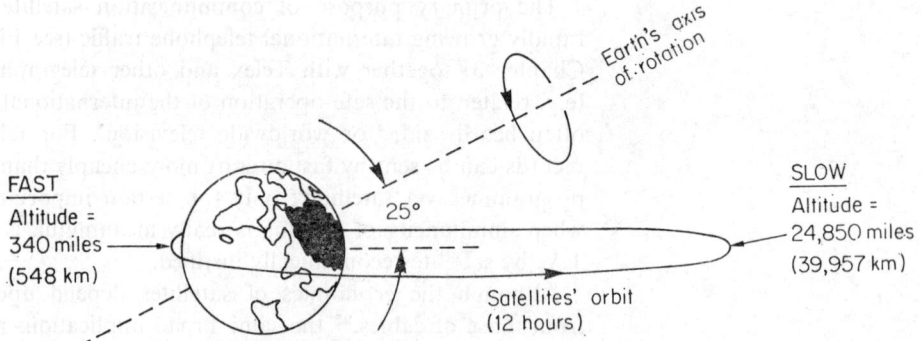

Figure 5.17. The U.S.S.R. satellite 'Molnya'.

however, during its high altitude it travels *slowly* over the U.S.S.R., whereas
it whizzes very fast over the rest of the world at low altitude, making it
usable to the Russians, for their own *internal* use, for 9 hours, for telephones,
telegraphs, photo-telegraphy and television.* By contrast, the countries of
the West seem to be settling for satellites positioned at about 22,300 miles
altitude exactly over the equator, where they remain virtually stationary.[55]
However, the countries within the Western sphere of interest are widely
scattered among the continents, straddling the equator and separated by
oceans, conditions for which both stationary satellites and transoceanic
cables are suitable. Those countries within the Communist sphere form one
great connected land mass, 8000 miles long and 4000 miles wide, lying well
North of the equator, over which the population is distributed; they have
therefore adopted this different solution. As in the West, all the other modes
of long distance communication are used also in the U.S.S.R., microwave
links, concentric cables, etc. For their airways they use radio-beacons similar
to those of Western countries, thereby suiting through traffic from the
West and elsewhere.† A popular book has recently been published in the
U.S.S.R. entitled *Growth of Communication in the U.S.S.R.* (in Russian)
which surveys the history of all modes; post, telephones, radio, T.V., etc.,
during the past 50 years.[341]

Since the costs to small or developing countries can be high for their
overseas communication, owing to the high rental of the few number of

* See *Telecommunication Journal*, **32**, No. 5, May, 1965; **33**, No. 12, Dec., 1966, p. 425.
Also 'The Soviet Communication Satellite Molnya I', in *Telecommunication Journal*
(I.T.U.), **32**, No. 10, Oct. 1965.
   † See *Telecommunication Journal*, **32**, No. 2, Feb. 1965.

COMMUNICATION AND WEALTH   165

satellite channels they at present need, one logical answer would be for groups of neighbouring countries to connect together, by cable or microwave link, to a central point, thereby combining their traffic for transmission overseas. This will be done, for example, by the three Territories of East Africa, Kenya, Tanzania and Uganda, as a consequence of which they will use a full-sized, economic, ground station, and they may later perhaps be joined by Zambia, Rwanda and Ethiopia. But in some other areas the poor relations between neighbours, or uncertainty of the future, prevents this economic move owing to the risks which appear to be involved when one country's lines of communication cross another country's territory. However, this is nothing new and many successful precedents have been set; for example, in that old hornets' nest, Europe, where great wars, traditional suspicions and variety of languages has not prevented interstate communication from progressing: roads, rails, postal service, rivers, airways, telegraphs, television . . . and, most recently, combination of telephone traffic for transmission by satellite from only four ground stations, situated in England, France, West Germany and Italy, to other continents. Real difficulties can arise at present where no alternative modes of communication exist.

There are other hopeful signs. Thus, one of the points upon which today's electronics industry is concentrating is the reduction of costs, partly in search of new markets and partly as deliberate policy towards improving communication with the economically developing countries. For example, the costs of small satellite ground stations are reducing, to the advantage of small or poorer countries whose overseas needs for communication are limited, though vital. Again, since communication is an affair of *mutual* interest, the costs can be shared by international agreement, or by aid programmes. Developing countries having need for fewer overseas channels benefit from 'multi-access' satellites*. (See Figure 3.1). Briefly, this means that a satellite is used entirely to connect only two particular countries which have heavy traffic, but is shared with others having lower traffic demands. Such a multi-access satellite then has several countries beaming their message traffic up to it, from different parts of the world, whilst it retransmits back again to other countries as required. It operates as a kind of telephone 'exchange'. This, and other proposals, will enable routing between countries to be more free and flexible.* It is one of the advantages of satellites that they are able to do this because they are really *broadcast* systems, capable of communicating over a wide area, as opposed to cables, which are *point-to-point*. A further advantage they offer is that the cost of their usage is independent of distance.

There is no reason to believe that any one global satellite system, such as that set up by Intelsat (see Chapter 3, Section 4), will have a monopoly of world communication. On the contrary, several or many systems may be set up, to serve the needs of different groups of countries, or for different purposes, including ship and air navigation. Nor does there seem to be any technical reason why small or developing countries should not join in their use; international law already operates widely and well, over great areas, in all fields of communication. Whether all countries can use them (but not necessarily own them) ultimately reduces to a question of cost analysis and equitable sharing.

* See Lutz, S. G., 'Small Station Aspects', *Telecommunication Journal*, **31**, No. 8, Aug. 1964, p. 225.

6

Some Social Aspects of World Communication

'To the average Saudi . . . the world outside his vast sun-baked sand pit is probably as insubstantial and dubious as a traveller's tale. "And are there deserts in London?" one old sheikh asked me.'

Malcolm Hews, *'South of Suez'*,
The Guardian, Thurs. 10 Aug. 1965.*

1. Communication, nationalism and internationalism

The emotional ways in which one race, or people of one nation, regard those of others are exposed by the images they commonly use, the slang, the cartoons, the characters in comic operas and fairy tales. They are exposed most simply by names; thus, among the English-speaking peoples alone we find used at various times such charming modes of address as these: Wogs, Dagoes, Yids, Niggers, Huns, Reds (see p. 16), Chinks, Limeys, Yanks, Froggies, the Yellow Peril . . . and the Bloody Pork and Beans: this last referring to our gallant allies, the Portuguese, 1914–18 War. The list could be extended. No doubt there are similar vocabularies in other languages; we in the West have been called Palefaces, the Pink Ones, and other things. Such are the endearing terms, the pet names, with which we have addressed one another mentally (and, unfortunately, too often overtly), in the human family.

Such names and images are a sociological study in themselves; they have specific historical origins, largely deriving from war, plunder, occupation, gastronomic habits, economic threats and early imperialisms. No doubt the Ancient Britons had rude names for the Romans, and the Crusading soldiery more popular epithets for the Saracens than mere 'infidels'. They signify the almost total social isolations of peoples and nations over the centuries and even today. Today we cannot be said to *know* each other, when our contacts in the past have been largely absent, or violent, and when our most vivid impressions have been formed in wars (both temporal and spiritual), occupations or exploitations. This is our legacy.

Nor are such images necessarily long-standing or historical, nor of remote cultures. Many an American must have a picture in his mind of Britain being as it was in the early Edwardian days of this century: quaint, foggy, tweedy, thatch-roofed cottages, housemaids in aprons. Why? From our more popular literature perhaps? More likely it is the result of the great emigration from Britain to the U.S.A. at the turn of this century, when millions left. (Between 1904 and 1914 some 10 million immigrants entered the U.S.A. from all European countries, including nearly 1 million from Britain.[333]) Emigrants carry pictures in their heads of their mother country as it was when they left her; those images may be cherished as their links with their own childhoods. There is no reason why they should be brought up-to-date. They retain the impressions and pass them on to their own children. In the reverse

* With kind permission.

direction, many Englishmen may think of America as made up of gangsters, millionaires and hillbillies, skyscrapers and frontier towns where every male carries a gun. Why? I can only conjecture that Hollywood has herself partly to blame. (For a fascinating study of early British attitudes to North America, her institutions, customs, social habits, etc. and their changes since mid-18th century see the anthology of literary extracts: *America through British Eyes*, Ref. 223.)

Such mythology is not just something which we have inherited from the past; it is still continually being created. It may be created by films and T.V. programmes sent overseas, by radio broadcasts, by newspapers, not because the people who make and write these are liars but because the listeners, viewers and readers are already predisposed to interpret them in ways which support their existing beliefs. Adults are not so ready to have their familiar notions shattered, for all comfort would be gone. *The great bulk of human communication has nothing whatever to do with logic, reason or semantics*; people do not hear or see what you tell them or show them, but only what they are predisposed to hear or see. As has already been emphasized in Chapter 4, 'human communication' does not consist of messages passing from one person to another, as though those persons were, for that moment, alone; a message may leave the speaker's mouth, but that is no reason why that same message should reach his listener's ear. Any public lecturer and any writer knows this full well. The message which is received will depend just as much upon all the other 'messages received' during the listener's lifetime as it does upon the particular words uttered at that moment. The message received is not that contained solely in the semantic content of the sentences uttered, but will depend upon who the receiver is, his past history and present condition and situation.[69] It depends, too, upon the *future*: that is, upon the consequences of his hearing the message aright, upon how it affects his feelings of security or self-confidence, or whether he *wants* to hear it.

When it comes to nation speaking to nation, the personal attitudes of their people one to another, the same principle applies, reinforced. Their attitudes are emotional and little based on reason, not because man is not a reasoning animal (which he can be, in certain situations) but rather because he is overwhelmingly controlled by his existing beliefs and images. He is deeply rooted in his national, tribal or other group culture, held firmly by a host of ties to family and friends, to the world as he knows it. If these roots be loosened, his idea of himself is weakened, however little.

People are of course not utterly resistant to change; they may be converted in their beliefs, both about others and about themselves. Such changes may come about more by flashes of insight than by deliberate logical reasoning, by being jogged by some chance event into 'seeing' things another way. They may be brought about very quickly under the impact of some cataclysm, like a war or an earthquake. But we cannot reasonably expect the various peoples of this world suddenly to drop their present ideas of one another by appealing to their *reason*.

We may ask ourselves the question: Now that we have invented many forms of technical communication, which have suddenly been flung around the world, linking continent with continent, country with country, how will this new-found freedom affect our mental images of one another? Will our ideas and attitudes change? Shall we understand one another better?

My own view, as stated before, is that they will not make any sudden changes in our *emotional* attitudes, nor radically alter our mental images of one another by appealing to our reason; at least, not in the first place. The first great benefits which world communication brings are practical and economic ones, by providing the means, for the first time in world history, for rapid and effective multilateral exchanges of many kinds. These provide first the 'mechanics of living', as they may conveniently be called, e.g. to enable the International Organizations to operate (see Chapter 4, Section 5) without which even a world populated with angels could not hope to operate stably. They do not guarantee a better world, but at least *permit* its ultimate possibility. These mechanics come first; our traditional images and emotional attitudes may, let us hope, follow in their wake.

It is only too easy to speak of *means*; of world radio, world telephones, world news services, film distribution, book circulation and of the International Organizations and even of organized tourism (that most rapidly expanding industry), that these might be thought in themselves to be powerful forces for bringing about a mental climate of 'internationalism'. They cannot do so alone; only changed *people* can do that. They are some of the 'essential prerequisites'. It is also questionable whether the idea of internationalism is a pragmatic one, at this time in history, when half the world has still not yet developed a sense of nationhood.[34]

The idea of a whole world of sovereign nation–states is of relatively recent historical origin.[69, 186] Prior to the last War, 1939–45, many large areas and hundreds of millions of people were living under colonial rule, many were living in disputed territories, many had no specific allegiances other than local; going further back into the century, many areas of the world were still unexplored, many were occupied by neighbouring tribal and other groups at regular war with one another. Even today, millions live either in refugee camps, or in areas over which no clear political system is dominant or stable, or in multiracial countries in which the racial relations are still being worked out. One important characteristic of the post-War world in the mid-20th century is the emergence, often the painful emergence, of nations-in-the-making, searching for their own identity, groping outward for relationships with others and experimenting with new political forms.[23, 248] The map of the world as a set of nation–states is still to be made; the 'political maps' of geography books, showing countries coloured and named, conceal as much as they reveal. In the meantime, to talk of internationalism, even as an ideal, is to overlook the fact that millions of people still do not know exactly who they are and how they relate to others in the world. We, in the long established industrial democracies, with long held traditions, may feel secure in the efficiency of our own administrations, with some idea of who our friends are and what our powers and our limitations may be; nevertheless we may be deceiving ourselves in some respects. 'Progress', 'economic growth rates', etc., are things that many of us accept without question. Things *ought* to get better, we may feel; they always have. It is people with the most clear sense of their own nationhoods that speak most lightly of internationalism. They can afford to.

'Recent events all over the world', wrote Jawaharlal Nehru in 1956, 'have demonstrated that the notion that nationalism is fading away before the impact of internationalism and proletarian movements has little truth. It is still one of the most powerful urges that move a people, and round it cluster sentiments and traditions and a sense of common living and common purpose'.[222]

Nationality, nationhood and nationalism are three distinct ideas. 'Nationalism' is often spoken of by the secure as something disreputable, something aggressive, to be deplored. It may be so sometimes, but it may also be constructive; it may be either, depending upon the form it takes and how it involves other nations. But as a concept it is neutral; what is 'nationalism' other than the 'powerful urge', as Jawaharlal Nehru calls it, to hammer out a nationhood, where that sense of political identity does not yet exist?

If one characteristic of the modern world is this movement towards independent nation–states with autonomous governments, occasionally splintering and increasing their numbers, there is another, which is not so commonly shown on school geography book maps. This is the rapid federative movement today towards nation groupings of many different kinds. These groupings are not only the so-called 'power blocks', but take many different forms not directly concerned with defence. Thus, to discuss world affairs today and to report them in newspapers and radio bulletins, it is increasingly necessary to refer to such Organizations as the North Atlantic Treaty Organization, European Free Trade Association, Western European Union, Common Market, Comecon, Benelux, the Organization for Economic Co-operation and Development, and many others representing treaty agreements based on trade and other social affairs, all of which are creations of the post Second World War period. They are in the first place political organizations set up by treaty or agreement between governments with specific constitutions and aims.[82] They are some of the 3000 or so International Organizations referred to in Chapter 4 (Section 5) being examples from the intergovernmental sector. They are not super-nations, nor empires, and they have no central governments; their increasing numbers, with their complex of titles, is a sign of the interdependence of the 'independent' nation–states. Other grand names have increasingly to be used today: South East Asia, the Near East, the North Atlantic community, Central America, West Africa . . . as much, if not more, than the names of individual nations. These names we use as though they were the names of personal acquaintances whose friendships and quarrels we are trying to understand. Such personifications and others, like 'the Arab countries', the 'Communist bloc', 'the English-speaking world', 'the Capitalist Countries', etc., may instil in our minds the notion that the countries within each are alike in all, or many, respects and that their peoples feel strong emotional ties with one another. Both nations are, of course, wrong; but such is the power of names.

In Chapter 3 some account was presented of the explosive growth and spread of international communication media, which has taken place almost wholly since the end of the Second World War. These are the airways, the overseas telephones, the Telex, the interchange of radio and T.V. programmes and films, and the growth of the tourist industry, etc. These are the technologies which are often said 'to bring the nations together' today. However, as remarked before, technology has no power in itself to do anything at all; it is no mere play with words to say that the power of technology resides in the people who use it. All these communication media basically do one thing: they remove certain constraints which hitherto existed upon the *possibilities* for better international co-operation. But the greatest powers for preventing the realization of these possibilities are still non-technical; they are the emotional blocks in people's minds, values, national parochialisms and other human factors. Whether our new-found powers will become used for mutual benefit, or not, cannot depend upon technical criteria alone. They may bring us closer together in some ways, but equally well drive us farther apart in others.

In this Chapter, some of the underlying arguments will be set down. Let us start with the medium of *tourism*.

2. On tourism as a mode of communication*

On page 3 the point has been stressed that any person's image of the world owes very little to his own direct observations and experiences, but is mainly built up by what he has been taught, or has read, or has seen on T.V. or at the cinema. It has been instilled into him by parents, teachers and friends, largely in his own language and symbols, by people of his own culture.[268] Nobody, in their three score years and ten, can visit more than a minute fraction of the places of this world, nor meet more than an infinitesimal part of its people. Our images are abstract, conjured up by school books, advertisements, pictures. I myself have never stood in the middle of the Sahara desert, yet I cannot avoid visualizing it; I have never sailed up the Amazon, though I can imagine the adventure. In both cases I shall be under an illusion. Mention the word 'Egypt' and I shall see in my mind pyramids, sand and a couple of palm trees; or say the word 'India' and, without conscious thought, I shall see elephants, or the Taj Mahal. Of course, no reasoning person *believes* these are major characteristics of those countries; any educated person can tell himself that there are far more important features. But to do so requires conscious effort, however small; and, even then, the results are more likely to be wrong than right. Other countries and peoples can only be, in imagination, abstracts.

Even if we take trouble and try to think deliberately what people are like in other countries which we may not have visited, our ideas are certain to be out-of-date and old-fashioned. They cannot fail to be so in this rapidly changing world. We can imagine people and places only as they *were* and not as they *are* today. Sitting in a New York subway train, I was once asked by a well-meaning passenger: 'Say . . . have all your folks got shoes?' During subsequent weeks many of my own mental images of the U.S.A. were forced to change too, one by one.

The illustrations in Figure 6.1 have been taken from a brochure which was issued to passengers by one of the world's major airlines. They are all kindly images: jolly people, every one. No passenger can really *believe* that the natives look like these, nor is this the artist's intention. What is intended is that passengers shall *recognize* the 'people' portrayed. They are not purely symbolic figures either (like Uncle Sam, John Bull, Britannia), but are fairy tale people which we have all been taught to visualize. The Beefeater represents England, though there are mighty few to be found there; the girl in the bonnet and clogs is Holland, but you would have to search that country to find her. We see America, dressed for Olympics, Japan like a Gilbert and Sullivan figure; we recognize Greece, Egypt, Burma, Switzerland. . . . What the artist has drawn here are, of course, so-called *traditional* figures.

'International tourism is today the largest single item in foreign trade and prospects for further expansion in world travel appear almost limitless'.[228] It is one of the most organized international industries of the world.†[256] Why do people take holidays abroad? First, to have a change from their

---

* Some notes on this subject were made in Chapter 3, Section 5.
† For statistics of tourism, country by country, see United Nations *Statistical Yearbook 1966*.[330]

PLATE 1

'Traditional' People of Various Nations
(From a British Overseas Airways Corporation flight brochure, with very kind permission).

(To face page 170

familiar lives and to see something different. They are therefore motivated to seek out aspects of life which are *different* from their own, and rarely do they search for elements which are held in common. They also go to see *things*: ancient monuments, buildings, archaeology, museums: mostly old things. A visitor to Cairo will leap on a camel and go to see the pyramids, whilst a tourist in London will visit the Tower; the natives show less interest. They may sit in cafés and watch the crowds, as *objects* of scrutiny: as things. And the differences which they go to see are those which they have learned about at home, from school history, from books, legends, pictures, films. . . . They go to confirm what they already believe. Tourism may do as much to enhance our ideas of national differences as it does to help unite us.

Tourism costs money, though it is becoming cheaper and easier; but it is true to say that only a small fraction of the people of any country have ever travelled abroad.*[229] Furthermore they must be largely drawn from the wealthier and more leisured classes; although increasing numbers of students and schoolchildren are travelling, they mostly must be able to afford the fares. The amount of leisure time enjoyed by people, even in the industrial countries, should not be exaggerated either. In 1965, less than 55 per cent of people in the O.E.C.D. countries (Western Europe, Japan, the U.S.A. and Canada[226]) took a holiday of more than 4 days, anywhere.[229] It is also a fact that many, if not a majority of the places visited lie in poorer regions of the world (see *Tourism*, Ref. 330) because so many historic places, quaint customs and picturesque peoples, and things which are known to be so different from those in wealthier areas, are to be found there. Tourism then, in its present phase, is a very rapidly expanding industry which is mainly bringing richer people into contact with the more antique and poorer elements of other countries;[229] the more modern and progressive elements are likely to offer less attraction to visitors, who do not often go on holiday abroad to see factories, hospitals, shipyards and office blocks.

It is from the wealthier end of the whole social spectrum that many tourists are drawn. 'Wealthier' here merely means 'having the money' (there are increasing numbers of working class people travelling abroad today). They go to see what they have read about and learned from their school history books, from pictures in magazines and films, from T.V. documentaries and newspapers: the Eiffel Tower, bullfights, Swiss chalets, pyramids, native markets, the Leaning Tower, castles on the Rhine and peasants. A glance around any Travel Agent's office walls will confirm this hypothesis.

Going further with this train of thought, it is a fact that once a country has discovered the attractiveness of these things to tourists, it feels economic incentive to preserve these ancient images of itself and to *advertise* them. Tourist brochures, junk shops and all the ballyhoo of business set those images firm. As the tourist trade increases and spreads into new areas, it becomes economically advantageous to appear to be out-of-date.

It may appear to the reader that I am advocating organized vandalism by Governments, but I am not. I am commenting only upon the inevitable and

* Issues of passports reveal this. Thus, in the U.S.A. new passport issues per annum ('Personal' and 'Pleasure') have increased between 1960 and 1965, from about 670,000 to 1 million, only.[334] In the U.K., over the same period, new issues rose from 780,000 to 990,000 whilst, in addition, the special British Visitor's Passports (valid 1 year, Europe only) rose from nearly 300,000 to over 700,000. (Information from British Passport Office; with thanks.) In either case, these figures are a small fraction of the total numbers of families in the populations. See United Nations *Statistical Yearbook* 1966 under *tourism*.[330]

expressing the belief that tourism, in its present day form, may not be quite such a powerful force for bringing the nations together as it is often said to be. It may perhaps do much to keep them apart. It is not possible to gain any real idea of what life is like in any foreign country merely by visiting it for a few weeks. To do so requires one to live there as a native, to make a living and to contend with their difficulties and strains day by day.

Further artificiality is added to the scene presented to the tourist by the fact that Government policies are increasingly aimed at making his path smooth, by improving customs and visa regulations, issuing tax-free petrol coupons, by giving him other privileges and holding 'courtesy campaigns'.[227] Such facilities are no doubt both desirable to the tourist and of economic advantage to the host country; they may leave the traveller with a good impression of that country but, at the same time, distort the picture of what life is really like for the natives. They may help to keep the people apart in understanding of one another.

What the net balance is, and will be, cannot be generalized upon, for it depends upon individuals and experiences. On the one hand, for people to meet and to see one another in the flesh may leave them with a sense of human relationship far greater than does a film or T.V. picture; on the other hand, such brief encounters are rarely deep, nor do they involve the person, who may return home with no better understanding of the foreigner's curious ways, habits and customs than he had before he went there. As countries become richer, so increasing numbers of their people can afford to travel overseas.[227] On a recorded world basis, tourist numbers increased by 12 per cent in 1965, having steadily increased over the years. However, the geographical position of some countries, such as the U.S.A. and Australia, handicaps their would-be travellers, because of the high cost of long overseas journeys; that is to say, geography, as well as wealth, selects the nationality of the traveller. The almost complete elimination of administrative barriers upon travellers within the O.E.C.D. area, and increasingly cheap travel, favour their tourism whilst, at the same time, shortage of currency in many countries (especially Eastern Europe) does not. Again, in spite of such foreign currency difficulties, bilateral agreements between groups of politically related countries make movements among them possible (e.g. there is no limit at present on currency allowance for travellers within the whole Sterling Area). There are thus many factors which select who shall travel abroad and where they shall go. The gross result of these factors ensures that, on the whole, tourists will be richer than their hosts; though clearly there are many exceptions and this situation is likely to change.

One other factor of great importance must be noted, namely that, during the past few years, many of the poorer developing countries are becoming increasingly attractive to tourists, for they offer totally new sights and experiences. Their facilities are developing fast and jet travel there is cheapening.[256] They need their share of this new great world industry. India, Africa, the U.S.S.R. and others are fast opening to tourists.

Since tourism is expanding at such a phenomenal rate, the question may be asked: What will happen when, in the more popular areas, the tourist population exceeds the native? This and many other problems were considered at a Seminar held in Portugal, in 1966, by representatives of the Mediterranean countries, Greece, Portugal, Spain, Turkey and Yugoslavia. (It is in these countries that the *rate* of expansion of tourism has been particularly high during the present decade.) One thing that will happen is that the native populations will be faced by greater numbers of, on the whole, richer and more 'sophisticated' people, to whom they may need to be excessively polite and helpful in their own economic interests, but to whom they may bear increasing resentment privately. Prices may be forced up; both the visitors and the visited may come to feel exploited. Again, great strains may come to be placed upon existing road, rail, hotel and other public services which the native population also use; perhaps Government policy will be to develop these as 'special tourist services' operated principally for the visitor's benefit. If the tourist population comes to approach or exceed that of the native, the latter may come to feel that they are *selling part of themselves.* This is conjecture; only time will show.

Fortunately one can see counterbalancing tendencies in the tourist traffic which may help personal understanding between the peoples. Thus, luxurious accommodation is only one form; there has been a rapid growth of other kinds too, of mixed nation holiday camps, rented houses, private accommodation, camping sites, etc., appealing to younger people, students and others of lower income. Packaged tours, chartered flights, student group holidays, and other cheaper forms of getting abroad are all increasing, and the travellers are not obliged to keep together in a herd except whilst actually travelling. The possibility of foreign travel among industrial workers, schoolchildren and others tied to a working schedule has been increased in some countries, during the past few years, by experimentally introducing 'staggered holidays'.[229] The class structure of tourism is changing fast.

At present, the bulk of tourism is confined to those countries which have established facilities, such as hotels, roads, railways, etc., together with traditional attractions of archaeology, well known native customs, mountains, lakes, rivers, sea coasts, scenic beauty, etc. That is, to a very small part of the earth's surface; mainly, to Europe. Tourist traffic to the U.S.A. is also quite high, though it comes mainly from the neighbouring country, Canada. Nevertheless, of the $7\frac{1}{2}$ million tourists reaching the U.S.A. in 1965, over $\frac{1}{2}$ million came from Europe and nearly 1 million from elsewhere.[229, 230] But increasingly other areas are being opened up in the developing countries, through faster and cheaper jet travel; increased wealth is enabling greater numbers of people to visit other continents; the Governments of many developing countries, of Africa, Asia, Central and South America, are assisting with establishment of airfields, roads, hotels and camp accommodation, as the economic value of this new and so rapidly growing industry is being realized. Money may flow as a consequence, in the desirable direction, but so will people too, and they will for a long time mostly be the richer visiting their poorer relations, with what social impact cannot yet be known. What is certain is that the present and future consequences of tourism should not be described by such simple phrases as: 'bringing the peoples of the world together, on our shrinking planet, etc., etc.'

3. International relations are institutional, not personal

After tourism, let us consider some of the other modes of world communication and whether they too are likely to lead to accord or to discord in the human family. It is still at the personal level of emotional attitudes that we are looking, not at the functional or economic levels where the values of the techniques are not here doubted.

International relations are almost entirely institutional and not personal relations; the two are quite different in kind.[186] Institutional relationships, however benevolent in intention, are utterly different from human relation-ships. They are set up by various official bodies, who have responsibility delegated to them, either voluntarily, or by unconscious custom, or by force of law. Such institutions act 'on behalf of' their people and the consequences of their decisions and actions do not commonly fall upon their staffs individually and personally. Certainly, a Cabinet Minister, a Trade Union leader, or a Company Director may do something rash which brings him into disgrace; he is expected to be a responsible person. Nevertheless, his sins are to some extent shared by the whole institution, and its 'reputation' may suffer, or it may admit inefficient organization and introduce changes: after the damage has been done. Institutional suffering is partially or even largely shared and so is quite different in nature from personal suffering. The loss of an overseas market may be quite serious for a country; but individual bankruptcy can be utterly disastrous for one man. An Army General may protest his concern when sending his troops into battle, but it is worse to be shot or bayoneted.

There is, of course, nothing new in that idea. But it may be important to bear it in mind when considering the likely effects of expanding world communication upon our personal attitudes towards other peoples.[193]

'Institutions' is a broad term and may cover everything from the most faceless bureaucracies of government: Trade Unions, educational systems, Social Security systems, police, etc., down to national customs, festivals, sports, and other more human activities. All are 'institutions' and all have one thing only in common; namely, they are all social, collectives bound and defined by rules either long established by custom or set up by law. Further-more, these rules, if they are known at all, are most clearly known and under-stood by the people actually involved in operating them, or conforming to them by habit. They are less easily recognized, understood or sympathized with by the people outside, above all by people from other countries which may have different institutions, often very different.

As the network of world communication expands between and over the various continents, bringing us ever more news from wider areas of 'the shrinking world' (as it is popularly called) so, admittedly, the physical *possibility* might be felt to be there for people increasingly to come to know one another. On the other hand, this expansion has taken place only during the last generation or so, an infinitesimal flash of time in human evolution. For thousands of generations man has lived in small communities and has developed limited emotional capacities; he can be said to *know* only a few people, as persons, at most a few hundred. But on no account can he be expected to *know* millions of his fellows, all over the world, as personalities, with any sense of compassion and personal involvement. Certainly, a few privileged people may have circles of foreign friends, who have travelled widely or lived abroad; but they are very few out of any country's population. To the vast majority of people, those in other countries are abstracts. We may see foreign faces on our T.V. screens, but we see them as representatives; we cannot *know* them. We may read about tragedies in our newspapers, coal mine disasters, famine in India, aircraft crashes, and other events every day; we may even feel moved to contribute to Public Subscriptions but, unless we happen to know one of the sufferers personally, we read of these only as tragic *events*. We may feel that 'They' ought to do something about it, that is, governments, international relief organizations or other official bodies. But as individuals we are helpless to feel personal involvement in all the world's tragedies, there are too many people to know.

This is no comment upon human callousness, but only upon the inevitable results of our suddenly being confronted with news on a global scale, when we have minds and emotional capacities more suited to life on a village scale. The world can never be my village.

As world communication networks expand, which they are doing rapidly, so we must increasingly come to see other peoples and nations in terms of their various institutions. Further, if we have no personal acquaintances whatever, we can see them only *as* collections of institutions. Does it not then follow that we must also increasingly come to interpret their actions, and their people's and leader's sayings and speeches, through the eyes of our own institutions with which we are so familiar?

This natural human tendency is encouraged by the fact that institutions can only be spoken of by their *names*. The same name is often used to refer to institutions in different countries which are, in fact and in significance to their people, quite different in nature. For example, we read of Trade Unions in both Britain and the U.S.S.R., but they are quite distinct in form and in their purposes; so they are, to lesser extent, in various European countries and the U.S.A. Or again, the expression Civil Service means something rather different in Britain and in the U.S.A. Governmental, legal, industrial and other institutions may have names in common, but their natures and the ways in which the people regard them may differ in different countries. We may speak of 'democratic' institutions, as though that word had only one universal meaning, which it has not. So we might go on with an endless list; the names of social institutions do not, strictly speaking, translate from one country to another.

Most people are aware of this as a fact, when they read or hear foreign news every day. But, unless they have lived in other countries, or are serious students of politics and world affairs, or are scholars of some kind, which most of us are not, they will be under unintended pressure to regard foreign institutions as being like their own, and understanding can be impaired. The spread of world news, therefore, may do as much to keep peoples apart, in their emotions and attitudes, as it does to keep them informed about facts. Our whole world communication network, which has expanded so rapidly within one generation, and continues to do so, may drive us apart emotionally just as well as it may draw us together economically and institutionally, at least at the present time. I do not say that it will; only that it might well do so. On any account, it is grossly naïve to assume that expanding world communication necessarily leads to 'peace and understanding'. It may do so but, in my opinion, if it does it will in the first place be due to the better and more secure operation of international institutions, and to the consequent reduction of practical frustrations, rather than by direct appeal to our consciences, feelings, beliefs and emotions.

4. International communication is both slender and institutional

Reference has been made in earlier Sections (e.g. Chapter 3, Section 4) to the apparently parochial attitudes of nations today, to their preoccupation with national, rather than international affairs. The opinion has been offered that most of us live, indeed, *must* live, in mental villages, in spite of all the technology of world communication, of an international Press, and of cheap and expanding tourism. This is not to say that we are not far more aware of world problems today, nor to deny that educational standards have risen and that far more people are informed about world affairs; indeed, this is certainly true. But, nevertheless, our emotional sense of *personal* involvement is, and must be, with ourselves, our families, our circle of friends and acquaintances, our 'kith and kin' and, as the circle expands, only to lesser and lesser degree with the rest of mankind. As the circle expands, so we are called upon to relate our personal selves to larger and more abstract *groups*. To repeat, for this point is easily misunderstood: I can have perhaps a few hundred personal friends and know them as individuals like myself; but I cannot possibly have a million friends. I may try to be idealistic, and profess friendship with other nations and peoples but, to pretend that I feel any personal involvement with each man and woman, as personalities, would be gross self-deception, if not a plain lie. Such large populations are understood by each one of us only as collections of institutions of many kinds, or in terms of assumed 'national characteristics', political organizations and other broad generalities. My relationships, and yours, to peoples of other nations are relationships to institutions: to them as abstracts.[186] The reasons are not economic, nor educational, nor political, but are inherent in human nature with its limited emotional capacity. The few foreign friendships which we can cultivate, however deep, will not necessarily lead us to accept all the other compatriots as brothers also. They will be 'the others', embodied in our mental images of those countries and their institutions. One's friends are, of course, always exceptional people! Satellite television, international telephones, world news, near-instantaneous jet travel and all the paraphernalia of world communication are powerless to change this situation and to make us one happy 'family', for human relations beyond our immediate circle are not *familial* relations in their nature.

This parochialism in human dealings is reflected both in the type of message traffic which flows over the international networks and in its sheer slenderness. As already remarked (in Chapter 3, Section 4),[287] most of the international telephone, telegraph and Telex traffic is not personal, between private persons, but is between institutions: governments, Press Agencies, industries, businesses, etc., or their representatives, acting 'on our behalf', i.e. in the economic sphere much more than the domestic sphere. Unfortunately, comparative figures are not available for air passenger traffic, nor for air mail, but it is suspected that the same comment would apply. Nevertheless, the quantities of traffic which flow between countries may be compared with that which flows within each country; with certain limited exceptions, the latter far exceeds the former.

For example, let us examine telephone traffic. Telephony is special, for it is human conversation, the most personal mode of communication. In Chapter 1 something of the real nature and meaning of conversation was described; conversation is not a casual matter of chance, for there is always a reason why this particular person talks to that one (Chapter 1, Section 5), when each recognizes the other as a fellow being, in an act of commitment. Telford and Isted, in a paper cited earlier (Chapter 3, Section 4)[287] have pointed out that in the majority of the more prosperous nations the major fraction of their telephone conversations are inland, to their own countrymen, whereas only a very small fraction of their calls are international. Naturally we should expect fewer extra-territorial calls, if for reasons of cost and language alone; but what is interesting is the magnitude of the ratio, how this varies between nations, and how it is changing as the years go by.

These two authors have listed some 70 nations, giving the ratios of their national, local and trunk calls combined, to outgoing international telephone calls during the year 1959.[287] These ratios vary enormously, as Table 6 shows.

What strange assortments of bedfellows have we here? It might at first be expected that the richer, more influential, nations would be having far more overseas and international conversation, in proportion to their own internal traffic, than the poorer, less industrialized, ones. Far from it! Those countries which were already highly industrialized (in 1959) and had very developed telephone systems, seem to have used these resources far more for talking to themselves than for talking to other countries. The U.S.A., the U.K., Sweden, Denmark, Argentine, Norway, German D.R., South Africa,

Table 6. *Ratio of internal (local and trunk) telephone calls to international calls, in 1959. (From Telford and Isted,[287] with kind permission.)*

1–50	50–500	500–2000	2000–5000	Over 5000
Dominica	Rep. of Ireland	Cameroons	United States	Singapore
Monaco	Belgium	Austria	Portugal	Japan
Lebanon	Switzerland	Ivory Coast	Spain	Australia
Luxembourg	Netherlands	Granada	South Africa	Polynesia
Sudan	France	Antigua	Israel	
Pakistan	German F.R.	Denmark	German D.R.	
Libya	Indonesia	Norway	Argentine	
Thailand	Central Africa	Mali	Trinidad	
	Egypt	Belgian Congo	New Zealand	
	St. Thome &	Ethiopia	New Caledonia	
	Principe	Greece	Nigeria	
	Somaliland	Sweden	Malaya	
	Syria	Turkey	Vietnam	
	Mauritania	Italy	Ghana	
	Angola	United Kingdom	East Africa	
	Dahomey	Burma		
	India	Mozambique		
	Bermuda	Upper Volta		
		Niger		
		Yugoslavia		
		Macao		
		Iceland		
		Madagascar		

Australia, Japan, New Zealand all have extensive telephone systems, yet all have very high ratios of internal to international calls per annum. On the other hand, those countries listed in the first column are not yet great industrial powers. Is it not surprising too that the United Kingdom, with all its overseas Commonwealth connexions, should be listed in the third column (ratio 1400)? Or that in the U.S.A., with her rapidly expanding world interests, people should have made 3400 telephone calls to fellow Americans before they made one to a foreigner?

If we did our sums again and separated the telephone conversations of different countries, both internal and international, into the two classes called before *domestic* (i.e. personal) and *economic* (i.e. business, etc.) our surprise might be even greater. For we should find that our domestic, personal conversation with people of other countries reduced still further, by a large factor, in proportion to our conversation with friends at home, especially in the highly industrialized countries.

The same authors, Telford and Isted,[287] comment upon the small fraction of calls that Britain made in 1959 to Europe and beyond, compared to her internal traffic, by asking: 'Is it reasonable to assume that our (British) interest in those who live on the continent of Europe is reduced by a . . . factor of 130: or that our interest in the rest of the world diminishes yet further by a factor of 10·7? If this, in fact, is true, for a country which prides itself on a high degree of international feeling and interest, we may indeed despair!' They comment too upon the ratio for the U.S.A. (internal/ international calls = 3400) which is even higher.

Those words were written in 1961 and the authors concluded, from these and other data, that 'it (was) not lack of interest but lack of facilities at reasonable cost that . . . brought about this sorry state of affairs'. (Quoted by kind permission.)

This is certainly true. With regard to Britain, for example, it is correct to say that her telephone facilities for speaking to all the Commonwealth countries were grossly unsatisfactory until very recent years. Six years have passed since Telford and Isted made their comments; further intercontinental cables have been laid (see map, Figure 3.1) and satellites have been installed and are now in regular commercial use, but there seems no end yet to the demand for overseas telephony. Advances in electronics have outstripped all predictions and it is not unfair to say that, today, techniques are known which, *in principle*, could form the basis of design of systems adequate to deal with the world's telecommunication traffic in the foreseeable future. These may sound brave words, but I have said *in principle*; the problems in future will be those of engineering design, of economics and of social studies: how to apply known principles cheaply and efficiently, and how to use them for the best purposes.

The strange assortments of countries listed in Table 6 suggest that many and varied controlling factors are at work. Overseas or overland communications between countries depend, first, upon there being a need and second, upon there being adequate and reliable means available. The needs naturally depend upon countries' foreign relations in trade, politics, travel (e.g. air routes) and other social factors defining common spheres of interest, for example, financial (such as the Sterling Area), groupings by Treaty, etc. With regard to there being adequate communication facilities to supply these needs, these depend not only upon technical progress but upon geography too. It is easier and cheaper for countries having common land boundaries, as in Europe, whereas intercontinental communication to and from Australia or the Americas is more expensive and technically difficult; until some 10 years ago, conversation across oceans was possible only by radio-telephone, which was often unreliable and unsatisfactory owing to sunspot disturbances causing fading and often total 'blackout', see pp. 82 and 83.

The new techniques of overseas cable and satellites have changed the whole nature of intercontinental speech leading, as we saw in Chapter 3, Section 4, to an explosive growth in demand. Telford and Isted were undoubtedly correct in saying, in 1959, that international communication has long been hampered by inadequate means, and the current decade has seen a tremendous growth which shows no sign of slowing down, either in fact or prediction (see flow map, Figure 4.2). Nevertheless, it is still true to say that, in bulk, the amount of it is still a very small fraction of most countries' internal communication, especially in the industrially advanced countries. We still talk and write to our own peoples far more than we do to those of other nations.

5. Will world broadcasting lead to extinction of minority languages?

It is a legitimate question to ask, whether or not broadcasting between nations will lead to gradual dominance of certain 'majority' languages over 'minority' ones and, eventually, to the extinction of the latter. Will worldwide broadcasting mean one day that we shall all be speaking the same, or a few, languages and that all the present day variety of tongues will have vanished, one by one?

The answer is probably: no, at least, not due to broadcasting alone; other pressures are likely to be more dominant. International broadcasting may actually help to preserve a wide variety of languages in common use, though it cannot possibly encourage *all* the world's minority languages. However, with regard to the normal *internal* broadcasting services of countries, or political groups of countries, the prospect may be otherwise, for it may be deliberate policy of Governments in some of the newer countries to use their broadcasting facilities so as to encourage the use of one single national language as part of their programme of nation building. Many of the developing countries and areas are polylinguistic; for example, many of those of Africa, because their political boundaries were determined by various European colonizers with little regard to the cultural, linguistic, tribal areas which existed.[53] A language is part of a nationhood, part of a people's unity and identity. Where great linguistic variety exists it may be necessary to encourage one *lingua franca*, as part of the educational programme; if radio is used to assist, it will be as a valuable tool of policy.

We might consider first what is meant by the expressions 'majority' and 'minority' languages. Strictly, a minority language is one spoken by very small populations, and many of the world's 3000 or so languages are spoken by only a few hundreds or thousands of people. (The precise number of languages cannot be stated. It depends upon what you consider to be a language, or a dialect, or a variant.[33]) But this does not mean that they are unimportant people or that they have no legends, no spoken art forms or group identity; that is, that they have nothing of their own which they preserve among themselves. Welsh and Irish are minorities; they have not been made so by broadcasting, but more by the fact that English is so widely taught in schools, together with the fact that the bulk of newspapers, books, public notices and other *printed* media appear in English. There are comparatively few books written in Welsh or Irish. And for practical and industrial purposes, English must be used as their *lingua franca*; they may speak their own tongues as well. Dutch is also a minority language, and the majority of educated Dutchmen speak other languages; but they nevertheless speak Dutch at home.

In many areas of the world, *linguae francae* have had to be adopted by minorities for practical purposes of trading and other dealings. Arabic is widely used as such; for example, in Iraq, and among many tribes of the multilingual Northern Sudan, who nevertheless retain their own languages among themselves.[53] In India, that continent of a hundred languages, Persian was used as a *lingua franca* until the time of Queen Victoria, when English replaced it. English remains their chief *lingua franca* today; it is the most widely-used language (by circulation[133,320]) in newspapers, for debate in their Parliament, and other official purposes. (There are, however, pressures in India now to reduce the use of English and to replace it by Hindi as a *lingua franca*, though this is going to be resisted in the Southern States. English was dropped as a compulsory subject, for example, in High Schools in India's large State, Uttar Pradesh, in 1967.) Such uses may put some pressure upon their national languages, but cannot alone destroy them.

The effect of broadcasting upon true minority languages may be to encourage such adoption of *linguae francae* as second languages. As radio sets sweep into Africa, South America and other areas of great linguistic variety, so their users may increasingly wish to understand what they hear. Broadcasting authorities, beaming their transmissions upon them from overseas, would like them to hear and understand too: but no broadcasting authority can afford to transmit to every small linguistic group of a few hundreds or thousands of people. No doubt they would like to reach as many listeners as possible, but they cannot reach them all.

It is clearly incorrect to call Arabic a minority language, for millions speak it, over a wide area, either as their first language or as a *lingua franca*; nor can Chinese be considered so, nor Hindi, nor Swahili . . . for millions speak and understand these, and no other. These people make substantial audiences whom broadcasters can afford to reach, and cannot afford to neglect. We people of European origin may think of English, or Russian, French or German and others as major languages, and influential, for two particular reasons. First, because they are widely used as *lingua franca* at international conferences and in business, travel, etc., that is to say, they are the languages of large and *industrial* countries. Both are requisite to such a notion: size and industrialization.

Second, because the great bulk of the world's books are written in half a dozen languages only, namely, English, Russian, German, Japanese, Spanish, French.[80, 312] It is also a sobering fact to remember that very many of the world's languages have no written form, although this point is admittedly vague, for it depends upon what you accept as a 'language'. These half-dozen languages therefore become 'major', as *written* languages. These books are sought in developing countries which may have little literature and no text books in their own languages; they may translate them but, nevertheless, the bulk of such translations are of works *originally* written in English, French, Russian and German, to which attention is therefore drawn and whose influence is spread. Many countries with low literacy rates, or countries with small populations and 'minority' languages, in fact produce authors who write in one of the 'major' languages, to find markets.[312] Figure 6.2 shows this; more books written originally in English, including those from the U.S.A., Australia and elsewhere, are translated into various languages than any others, then follows French, then Russian, then German. (Most of the Russian works are translated into other languages of the U.S.S.R.[312])

I submit then that the only justification we have for regarding these half-dozen languages as 'major' is that they are the *written* languages of peoples who have so far produced the bulk of the world's literature, text books and newspapers, and have spread them abroad. Their widespread international adoption as spoken *linguae francae* also stems partly from that source.

However, most people in this world cannot read any of these languages, if they can read at all, nor speak them. Their use is confined to small, educated minorities. English may certainly be the most widespread *lingua franca* among the world's countries, but the great majority of *people* do not read or speak it.

To return to our subject of broadcasting. Overseas broadcasting is essentially directed to *people*, masses of individual people, the majority of whom understand no language but their own. The most massive audiences outside the industrial countries are of course those who understand a most widespread spoken language, like Arabic, but, as broadcasting countries increase in number, become richer and able to afford more transmitting stations which they can devote to overseas programmes, they seek out audiences in increasing numbers of languages. There is the further reason that radio sets, especially cheap transistor sets, have poured into areas of low literacy and diverse languages during only the past few years. Mr. Michael Stewart,

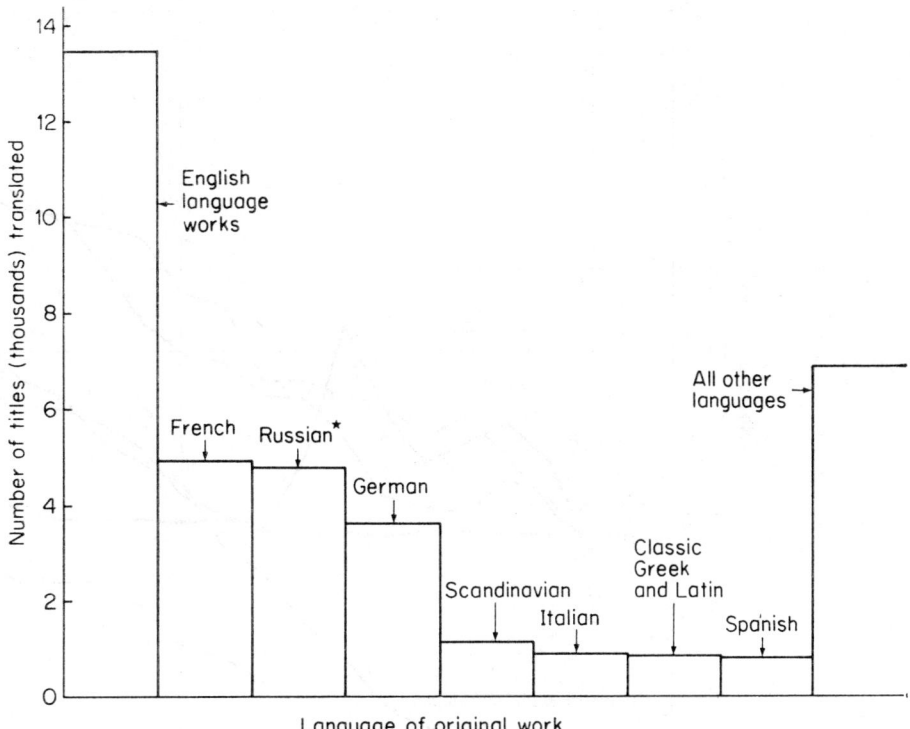

Figure 6.2. The spread of English language writings. Based on the numbers of titles of works translated and published within all the countries of the world, in 1964, according to original language of writing. *About 40 per cent of these translations from the Russian language were translated within the U.S.S.R., and most of these were made into other languages of that polylingual country.
Data used here under copyright of the United Nations (*Statistical Yearbook*, 1966). Reproduced by permission.

the British Foreign Secretary at the time, gave as one of his impressions of an Asian visit in 1965 the memory of a young man cultivating a paddy field with a wooden plough, with a Japanese transistor set slung on its handle.[26] But in no continent has this flood been greater than in Africa (excluding South Africa),[26] where radio sets have entered into every country in great and increasing numbers. Between the years 1955 and 1965, their numbers rose from 360,000 to 4,800,000. (B.B.C. information, see Chapter 4, Section 3.)

There is yet another reason why world broadcasting by itself is unlikely to destroy the variety of world languages for a long time to come, which is illustrated by Figure 6.3. The curves here show how the major broadcasting countries have steadily raised the hours per week of their External Broadcasting (i.e. to other countries). In the early post-War days Britain's B.B.C.

was leading, but as time has passed other countries have been able to build up, and the languages in which they broadcast are those relevant to their own foreign spheres of interest (political, trading, cultural, etc.).[28] The major broadcasting countries, whose numbers are increasing, cannot wait until everybody in the world speaks English, or Russian, or Chinese: but

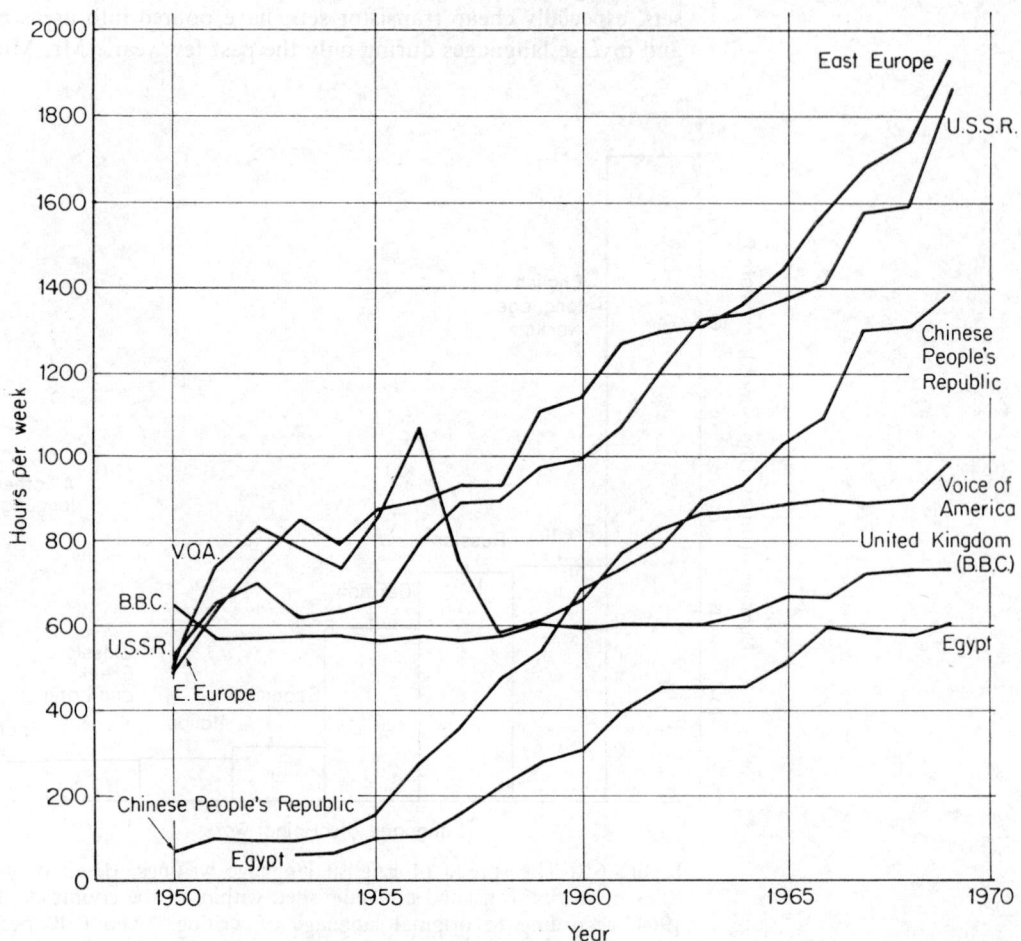

Figure 6.3. Estimated programme hours per week, intended for other countries, by some leading external broadcasters. East Europe comprises Albania, Bulgaria, Czechoslovakia, East Germany, Hungary, Poland, Rumania and Yugoslavia. (Data from British Broadcasting Corporation,[27] with kind permission.)

they must reach people now, in their own languages, provided that there are populations large enough in numbers to justify the costs. Those minorities to whom no broadcasting is yet addressed, and who understand no second language, may feel a desire to learn one; but this alone is no reason why they should cease to speak their own tongue.

There can be far larger forces upon people than broadcasting, to suppress their minority languages. There is also considerable difference between the multilingual countries of industrialized Europe and the aspiring, developing countries. Thus, in Europe, English is commonly used as a *lingua franca*, but this does not destroy the languages of the other countries, whose people continue to use Dutch, Norwegian, Hungarian, etc., within their own borders and among their own kind.[28]

In the more rapidly developing countries, however, the learning of a second language, such as English, may offer to a person the great chance of economic advancement; it may open doors to education, to technical literature, to a job, to political articulation or to prestige. Again, a second language is commonly used as a vehicle language in schools, where children are separated from their parents and taught new ideas; this language embodies those ideas and all the concepts of change that go with them. Their tribal languages do not carry this power. Governments may adopt deliberate policies for encouraging some *lingua franca* in their educational programmes, in areas handicapped in their progress by polylingualism (e.g. as with Swahili in Tanzania, or English in Kenya and Uganda). If used as part of such policies, by their own national broadcasting services, radio can be a most powerful tool of persuasion; but casual listening to the broadcasts of foreigners does not have any comparable influence.

There can be few better ways of demonstrating the truth of this conclusion than to examine the hours of broadcasting made by the B.B.C. in foreign languages other than European ones, and to see how the number of these languages has increased with the years. There are several reasons for citing the B.B.C. on this point (apart from the fact that the data has been made available to me by courtesy of the B.B.C. External Services Department):

(1) It is English which has now spread most widely among the countries of the world as a second language. Consequently, if there is any truth in the belief that broadcasting is leading to dominance by any major language, then it would be English that ought to be doing it, in mid-20th century.

(2) The B.B.C. has strictly limited finance available for its Overseas Broadcasting Services.[180, 212] Financial conditions do not therefore favour the extension of its range of foreign languages; it might be expected to concentrate on English and other so-called majority languages like French, Russian, Arabic and German, so as to reach a majority of people.

(3) Britain's long maritime and early colonial history, and its extensive Commonwealth and international connexions, undergoing considerable changes this mid-century, led her before the last War into a wider *range* of international involvements than any country in history. It might then be thought that her overseas broadcasting would have already been made in a wide range of foreign languages in the early days of the 1930s and 40s.

(4) Britain emerged from the 1939–45 War with the biggest Overseas Broadcasting Service in the world (Figure 6.3), which had been built up particularly for the purpose of maintaining contact with allies in the occupied countries of Europe. Since the War, the B.B.C.'s weekly output has remained fairly steady at about 600 to 650 hours per week (whilst that of other countries has grown rapidly (Figure 6.3)). It might therefore be felt that the B.B.C. could not afford broadcasting *time* to devote to many different languages.

Such expectations are all contrary to the facts, which are summarized in Figure 6.4.

At the outbreak of the Second World War, September 1939, the B.B.C. was transmitting to overseas listeners in the English language for a total of about 210 hours per week; broadcasts in all foreign languages combined totalled only 62 hours per week. These languages were 13 in number and included the 'major' languages, French, covering also Canada and North Africa, Spanish and Portuguese, covering also South and Central America, German, covering Austria also, and Italian, but not Russian. That was in

1939. During the subsequent years of war the hours of overseas broadcasting increased; by 1945 the weekly hours devoted to the English language rose to the peak number of 484 whilst, however, at the same time the number of foreign languages used rose to 39 occupying 377 hours per week in all. Since that date a further interesting change has taken place. Continued financial strictures have not prevented the numbers of languages of foreign

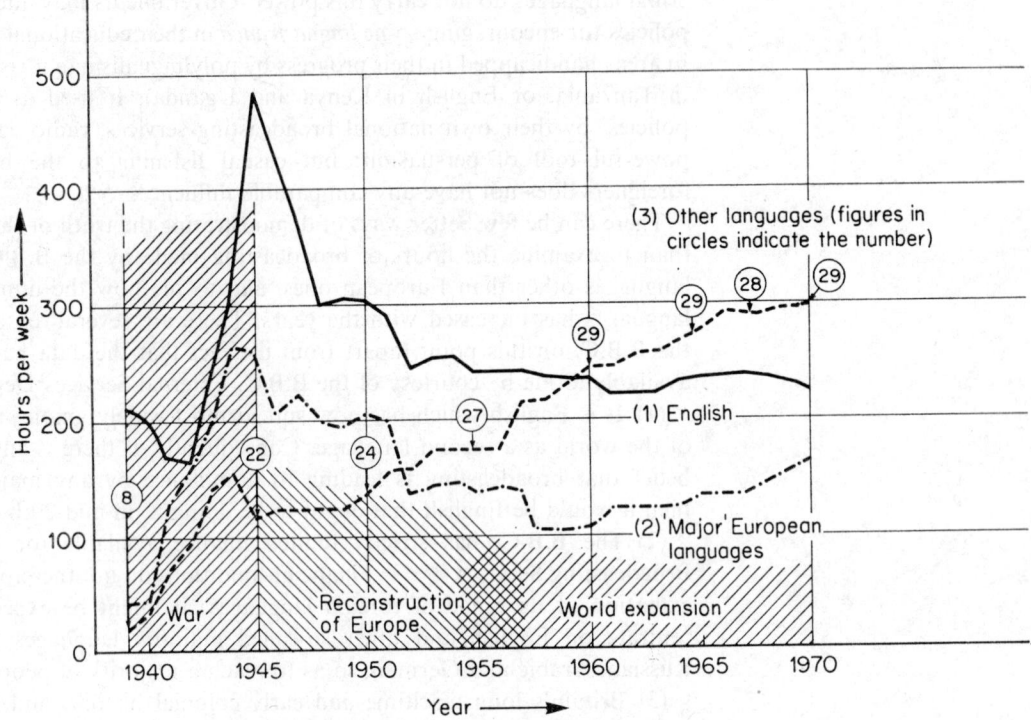

Figure 6.4. Worldwide broadcasting is unlikely to extinguish 'minority languages' (see p. 183). Example of B.B.C. Overseas Broadcasting.

1. *English Language*. English for continental Europe and countries overseas.
2. *'Major' European Languages*. Danish, Dutch, French, German, Italian, Norwegian, Portuguese, Russian, Spanish, Swedish. (By 1970 only Spanish, Portuguese, French, German and Italian.)
3. *Other Languages* (*Figures in small circles indicate their numbers*).
   Afrikaans, Albanian, Arabic, Flemish, Bengali, Bulgarian, Burmese, Chinese (Cantonese, Hokkien and Kuoyu), Czech, Finnish, Greek, Gujarati, Hausa, Hebrew, Hindi, Hungarian, Icelandic, Indonesian, Japanese, Luxembourgish, Malay, Maltese, Marathi, Persian, Polish, Rumanian, Sinhala, Somali, Swahili, Tamil, Thai, Turkish, Urdu, Vietnamese, Serbo-Croat and Slovene.

broadcasts from falling to only 35; *falling*, yes, but the languages which have been dropped are mainly the West European ones closest to the British culture: Danish, Dutch, Norwegian, Swedish, whilst the weekly hours of French and German have also been reduced. No 'non-major' language has been dropped other than Albanian, Afrikaans, Flemish, Hokkien Chinese, Gujarati, Icelandic, Hebrew, Luxembourgish and Marati whilst others have been added including Hausa, Indonesian, Somali, Swahili, Urdu and Vietnamese.

Thus the range and variety of *non-major* languages used by the B.B.C. for overseas broadcasts has not reduced with the years. Furthermore, the total time devoted to all foreign languages rose in 1969 to 466 hours per week whilst that assigned to broadcasts in English fell to 225 hours per week.

Naturally, political and other reasons could be found for choosing the specific languages and for their changes,[26] but this is not the point under discussion. The evidence summarized by Figure 6.4 supports the conclusion given earlier, namely that broadcasting *per se* is not likely to extinguish the non-major languages: those languages of the less powerful, low industry or 'developing' countries. English, French, German and other languages may be 'major',* with regard to the numbers of countries using them for specific purposes; but the majority of people in this world neither speak nor understand them. And broadcasting is directed to *persons*, not to countries, therefore it must seek them out in their own languages. Consequently, the more resources that a country can afford to devote to overseas broadcasting, the greater the variety of languages it may be expected to use. Nevertheless, there will be many languages of small minorities, possibly hundreds, for which broadcasting is unlikely ever to cater and hence cannot affect their usage. Upon these languages greater pressures than broadcasting alone may come to bear.

These arguments have been applied entirely to *spoken* language; when it comes to written language the story may be somewhat different. Some attention has already been given to newspapers,† so let us now consider another most important medium, that of books.

6. On books in the 'Age of Television'
Whereas radio, films and T.V. can be directed to all people, whether literate or not, with various degrees of effectiveness, and newspapers too may spread their news to illiterate populations by being read aloud, books are far more confined, for several reasons.

One obvious reason is economic. Most books, even paperbacks,[300] are very expensive in relation to the incomes of most people in this world. (Unesco defines a *book* as 'a non-periodical printed publication of at least 49 pages, excluding the cover pages'.) Another reason is that most of them are written in one of a few languages only. Yet another is that libraries are most readily established in towns and cities, making it difficult and expensive to serve scattered rural populations who, in some countries, are a majority. In many poorer areas of the world illiteracy and cost are the obvious major restrictions. Though public lending libraries do exist in many poor countries, in Colleges, Schools, Embassies (or their Information Bureaux), Social centres, and other institutions, e.g. The British Council, they are often relatively small, little used, contain mostly European and often unsuitable stocks, and many have been established only recently.

Even within the industrial countries, the familiar free Municipal Public Library, used by citizens of all interests, classes and conditions, is not a very ancient institution (although by the 18th century, the habit of reading was already established in Britain among an educated class).[155] After all, Public Municipal Lending Libraries did not start in Britain or the U.S.A. until the early 1850s. That is to say, Public Libraries in the modern sense of Municipal, rate-supported, free lending libraries for the man in the street.

* The words 'major languages' are used throughout this Section to refer only to those most closely connected with West European culture; they are the languages of the majority of the world's books (see Figure 6.2). It is not used here as a value-term.

† See Chapter 1, Section 6, Chapter 2, Sections 5 and 6, Chapter 3, Section 2, Chapter 4, Sections 1, 2 and 4.

There have been many 'non-private' libraries in Britain since the 15th century, especially including those at Oxford and Cambridge Universities.[295] (Prior to 1850 there had of course been Subscription Libraries, Mechanics Institutes and libraries in many institutions, but the First Public Libraries Act was passed in the U.K. in 1850; in the U.S.A. in 1849.)[173, 208] Even then, for many years few people had any idea of their purpose; there was no demand for them.[208] It was not until after such Libraries had been started that people realized their purposes and values, and demand began slowly to rise. Books are a medium of communication and, just as with all the other media, as we saw in Chapter 3, it is supply which creates demand. As McColvin has said about public libraries: '. . . here is, definitely, a case when supply created demand, not where demand created supply. And the same, let us never forget, is true today in every country in the world, be it Indonesia or Italy, Pakistan or Peru'.[208] The same thing can be said about book writing and publishing in general; they are not done as a result of public demand.

The extent to which libraries exist and are used in any country, and also sales of books, do not depend solely upon literacy, but upon other social conditions too, including a certain level of education, an arousal of curiosity, interest and motives for enquiry, aspirations, spare mental energy, free time, proximity to urban centres and other characteristics of people of the more 'advanced' societies, possessing a substantial 'middle class'. But literacy alone is not enough. Furthermore, the mere *size* of the community in which a person lives may determine the size of the library that it can support, and hence the range of titles and subjects.[208] Scattered, rural populations cannot be so well or easily served; travelling libraries, organized arrangements for book exchanges between libraries on a nationwide basis, etc., require the conditions of rapid transport and communication that exist only in the more advanced countries. Even within those countries, these conditions can vary much. Thus a greater proportion of the British population lives in large conurbations than does that of the U.S.A.,[334] where towns and cities are also much farther apart and there is a far greater number of small and widely dispersed communities. At the 1960 census, for example, about 30 per cent of the population of the U.S.A. were living in communities of less than 1000 people. The corresponding figure for Britain cannot be stated exactly because many communities are so close together as to merge and often form suburbs of adjoining urban areas (e.g. one sixth of the whole population of Britain lives within the single conurbation of Greater London). If parishes be taken as the unit then only about 7 per cent of the population of England and Wales lives in parishes having less than 100 population. (*Census* 1961, *England and Wales, Age, Marital Condition and General Tables*, H.M.S.O., 1964. With kind permission.) These geographical and demographic differences between the U.K. and the U.S.A. may partly account for the great difference in the usage made of public lending libraries in these two countries;[64, 208, 337] thus, in 1962, the public library circulation in the U.S.A. was nearly $4\frac{1}{2}$ books per head of population,[334] whilst in Britain it was $9\frac{1}{2}$. (As noted later in the Section, neither of these figures should be interpreted with great precision. For U.S.A. circulation figures in 1956 see Refs. 238 and 337.) This difference certainly has nothing whatever to do with the quality and services of American libraries, many of which are unmatched anywhere in the world. Their problem of *distribution* is far greater than ours in Britain, especially among rural, small town populations. At the same time, one cannot refrain from commenting again upon the extraordinary addiction to the printed word shown by the British, which has origins going back centuries;[155] as was noted before, the British buy more newspapers than any other people[320] and produce far more books (by titles), for their population size, than do Americans.[330] By the 18th century Britain was the most literate country in the world.[80] Her early industrialization and urban conditions favoured the introduction of public libraries. In other countries, where libraries and literature of religious or political types were dominant, as in Holland, Belgium and Eastern Europe, public libraries 'made little and difficult progress'.[173] This has also been true where sharp distinction has been traditional between 'scholarly' and 'popular' libraries, as in Italy, Austria and Germany.[173] The social origins and patterns of development of public libraries have been closely similar in Britain, the U.S.A.[14] and Scandinavia,[116,173,208] where they started, from very different backgrounds, under the inspiration of private people of great social insight, including clergymen and teachers.

Within the industrial countries, with their abundance of media claiming the attention—books, cinemas, newspapers, magazines, and many and varied forms of entertainment—that hoary question is so often heard asked: 'Since television, does anybody read any more?' Indeed, I have heard the opinion widely expressed that, 'now that we are all glued to the goggle-box, libraries are falling out of use'. This belief is, of course, the reverse of the truth;[195] library usage and book buying are both on the increase. It is cinema attendance which has declined in the industrial countries, but not, I am led to believe, in the U.S.S.R. (see Figure 2.1). If anything, television acts as a stimulus to reading; as a medium, it replaces, not reading, but rather many of the functions of the cinema. Very little research has been published yet concerning the effect of *particular* T.V. and radio programmes (e.g. plays, documentaries, educational programmes, serialized books, etc.) upon the subsequent sales of 'the book' or lendings from public libraries (see Figure 2.1). This seems to the author to be a matter of major sociological importance to educators, broadcasters, librarians, sociologists and others. See Ref. 195 which contains one such study.

Figure 6.5 shows the increase of book lendings from the Municipal Public Libraries in the United Kingdom, since the introduction of universal primary education in 1870, from figures supplied by the Library Association, London; later figures are published annually, by library authority, in the *Municipal Yearbook*.[220] The dates of various Education Acts, Library Acts, and of the start of broadcasting and T.V. are also marked.

The coming of broadcasting in 1922, and the restarting of the B.B.C. Television Service after the War, both preceded spurts in book lendings. This curve shows that, far from declining, library books circulated in ever increasing numbers during the period when T.V. sets came to enter into virtually every home in Britain. Population increase does not account for this (see the population growth curve, Figure 2.4).

It must be admitted that great precision cannot be attached to this curve; for one thing, the basis of calculation of book lendings differs from one Local Authority to another and, in addition, the coverage for the various years is incomplete in different ways and an estimate has been made for most of these years to cover those Authorities that did not report.* Nevertheless, the general trend is undeniable; book circulation continues to increase, rapidly.

* These cautions have been made to me by the Library Association.

It would be wrong to jump to the conclusion that radio and television were the sole immediate *causes* of this increase in book reading, for other pressures have been at work. Perhaps none are more important than the rising standards and spread of education (in Britain, for example, the 1944 Education Act introduced secondary education for all). Nor should we discount the effects of the Second World War upon people's interests in world and home affairs; for example, we shall note later the very great increase in newspaper reading during World War II, especially by women

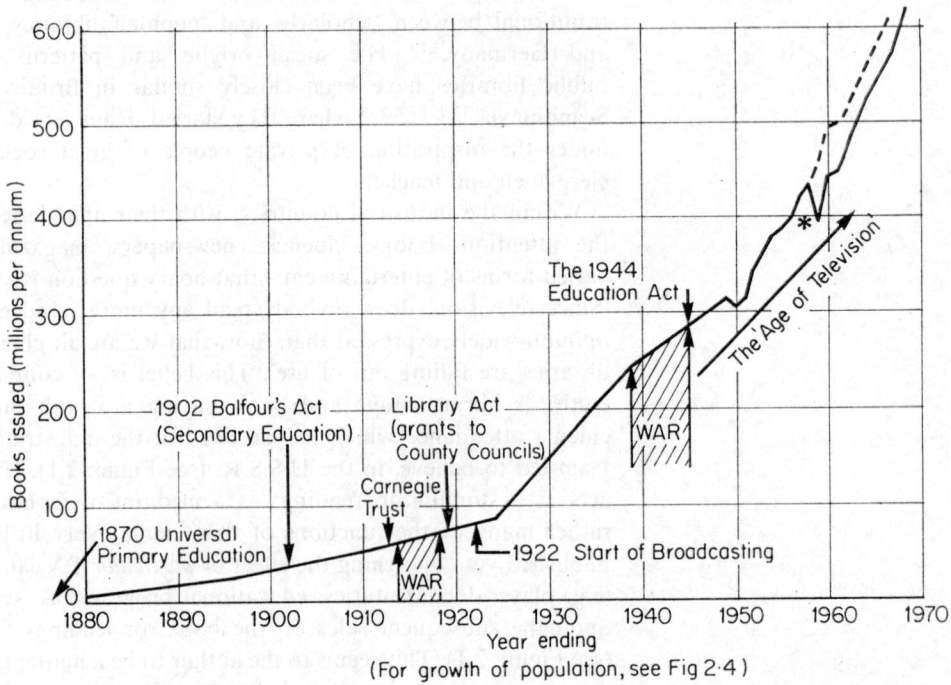

Figure 6.5. The number of books issued from Municipal Libraries in Britain, over the past century. Figures kindly supplied by the Library Association, London.

*After 1958, issues from school libraries run by Public Libraries were not listed. This accounts for the sudden drop. The dotted line is estimated, but not over-generously. Figures are published annually in the *Municipal Yearbook*, but there is a slight uncertainty introduced because it is not always possible to distinguish clearly between issues from Public Libraries and school libraries.

(see Figures 6.6 and 6.7). Rising standards of education and increased wealth for increasing numbers of the population have played their part; so has the so-called 'paper-back revolution', in drawing the attention of new readers, by display in bookshop windows, and otherwise.[80] Nor should we discount the far greater attractiveness of modern library architecture, exterior and interior, and the improved stocks.[208] Far more money has been made available since the last War, not only for libraries but for education in general in the public sector. In Britain, as elsewhere educational standards for very many people have greatly risen, and radio and television are a part of that process. As further evidence of rising standards we might note that, since the War, the total enrolment at all major (adult education) evening Institutes has increased steadily.[123] Yet again, evidence is offered by the great increase in buying of 'quality' newspapers since before the War (see Section 7).[126] (The Press itself recognizes the two classes, 'quality' and 'popular'.[125, 355])

We are here speaking of *averages* which, of course, completely conceal all knowledge of who it is that is borrowing or buying more books nowadays. There is no reason to believe that the people who are heavy viewers of T.V. are necessarily the same ones who are reading more. The habits of doing either, or both, may depend upon a host of other social factors.[238] For this, and other reasons, the effects of television upon people's reading habits cannot reliably be studied by direct comparison of two communities, (a) one which had television early and (b) another which had no television until some years later; more subtle means of research must be used.[237]

The curve in Figure 6.5 holds another trap of misinterpretation, if we are not careful, which is this: although library circulations have undoubtedly increased rapidly since the coming of television, we do not know whether the increase might not have been even greater if T.V. had not been invented. One study, made in Illinois, indicates that it would have been; the predicted increase being about one book a year per person, with a likelihood for this to have come from the Fiction shelves of the libraries.[237]

Mere increase in the volume of circulations is one thing, equally important is the *quality* of reading: how has this changed since the coming of T.V.?

First, let us note that Public, rate-supported Lending Libraries are normally administered by committees of Local Authorities (the administering authorities and organizations vary between countries[208]) and City Fathers, who are ultimately responsible, are not, on the whole, inclined towards pornography.

To be serious, a number of major studies of changes in public reading tastes during the coming of television arrive at rather similar conclusions, namely, that television tends to widen children's tastes, introducing them to literature other than fiction; further, they have noted the increase in reading of more serious papers and magazines, with corresponding reduction in circulation of comics and 'low brow' magazines and books. This has been reported in Britain,[121] in the U.S.A.[267] and Japan[94, 237] and, no doubt, elsewhere.

Unfortunately no detailed statistics are available, to the writer's knowledge, to show how reading interests have waxed and waned among various different subjects. But it is known that, generally speaking, non-fiction has become somewhat more popular at the expense of fiction;[80, 237] non-fiction means not only technical subjects, but includes history, travel, hobbies of all kinds, accountancy, affairs, and many other fields.

With regard to book *production*, more details are known for, among other sources, the *U.N. Statistical Yearbook* for 1966 publishes the figures for each country, listed under classes of subject: General, Philosophy, Religion, Social Sciences, etc.[330] These relate only to the various national productions; it is not known how many are actually written within those countries, nor in what languages. The figures show that the proportion of non-fictional books has been rising since the Second World War.[9, 80, 330]

This tendency is not confined to countries having many T.V. or radio sets, but is a general one throughout the world.[80, 330] The *proportion* of technical books, books on science, accountancy, law and other non-fiction, both imported into and produced in 'developing' countries, must be expected to be high and increasing, as their sights are set on rising material standards, industrialization and self-determination.

As with other modes of communication, books create their own particular relationships between the advanced and the developing countries. The first is obviously the result of the very uneven distribution of literacy among peoples of the various countries (see U.N. *Statistical Yearbook* for 1964 and 1966).[33,300,322] In this connexion it is important to remember that, although many of the poorer countries produce only a very small number of *written* works,[80,300] many, or most, of them have an extensive *spoken* literature, of long tradition, as did the Ancient Greeks whom we often regard as having laid the foundations of our own Western culture. However, to read books requires more than literacy (which may mean little more than the ability to sign a name[33]). There must be a reason, a desire, a motive. Books are not easy to read but require concentration for long periods; reading the words is one thing, but comprehension is another, and critical understanding yet another. It is a private, withdrawn occupation. The wish and ability to read extend beyond simple literacy into the whole continuing process we call 'education', and the desire, often passionate desire, for education is one of the marked characteristics of the newly independent and developing countries. It is unfortunate, then, that in this process they have to rely heavily upon books written in languages other than their own; for most of the world's books have been written in one of the European languages, or in Japanese or Chinese.[80] It has been pointed out that, in 1963, 75 per cent of the world's books (by title) were written in one of 12 countries[80,300] and that roughly a third of the world's book production is in one of four languages only, English, German, Spanish and French, with the proportion of English language works increasing[80] (see Section 5).

The great book production of the U.S.S.R. is frequently referred to. They certainly *buy* many, but their book titles per head of population are actually low (0·13 per thousand population, compared to 0·47 in Britain). The mistake may arise because the U.S.S.R. list their cumulated production in 93 languages.[80] See also U.N. *Statistical Yearbook*, 1966.

Students in many of the developing countries therefore need to be literate in what is, to them, a foreign language and their education will proceed to a major extent through one of these European languages, with all the cultural influences that may imply (not necessarily desirable). Furthermore, to read the bulk of educational books with understanding the student must have at his command an exceptionally large vocabulary;[288,289] the learning of a foreign language for conversation need not involve a large vocabulary, but the understanding of books does.

For this reason it can help if special editions are produced of standard classics, of specially written school primers and even of technical books, which use English or other European vocabularies limited to a few hundred or, at most, a couple of thousand words or so.[232] Such work has been going on in many centres in developing countries since the Second World War, particularly at the initiative of major commercial Publishing Houses. Other special classes of book are also published, both by local branches of commercial publishers from the industrial countries and by locally organized commercial Firms and Trusts.

For example, in East Africa, school primers and other books, written with reduced vocabularies, are now being published locally* to suit curricula laid down by the (African) Education Authorities and to be used as directed by them, together with 'Supplementary Books' for general and home reading. These vocabularies start with the words in most common literary usage and

---

* E.g. by the East African Publishing House (an all-African commercial Trust), by Longmans, the Oxford University Press and others, at local Houses.

extend to less frequent words, according to known statistics. For example, see M. West, in Bibliography.[347] Such books fall into distinct classes, among which a few could be mentioned here:

(a) Simple stories, fairy tales, legends, plays, classics and African folk tales, written in reduced English vocabularies of about 500, 750, 1000, 1500, 1750, 2000, 2500 (and other) words, suited to different school standards as decided by the local Education Authorities.

(b) Books specially written in small vocabularies of about 500, 750, 1000, 1500 etc. words, by both African writers and by Europeans who have lived in Africa for long periods.

(c) Practical and semi-technical books in small vocabularies on carpentry, building, nursing, agriculture and other practical topics, not written in a dry technical way, but in the form of simple stories. E.g. *Turning Wheels*: Frankie's father is a farmer, but he wants to be an engineer. Then an exciting adventure influences his choice. (Published by Longmans of Kenya, Ltd.)

(d) Books in native languages: e.g. Swahili, Kamba, Luo, Kikuyu . . . with African backgrounds.

(e) Booklets about manufactured articles: *A Bar of Soap, A Packet of Needles, A Cup of Coffee*, etc. (Longmans of Kenya, Ltd.)

There are several other categories of special publication. Such school texts can offer far more relevance to the local situation than old editions of *Jane Eyre, Nicolas Nickleby* and *Kenilworth*. Similar work, directed away from European background, history and culture, has been going on in West Africa, Malaysia and many other developing countries, at least wherever there are overseas branches of the commercial Publishing Houses of the advanced countries of long literary tradition; increasingly, local national firms and Trusts may be expected to emerge, as more national authors appear. What is certain is that a major part of such publication will be school primers and other educational texts many if not most of which will be, for a long time yet, in English.

Not only does the large vocabulary of English, with its great range of near synonyms, present problems, but there are other difficulties which may handicap pupils of non-European origin, who have at present no alternative but to use our standard classics and technical texts.

For example, I personally question whether the right mental images, or concepts, are readily induced in, say, an African mind by the metaphors, analogies and verbal forms used by European writers, even in science books, because of the great differences in environment, customs, interests, histories and language. We might remember that the earlier concepts of science were created in the 16th and 17th centuries by people who wrote in *Latin*. For such reasons, it is the general rule that better results are achieved by local translators, working *into* their own language. Such translators and also writers of original works, in science and technology, are unfortunately in short supply in many developing countries.

Books flow most readily between countries having the same, or closely related, languages, promoting intellectual and cultural exchanges within those language blocs (e.g. English-speaking, Spanish-speaking, etc.). Escarpit points out the importance of this inevitable fact of language, for producing an interdependence of the countries within those blocks.[80] English being the most widely used literary language (see U.N. *Statistical Yearbook*, 1966) the United Kingdom, the U.S.A. and other English-speaking countries have this advantage for the spread of their literary and technical books. But at the same time both the U.K. and the U.S.A. have enormous internal and external markets, so there is less pressure upon them to translate their own works into foreign languages, for export.[80] (Unesco's annual *Index Translationum* lists the translated books published in some 80 and more countries.[304])

Translation provides the main outlet for books to flow between countries within different language blocs and, again, the English language is in a favoured position, for it is English language works which are translated into foreign languages by many countries, in far greater numbers than any others, followed by French, Russian, German (see Figure 6.2 and U.N. *Statistical Yearbook*, 1966). Small countries, with minority languages, have small internal native language markets and see outside their borders really large market possibilities not only for translation of their own works but those of other countries too. There can be other reasons than economic ones for the production of translations by different countries; historical and traditional ones, for example. The remarkable foreign language publishing industry of that tiny country, the Netherlands, is very well known, and this may be traced to her unique position in oppressed 17th century Europe, at the time of Cardinal Richelieu, as the main outlet for new thought and ideas. Thus Alexander Dumas, in his Preface to *The Three Musketeers* tells of his discovery of a document entitled *Memoirs of Monsieur d'Artagnan*, upon which he based his novel. To quote Dumas: '. . . . printed by Peter the Red at Amsterdam—as the principal works of that period, when authors could not adhere to the truth without running the risk of the Bastille, generally were'. Another tiny country, Israel, translates nearly as many books as we do in the United Kingdom, though her population is a small fraction of ours. (See U.N. *Statistical Yearbook*, 1966.)

Escarpit has pointed out the very small fraction of the world's literature which constitutes translations; in the case of Chinese and Japanese work the number is infinitesimal which, in his opinion, is not due to political reasons.[80]

Many developing countries are polylingual and must make decisions about the vehicle language they intend to use in their educational programmes. In many cases they can choose one of these major European languages, if only because colonial history has left them with a certain inheritance of this kind after independence has been achieved. For them, books are at least available from overseas, even if costly and not ideal. But others must adopt a non-European language as a *lingua franca*;[300] Tanzania, for example, proposes to adopt Swahili (for good reason), but there are few books yet written in Swahili, or in any other African languages for that matter, except Arabic.[208] A similar dearth exists among the countries of Asia, apart from religious books. In other areas no *lingua franca* has been established and polylingualism presents a great problem, owing to grossly inadequate printing and editing facilities and to the small markets.[300]

Such is the situation that will exist until the developing countries write and publish their own books on a far wider range of subjects and in greater numbers than at present, in their own languages or their adopted *lingua franca*.[308]

It is perhaps of interest here to reflect upon the fact that a similar language problem once existed in Britain too, centuries ago. Prior to the 14th century, Latin and French were used by all, except the 'common man'. Then English began to return as the vernacular language. Caxton may not have been the first man in Europe to introduce printing, but his fame and uniqueness arise from the fact that he printed *lay* books, not religious works, in great numbers and, furthermore, in the vernacular English. He and others produced both translations and originals in the vernacular, giving evidence of the spread of literacy among a *lay* population (see p. 25).[2, 155, 295] There is a growing need for the same thing to be done, today, in the developing countries of the world.[300]

A number of Unesco Reports have examined the difficulties both of importing books into the poorer countries and of producing them there.[1, 9, 262, 300, 301, 302, 308] It would be impudent of me to attempt a survey of this immense and complex problem covering a hundred very different countries. Nevertheless, there are certain broad generalities which are relevant here.

The countries of lowest literacy and economies lie within the continents of Africa and Asia (see Figure 3.2). Languages are diverse and many countries and language groups are small, especially in Africa. Hence markets for most books, both imported and local, are very small and books are in very short supply, both educational and vocational. However, the present great drive for education in these countries is raising demand, especially for school textbooks and literacy primers; it is these that are most urgently needed, because schoolchildren form the main reading public, and there are now large numbers of them. It has been estimated that, by 1980, 40 per cent of Asia's predicted 1370 millions will be of school age.[308] Assuming this to be 5–14 years inclusive, the corresponding figures in 1965 in U.S.A. and U.K. (where compulsory education has long existed) are: U.S.A.[334] 20·3 per cent and U.K.[123] 14·6 per cent. In Asia, as in Africa, populations are very young. Literacy rates are rising, as a percentage of populations, although the actual *number* of illiterates is increasing, due to the 'population explosion'.[300, 319, 322] One estimate reckons that, in countries of lower literacy, a 1 per cent rise in literacy figures could lead to a 5 per cent increase in purchasing power. Thus the prospects for book publishing in Asia and Africa are improving from the literacy and educational points of view,[300, 308] and from that of rising demand.[300] But the prospects for *production* there are not so happy.

There are other and very serious obstacles. First, financial: book exports from the poorer countries are as yet very small, so publishers earn little foreign currency from sales abroad. Second, there is a shortage of paper in Asia and, particularly, in Africa; demands for paper, although still a very small fraction of world demand, are rising in both continents at rates far higher than in any other part of the world.[80] Unfortunately for the smaller countries paper is much more expensive to buy in small quantities.[300, 301] Third, printing presses are mostly, though not all, antique and inadequate in number for coming demands; modern ones are costly to import.[164, 300] Fourth, costs of transport are high, both inland and from overseas.[80, 300, 316] Fifth, bookshops and other centres of distribution are too few, as are libraries too, over the greater parts of the two continents; there is also a shortage of publishers. Sixth, there is a shortage of trained manpower, of editors especially, and of illustrators, printers and authors.[300] These are some of the main difficulties facing the development of the book industry in Africa and Asia, to resolve which Unesco have made a number of suggestions.

As with other modes of communication (see Chapter 5, Section 3), recent developments in the technology of printing and book production in the advanced countries are resulting in cheaper methods, which may help the situation considerably, in the poorer countries.[80, 300] So, too, might many organizational suggestions made by Unesco, including those for tariff and trade agreements, licensing, copyright, subsidies, and other financial and legal arrangements.[80, 300, 316] There are many restrictions upon the supply of books to the developing countries, which must be rationalized if their rapidly rising demands of education are to be met. And television, as it enters and develops in those countries certainly will not be a deterrent to literacy, reading and education; just as in the industrial countries, it is likely to be a stimulus to interest, curiosity and mental appetite.[262, 265] Furthermore, as the population explosion[239] continues to increase the numbers of children who are unable to find school places, in spite of many impressive programmes of school provision,[130] television, with radio, film and other aids, could increasingly help to fill the gap. There seems to be no other way, and such technical aids can be used as very effective ways of multiplying the effective number of teachers (good teachers) and the number of school places. The process we call development involves not only rising economic levels and purchasing powers but, fundamentally, it is an education process, a process of adaptation to changing circumstances and inculcation of desire to take a personal part in those changes. Books were the major technical force behind that process in early Europe; today these other technical aids exist, to help accelerate similar processes in the other countries which are 'in a hurry'.

7. Democracy and the mass media
In several places in this book, I have argued that the expression 'mass-communication' is an unfortunate misnomer, and one calculated to arouse prejudice (e.g. see p. 35 and p. 42). It suggests analogy to mass-production, implying the creation of that mythical monster 'mass-mind' created by those other mythical monsters, the Great Manipulators.

The term 'the masses' has a long history stemming from the French Revolution; it is an expression partly of fear and partly of contempt. Thomas Carlyle demonstrated such emotional attitudes when he spoke of 'the masses' as Swarmery, Sons of the Devil, etc.[357] (See p. 42.)

Unesco takes the opposite view and has emphasized in many publications the enormous values of the mass-media: the press,[306, 309] radio, cinema,[321] books etc.,[300, 308] values which are great, though different in kind, to countries in all states of economic and political development.*[301, 302, 307, 310, 315, 320]

In those countries which have long had an established Press, cinema and radio, the forms of these media have been seen to change over the years. Newspapers in Britain say, are very different from those 50 years ago; they serve rather different functions now. Films, too, have changed, as the theatre has changed, with the social climate. It would be quite wrong to assume that the various mass-media have today reached final, immutable forms, and to base argument and criticism upon such assumption. The really important thing about the 'newspaper of the future' is not that it may come into our homes electronically, via our T.V. screens, or by the home printing press actuated by a World News Centre via our private data links, etc., etc; the factor of real importance will be what that newspaper *contains*. The concept we call 'the news', or the content of newspapers, has regularly changed over the decades (see Chapter 2, Section 5) and will continue to do so. Our ideas may alter with regard to the importance of different classes of item (e.g. crime, financial, industrial, political, etc.) and new categories may appear; factual news may reduce in volume, whilst criticism and commentary increase, etc. Even during the past quarter of a century there has been a steady swing of public favour towards the more serious newspapers,[77, 125, 355]

* For good bibliography on the values of mass-media to national development, see Ref. 262 and see also the many references in Bibliography under Unesco.

presumably correlated with the rising standards of education among wide sections of the community. E.g., in Britain, the 'quality newspapers' increased their circulation from about 6 per cent to 9 per cent of the whole circulation in the quarter century preceding 1957 and the increase is continuing today. (See p. 188.)

As the 1947–49 Report of a Royal Commission on the Press showed, the contents of British national dailies steadily became both more serious and

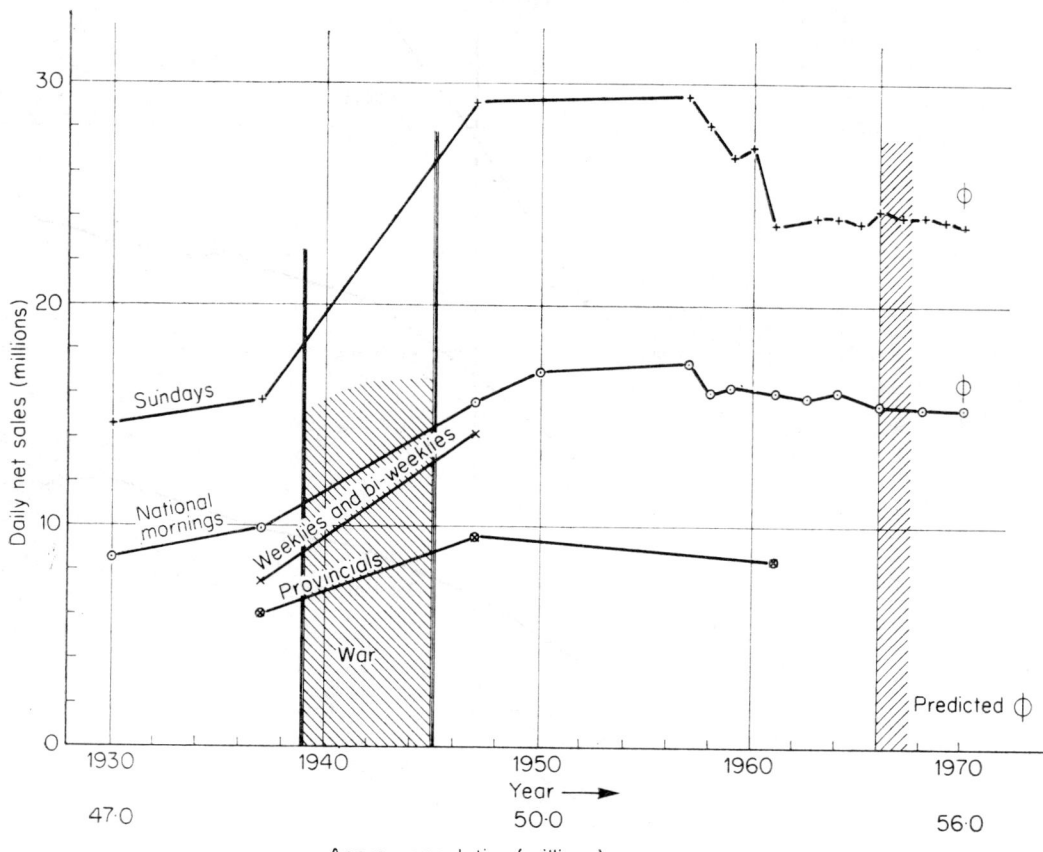

Figure 6.6. Effects of war upon newspaper reading habits in Great Britain. Sources: points marked + and ⊙, from The Economist Intelligence Unit, London;[77] others from H.M.S.O.[44,125,126] Other figures from (1) 1961 Royal Commission (H.M.S.O.) (2) C.O.I. *The British Press*, (3) 1947–49 Royal Commission (H.M.S.O.). φ signifies predicted. Newspaper statistics cannot be stated with great accuracy.

more international in tone as assessed between the years 1927, 1937, 1947, whilst the space devoted to advertisements was reduced over this time.[125] The latter decade covered the years of the Second World War and, during that decade, 1937–1947, the daily circulation of British national and provincial newspapers nearly doubled, rising from 16·7 million to 28·5 million,[125] probably owing to the great increase of women's reading during the War (see Figure 6.6). This great increase was continued after the War in spite of a severe shortage of newsprint.[125] It should however be borne in mind that accurate and reliable statistics of newspaper circulations are very hard to come by. It will be noticed that there are many missing figures in both Figures 6.6 and 6.7; these curves therefore indicate *general* growths of circulations, prior to 1956, for which period annual statistics have not been found.

The same great upsurge of newspaper circulation during the War appeared in the U.S.A., as Figure 6.7 shows.[334] In this case the classifications are different, because the sharp division between 'national dailies' and 'provincials'

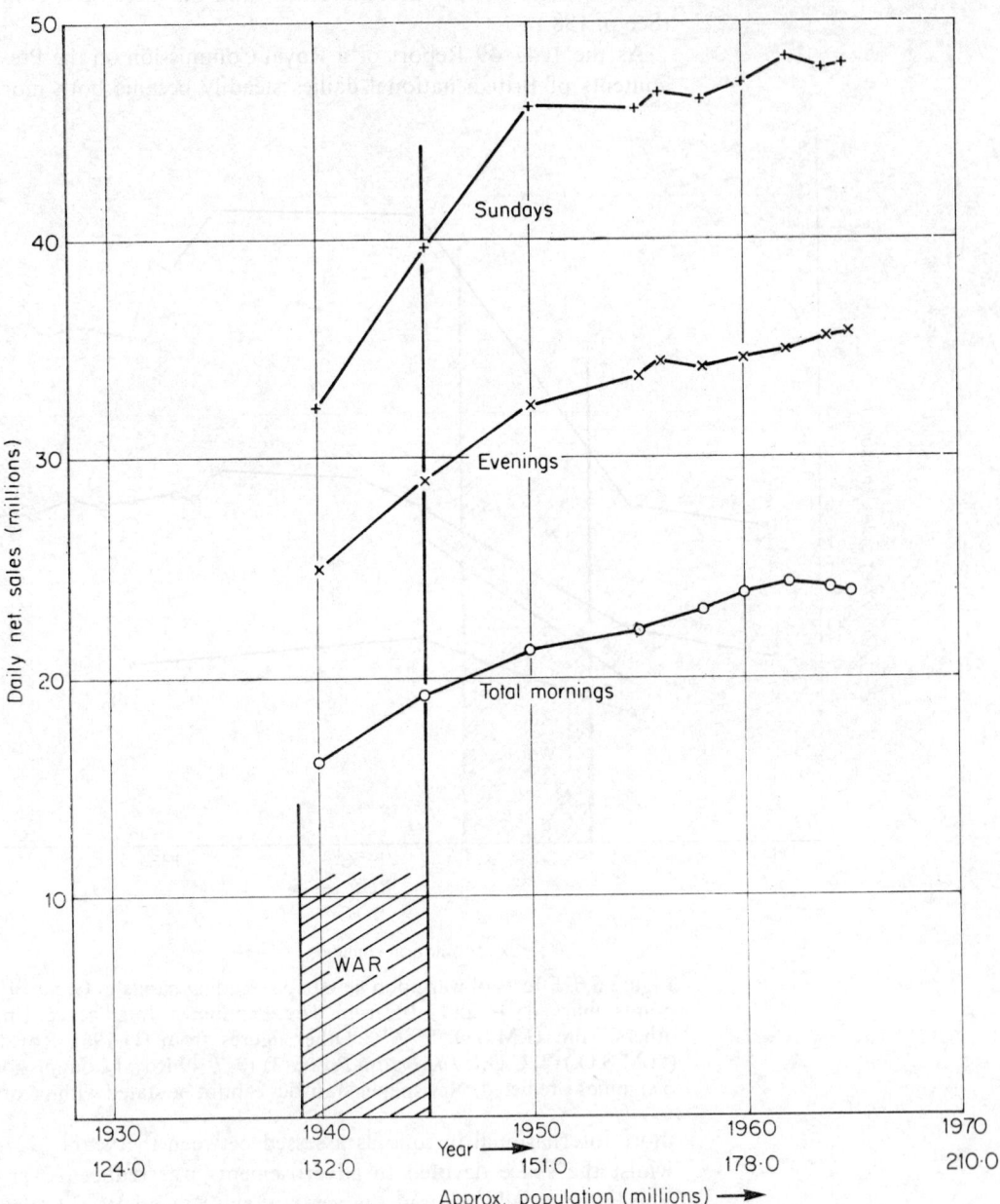

Figure 6.7. Effects of war upon newspaper reading habits in the U.S.A. Source: reference 334.

is not a feature of American newspapers. Notice particularly, in both Figures 6.6 and 6.7 that Sunday papers spread their circulations most rapidly. It should also be noted that the *population* of the U.S.A. has expanded far more rapidly than that of Britain (see Figure 2.4); figures have been added against the years, in both these diagrams, for readers who may wish to assess newspaper circulations per head of population.

Neither should we assume that the changes which newspapers will certainly undergo, in future, will come about just because the Great Manipulators desire these changes. The changes will occur under the direction of a host of social forces, such as education, the growth of international institutions, extended travel, changing industry and economics, etc. and, above all, the introduction of new media. Radio, films and television have been taking over some of the functions of the earlier newspapers and have introduced their own forms of news presentation, documentaries and criticism; what new forms may yet appear can only be guessed at. Nobody, in the industrial countries at least, is under the influence of any one single medium alone, but is exposed to very many and varied forms.

In developing countries which do not have a long established Press, or radio service, the responsibilities and values of the media are different.[301, 302, 307] Above all, they must work towards building up *trust* for, without this, they will not become accepted, nor prosper. In initial stages their circulations or audiences will necessarily be low: nevertheless, the circulation and readership of a newspaper may be far less than the number of people who *learn* the news and other contents, for chiefs or scribes and other literates may call a meeting and read the news aloud to them. I am informed that, for example, in East Africa 'probably 8 or 10 people hear the news for every paper sold'. (See p. 155.) Advertising revenue will be correspondingly small and there are many other difficulties to contend with. They may need to operate in several languages and may face difficulties of circulation owing to absence of good roads and dispersed tribal populations. They may have to operate with inadequate technical equipment and staff and, in many cases, with endless frustrations and delays through lack, or total absence, of telephones, through semi-literate compositors, slow trains, and with the dangers of false, libellous and unintelligible reports.[164] Further, the Press and radio of a new country may have to accept, as part of their responsibility, avoidance of over-sharp or hasty criticism of the Government, either for the obvious reason of prudence, lest they might otherwise be put out of business the same day, or as part of their policy of trust-building; opposition and criticism are things that have to be 'afforded', for all freedoms are relative to overall social conditions, including that of the Press.[164, 281] This is so not only for political reasons. During the 1939–45 War and post-War years until 1959 the British Press, for example, had necessarily to reduce the sizes of papers owing to economic restriction on imports of newsprint. Thus the Press could not be said to be 'free' to publish all that it might have desired; however, it adapted responsibly to the situation and circulations continued to grow[125] (see Figure 6.6).

As part of their programme of 'helping the less developed countries to build up their information media',[301] the Economic and Social Council of Unesco sponsored three Regional Conferences; that for South East Asia, in Bangkok (January 1960);[302] for Latin America, in Santiago, Chile (February 1962); for Africa, in Paris (January–February, 1962).[301] In Africa with so many countries newly receiving their independence, (to quote): 'the modern media of communication, unsurpassed in speed, range and force of impact, had a basic part to play. These media . . . could be used to bring technical instruction and training, as well as general education, to the mass of the people on a vast scale and thus associate them closely with the major tasks of economic and social expansion'.[301] The mass-media, so readily taken for granted, or even scorned through intellectual snobbery in the older, politically stable and industrialized countries, are essential to the development of a sense of nationhood.

At the time of that Conference, 1962, 'Unesco studies had shown that for every 100 people in Africa, there were only one copy of a daily newspaper, two radio receivers and 0·5 seats in permanent cinemas'.*[301] (Unesco minima criteria were 10 papers, 5 receivers and 2 seats.) Such averages over a whole continent are, of course, not fully descriptive of the true situation; the countries of Africa vary greatly in their shares of these facilities.[320] Thus some countries have a long-developed Press (e.g. East Africa, United Arab Republic, Ghana, South Africa) whilst others have very few services of any kind (e.g. Ethiopia, Congo and others). Even South Africa has, at the time of writing, no television service.[320]

The Unesco Report urged the African States to 'immediately take action to develop the press, radio and film and . . . prepare for the introduction and effective use of television'.[301] At the same time, Unesco referred to the need for 'freedom of information' in these developments; it did not speak of 'freedom of the Press' in the sense of unrestricted liberty of criticism: 'Good government was essential to the maintenance . . . of a good press and each was a guarantee of the other. A major task, therefore, was to ensure that the media played a *constructive rôle* in the development of democratic government' (my italics).[301]

The economic state of a nation is closely correlated with its investment in communication services (see Chapter 5, Sections 1 and 2). Nevertheless, communication services are needed for reasons other than economics; 'social development' or 'progress' cannot be conceived in economic terms alone, but in the growth of a sense of nationhood, to express the uniqueness of a people and so, reciprocally, to enable each person to know better 'who he is', in relation to his fellows.[248] To develop this sense and, with it, self-respect within the company of nations, the various domestic services are of particular value.[262] Perhaps the nearest that we, in industrial societies, can come to sensing these values is during wartime or other threats of disaster, when Press and radio change their conventional rôles. It has been the radio and the Press which have forced awareness of the outside world upon the 'traditional societies' and brought about their downfall.[187, 248]

Although radio, together with newspapers or sheets read aloud by scribes or other literates, may overstep literacy to the extent of introducing some knowledge of the outside world, of instilling some sense of social condition and even of political awareness,[262] these media cannot be substitutes for literacy. As Mary Burnet and others have explained, the world has always been largely illiterate, but it is only today that illiteracy has really become a *problem*.[33] Only today are the traditional societies, hitherto isolated and self-sufficient, being forced into contact with the rest of the world: 'Illiteracy became a problem when modern means of transportation and communication began bringing peoples closer and closer together and those who had remained outside the stream of technical progress were pulled into the main current—when independence awaked dormant political consciousness . . .'[33] Certainly, skills and trades can be taught without literacy, but education cannot be continued both among and solely by illiterates; without external aid, they cannot become self-sufficient once their traditional modes of living have started to break down. They must become literate, not only to be able to

---

* For details of conditions of the Press in Africa, country by country, prior to the coming of many independencies, see Ref. 164.

follow simple instructions, but to write them too, to explain to others, understand, modify and develop ideas; not only to read the words of a newspaper, but to comprehend the reports, critically. Mary Burnet and others refer to such true literacy as *functional literacy*, literacy that works.[33,253,319] Until such levels of literacy are reached by a substantial proportion of a population, democracy cannot develop, in the sense of allowing a person to form ideas and take responsible actions towards them, involving strangers outside his village, or those beyond the small community with whom he is familiar and whose ways he knows well.[7] (For example, see the article by Lerner in Ref. 248.)

The Greek city–states may have known democracy in the market place, but they were small communities and citizens could meet one another, listen to oratory, discuss and criticize. It is sometimes said that radio and T.V. have come to introduce some such powers into our modern nation–states; but, though these media have at least enabled millions of people to see and hear their representatives, or their leaders and others who have great influence, they cannot transform a nation–state into a city–state. It is true that during wartime and other emergencies, Kings, Presidents and Prime Ministers can do much to raise a nation's morale and to instil a sense of unity and purpose; but this is but one half of the nervous system of democracy. Radio and T.V. can inform, instruct, advise, cajole, promise, expose insincerity, etc., but they cannot convert 100 million listeners into a public meeting. The real problem of communication within today's nation–states is the problem of *size*. They are too big.

Our radio, T.V., Press and other mass-media are the means *par excellence* for keeping large populations, at all social levels, informed of current affairs and events; often for arousing in them common emotions, and for directing their attention to single objectives as in wartime.[37] The mass-media can serve to give authority to what otherwise might become mere rumour ('They say that . . .', 'Have you heard about . . .?'). Statements made in the Press, or on T.V. news may or may not be wholly correct, but they provide sources of reference. They can provide the critical with ammunition with which to attack prejudice and hearsay. Our various and diverse mass-communication media are like the sense organs of the body politic, feeding it with information from the outside world: its 'afferent' nervous system. But democracy requires more than an afferent nervous system; true democracy rests upon there being adequate means of *exchange* between people, for discussion and opinion forming, for criticism, for education, for expression, and for all that can admit control over processes of change. Only in societies, large or small, which have some minimal technology of communication, whereby people may both air their views, compare, learn about the actions of their chosen representatives and influence them, can democracy exist in any shape and scale. Communication is requisite for any organization, but democracy requires it to exist in many different forms, for both personal and institutional use; the *diversity* of its sources of information is one of democracy's main protections.[126] Within those areas of the world which are virtually void of established communication, democracy may exist on a village scale, but not on the grand scale.

On the other hand, bureaucracy also depends upon there being a complex web of communication, and the mere existence of communication systems does not ensure democracy. It is certainly the case that a country that has raised itself from serfdom into a modern industrial state must have developed its informative systems, as in the U.S.S.R.;[342] it cannot do so without. (The functions of both *agitators* and *propagandists* in Communist societies are 'to ensure that people are informed'. See p. 177.) It may subsequently decide that it can afford to evolve its 'efferent' system by diversifying its media, encouraging expression of points of view, enabling comparisons to be made, allowing criticism, and by developing many possibilities for public opinions to be formed and felt. Even within our so-called democratic countries our means for personal and minority expression are still far less developed than are our systems for public informing; expression, and much formation, of *public opinion* must largely remain with professionals, writers, journalists, politicians, delegates and others acting *on behalf of* the many. In mid-20th century we are still climbing out of the authoritarian, bureaucratic phase into the democratic phase, in the industrialized countries. Democracy is still young, and has far to go. There are very many and long steps yet to be taken in the direction of what we commonly call *education*, a process still imperfectly understood and quite inadequately provided for. Democracy rests upon these three: trust, watchfulness and education, and the most basic of these is education.

At the present day, the most developed means of public *expression*, the outward or 'efferent' part of the body democratic, is 'voting'. If there ever were anything which really justifies the appellation mass-communication, it is democratic voting. Voting for specific candidates, or for specific issues, is done by putting a cross on a piece of paper. You may not write down your personal opinions, nor explain your decision, without disqualification. Everything is done to conceal your personal identity. In parliamentary elections ballot papers are actually numbered, to guard against charges of multiple voting. The assumption that your vote shall not be used against you is an act of trust. In other institutions voting may be public (e.g. at the U.N.). The communication, the end result, is achieved only by counting. It is a 'mass-result', not a personal one. The voter may be a genius or a nitwit; the equity of the business does not take his intelligence into account.

In those advanced communities which we call industrial democracies, there have developed elaborate and, in many ways, efficient systems of government, covering large areas and great numbers of people. But, as the current wave of student demonstrations shows, in the U.S.A., in France, Britain, Sweden, Japan and elsewhere, all is not well. Communication is still mainly outward, from the centres of government and authority. Radio, newspapers, the law and other institutions send out their information and instructions daily yet, apart from voting every five years or so, the public cannot easily reply, except through such devices as referenda (when the questions to be answered are *preformulated* by governments) public opinion polls, 'letters to the Editor', 'lobbying', or, as we see so much today, by demonstrating, by marching in the streets with banners and, unfortunately, sometimes by violence. The body politic urgently needs an effective efferent system, giving people a far greater sense of participation in affairs.

In societies that call themselves 'democratic', very many things are decided by voting, by majorities, by 'pressures of public opinion', which are strictly forms of mass-communication.* If those decisions are accepted as binding, as shown by respect for the law, then it must have been assumed that, on the whole, voters have acted responsibly, whatever their knowledge or intelligence.

* See Berelson, B.: *Democratic Theory and Public Opinion* in Ref. 16.

And a society which assumes this ought to hold education as one of its greatest values.

The idea of 'the greatest good for the greatest number' is nonsense if that number, the people, are unable to know good when they see it and are unable to recognize what is better, when it appears. Education, in many forms, is the essential constituent of any progressive democracy. And for this our 'mass-societies' have opportunities never before possessed, of their mass-communication systems. The responsibilities falling upon these: radio, T.V., cinema, Press, literature and all, have never before been greater. We are still learning how to use them and we have very far to go yet before we extract many of the real social values which these technologies can offer.

8. Thoughts on the future of world communication: a summary

In this closing Section we shall attempt to draw together some of the threads of argument which have necessarily been very dispersed throughout this book. For 'human communication' and 'technology' are not simple things to be understood in the language of a single academic subject. The title of this book: *World Communication—Threat or Promise?* poses a question which cannot be answered in simple yes–no terms, for it is a value question. There are many answers, depending upon who *you* are and who you are speaking *about*. Some people live in rich countries, some in poor; some believe in 'progress', some do not have the idea; some possess the economic power to instal and own the global communication systems, some have to put up with what they can get. There are infinite varieties of condition; above all, there are the social histories and the inheritances which they have left the peoples of different nations and non-nations. Perhaps our greatest difficulty is to avoid the images of communication media, radio, telephone, television, books, newspapers, railways and roads...that naturally arise in our own minds in the affluent Western countries. It is utterly useless, in the writer's opinion, to theorize or speculate about the future of world communication in terms of these Western images alone, as though 'Western man' were 'the world'. One of the most unfortunate results of the fact that the bulk of the technology (both electronic and transport) has been created within the affluent countries, is that it can lead us to imagine the future solely in terms of such images.

The opinion has been offered here that these Western images of such technologies as television, telephones, books and newspapers are largely domestic ones. We tend to think of these as they are used in the homes, or to analyse their power upon the individual; that is to say, their apparent personal, emotional values are stressed. Their immense powers for *organizing* are perhaps inadequately emphasized: powers for organizing industrial, commercial, governmental, educational and a host of forms of institution. The reason for this is obvious; it is that we in the so-called advanced countries take our complex and varied institutions for granted; we feel that we live in organized countries. We *expect* our institutions to operate. We expect our electricity supplies to be there, our shops to be stocked, our trains to operate. our Civil Service to answer queries, our teachers to teach . . . and when there is a breakdown, or a strike, or any kind of *failure*, we may feel that our trust has been betrayed and we become righteously angry.

This notion of *trust* seems essential to the idea of an advanced country: a term usually taken to mean only economically advanced. But mere wealth is inadequate for the idea; an advanced country surely is one whose people trust their institutions, a trust which must allow for social change and for those institutions to be modified and adapted. This, of course, need not imply that the people of developing countries are not trustworthy people: far from it. Rather it is to say that their trusts may be of a different nature. It is to say that within pre-industrial societies trust is placed more upon individual persons, known personally, whereas in industrial, advanced societies we can operate only inasmuch as we have trustworthy institutions and we trust them, often very large-scale institutions. And institutions are abstracts, not persons. We telephone 'the manager' or 'the secretary' or 'Head Office' and converse with the disembodied voices of those whom we have never met as persons. They are *functions*. In this view, 'advancement', through industrialization, requires a steady transfer of the concept of trust, from trust in acquaintances to trust in abstract institutions and their symbolic representatives.

It has been argued in this book that the primary contribution which the technologies of communication can make to such advancement, nationally and internationally, is to this very development of trust. That is, however, not through their possible emotional powers, for attacking other people's beliefs, or identities, not for *teaching* them to trust our present institutions and so ourselves, but essentially through their power for assisting the practical and successful operation of institutions and for creation of new ones. A 'trustworthy institution' as being one that *works*, is the Pragmatist's view.[32, 97] In particular, our global communication network, though as yet largely confined to Western traffic usage, at last offers the beginning of practical means for realistically operating the International Organizations, without requiring people to shed all their national and cultural identities. Our argument here has been that emotional attitudes, not only between peoples of different countries and cultures, but also between the different social sections, classes, ethnic groups, age groups, occupation groups, etc. of any one country, are not prime *causes*; they are rather *consequential* upon the existence or the removal of practical frustrations.

Admittedly, such conclusions can be drawn only if one adopts a certain philosophical viewpoint of the relation between the individual and society.

The viewpoint that has been taken in this book is one first clearly adopted by the great pioneer sociologist Emile Durkheim (see p. 3). This is the view that our ways of thought, the feelings we have about our own selves and others, the attitudes we adopt, our beliefs and images (our whole ego) are not born into us, nor are they much the result of our personal observations (see p. 3). Rather they are the result of the way we each have been taught, first by mother and the family institution and then through all the institutions which constitute our particular society. All our knowledge, beliefs, feelings, are socially derived; the person and his society are two sides of the same coin.

Inasmuch as the people of a country, or a tribe, or a language, or any social group *share* common institutions, they have a certain affinity and common image. They see themselves to be related and the others to be, somehow, different. We are each made as our institutions have made us. We therefore cannot make wholly objective judgements about the peoples of other countries, languages and cultures, whose institutions are different. We can only try to understand them through the eyes of our own institutions. We cannot *be* one of them.

But social institutions change and, largely owing to the rapid growth of technology and science and to the practical forces they have released, some are today changing fast. It has been argued here that all social change, whether 'progressive' or not, arises by the actions of those individuals who challenge the existing norms, by those who dispute, deny, disagree, dissent. The essential prerequisite to change is *dissent*. On the other hand, agreement, acceptance, refusal to listen or to be criticized, that is to say, *assent alone*, can merely lead to a world ruled by cliché, slogan, dogma, a world incapable of change.

Unfortunately, dissent, though vital to change, can make the majority of people feel disturbed, for it requires them to change their habits, to adjust in some way to new conditions and to question themselves. Such adjustment can often make them feel uncomfortable and, at worst, it can instil in many people a sense of outrage. This is the perpetual contradiction of 'progress', that it must make many people more unhappy.

The words 'law and order' are flung about today, as though they referred to commodities. 'We must *have* law and order' is so often said, as though these were things that could be bought, or discovered, somewhere. They are words symbolic of our 'progressive' society which, to be so, requires our continual readjustment and exposes our preconceived ideas to challenge and criticism. But law and order are not primary things; underlying them, in any form, there must be the more fundamental element of trust.

How can global communication make any contribution towards such increased trust, as to better law and order, in the international sphere? The International Organizations, which are rapidly growing in numbers, are enabling the great complex that we call 'international relations' to be increasingly better *defined*, by identifying specific fields of common interests between different groups of nations and cultures. They have been enabled to operate since the end of World War II through the practical aids offered by global communication and transport. Within these specific fields of interest, international law has greatly improved, not because we are better people but because of the refined definitions and resultant practical operations.

The viewpoint taken in this book is that global communication and transport do not mean an inevitable drive towards centralized 'world government' if this be taken to mean shedding of all cultural and national identities, adoption of one political system acceptable to or forced upon all countries, having a bureaucracy of unthinkable size, having central power of terrifying scale. That is, not a centralized world government based upon the false analogy to any of our present national governments. No: global communication increasingly offers opportunity both for centralizing certain of our functions, especially economic ones, and creating larger groups, and equally well for decentralizing other of our functions, especially those which concern different groupings of countries having different conditions bearing upon them. That is to say, it seems to the writer that it becomes increasingly possible for world government to take on the form of a multiplicity of *federations* between countries, overlapping federations. Perhaps the term 'world order' is more appropriate than 'world government', being based upon increasing specification of mutual interests, each restricted and defined: a dispersal of power, not so much among nations, as among the great variety of *functions* that are covered by the term international relations.

The values of global communication, in this view, lie in the contribution which the various systems can make towards this end, towards the practical removal of frustrations. The values lie not in their unlikely power for persuading everybody else to be like us, but rather in putting our various distinct characteristics, arising from our different histories, geographies and peoples, to positive value. That is, to work *through* these differences, not *upon* them, and to use these differences, which may seem to be dissent or even heresy, as a creative source of change of our own institutions. For whatever progress is, it must include a preparation for such change, as other peoples' institutions change.

What is progress? It is essentially an idea that can emerge only in societies which have already adopted the concept of change. In pre-industrial, pre-literate societies, living wholly in an environment over which they have virtually no control, the concept of change may not clearly exist. There can be little or no personal, individual, action. But once some practical powers of control have been realized, then change becomes conceivable; as these powers increase we are offered increasing *choices* and these choices must be made; thus we are increasingly *challenged* and we must accept these challenges. We then feel ourselves to be persons as well as social groups. We then start criticizing and demanding our 'rights'; we look forward to a 'better future'. That is, we have expectations. We expect things to improve and the Gross National Product to rise annually. But, seriously, why should we? In one word, we in the industrial countries have invented a certain *notion* of progress: we have evolved also a deep sense of 'the future'.[51]

It is interesting to note how this word *progress* has changed its meaning during the past 250 years; the period of rapid science and technology growth, in Western countries. (Very like the period centred on A.D. 500 in China.)

When John Bunyan wrote his allegorical book *The Pilgrim's Progress*, (published 1678) the word progress merely meant 'a journey'. Only during these later centuries, largely as a consequence of spread of scientific knowledge, has it come to have the sense of moving *forward*. 'Forward' implies a mental direction or goal, something that we are moving towards. We may feel today that our science and rationality have given us control of this vehicle called progress. It lies at the base of the Protestant Ethic: work hard and Heaven is yours as reward. Heaven now lies in front of us, but we never seem to reach it whereas, prior to, say, the end of the 17th century most people in Christendom did not have our deep-set feelings that things *ought* to get better every year and of dismay when they do not; they were falling *out* of Heaven. Neither do many peoples of developing countries today necessarily have such feelings; rather they are happy when things *do* go right or get better. But we in the advanced countries see Heaven lying in front of us, though we never reach it, for it continually recedes. Indeed we cannot, for if we did reach a state of final and total bliss we should have no way of knowing the fact—there would be nothing better in front of us.

Another word that has changed its meaning over the past 250 years is also revealing: the word *individual*. As Milton, for example, used this word it meant 'inseparable'. Thus he speaks of 'the individual man and wife', because one cannot exist without the other or, again, he uses the phrase 'the individual and Holy Trinity', as implying an inseparable Unity. The word *individual* has come to change its meaning, from 'a group whose persons cannot be separated' to 'a person whose parts cannot be separated'.*

The idea that we call 'the future' is rather a curious one. (See Chapter 2, Section 2 for a discussion of the Western concept of time.) It is something that does not exist, nor can it ever exist. It is as non-existent as the Phoenix,

---

* These two words, *progress* and *individual*, with their changing meanings, have been discussed by the author in an article in Ref. 47. See also *Oxford English Dictionary* (complete edition).

and can never be observed, for it must always be ahead of us. As Dennis Gabor has so correctly said 'You can only *invent* the future'.[95]

This we must do, at least within the industrial, technological societies, if our concept of progress is to contain any element of responsibility. Without speaking of the future we could make no plans; insurance companies would close down; no timetables or schedules could have any meaning. We are forced by our expanding technology to take the future into increasing consideration as our economic areas expand, although it does not exist. It is more meaningful to speak of 'many possible futures', for it is a plurality; it is we who choose from among them.

However, it is far from being the only non-existent that we talk about. As remarked upon in an earlier Section, we speak all day long about things and persons of which we have no direct and personal experience. Newspapers and television news force us to speak of foreign people we have never met, or of foreign countries' institutions of which we are not members, or of foreign places that we have never visited. We speak of past history, of early civilizations, of death, of outer space, of endless things of which we have only 'knowledge by reportings' (to use an expression adopted in Chapter 1). And all such knowledge requires us to place trust of some kind, or some degree, in the source of information, a trust which on many occasions is blind, for we personally have no way whatever of checking the facts, directly, at that moment. If this be accepted as reason, then it is to our educational institutions that we should increasingly direct our thoughts, energies and money. Amongst these there must be more 'mediating' institutions, coming between the individual and the sources of information, not merely as protectors, but as aids to criticism, value-judgement, and therefore to trust that is less blind.

This, then, is a summary of our main points of view, as expressed in this book, inasmuch as they relate to the future. In closing, it may be useful to note two contrasting views of the future, illustrating its lack of objectivity, made by two great men of earlier centuries. Thus, Samuel Johnson (1709–1784): 'Whatever withdraws us from the power of our senses; whatever makes the past, the distant, or the future, predominate over the present, advances us in the dignity of thinking beings'. Whereas Edmund Burke (1729–1797): 'You can never plan the future by the past'. (The Oxford Dictionary of Quotations list many quotations, of great diversity, concerning the future.)

I have not attempted to *predict* the likely future here, what new inventions will be made, what new social institutions are likely to be created, or what will happen. For prediction of the future implies, in a sense, communication with people of the future, people who are not yet born or, if already born, have yet to be moulded by all their experience during the intervening time. I can only speak of the present and express *hope* for the future.

Nevertheless, there is one thing about the future that can be stated with absolute certainty: it will be peopled by those whom we today often refer to pompously as 'the young'.

Bibliography

1. Abraham, H. J., 'Historical Textbooks', *Unesco Chronicle*, Jan. 1956.
2. Adamson, J. W., 'The Extent of Literacy in England in the Fifteenth and Sixteenth Centuries: Notes and Conjectures'. *The Library (Trans. of Bibliog. Soc.)* **X**, p. 163. Oxford University Press, London, 1930.
3. Alexandersson, G. and Nordström, G., *World Shipping*, John Wiley, New York, 1963.
4. Allport, G. W. and Postman, L., *The Psychology of Rumour*, Henry Holt, New York, 1947.
5. American Telephone and Telegraph Co., *The World's Telephones*. (Statistics published annually). From A.T.T., 195 Broadway, N.Y. 7. U.S.A.
6. Asian Broadcasting Union: H.Q.: C/O N.H.K., Uchisaiwai—Cho Chiyoda—Ku, Tokyo. Sec. Gen: Box 3636, G.P.O. Sydney, Australia.
7. Bailey, F. G., 'The Peasant View of the Bad Life', *Advancement of Science*, **23**, No. 114, Dec. 1966.
8. Bailey, T. A., *A Diplomatic History of the American People*, Appleton–Century–Crofts (Meredith Pub. Co.), New York, 1964.
9. Barker, R. E., *Books for All*, Unesco, Paris, 1956.
10. Barton, A. H. *et al.*, 'Social Organisation Under Stress: a Sociological Review of Disaster Studies'. *National Acad. Sci., Nat. Res. Council*, Washington D.C., 1963.
11. Bauer, R. A., 'The Obstinate Audience', *Amer. Psych.* **19**, No. 5, May 1964.
12. Beke, G. E. van der, *A French Word Book*, New York, 1929.
13. Bell, A. Graham, 'Telephone Researches', *Four. Soc. Tel. Eng.*, Oct. 31, 1877.
14. Berelson, B., *The Library's Public*, Columbia University Press, New York, 1949. (Books in the U.S.A. prior to television.)
15. Berelson, B., 'What Missing the Newspaper Means', from Schramm, W. (Ed), *Process and Effects of Mass Communication*, Urbana, University Illinois Press, 1954.
16. Berelson, B. and Janowitz, M. (Eds.) *Reader in Public Opinion and Communication* (2nd Ed.), The Free Press, N.Y. City (The Macmillan Co.), 1966.
17. Bloch, B. and Trager, L., *Outline of Linguistic Analysis*, Linguistic Society of America, Waverley Press, Baltimore, 1942.
18. Bloomfield, L., *Language*, Henry Holt, New York, 1933.
19. Bodmer, F., *The Loom of Language*, W. W. Norton, New York. (George Allen and Unwin, London) 1944.
20. Bogaerts, R. F., 'Probable Evolution of Telephony', *Elec. Communication*, (I.T.T.) **38**, No. 2, 1963, p. 184.
21. Bogue, D. J., *The Population of the United States*, The Free Press, Glencoe, New York, 1959.
22. Bowett, D. W., *The Law of International Institutions*, Methuen, London, 1963.
23. Briggs, A., 'The Communications Revolution', *New Scientist*, London, 13th May, 1965.
24. Briggs, A., *History of Broadcasting in the United Kingdom*, Vols I and II, Oxford University Press, London, 1961 and 1965 respectively.
25. Brinkley, J. R., *Economic Aspects of Space Communication*, U.R.S.I., Paris, Sept. 1961.
26. British Broadcasting Corporation, *Annual Report and Accounts of the British Broadcasting Corporation* 1965–66 (and later years). H.M.S.O., London.
27. British Broadcasting Corporation, *B.B.C. Handbook*, London (annually).
28. British Broadcasting Corporation, *The European Service of the B.B.C. (two decades of broadcasting to Europe 1938–1959)* B.B.C., London, 1959.
29. British Broadcasting Corporation, *Facts and Figures about Viewing and Listening*, B.B.C., London, 1961.

30. Brooke, R. L., 'Costs of Clerical Services', A Letter to the Editor of the *Organisation and Methods Bulletin*, published by H.M. Treasury, London, **12**, No. 1, Feb. 1957.

31. Brown, J. A. C., *Techniques of Persuasion* (*from Propaganda to Brainwashing*), Penguin Books, London, 1963.

32. Buchler, J. (Ed.), 'The Philosophy of Peirce', *Selected Writings*, Routledge and Kegan Paul, London, 1950.

33. Burnet, M., *A.B.C. of Literacy*, Unesco, Paris, 1965. (A short exemplified account of the significance of literacy, in modern times.)

34. Calder, Lord Ritchie, 'Worldly Wiseman', *University Edinburgh Gazette*, No. 37, Oct. 1963, p. 28.

35. Campbell, A. and Metzner, *Public Use of the Library*, Inst. for Soc. Res., Ann Arbor, Michigan, U.S.A., 1950.

36. Campbell, J. W., 'Possible Uses of Satellites for Navigation and Traffic Coordination', *Telecomm. Jour.* **31**, No. 2, Feb. 1964, p. 37. (I.T.U.)

37. Cantril, H., *et al.*, *The Invasion from Mars* (*A Study in the Psychology of Panic—with a complete script of the famous Orson Welles broadcast*) Princeton University Press, 1940.

38. Capell, A., *Studies in Socio-Linguistics*, Mouton, The Hague, 1966.

39. Carl, H., 'Microwave Telephone Relay Network in Mexico', *Elect. Comm.* **39**, No. 3, 1964, p. 379.

40. Carrington, J. F., *Talking Drums of Africa*, Corey Kingsgate, London, 1949.

41. Carroll, T. J., 'Microwave Propagation Well Beyond the Horizon from Marconi to the Present', *The Science Counselor*, March 1958, Duquesne University Press, Pittsburgh 19, U.S.A. (Historical interest.)

42. Carter, L. J. (Advisory Editor), *Communications Satellites*, Academic Press, London & N.Y. (Proceedings of symposium organized by the British Interplanetary Society), 1962.

43. Central Office of Information, *Britain—an Official Handbook*, London. Published annually by the C.O.I.

44. Central Office of Information, *The British Press*, C.O.I. London, May 1966 (Quote: No. RF.P.5572/66.)

45. Chapuis, R., 'Work of the Plan Committee in the Intercontinental Sphere' (Rome, Dec. 1963). *Telecomm. Jour.* **31**, No. 4, April 1964, p. 98.

46. Charyk, J. V., 'Communications Satellite Corporation: Objectives and Problems', *Astronautics and Aerospace Engineering*, Sept. 1963, p. 45 (Mr. Charyk is the first President of Comsat).

47. Cherry, C., 'But there is Nothing I have is Essential to Me', in volume *To Honor Roman Jakobson*, Mouton, The Hague, 1967.

48. Cherry, C., 'Communication, Politics and People', in *Communication* (Ed. Thayer, L.), Charles C. Thomas, Springfield, Illinois, 1967.

49. Cherry, C., 'On Communication Before the Days of Radio', *Proc. I.R.E.* (50th Anniv. Issue), **50**, No. 5, May, 1962, p. 1143.

50. Cherry, C., *On Human Communication* (*A Review, a Survey and a Criticism*), The Technology Press of M.I.T. and John Wiley, 1957. Also in German translation, Fischer-Verlag, 1963 as *Kommunikations Forschung–eine neue Wissenschaft*.

51. Cherry, C., 'The Scientific Revolution—and Communication', *Nature*, **200**, No. 4904, Oct. 26, 1963, p. 308.

52. Cherry, C., Three Cantor Lectures to the Royal Society of Arts.
    (1) *The Nature of Human Communication*
    (2) *The Communication Explosion*
    (3) *The Future of World Communication*
    Jour. Royal Soc. of Arts, **CXIV** Feb. 1966, pp. 158–205.

53. Church, R. J. H., Clarke, J. I., Clarke, P. J. H. and Henderson, H. J. R., *Africa and the Islands*, Longmans, London, 1964.

54. Ciba Foundation, *Disorders of Language* (Ed. A. V. S. de Reuck and M. O'Connor) J. and A. Churchill, London, 1964.

55. Clarke, Arthur C., 'Extra-Terrestral Relays', *Wireless World*, Oct. 1945, p. 305. (First reference to communication satellites.)

56. Clarke, Arthur C., *Voice Across the Sea*, Harper and Brothers, New York, U.S.A., 1958.

57. Codding, G. A., *Broadcasting without Barriers*, Unesco, Paris, 1959.
58. Codding, G. A., *The Universal Postal Union*, UPU, N.Y. University Press New York 3, 1964.
59. Codding, G. A. Jr., *The Telecommunication Union*, E. J. Brill, London, 1952.
60. Colgrove, K. W., *International Control of Aviation*, World Peace Foundation, Boston 1930 (for early aviation Conventions).
61. Cook, Sir James, 'The Science Information Problem', *Advancement of Science* (Brit. Ass.) **23**, No. 112, October 1966, p. 305. (A short account of the social implications of the 'document explosion'.)
62. Cranston, M., *Freedom: a New Analysis*, Longmans, Green, London, 1953.
63. Dampier, Sir W. Cecil, *A History of Science*, Cambridge University Press London (1st Ed. 1929, 4th Ed. 1948).
64. Daniel, H., *Public Libraries for Everyone*, Doubleday, New York, 1961. (Statistics of U.S.A. Libraries.)
65. Davidson, W. P., 'On the Effects of Communication', *Publ. Opin. Quart.*, **23**, 1959, p. 343.
66. De Koster, L., *The Vocabulary of Communism*, W. B. Eerdmans Pub. Co. Grand Rapids, Michigan, U.S.A. 1964.
67. Deloraine, E. M., 'Evolution of Telephone, Telegraph and Telex Traffic', *Elec. Comm.*, **39**, No. 2, 1964, p. 265.
68. Deloraine, E. M., 'Telecommunications in Western Europe', *Elec. Comm.*, **40**, No. 1, 1965, p. 14.
69. Deutsch, K., *Nationalism and Social Communications: an Enquiry into the Foundations of Nationality*, Tech. Press M.I.T. & John Wiley, New York, 1953.
70. Diringer, D., *The Alphabet*, Hutchinson, London, 1948.
71. Doob, L. W., *Communication in Africa: a search for Boundaries*, Yale University Press, New Haven and London, 1961.
72. Doob, L. W., 'Goebbels' Principles of Propaganda', *Publ. Opin. Quart.*, Autumn 1950, p. 419.
73. Doob, L. W., *Public Opinion and Propaganda*, The Cresset Press, London, 1949.
74. Dormer, D. J., 'The C.C.I.T.T. and its Secretariat', *Telecomm. Jour.*, **32**, No. 8, Aug. 1965, p. 312.
75. Downs, R. B. (Ed.), *The First Freedom* (*Liberty and justice in the world of books and reading*), American Lib. Assoc., Chicago, 1960.
76. *Economist (The)*, 'The Economist Diary 1968', The Economist Newspaper Ltd., 25 St. James's St., London.
77. *Economist Intelligence Unit*, 'The National Newspaper Industry', Joint Board for the Newspaper Industry, London, 1966.
78. *Encyclopaedia Britannica* (11th Ed. preferred), 1910–1911.
79. Engels, F., 'The Condition of the Working Class in England in 1844', Allen and Unwin, London, 1892.
80. Escarpit, R., *The Book Revolution*, George Harrap, with UNESCO, 1968.
81. Estoup, J. B., *Les Gammes Sténographiques*, Paris, 1916.
82. Europa Publications Ltd., *The Europa Year Book*, 18 Bedford Square, London, 1967. (2 volumes. The title is misleading; these volumes give details of all *world's* International Organizations. Vol I covers Europe, Vol II the other continents.) Latest edition, 1971.
83. European Broadcasting Union, *The E.B.U. Review* (monthly), 1–3 rue de Varembé, Geneva.
84. Fagen, R. R., 'Mass Media Growth: a Comparison of Communist and other countries', *Journalism Quart.*, **41** Autumn 1964 (University of Minnesota), p. 563.
85. Federal Communications Commission (U.S.A.), *Statistics of Communications Common Carriers*, issued annually since 1939 by U.S. Gov. Printing Off., Washington, D.C.
86. Fed. of Commonwealth Chambers of Commerce, *Handbook of Commonwealth Organisations*, Methuen, London, 1965.
87. *Financial Times*, Tuesday, May 30, 1967. (Issue devoted to articles on world air transport.)
88. Fiske, M., *Book Selection and Censorship*, University California Press, 1959.
89. Fitzgerald, J. J., *Peirce's Theory of Signs as Foundation for Pragmatism*, Mouton, The Hague, 1968.

90. Florinsky, M. T., (Ed.) *Encyclopaedia of Russia and the Soviet Union*, McGraw Hill, New York, 1961.
91. Foster, P., *White to Move?* (a portrait of East Africa today), Eyre and Spottiswoode, London, 1961.
92. Fraser, L., *Propaganda*, Oxford University Press, London, 1957.
93. Frisch, Karl von, *Bees: their Vision, Chemical Senses and Language*, Cornell University Press, Ithaca, U.S.A., 1950.
94. Furu, Takeo, *Television and Children's Life*, Japan Broadcasting Corp., Tokyo, 1962.
95. Gabor, D., *Inventing the Future*, Secker and Warburg, London, 1963.
96. Galbraith, J. K., *The Affluent Society*, Hamish Hamilton, 1958 and Pelican Books, Great Britain, 1962.
97. Gallie, W. B., *Peirce and Pragmatism*, Pelican Books, Harmondsworth, Middlesex, Great Britain, 1952. (A good account of Charles Sanders Peirce's philosophy.)
98. General Post Office of the United Kingdom, *Post Office Telecommunications Statistics*, published every 5 years, with annual amendments, within the Administration only. Covers telephones, telegraphs and Telex.
99. Gombrich, E. H., *Art and Illusion*, Phaidon Press, London, 1960. (The A. W. Mellon Lectures delivered in Washington, 1956.)
100. Gombrich, E. H., *Meditations on a Hobby Horse*, Phaidon Press, London, 1963.
101. Gombrich, E. H., *The Story of Art*, Phaidon Press Ltd., London, 1950.
102. Good, I. J. (Ed.), *The Scientist Speculates* (*An Anthology of Half-Baked Ideas*), Heinemann, London, 1962.
103. Goodall, E., Cooke, C. K. and Clark, J. D. (Ed. R. Summers), *Prehistoric Rock Art of Central Africa*, Chatto & Windus, London, 1959.
104. Gowers, Sir Ernest, *ABC of Plain Words*, Her Majesty's Stationery Office, London, 1951. (A criticism of 'business and official' English.)
105. Greenberg, B. S. and Parker, E. B. (Eds.), *The Kennedy Assassination and the American Public: Social Communication in Crisis*, Stanford University Press, 1965 (detailed analysis according to age, sex, social class, etc.).
106. Grimble, A., *A Pattern of Islands*, John Murray, London, 1952. Published in the U.S.A. under the title *We Chose the Islands*.
107. Haldane, J. B. S., 'Animal Ritual and Human Languages', *Diogenes*, **4,** 1953, pp. 3–15.
108. Haley, A. G., *Space Law and Government* (Appleton–Century–Crofts), Meredith, New York, 1963.
109. Haley, Sir William, *The Responsibilities of Broadcasting* (Lewis Fry Memorial Lecture), B.B.C., London, 1948.
110. Halina, J. W., 'Data Transmission—Current Trends and Future Prospects', *Elec. Comm.*, **41,** No. 2, 1966, p. 177 (whole issue is devoted to data transmission).
111. Hall, A. R., *The Scientific Revolution*, 1500–1800, Longmans, Green, London, 1954.
112. Halsey, R. J., 'British Commonwealth Ocean Cables', *I.E.E.E. Trans. on Comm. Tech.* Vol: Com-12, No. 3 Sept. 1964, p. 6.
113. *Hansard*, House of Lords Official Report, **280,** No. 121, 'Overseas Information Services', March 1967.
114. Harder, W. J., *Daniel Drawbaugh*, University of Philadelphia Press, U.S.A., 1960.
115. Harris, Zellig S., *Methods in Structural Linguistics*, Univ. of Chicago Press, Chicago, 1951. (See also reviews of this in *Language*, **29,** No. 1, Jan–March 1953).
116. Harrison, K. C., *Libraries in Scandinavia*, Andre Deutsch (Grafton Book), London, 1961.
117. Hebb, D. O., *The Organisation of Behaviour*, John Wiley, New York (Chapman & Hall, London), 1949.
118. Herd, H., *The March of Journalism*, Allen & Unwin, London, 1952 (a history of the Press).
119. Herodotus, *The Histories*, translated by Aubrey de Selincourt, Penguin Books, Harmondsworth, England (and Penguin Books, 3300 Clipper Mill Road, Baltimore, U.S.A.), 1954.

120. Hertz, H., Letter (translated into English) dated 1889, reproduced in *Invention and Innovation in the Radio Industry*, by W. R. Maclaurin (Macmillans, London, 1949). The original letter is in the Deutsche Museum, Munich.

121. Himmelweit, H., Oppenheim, A. N. and Vince, P., *Television and the Child; an Empirical Study of the Effects of Television on the Young*, Oxford University Press, 1958.

122. Hinrichsen, J., 'H.F. Circuits Network for Africa', *Telecomm. Jour.* (*I.T.U.*), **31**, No. 8, August 1964, p. 231.

123. H.M.S.O., *Abstracts of Statistics*, Her Majesty's Stationery Office (Central Statistical Office, London). Issued annually.

124. H.M.S.O., *Census 1961, England and Wales, Age, Marital Condition and General Tables*, Her Majesty's Stationery Office, 1964.

125. H.M.S.O., *Report of a Royal Commission on the Press*, 1947–49, Her Majesty's Stationery Office, London, 1949.

126. H.M.S.O., *Report of the Royal Commission on the Press, 1961–62*, Her Majesty's Stationery Office, London, 1962.

127. H.M.S.O., *Satellite Communications* (White Paper), Her Majesty's Stationery Office, Aug. 1964.

128. Hodge, B., Lewis, G. L., and Lauwerys, J. A., *Cyprus School History Textbooks*, Educ. Advis. Comm. of Parliamentary Group for World Govt., House of Commons, London (undated, probably 1966). Also entered as Ref. 179.

129. Hodgkinson, H., *Doubletalk—the Language of Communism*, Allen and Unwin, London, 1955.

130. Houghton, H., 'The Effect of the Population Explosion on Education', *The Advancement of Science*, **23**, No. 115, Jan, 1967, p. 443.

131. Huxley, Aldous, *The Devils of Loudun*, Chatto & Windus, London, 1952.

132. I.C.T., 'Taping the T.V. Audience', *ICT Data Processing Jour.*, No. 19, 1964, p. 22. (House journal of the International Computers and Tabulators Ltd.)

133. India (Gov. of), *India—a Reference Annual*, Min. Inf. & Broadcasting, Gov. of India.

134. Inkeles, A., *Public Opinion in Soviet Russia* (a Study in Mass Persuasion), Harvard University Press, Cambridge, U.S.A. Second edition, 1950.

135. Institut du Transport Aérien, *I.T.A. Bulletin*, Pub. by the Institute, 4, Rue de Solferino, Paris 7. (For detailed analyses of all member countries' scheduled air lines, statistics of traffic growth, economics, etc.)

136. Inst. Electrical Engineers (United Kingdom). Several papers concerning the Anglo–Canadian Telephone Cable (CANTAT), *Proc. I.E.E.*, **110**, July 1963, pp. 1115–1164.

137. Intergovernmental Maritime Consultative Organization, *Basic Documents*, I.M.C.O., 22 Berners St., London, W.1. (Legal agreements, rules of procedure, etc.)

138. Intergovernmental Maritime Consultative Organization, *Convention*, I.M.C.O., 22 Berners St., London, W.1. (Constitution, etc.)

139. Intergovernmental Maritime Consultative Organization, *IMCO Bulletin*, I.M.C.O., 22 Berners St., London, W.1.

140. International Bank for Reconstruction and Development, *World Bank Atlas of per capita Production and Population, 1969*. Earlier issues also appeared.

141. International Civil Aviation Organization (I.C.A.O.), *Air Navigation Plan* (in World Regions), published by I.C.A.O., regularly, 1080 University Street, Montreal 3, Quebec.

142. International Civil Aviation Organization, *Memorandum on I.C.A.O.*, Montreal 3, 1966 (a booklet on its history, aims and organizations).

143. International Civil Aviation Organization, *Traffic Flow*, published twice annually by the I.C.A.O., 1080 Univ. St., Montreal 3, Quebec.

144. International Radio and Television Organization (O.I.R.T.), *Catalogue of Transmissions suitable for Exchange* (U. Mrazovk 15, Prague 5).

145. International Radio and Television Organization (O.I.R.T.), *Radio and Television* (quarterly). Liebknechtova 15, Prague 16. (See also *European Broadcasting Union* entry.)

146. International Telecommunication Union, *From Semaphore to Satellite*, Geneva, 1965. Also serialized during 1965 in *Telecomm. Jour.* (*loc. cit.* under Int. Tel. Union. Ref. 153.)

147. International Telecommunication Union, *General Plan for the Development of the International Network for 1963–68* (the full and official Report of the Rome Committee: the first global plan) Geneva, 1964.

148. International Telecommunication Union, *General Plan for the Development of the International Network in Africa, 1965–1970* (Addis Ababa Plan), Geneva, 1967.

149. International Telecommunication Union, *General Telephone Statistics*, (Published annually by this specialized agency of the U.N.), Geneva.

150. International Telecommunication Union, 'Improved Telecommunications for Africa', *Telecomm. Jour.*, Sept. 1965, No. 9, p. 369.

151. International Telecommunication Union, Report of the 2nd World Plan Committee, Mexico City, Oct. 1967: published 1969.

152. International Telecommunication Union, 'Rome Plan Committee Meeting', *Telecomm. Jour.*, **31**, March 1964, p. 62 (see also Chapuis, R.).

153. International Telecommunication Union, *Telecommunication Journal*, monthly (technical; not too specialized), Geneva (originally the *Journal Télégraphique*, 1869–1933).

154. International Telephone and Telegraph Corp. Journal, *Electrical Communication*, **39**, 1964; **45**, 1970.

155. Irwin, R., *The Heritage of the English Library*, Allen & Unwin, London, 1964.

156. Jacob, Sir Ian, *The B.B.C.: A National and an International Force*, B.B.C., London, 1957.

157. Jakobson, R., *Kindersprache, Aphasie und Allgemeine Lautgesetze*, Sprakvete- skapliga Sällskapets 2 Uppsala Forhande, 1940–1942.

158. Jespersen, O., *Language: its Nature, Development and Origin*, George Allen and Unwin, London, 1922.

159. Jipp, A., 'Wealth of Nations and Telephone Density', *Telecomm. Journ.*, July, 1963, p. 2.

160. Johansen, O. L. (Ed.), *World Radio and T.V. Handbook*, O. L. Johansen, Hellerup, Denmark.

161. Jones, N. J. H., 'Economic Growth and the Development of Telephone Systems, *Teleteknik*, **VII/2**, 1963 (in English).

162. Jones, N. J. H., *People and Telephones*, Thesis for the Diploma of Imperial College, London, 1963.

163. Keller, H., *The Story of my Life*, Hodder & Stoughton, London. Reprinted 1945.

164. Kitchen, H. (Ed.), *The Press in Africa*, Ruth Sloan Associates, Washington, 1956.

165. Klapper, J., *The Effects of Mass Communication*, Free Press, Glencoe, New York, 1960.

166. Knight, N. V., *Operational Research in Telecommunications Economics*, Inst. Post Office Elec. Eng., London, Oct. 1966.

167. Köhler, W., *The Mentality of Apes*, Kegan Paul, Trench, Trubner, London, 1925. (Harcourt, Brace, New York.)

168. Komatsuzaki, S. and Ito, H., 'Market Research on Telephone Service', *Japan Telecomm. Review*, 1965. (Also *N.T.T. Publication D*, No. 6, July 1964.)

169. Kracauer, S., *From Caligori to Hitler*, Princeton University Press, 1947. (A study of the German film.)

170. Kraus, S. (Ed). *The Great Debates*, Indiana University Press, Bloomington, 1962.

171. Kühn, H., *The Rock Pictures of Europe*, Sidgwick and Jackson, London, 1956.

172. Kuznets, S. and Thomas D. S., *Population Redistribution and Economic Growth in the U.S.A., 1870–1950*, Amer. Philosoph Soc., Philadelphia. (2. Vols) 1957, 1960.

173. Landau, T., *Encyclopaedia of Librarianship*, Bowes and Bowes, London, 1958 (3rd Ed. 1966).

174. Langer, Susanne K., *Feeling and Form (A Theory of Art)* Routledge and Kegan Paul, London, 1953. (Especially Chapter 7, 'The Image of Time'.)

175. Langer, Susanne K., *Philosophy in a New Key—a study in the symbolism of reason, rite and art*, Harvard University Press, 3rd Ed., 1957.

176. Laslett, P., *The World We Have Lost*, Methuen (University Paperbacks), London 1965.

177. Lasswell, H. D., Leites, N. and associates, *The Language of Politics*, M.I.T. Press, Cambridge, Mass, 1949.

178. Latey, M., *Broadcasting to the U.S.S.R. and Eastern Europe*, B.B.C. Lunchtime Lecture. Published by B.B.C., London, 11 Nov. 1964.

179. Lauerys, J. A. (Introducer), *Cyprus School History Textbooks*, Educ. Advisory Comm. of the Parliamentary Group for World Government. House of Commons, London (Undated, probably 1966.) Also entered as Ref. 128.

180. Lean, T., *The Revolution Overseas*, B.B.C. Lunchtime Lecture. Published by B.B.C., London, 13th March 1963.

181. Lean, T., *Voices in the Darkness*, Secker, London, 1943 (The story of the 1939–45 radio 'war'.)

182. Lecky, W. E. H., *History of European Morals, from Augustus to Charlemagne*, Vol. II, Longmans, Green, London, 1869.

183. Leach, G. N., *English in Advertising* (*A Linguistic Study of Advertising in Great Britain*), Longmans, Green, London, 1966.

184. Lerner, D., 'Communication Systems and Social Systems, a Statistical Exploration in History and Policy', *Behavioural Science*, **2**, 1957, p. 266.

185. Lerner, D., Editor's Introduction to the *Public Opinion Quarterly*, **XXII**, Autumn, 1958 No. 3, p. 217.

186. Lerner, D., 'International Cooperation and Communication in National Development'. (Article on p. 103 of Ref. 188.)

187. Lerner, D., *The Passing of Traditional Society*, The Free Press, Glencoe, New York, U.S.A. 1958. (For effects of literacy upon attitudes and modes of thinking: Egypt, Iran, Jordan, Lebanon, Syria, Turkey.)

188. Lerner, D. and Schramm, W., *Communication and Change in the Developing Countries*, East–West Center Press, Honolulu, 1967.

189. Library of Congress, *International Scientific Organizations*, Washington, 1962. (See pp. 468–479 for history and structure of the International Telecommunication Union.) U.S. Information Office.

190. Licklider, J. C. R., *Libraries of the Future*, M.I.T. Press, Mass. U.S.A., 1965.

191. Lindauer, M., *Communication among Social Bees* (Harvard Books in Biology, No. 2), Harvard University Press, Cambridge, Mass, 1961.

192. Lindauer, M., 'Schwarmbienen auf Wohnungssuche', *Z. Vergleich. Physiol.*, **37**, pp. 263–324, 1955.

193. Lippmann, W., *Public Opinion*, Macmillan, New York, 1961.

194. Lorenz, K., *On Aggression* (translated by Marjorie Latzke) Methuen, London, 1966.

195. Luckham, B. and Orr, J. M., 'Broadcasting and Public Libraries', *Library Assoc. Record*, **69**, Jan., 1967, p. 11.

196. Lynd, H., *On Shame and the Search for Identity*, Routledge and Kegan Paul, London, 1958.

197. MacLean, S. Jr., 'Systems of News Communication', from *Communication: Theory and Research* (Ed. Lee Thayer) C. C. Thomas, Springfield, Illinois, 1967.

198. Maheu, R., 'Radio and Television in the Service of Social Development and Education', *Telecomm. Jour.*, **32**, Feb. 1965.

199. Mance, O., *International Communications*, Oxford University Press, London, 1944.

200. Mangone, G. J., *A Short History of International Organizations*, McGraw Hill, New York, 1954.

201. Manvell, R., *This Age of Communication* (*Press, Books, Films, Radio, Television*), Blackie, Glasgow, London, 1966.

202. Mao Tse-Tung, *Quotations from Chairman Mao Tse-Tung* (introduced by A. D. Barnett, printed in English), Corgi Books (Trans–World Publishers), London, 1967.

203. Marconi, D., *My Father, Marconi*, Frederick Muller, London, 1962.

204. Marco Polo, *Travels* (about A.D. 1297). In modern form pub. by Everymans Library, J. M. Dent and Sons, London, 1908.

205. May, J., *Living in Cities*, Longmans, Green, London, 1966. (A study of the urban environment and its social effects.)

206. Mayani Z., *The Etruscans Begin to Speak*, Souvenir Press, London, 1962.

207. Mayer, K. P., 'Language Statistics: a Brief Survey and an Outline of a Dynamic Model', *The Incorporated Linguist*, **3**, No. 4, October 1964. (Contains several references to statistical counts of languages.)

208. McColvin, L. R., *The Chance to Read: Public Libraries in the World Today*, Phoenix House, J. M. Dent, London and Oxford University Press, New York, 1956.

209. McNeil, E. B. (Ed.), *The Nature of Human Conflict*, Prentice-Hall, Englewood Cliffs, New Jersey, U.S.A. 1965. (Collected essays by different authors.)

210. Mead, Margaret (Ed.), *Cultural Patterns and Technical Change*, Mentor (for Unesco), New York, 1955.

211. Merrill, J. C., *A Handbook of the Foreign Press*, Louisiana State University Press, U.S.A. 1959 (includes the Mainland of China).

212. Monahan, J., 'Britain's Voice in Europe', *The Listener*, Oct. 31, 1963, London, p. 681.

213. Morant, G. M., *The Significance of Racial Differences*, Unesco, Paris, 1958.

214. Morgan, T. J., 'The Long-term Assessment of Future Telecommunication Requirements', *A.T.E. Journal*, **21,** No. 3, July 1965, p. 123.

215. Morgan, T. J., *Telecommunication Economics*, McDonald, London, 1958.

216. Morris, C. W., 'Foundations of the Theory of Signs', *International Encyclopaedia of Unified Science Series*, **1,** No. 2, University of Chicago Press, Chicago 1938.

217. Morris, C. W., *Signs, Language and Behaviour*, Prentice-Hall, Englewood Cliffs, New Jersey, U.S.A., 1946.

218. Mumford, Sir Albert, 'Communication in the Public Service of the United Kingdom', *J. Inst. Elec. Engs.* (*London*), **9,** Nov. 1963, p. 460.

219. Mumford, L., *Technics and Civilisation*, Routledge and Sons, London, 1946.

220. Municipal Journals Ltd., *Municipal Yearbook and Public Utilities Directory*, 3, Clements' Inn, Strand (annually).

221. Neal, H. E., *Communication from Stone Age to Space Age*, Phoenix House, London, 1960.

222. Nehru, Jawaharlal, *The Discovery of India*, Meridan Books, London, 1956. (First published 1946.)

223. Nevins, A. (Ed.), *America Through British Eyes*, Oxford University Press (N.Y.) 1948.

224. Oakley, K., 'A Definition of Man', *Penguin Science News*, Great Britain, No. 20, 1951.

225. Oakley, K., *Man the Tool Maker*, Phoenix Books, University of Chicago Press, 1959.

226. OECD *Observer*, published by the Organization for Economic Cooperation and Development in English and French, bi-monthly, by OECD Information Service, Château de la Muette, 2 rue André Pascal, F75, Paris 16.

227. OECD *Observer*, 'Forecasting Passenger Transport Demand up to 1975', **29,** Aug. 1967, p. 10.

228. OECD *Observer*, 'Formulating and Running a Government Tourism Programme', **29,** Aug. 1967, p. 33.

229. OECD *Observer*, 'Tourism: A Rapidly Growing Industry', **24,** October 1966, p. 26.

230. OECD, 'Tourism Development and Economic Growth', *Report*, 1967.

231. Ogden, C. K. and Richards, I. A., *The Meaning of Meaning*, Routledge and Kegan Paul, London, 1949 (1st Ed. 1923).

232. Ogden, C. K., *The System of Basic English*, Harcourt, Brace, New York, 1934.

233. Ouspensky, P. D., *The Psychology of Man's Possible Evolution*, Hodder and Stoughton, London, 1951. The Hedgehog Press (Doric Publishing Co. Inc.), N.Y.

234. Packard, V., *The Waste Makers*, Pelican Books, Harmondsworth, Middlesex, England, 1960.

235. Paget, Sir Richard, *Human Speech*, Kegan Paul, Trench, Trubner, London, 1930. (New Edition 1965.)

236. Paloczi-Horvath, G., *The Writer and the Commissar*, The Bodley Head, London, 1960.

237. Parker, E. B., 'The Effects of Television on Public Library Circulation', *Pub. Opinion Quart.*, **27,** 1963, p. 578.

238. Parker, E. B. and Paisley, W. J., 'Predicting Library Circulation from Community Characteristics', *Pub. Opinion Quart.*, **29,** Spring 1965.

239. Parkes, A. S., 'Biological Aspects of the Population Explosion', *Adv. of Science*, **XXI**, March 1965, p. 509. (Very readable analysis of consequences of explosion, leading to conclusions on contraception.)
240. Partridge, E., *A Dictionary of Clichés* (4th Ed.), Routledge and Kegan Paul, London, 1948.
241. Peirce, C. S., *The Collected Papers of Charles Sanders Peirce*, Vols I to VI (Ed. C. Hartshorne and P. Weiss), Harvard University Press, 1931–35.
242. Peirce, C. S. (Selected writings, Ed. Justus Buchler), Routledge and Kegan Paul, London, under the title *The Philosophy of Peirce*, 2nd Imp. 1950. (Also listed here under Buchler.)
243. Pflaum, H. G., *Essai sur la 'Cursus Publicus' sous le Haut-Empire Romain*, Imprimerie Nationale, Paris, 1950.
244. Pilkington, Sir Harry (Chairman), *Report of the Committee on Broadcasting 1960*, Her Majesty's Stationery Office, London (Cmnd 1753), 1962.
245. Pledge, H. T., *Science since 1500*, Her Majesty's Stationery Office, London, 1939.
246. Pratt, F., *Secret and Urgent*, The Bobbs-Merrill Co., Indianapolis, Ind., 1939 (Blue Riband Books) (gives frequencies of letters and letter digrams and trigrams).
247. Presbury, F., *The History and Development of Advertising*, Doubleday Doran, Garden City, New York, U.S.A., 1929.
248. Pye, L. W. (Ed.), *Communications and Political Development*, Princeton University Press, Princeton, 1963.
249. Ramsay, A. M., 'The Speed of the Roman Imperial Post', *J. Roman Studies*, **15**, p. 60, 1925.
250. Read, D., *Press and People*, 1790–1850, Edward Arnold, London, 1961. (Growth and values of the Press during the Industrial Revolution in North England.)
251. Reiger, S. H. and Meckling, W. H., 'Economic Aspects of Communication Satellite Systems. Space Radio Communication', *U.R.S.I. Symposium*, Paris, 1961. Elsevier, Amsterdam, New York & London, 1962.
252. Robbins, A. P., *Newspapers Today*, Oxford University Press, 1956.
253. Rogers, E. M. and Hertzog, W., 'Functional Illiteracy among Colombian Peasants', *Econ. Dev. and Cultural Change*, **XIV**, Jan. 1966, p. 190.
254. Rolo, C. J., *Radio Goes to War*, Faber and Faber, London, 1943.
255. Ryle, G., *The Concept of Mind*, Hutchinson's University Library, 1949.
256. Sales, H. P. (Ed.), *Travel and Tourism Encyclopaedia*, Travel World (Blandford Press), London, 1959.
257. Sampson, H. (Ed.), *Jane's World's Railways*, 1966 and regularly. (Formerly called the *World's Railways*) Low, Morton, London.
258. Sapir, E., *Language*, Harcourt, Brace, New York, 1939.
259. Sathan, S. A., 'The International Consultative Committees (of I.T.U.) and Problems of the New and Developing Countries', *Telecomm. Jour.*, **31** No. 1, Jan. 1964, p. 21.
260. Schramm, W., 'Communication in Crisis', in *The Kennedy Assassination and the American Public: Social Communication in Crisis*. (Ed. Greenberg and Parker), Stanford University Press, 1965.
261. Schramm, W. (Ed.), *Mass Communications*, University Illinois Press, U.S.A. 1960.
262. Schramm, W., *Mass Media and National Development*, Stanford University Press, U.S.A. and UNESCO, 1964. (Considerable bibliography.)
263. Schramm, W., 'The Nature of News', *Journalism Quart.*, **26**, 1949, p. 259.
264. Schramm, W., *One Day in the World's Press*, Stanford University Press, Stanford, 1960.
265. Schramm, W. (Ed.), *The Process and Effects of Mass Communication*, University Illinois Press, U.S.A., 1961.
266. Schramm, W., *The Role of Information in National Development* (an abridged version of Ref. 262) Unesco, undated.
267. Schramm, W., Lyle, J., Parker, E. B., *Television in the Lives of Our Children*, Stanford University Press, California, 1961.
268. Schrödinger, E., *My View of the World*, Cambridge University Press, 1964.
269. Schrödinger, E., *What is Life?*, Cambridge University Press, London, 1944.

270. Scupham, J., *Broadcasting and the Community*, C. A. Watts, London, 1967.
271. Sebeok, T. A., 'Animal Communication', *Science*, **147**, No. 3661, 26th Feb., 1965, pp. 1006–1014.
272. Sebeok, T. A. Reviews of 3 books:

(1) *Communication Among Social Bees* by M. Lindauer
(2) *Porpoises and Sonar* by W. N. Kellogg.
(3) *Man and Dolphin* by J. C. Lilly.

in *Language*, **39**, No. 3, Pt 1, July–Sept. 1963.
273. Shannon, C. and Weaver, W., *The Mathematical Theory of Communication*, University Illinois Press, Urbana, U.S.A. 1949.
274. Shannon, C. E., 'Prediction and Entropy of Printed English', *Bell Syst. Tech. Jour.*, **30**, 1951, pp. 50–64.
275. Sheatsley, P. B. and Feldman, J. J., 'The Assassination of President Kennedy', *Pub. Opinion Quart.*, **28**, No. 2, Summer, 1964.
276. Sherrington, Sir Charles, *Man on his Nature* (The Gifford Lectures, Edinburgh 1937–8), Cambridge University Press, London, 1953.
277. Smith-Rose, R. L., 'Marconi, Popov and the Dawn of Radiocommunication', Inst. Elec. Engrs (*Electronics and Power Journal*), London, March 1964, p. 76.
278. Speeckaert, G. P. (Ed.), *The 1978 International Organizations Founded since the Congress of Vienna*, Union of International Organizations, No. 7, 1957.
279. Statham, Cmd. E. P., *Wireless Telegraphy on Board the 'Europa'*, The Navy and Army Illustrated, Aug. 26, 1899, London.
280. Stearn, W. T., 'The Origin and Later Development of Cultivated Plants', (Master's Memorial Lecture, Part II) *Jour. Roy. Hort. Soc.*, **XC**, Part 8 August 1965, p. 322.
281. Stebbing, Susan, *Thinking to Some Purpose*, Pelican Books, Harmondsworth, England (and New York) 1941.
282. Steel, R. W., 'Geography and the Developing World', *Adv. of Science, British Association*, **23**, No. 117, March 1967, p. 566.
283. Stenton, F., *Mass Media and Mass Culture* (Great Issues Lecture: The Hopkins Center, Dartmouth College, Nov. 26, 1962), American Fed. Arts, New York.
284. Stephenson, W., 'The Ludenic Theory of Newsreading', *Journalism Quart.*, **41**, No. 3, Summer 1964, p. 367.
285. Storey, G., *Reuter's Century* (1851–1951). Max Parrish, London, 1951.
286. Szapiro, J., *The Newspaperman's United Nations*, Unesco, Paris, 1961. (A journalists' guide to the U.N. and its Specialized Agencies.)
287. Telford, M. and Isted, G. A., 'Predicted Future Expansion of Intercontinental Telephone Traffic', *Point-to-Point Telecommunications*, Vol. 6, Oct. 1961, p. 4. Marconi Wireless Teleg. Co. England. (A very readable outline.)
288. Thomson, G. H. and Thomson, J. R., 'Outlines of a Method for the Quantitative Analysis of Writing Vocabularies', *Brit. Jour. Psych.*, **8**, 1915.
289. Thorndike, E. L. and Lorge, I., *The Teachers' Word Book of 30,000 Words*, Bureau of Publications, Columbia University Press, New York, 1944. (Frequencies of English Lexical Units.)
290. Thorpe, W. H., *Bird Song*, Cambridge University Press, 1961.
291. Timmerman, W., Dawidziuk, B. M., Hvidsten, T. N. M., 'Expanding Global Submarine Cable Network', *Elec. Comm.*, **41** No. 1, 1966, p. 77.
292. Tindergen, N., *Social Behaviour in Animals*, Methuen, London, 1953 (Methuen Biological Monographs).
293. Tiryakian, E. A., *Sociologism and Existentialism*, Prentice-Hall, Englewood Cliffs, New Jersey, U.S.A. 1962. (An excellent outline of Durkheim's social theory and of the chief existentialist philosophies.)
294. Töpffer, R., *Enter: the Comics* (*Essay on Physiognomy and the True Story of Monsieur Crépin*), translated by E. Wiese, University Nebraska Press, Lincoln, U.S.A. 1965.
295. Trevelyan, G. M., *English Social History*, Longmans, Green, London, 1942.
296. Timmer, J. D., 'Symbol and Meaning: Communication in the Modern World', *Geographical Rev.*, **LVII**, No. 1, 1967, p. 122.
297. Troldahl, V. C. and Jones, R. L., 'Predictions of Newspaper Advertisement Readership', *Jour. Advert. Research*, **5**, No. 1, March 1965, p. 23.

298. T.V. Publications Ltd., *Report of a Page Traffic Survey on the 'T.V. Times'*, prepared by the Bureau of Commercial Research Ltd., 1962–63.
299. Twain, Mark, 'Jim Baker's Blue Jay Yarn' appears in
    (1) *Family Mark Twain*, Harper, London, 1935.
    (2) *Favourite Works by Mark Twain*, Stroud and City, 1939.
300. Unesco, *Books for the Developing Countries—Asia, Africa* (Report No. 47 on Mass Communication), Paris, 1965.
301. Unesco, *Developing Information Media in Africa* (Report No. 37 on Mass Communication), Paris, 1962.
302. Unesco, *Developing Mass Media in Asia,* (Report No. 30 on Mass Communication), Paris, 1960.
303. Unesco, *The Effects of Television on Children and Adolescents* (Report No. 43 on Mass Communication), Paris 1964. (An annotated bibliography.)
304. Unesco, *Index Translationum*, Paris, annually. (List of translated books, under countries of publication and subjects.)
305. Unesco, *India: Paintings from the Ajanta Caves*, Paris, 1954. (Colour plates.)
306. Unesco, *The Influence of the Cinema on Children and Adolescents* (Report No. 31 on Mass Communication), Paris, 1961. (An annotated bibliography).
307. Unesco, *Mass Media in the Developing Countries* (Report No. 33 on Mass Communication), Paris, 1961.
308. Unesco, *Meeting of Experts on Book Production and Distribution in Asia, Tokyo, 1965.* (Unesco/MC/55), Paris, 1966.
309. Unesco (Ed: J. Szapiro), *The Newspaperman's United Nations*, Unesco, Paris, 1961. (A compact description, for journalists, of the U.N. and its Agencies.)
310. Unesco, *Social Education Through Television* (Report No. 38 on Mass Communication), Paris, 1963.
311. Unesco, *Space Communication and the Mass Media* (Report No. 41 on Mass Communication), Paris, 1964.
312. Unesco, *Statistical Yearbook* (annually), Paris.
313. Unesco, *Survey on the Ways in which States Interpret their International Obligations* (Paul Guggenheim), Paris, 1955.
314. Unesco, *Television in the Service of International Understanding* (a conference of Directors of Television Programmes, 1960), Unesco, Paris, 1960.
315. Unesco, *Television and Tele-Clubs in Rural Communities* (Report No. 16 on Mass Communication), Paris, July, 1955.
316. Unesco, *Trade Barriers to Knowledge*, Paris, 1956.
317. Unesco, *The Unesco Courier* (a monthly magazine covering all subjects within Unesco's mandate), Paris.
318. Unesco, *What is Unesco?*, Paris (2nd ed.), 1960.
319. *World Campaign for Universal Literacy*, Econ. Soc. Dev. Council Document E/3771, New York, 1963.
320. Unesco, *World Communications: Press, Radio, Film, Television*, Paris, 1964 (a book concerned with social statistical and educational aspects, country by country. Also contains bibliography of Unesco and other publications). Later Edition, 1966, in French.
321. Unesco, *World Film Directory—Agencies concerned with Educational, Scientific and Cultural Film* (Report No. 35 on Mass Communication), Paris, 1962.
322. Unesco, *World Illiteracy at Mid-Century*, Paris, 1957. See also U.N. Statistical Yearbook, 1966.
323. Union of International Associations, *International Associations* (monthly), 1, rue aux Laines, Brussels 1.
324. Union of International Associations, *The Yearbook of International Organizations* (Sec. Gen. Office, 1, Rue aux Laines, Brussels 1). Published in official collaboration with the U.N. Secretariat.
325. United Kingdom, Ministry of Labour, *Monthly Digest of Statistics*, Central Statistical Office, London.
326. United Nations, *Compendium of Social Statistics* (Sales no: 63 XVII. 3), New York, 1963.
327. United Nations, *The Future Growth of World Population* (Population Studies No. 28, 1958). Dept. Econ. Soc. Affairs, New York, 1958.
328. United Nations, *Repertoire and Practice of the U.N. Organs*, Vol. III, article 71, U.N., New York 1957

329. United Nations, *1963 Report on the World Social Situation,* Dept. of Econ. and Soc. Affairs, New York, 1963.

330. United Nations, *Statistical Yearbooks,* New York. (Published annually since 1948, with few gaps. Each issue deals with different spheres: economics, populations, social security, production, etc. For *communication* see especially 1948 (newspapers), 1960 (radio, T.V.), 1966 (railways, shipping, aviation, tourism, mail, telephones, newspapers).

331. United Nations, *World Population: Challenge to Development,* U.N., N.Y. 1966. (A summary of highlights of the World Population Conference, Belgrade, 1965.)

332. United Nations, *Yearbook* (annually), U.N., New York.

333. United States Bureau of the Census, *Historical Statistics of the United States, from Colonial Times to 1957,* U.S. Gov. Printing Office, Washington, 1960.

334. United States Bureau of Census, *Statistical Abstracts of the United States, 1967,* Washington, 1967.

335. United States Dept. of Commerce, *Survey of Current Business,* Washington 1966.

336. United States Gov. Printing Office, *Communication Satellites: Technical, Economic and International Developments,* Washington, Feb. 1962.

337. United States Office of Health, Education and Welfare, *Statistics of Public Libraries, 1855–56,* Washington, 1959.

338. Universal Postal Union (U.P.U.), *L'Union Postale,* pub. monthly, Berne, Switzerland.

339. Universal Postal Union, *L'Union Postale; sa fondation et son development, 1874–1949,* Berne, 1949.

340. U.R.T.N.A. (Union des Radiodiffusions et Télévisions Nationales d'Afrique), *Newsletter,* 15, Blv. de la République, Dakar, Senegal. (First number, Nov. 1967.)

341. U.S.S.R., 'Development of Communication in the U.S.S.R.' (in Russian). (Ed. N. D. Psurtsev.) Pub. by *Communication,* Moscow, 1967. (Historical survey of 50 years, 1917–67.)

342. U.S.S.R., Central Statistical Office, 'Transport and Communication in the U.S.S.R.' (in Russian), *Statistika,* Moscow, 1967. (Statistical data.)

343. Walters, F. P., *A History of the League of Nations,* Oxford University Press, London, 1952.

344. Ward, Barbara, 'The Menace of the Urban Explosion', *The Listener,* 14 Nov. 1963.

345. Waterfield, G., 'Suez and the Role of Broadcasting', *The Listener,* Dec. 29, 1966.

346. Webb, R. K., *The British Working Class Reader, 1790–1848,* Allen and Unwin, London, 1955.

347. West, M., *A General Service List of English Words,* Longmans, Green, London, 1953 (re-issued 1963).

348. Whatmough, J. An extensive critical bibliography of language studies, including many statistical analyses, published by Comité International Permanent de Linguistes, Harvard University Press, Cambridge, Mass., 1954.

349. Whatmough, J., *Language—a Modern Synthesis,* Secker and Warburg, London, 1956.

350. Whorf, B. L., *Language, Thought and Reality.* Selected writings (Ed. J. B. Carroll), M.I.T. Press, Mass., 1956 (also in paperback).

351. Wiener, N., *Cybernetics,* The Tech. Press of M.I.T. and John Wiley, New York, 1948.

352. Willcox, A. R., *Rock Paintings of the Drackensberg,* Max Parrish, London, 1956.

353. Williams, C. B., 'A Note on the Statistical Analysis of Sentence Length as a Criterion of Literary Style', *Biometrika,* XXXI, Parts III and IV, March 1940.

354. Williams, C. B., 'The Statistical Outlook in Relation to Ecology', *J. Ecology,* 42, No. 1, Jan. 1954. Includes long list of other studies of the 'logarithmic law' of biology, including language statistics.

355. Williams, Francis, *Dangerous Estate: the Anatomy of Newspapers,* Longmans, Green, London, 1957.

356. Williams, R., *Communications,* Chatto and Windus, London, 1966.

357. Williams, R., *Culture and Society (1780–1950)*, Pelican Press, Harmondsworth, England, 1961.
358. Winter, P., Ploog, D. and Latta, J., 'Vocal Repertoire of the Squirrel Monkey (*saimiri sciureus*) its Analyses and Significance', *Exp. Brain Res.*, **1**, 1966, p. 359. (Contains considerable bibliography of studies of monkey 'Speech' and others.)
359. Wright, L. B., *Culture on a Moving Frontier*, Indiana U.P., U.S.A., 1955 (see esp. Chaps. 5 and 6).
360. Wright, C. R., *Mass Communication*, Random House, New York, U.S.A., 1964.
361. Zeman, Z. A. B., *Nazi Propaganda*, Oxford University Press (and Wiener Library) London, 1964. (Contains good bibliography of books and documents concerning Nazi propaganda.)
362. Zimmerman, L. J., *Poor Lands, Rich Lands (The Widening Gap)*, Random House, New York, 1965.
363. Zipf, G. K., *Human Behaviour and the Principle of Least Effort*, Addison–Wesley Publishing, Cambridge, Mass., 1949. (Includes statistical 'laws' of language.)
364. Zuberi, M. I. H., *Principles of Telephone Traffic Estimation and Prognoses*, Kungl. Tekniska Högskolan, Stockholm 70. Institutionen för Teletraffiksystem, Rapport No. T.T.S. 3–66, May 1966.
365. Zuberi, M. I. H., *Studies in Telephone Demand Estimation and Prognoses*, Kungl. Tekniska Högskolan, Stockholm 70. Institutionen för Teletrafksystem Rapport No. T.T.S. 2–65, Dec. 1965.
366. Zuckermann, S., *Scientists and War*, Hamish Hamilton, London, 1966.

Index

Addison, J., 37, 39
Advertisements, 195
Advertising, 33, 36, 117, 171, 197
  artistry, 40
  as show business, 41
  costs of, 40
Advices, the, 37
Aechaian League, 125
Affluent society, 38
Africa, 61, 72, 133, 147, 148, 151, 161, 172, 173, 179, 180, 181, 193
  newspapers and G.N.P., 155
  populations, 102
  radio, newspapers, cinemas, 198
  telephones and G.N.P., 153
African Telecommunication Union (U.R.T.N.A.), 127
Aggression, 7
Agitation, 117
Aid, economic, 102
Aid programmes, 151
Aid to developing countries, 27, 160, 161
Aircraft, 100
Aircraft traffic, 90
Airlines, 156
Air mail, 94, 95, 156, 176
Air passenger traffic, 176
Air transport, 128
  statistics, 45
Air travel, falling costs, 160
Airways, 55, 80, 81, (map) 92, 94, 163, 164
  dependence on electronics, 95
  for poorer countries, 95
  traffic, 160
  traffic growth (graph) 97
Albania, 182
Anglo–Soviet Cultural Agreement, 112
Animal signs, 12
Arab countries, 169
Arab Postal Union, 127
Arabic, 179, 180, 181, 192
Archaeological remains, 171
Argentine, 142, 151, 177
Arnold, Matthew, 121
Asia, 71, 147, 148, 151, 173, 193
  newspapers and G.N.P., 154
  telephones and G.N.P., 152
Asian Broadcasting Union (A.B.U.), 113, 127
Asian writing, 192
Asociacion Inter-americana de Radio-diffusion (A.I.R.), 113
Associated Press, 64

Australia, 133, 143, 172, 177, 180
Australian radio, 111
Austria, 183, 187
Austro–German Postal Union (1850), 130

Balloons, 130
Baraza, The, 156
Barnum, Phineas Taylor, 41
Bees, 2, 12
Belgium, 145, 187
Bell, Graham, 34
Benelux, 169
Book-burnings, 117
Books, 185, 187
  and markets, 192
  and Unesco, 193
  cost of, 185
  growth of buying, 187
  in Africa, 191
  in developing countries, 189
  in reduced vocabularies, 190
  in West Africa, Malaysia, 191
  in U.S.S.R., 190
  language distribution, 181
  production, 189
  supply and demand, 186
Bookshops, 193
Brain-washing, 118
Brazil, 142
Breakdowns, 162
Britain, 175, 178, 185, 189, 200
Britannia, 170
British addiction to print, 187
British Broadcasting Corporation, 16, 56, 60, 106, 109, 182
  (External Services), 181, 183
  languages, 184
British Commonwealth, communication within, 87, (map) 89
British Council, the, 116
Broadcast languages, 109
Broadcast listener surveys, 109
Broadcasting, 49, 73, 105
  and reading, 187
  external, 181
  global, 179
  history of, 35
  language variety, 184
  of news, 60
  overseas, 108, 180, 182
Broadcasting Unions, 113
Bulgaria, 182
Bunyan, John, 204

Bureaucracy, 199, 203
Burke, Edmund, 205
Burma, 170
Butler, Samuel, 136

Cable, 135
Cables, 82, 158, 159, 160, 163, 178
  falling costs, 163
  intercontinental, (map) 62, 83, 87
  international, 62, 83, 87
Cambridge University, 186
Canada, 133, 142, 143, 164, 171, 173, 183
Canals, 100
Cantonese, 111
Caribbean, 133
Carlyle, Thomas, 42, 194
Carnegie Trust, 188
Cars, 100
Catholics, 114
Cave drawings, 21
Caxton, William, 25, 38, 192
C.C.I.T.T., 94
Censorship, 112, 118, 119
Census, in U.K. and U.S.A., 186
Central America, 72, 133, 147, 151, 173, 183
  newspapers and G.N.P., 153
  telephones and G.N.P., 152
Ceremonial, 15
Changing society, 28
Chartists, 104
China, 31, 69, 112, 123, 137, 147, 156, 204
Chinese, the, 17, 20, 111, 180, 182, 190, 192
Chinese News Agency, 69
Chinese Peoples' Republic, 182
Chinese Red Guards, 120
Churches, 117
Churchill, Winston, 112
Cicero, 32
Cinema, the, 51, 52, 149, 187
  as visual display, 53
  statistics, 43
Civil Service, 175
Clarke, Arthur, 84
Clichés, 7, 17, 114, 117, 203
Clock, 2, 12, 23, 27
  as a tyrant, 29
  an obsession 27–29
Coaxial cables, 158, 160
Codes, 15
Colonialism, 148
Comecon, 169
Common Market, 125, 169
Commonwealth, 177, 178, 183
  communication, 94
  Communications Conference, 88
  Press Union, 127
  Telecommunication Board, 88
  telephone plan 1958, (map) 89
Communication,
  a service industry, 90

advantage to richer countries, 127
affording and needing, 143
and courage, 11, 19
and mobility, 49
and modernization, 148
and organization, 48, 123
and public protection, 118
and security, 4
and sociability, 49
and social stability, 51, 53
and trade, 90
and wealth, 136
as sharing, 2
breakdowns, 162
costs to poor countries, 161
delay in, 103
domestic and economic spheres, 69
falling costs, 156, 160
for resolving, 55
for stability, 55
in antiquity, 29
in developing countries, 59, 150, 151, 156
inland, 69
intercontinental, (map) 62, 80
investment in, 137
long-term planning, 128
necessity or luxury? 137
one-way, two-way, 9
organizing power, 201
overseas, 80, 159
practical values, 168
public and private, 4, 47, 94
reliability of, 31, 33, 61, 84, 162
speed of, 35, 48, 50, 53
statistics of, 70
time-delay 32
Western images, 201
world planning, 126
Communication media,
  power of, 105
  their inter-relations, 151
Communist 'agitators' and 'propagandists', 200
Communist bloc, 169
Communist countries, 123, 129, 130, 131, 139, 144, 145
Communist Party, 53
Computers, 55, 58, 81, 95, 104
Computer 'languages', 15
Comsat, 86
Concepts are social, 13
Congo, 198
Congress of Vienna 1815, 125
Consumer society, 36
Conversation, 4, 12, 176
  as 'resolver', 49
Correlation Coefficient, 138
Costs, 178
  falling, 160
  of communication, 157
Courage in communication, 11, 19
Cromwell, Oliver, 33, 37, 40, 118

Crowd behaviour, 42, 51
Currency difficulty, 172
Cursus publicus, 35, 48, 58
Cybernetics, 58
Cyprus, 116, 120
Czechoslovakia, 142, 182

Data-processing, 81
Democracy, 25, 194, 199
  and communication, 199
Denmark, 177
Developing countries, 59, 141, 144, 148, 204
  aid, 151, 161
  and broadcasting, 185
  communication, 156
  journalists in, 150
  newspapers and G.N.P., 151
  prestige, 162
  publishing difficult, 193
  radio in, 58
  telephones and G.N.P., 151
  (U.N. definition), 145
Dialects, 13
Disaster threats, 198
Dissent, 19, 204
  its values, 203
Diversity of communication, 199
Diversity of traffic, 93
Dockwra, W., the post, 33
Document explosion, 99
Donne, John, 118
Doob, L., 106
Doubletalk, 117
Durkheim, Emile, 3, 202
Dutch, 179, 182

'Early Bird', 87
East Africa, 163, 190, 197, 198
  communication satellites, 165
East Europe, 182, 187
East Germany, 123, 145, 177
Economic gap, 101
Economic growth, 100
Eden, Anthony, 116
Education, 200, 201, 205
  and multilingualism, 183
  in developing countries, 190
Education Act, U.K., 1944, 188
Egypt, 170, 182
Electronics, 158
Embarrassment, 9
Embassies, libraries of, 185
Emigration, 166
Emotional capacity, 175
Emotions, as consequences, 202
England, 170
  communication satellites, 165
English, 111, 180, 182, 183, 190, 192
  business, 18
Ethiopia, 198
  communication satellites, 165

Europe, 71, 147, 178
  communication satellites, 165
  East, 111, 112, 113, 172
  West, 171
European Broadcasting Union (E.B.U.), 113, 127
European Free Trade Association (E.F.T.A.), 125
Eurovision, 106, 113, 127
Evening Institutes, 188
Exploitation, by tourists, 173
External broadcasting, 181, 182

Fading, 178
Falling costs, overland routes, 161
Federations, 102, 203
Fiction and non-fiction, 189
Film, 185
Films, 163, 185
  in poor countries, 106
Foreign broadcasts, 110
Foreign travel, 171
Foreigners, images of, 170
France, 133, 145, 200
  communication satellites, 165
Franco–Prussian war, 130
French, 180, 183, 190, 192
French Revolution, 130
Frequency Registration Board, International, 82
Friends, always limited, 176
Frustration, 115, 203
Functional literacy, 199
Future, the, 204, 205
Futures, a plurality, 205

Gabon, 155
Galbraith, J. K., 38
Gap, economic, 98, 101, (diagram) 146
George III, King, 54
German, 180, 183, 190, 192
Germany, 136, 187
Germany, D. R., 123, 177
Germany, F. R., 81, 122, 145
  communication satellites, 165
Ghana, 155, 198
Goebbels, P. J., 114, 116
Great Exhibition 1851, 64
Great Manipulators, 119, 194, 197
Greater London, 186
Greece, 170, 172
Greek city–states, 50, 125, 199
Gross National Products, 139, 141, 143, 204
  (definition), 142
Ground Stations, for poor countries, 93
Growth curves, 98, 99
  regenerative, 98
Growth rates, economic, 100
Gypsies, 24, 32

Haiti, 151
Havana Convention (1928), 130

Hebrew, 31, 48
Heidegger, Martin, 18, 42
Herodotus, 21, 32
Hertz, Heinrich, 49
Hindi, 179, 180
History books, 120
Hitler, A., 69, 115
Hogarth, William, 39
Hogg, Quintin, 5
Hokkien, 111
Holiday camps, 173
Holland, 170, 187
Hollywood, 166
'Hot line', 54
Hume, David, 13
Hunan, 111
Hungarian Rising 1956, 111
Hungary, 182

Iceland, 142
Illiteracy, see also literacy, 24, 106, 120
Immigrants, 110
Index Librorium Prohibitorum, 118
India, 147, 172, 179
Indicator signs, 2
Individual, changed meaning, 204
Industrial Revolution, 25
Industrialization, 25
Industry, international, 104
Institutions, 174, 175
   as abstracts, 202
   international, 175
Intelsat, 84, 93, 163, 165
   signatories, 85
Intergovernmental Maritime Consul-
   tative Organization (I.M.C.O.), 123,
   128, 130, 131
International Air Transport Associa-
   tion, 131
International Bank for Reconstruction
   and Development (I.B.R.D.), 147,
   156
International Civil Aviation Organi-
   zation (I.C.A.O.), 123, 128, 130
International Commission for Air
   Navigation, 130
International Court, 122
International Frequency Registration
   Board (I.F.R.B.), 82, 132
International law, 132
International Monetary Fund (FUND),
   121, 123
International Organizations, 56, 57,
   107, 121, 168, 202, 203
   as advisory bodies, 132
   growth of, (graph) 124
   U.N., Governmental and non-
   Governmental, 124
International Postal Union (I.P.U.), 123
International Radio and Television
   Organization (O.I.R.T.), 113
International Radio Consultative
   Committee (C.C.I.R.), 132

International relations, 173
International Savings Bank, 130
International Telecommunication
   Union (I.T.U.), 94, 123, 128, 129,
   132
International Telegraph and Tele-
   phone Consultative Committee
   (C.C.I.T.T.), 94, 132
International Telegraphic Convention
   (1865), 129
   (1932), 129
International trade, 131
Internationalism, 166, 168
Intervision, 113
Iraq, 179
Irish, 179
'Iron Curtain', 112
Israel, 192
Italian, 183
Italy, 133, 142, 187
   communication satellites, 165

James I, King, 117
Jamming, radio, 111
Japan, 136, 142, 147, 170, 171, 177, 189,
   200
Japanese, 180, 190, 192
   16th Century, 103
Jargons, 6, 18
Jesuits, 114
John Bull, 170
Johnson, Samuel, 19, 37, 118, 205
Journalism, 108
Journals, modern, 39
Junk shops, 171

Kamba, 191
á Kempis, Thomas, 118
Kennedy, President, 50, 51
Kenya, 183
   communication satellites, 165
Kikuyu, 191
Knowledge, by encounter and by
   reportings, 8
Kublai Khan, ix, 32
Kuwait, 147

Langer, Susanne, 2
Language
   and broadcasting, 184
   and identity, 16
   as social matter, 13
   barrier, 64
   dialects, 13
   impoverished, 18
   in broadcasting, 109
   minority 6, 16, 111
   of computers, 14
   ritual, 17
   statistics, 13
   teaching, 110
   universal, 12
   see multilingualism

Language of Bees, 2, 12
Language-systems, 14
Lasers, 158, 162
Latin, 191
Latin America, 161
Law, 174, 200
  and Order, 203
  international, 121, 122, 203
League of Nations, 121, 125
Legends, 23
Leisure, 171
Lenin, V. I., 109, 117
Leonardo da Vinci, 21, 48
Lerner, D., 148
Letters, 118
  true cost of, 78
Libel, 197
Libraries, 118, 119, 186, 193
  and rural populations, 185
  influence of religion, 187
  Lending, 185
  Municipal Public, 185–188
Library Association of U.K., 187
Library books, 108
  circulation, 186, 188, 189
  growth of usage, 187, (graph) 188
Linguae francae, 12, 15, 110, 179, 182, 192
Lippmann, Walter, 119
Literacy, 3, 20, 22, 31, 137, 142, 150, 162, 180, 181, 185, 186, 187, 190, 193, 197, 198, 204
  and comprehension, 199
  and loneliness, 22
  and questioning, 47
Literature, *see* Books, 190
Literature, spoken, 190
Lloyds, 61
Locke, John, 48
London Airport, 96
Ludenic theory of news, 41, 53, 107
Luo, 191
Lying, 117

Mail, international, 95
Malaysia, 154
Mandarin, 111
Manipulators, 119, 194, 197
Mao, Chairman, 20, 120
Marconi, G., 49
Martians, 50
Marxism–Leninism, 117
Mass-communication, 26, 33, 36, 38, 59, 114, 194
  as a misnomer, 42
Masses, the, 42
Mass-media, 119, 149, 150, 194, 199
Mead, G. H., 21
Mechanics Institutes, 186
Mediating institutions, 205
Merchant Banks, 60
Mexico, 161

Mexico City Plan, 132, 135
Microwave relays, 160, 162
Middle East, 61
Mill, John Stuart, 42
Milton, John, 204
Minority languages, 6, 179
Money, as communication, *x*, 137
Money, falling values, 157, 159
Montaigne, 36
Motor cars, 2
Multilingualism, 162, 179, 192
  in developing countries, 183
Municipal Public Libraries, 185–188

Napoleon III, 129
Nasser, President, 23
'National characteristics', 176
National images, 166, 167
National Income (definition), 142
Nationalism, 13, 120, 126, 166, 169
Nationality, 169
National Socialism, 115
Nationhood, 149, 169, 179
  of nation–states, 168
Nation–states, 169
  their size, 199
Nazi Germany, 116
Nazis, 117
Nazism, 114, 125
Nehru, Jawaharlal, 121, 168, 169
Netherlands, 192
News, 17, 37, 103, 104, 175, 176
  an obsession, 27, 28, 39
  as a duty, 29, 41
  by voice or print, 106
  early history, 80
  increasingly international, 195
  in developing countries, 197
  its regularity, 28
  Ludenic theory, 41, 53
  mechanization of, 60
  of disaster, 121
  omission, 119
  on radio and T.V., 197
  selected, 27, 28
  speed of, 55
  Western traditions, 121
News agencies, 8, 27, 59, 60, 80, 119, 150
  maps, 65–68
Newspaper, origin of, 36
Newspaper reading, 188
  by women, 188
Newspaper Tax, 40
Newspapers, 142, 145, 148, 149, 187, 205
  and trust, 197
  and wealth, 143, 144
  British, 195
  changing, 194
  content analysis, 39, 194, 195
  (definition of), 155
  falling costs, 157
  in U.S.A., 196
  of the future, 194

Newspapers—*Continued*
  per capita, 142
  'quality' and 'popular', 195
  read aloud, 185
  weekdays and Sundays, 196
  women's reading, 188, 195
New Zealand, 143, 145, 177
North Africa, 183
North America, 71
North Atlantic Treaty Organization
  (N.A.T.O.), 169
Norway, 177
Norwegian, 182

'One', the, 18
Opinion Polls, 200
Organization for Economic Co-
  operation and Development
  (O.E.C.D.), 169, 171, 172
Ouspensky, P., 117
Oxford University, 186

Pakistan, 147
Pantheism, 9
Paperbacks, 185, 188
Paper shortage, 193
Parkinson's law, 98
Parliament, 5
Party, the Communist, 53
Passports, 171
Paternalism of the state, 40
Peirce, C. S., 2, 3, 21
Perceval, Spencer, 54
Persian, 179
Personifications, 8, 18, 174
  of states, 169
Peru, 161
Peter the Great, 16
Peter the Red, 192
Phoenecians, 131
Pigeon post, 76
Plan committees, Regional,
  Africa, Asia, Latin America, 132
Planning, long term, 133
Poland, 111, 182
Political articulation, 105
Political consciousness, 23
Politics, 18, 105
Polo, Marco, *ix*, 32
Polybius, 32, 125
Polylingualism, 162, 179, 183, 192
Pope Gregory XV, 113
Population distribution, 160, 164
  U.K. and U.S.A., 186
Population explosion, 99, 148, 193,
  194
Population growth rates, 47, 148
Population, of Asia, 193
Population, redistribution, 100
Populations, U.S.A. and U.K., 47
Pornography, 189
Portugal, 172
Portuguese, 183

Postage stamps, 34
Postal Congress of Berne (1874), 130
Postal service, 32, 33, 40, 48, 95, 129
  international, 130, 157
Poverty, global belt, 61, (map) 63
Poverty, world distribution, 145, 147
Pragmatism, 2, 202
Prediction, hazardous, 135
Prejudice, 167, 169
Primary education U.K. 1970, 188
Press Agencies, 176
Press, the, 33, 36, 51, 81, 119, 137, 150,
  175
  British, 119
  changing function, 39
  freedom of, 197, 198
  in developing countries, its dangers,
  197
  in poor countries, 38
  in war, 196, 197
  political function, 38
  'quality' and 'popular', 188
  telegrams, 81
  the Royal Commission 1949, 119
  1951–2, 119
Press Congress of the World 1915, 1926,
  150
Printing and science, 48
Programme exchange, 112
Progress, 201, 203, 204
  its changed meaning, 22
Propaganda, 15, 20, 105, 108, 113
  by cinema, 116
  Communist, 116
  morally neutral, 114
Protestant Ethic, 204
Public Lending Libraries, 185–188
Public Libraries Act (U.K. 1850, U.S.A.
  1849), 186
Public opinion, 200
Publishing, 186
Puerto Rico, 151
Punctuality, as a virtue, 29
Purgatory, 118
Pye, L., 149, 150

Radio, 81, 118, 149, 150, 185
  and war, 49
  blackout, 82, 94
  in poor countries, 106
  main uses, 30
  navigation, 128
  receivers per capita, 142
  relay, 135
  short-wave, 93
Radio-telephone, 178
Railways, 34
  statistics, 44, 45
  traffic, 100
Rationalism, 14
Reading, 100
  and quality, 189
  and television, 189

Reading—*Continued*
  changing tastes, 189
  influence of television, 187
Reasonableness, 115
Reason, its limitations, 167
Recording, 31
Red Book, the, 20
Reds, the, 16
Referenda, 200
Regenerative growth curves, 90
Regional Organizations, 126
Relay satellite, 93
Reliability, 31, 61, 84, 162
  of data, 155
  in industrial society, 31, 33, 201
Renaissance, 48
Reuters, 60, 64, 81, 159
Richelieu, Cardinal, 192
Ritual, 5, 15, 17, 106
  and rôle, 5
  defines 'in' and 'out' groups, 6
  of language, 6, 17
Roads, 73
  sport and transport, 137
Robots, 58
Rôles, 1, 5
Roman Curia, 113
Roman Empire, 53
Rome, 32
Rome, ancient, 26
Rome Plan, 93, 132, 134 (map), 135
Rousseau, J. J., 126
Royal Commission on the Press, 1947–
  49, 195
Rumania, 182
Rumour, 20, 50, 55, 106, 149, 199
Russian, 180, 182, 183, 192
Russian satellites 'Molnya', 164
Russo–Japanese War, 116
Rwanda, communication satellites, 165

Sahara, 170
St. Paul, 117
Sartre, Jean-Paul, 9
Satellites, 77, 83, 84, 104, 128, 135, 158,
  159, 178
  and poorer countries, 61, 93
  communication (*see* under various
    countries), 165
  for developing countries, 159
  for poorer countries, 163
  ground stations, 163
  international use, (map) 62, 86
  in U.S.S.R., 164
  'multi-access', 163, 165
  stationary, 164
Satellite television, 176
Saul, 118
Scandinavia, 187
Scatter diagrams, 138
Schools, 117
Schramm, Wilbur, 38, 118, 137, 149
Schrödinger, Erwin, 3, 21

Scientific language, 191
Sea-traffic increase, 131
Secularization, 148
Security, of state, 118
Self and society, 202
Self-consciousness, 9, 23
Self-image, 5, 167
Semantics, 13
Service industries, 90
Shipping, 100, 131
  lanes (map), 91
  routes, 90
  statistics, 45, 46
Ships, 104
Shorthand, 32
Sign-systems, 14
Silone, Ignazius, 8
Slave trade, 125
Slogans, 17, 114, 117, 203
Society, traditional, 22, 23
South Africa, 164, 177, 181, 198
South America, 72, 133, 147, 151, 173,
  180, 183
  newspapers and G.N.P., 153
  telephones and G.N.P., 152
South East Asia, 61
Soviets, 117
Space-cult, 58
Spain, 133, 172
Spanish, 180, 183, 190
Specialized Agencies of U.N., 107,
  121
Speech, 20, 47, 82
Spoken literature, 190
Sport, 174
Sputnik, 58, 103
Staggered holidays, 173
Stalin, J., 111
Stamp Tax, on newspapers, 104, 157
Stars, cult of the, 53
Stateless persons, 168
States, their size, 199
Statistics, 138
Sterling Area, 172, 178
Stewart, Michael, 181
Stock Exchanges, 34, 55
Student travel, 173
Submarine cables, 135
Subscriber organizations, 35
Subscription Libraries, 186
Sudan, 179
Suez, 116
Suez Canal, 164
Sunspots, 82, 83
Swahili, 180, 183, 191, 192
  newspapers, 156
Swaziland, 155
Sweden, 142, 145, 177, 200
Switzerland, 122, 145, 170
Syria, 154

Taj Mahal, 170
Talking drum, 76

Tanzania, 183, 192
  communication satellites, 165
Tariffs, 127
Technology, definition of, 98
Telegraph, 48, 57, 80, 129, 160, 163
  and railways, 34
  early, 103
  falling costs, 157
  political power 53–56, 57 *et seq.*, 103
    et seq.
  routes, 90
Telephone, 48
  history, 34
  traffic, international, 163
    U.K. overseas, 82
    U.S.A. overseas, 83
    transatlantic, 77
Telephones, 118, 160
  and mobility, 49
  and security, 49
  and wealth in 1958, 139
  in 1966, 144
  in States of U.S.A., 140, 141
  by cable and satellite, 77
  calling rates, 74, 82
  call statistics, ratio inland/overseas,
    177
  calls, domestic and economic spheres,
    177
  continental growth, 71, 72
  conversations per capita, 142
  conversations per telephone, 142
  domestic and economic spheres, 73,
    136
  falling costs, 157, 158
  in developing countries, 143
  in U.S.A. and U.K., 70
  in various countries, 78
  statistics of, 79, 80
  statistics of countries, 75
  the 'Rome Plan', 77 (map) 134
  traffic prediction, 77
  world growth, 70
Telephony, intercontinental, 81
Telephony, international, 176
Television, 51, 53, 149, 185
  and books, 188
  and politics, 24
  and radio licences, 43
  and reading, 187, 194
  educational, 136
  effects upon reading, 189
  for language teaching, 110
  in emerging countries, 24
  programme exchange, 113
  'worldwide', 163
Telex, 60, 61, 69, 81, 119, 128, 136, 156,
  160, 163, 176
Telstar satellite, 93
Text books, lack of, 180
Theatre, the, 52
Times, The, London, 103
Tourism, 3, 94, 96, 107, 168, 170, 171, 175

its class structure, 173
  privileges for visitors, 172
  visas, 172
Trade, railways and telegraphy, 90
Trade routes, traditional, 90
Trade Unions, 148, 174, 175
Traditional images, 170
Traffic
  demands, 161
  diversity, 93
  flow, 132
  flow, global (map), 134
  prediction, 94
Translation, 16, 109, 192
Travel agents, 171
Travelling libraries, 186
Treaty of Paris 1814, 125
Treaty of Prague, 159
Trunking, 156 *et seq.*
  advantages to rich countries, 160
Trust, 31, 149, 197, 200, 201, 203, 205
  in developing and advanced countries,
    202
Turkey, 172

Uganda, 183
  communication satellites, 165
U.K., 133, 149, 171, 177, 191, 193
  books and newspapers, 136
  population growth, 47, 75
U.N. and journalism, 150
U.N. Conference on Freedom of
  Information 1948, 150
U.N. specialized Agencies, 121–123, 150
Uncle Sam, 170
Unesco, 38, 59, 107, 112, 119, 120, 121,
  136, 143, 149, 150, 185, 193, 194,
  197, 198
  Dept. of Mass-Communication, 123
  diverse functions of, 123
Union of International Associations,
  124
Union of National Radio and T.V. of
  Africa (U.R.T.N.A.), 113
United Arab Republic, 198
United Nations Organization, 13, 84,
  107, 121, 149, 200
  specialized Agencies, 121–123
Universal Postal Union (U.P.U.), 128,
  130, 157
Uruguay, 151
U.S.A., 133, 143, 145, 147, 149, 166,
  170–173, 175, 177, 178, 180, 185,
  189, 191, 193, 196, 200
  age of population, 75
  migration, 74
  population, 74
  growth, 47
  railways, 45, 138
  Southern States, 141
U.S.S.R., 109–112, 147, 164, 172, 175,
  182, 187, 190, 200
  polylingualism, 181

U.S.S.R.—*Continued*
   short-wave radio, 112
   wired receivers, 112
Uttar Pradesh, 179

Vatican, the, 116
Venezuela, 151
Vernacular, 193
Verne, Jules, 48
Vocabulary, 190
Voice of America, 182
Voting, 200

Wall sheets, 137
'Walter and Connie', 110
War, 19, 27, 32, 49, 50, 54, 84, 109, 116, 131, 167
   and newspaper reading, 195–197
   and telephone traffic, 82
   and the Press, 198
   of 1812, 53
   propaganda, 114
War, First World (1914–1918), 64, 81, 130
War, World War II, 27, 78, 106, 118, 130, 148, 168, 183, 188, 189, 197, 203
Wave guides, 158
Webb, Beatrice, 118

Welles, Orson, 50
Wells, H. G., 50
Welsh, 179
West, the inscrutable, 120
Western European Union, 169
Whorf, B. L., 21
Wogs, etc., etc., 166
World awareness, 104, 107
World Bank (I.B.R.D.), 123, 146
World Bank Atlas of Production and Population, 140
World communication, planning, 126, 133
World communication, Regional Organizations, 127
World government, 203
World order, 203
World peace; needs expertise, 126
World population, 147
Wotton, Sir Henry, 117
Writing, 20
   an intellectual act, 47

Xenephon, 32

Yemen, 154
Yugoslavia, 123, 172, 182

Zambia, communication satellites, 165
Zeal, of propagandist, 115